Standing in the Spaces

STANDING IN THE SPACES

Essays on Clinical Process, Trauma, and Dissociation

PHILIP M. BROMBERG

 THE ANALYTIC PRESS

1998   Hillsdale, NJ   London

First paperback printing 2001

Published by The Analytic Press, Inc. [Editorial offices: 101 West Street, Hillsdale, NJ 07642] (www.analyticpress.com)

Index by Leonard S. Rosenbaum

Journal, Book, and Publisher Acknowledgments

The author gratefully acknowledges the following publications in whose pages versions of most chapters first appeared: *Journal of the American Academy of Psychoanalysis* [chapter 6]; *Psychoanalytic Psychology* [chapter 2]; *Contemporary Psychoanalysis* [chapters 2, 3, 4, 5, 7, 8, 9, 14 and 17]; *Psychoanalytic Dialogues* [chapters 10, 15 & 16, and chapters 13 and 18, which are derived from the earlier forms of these essays but have been materially rewritten and expanded for this volume]; *Self Psychology: Comparisons and Contrasts* (ed. D. W. Detrick and S. P. Detrick, The Analytic Press 1989) [chapter 11].

The author thanks also the *Journal of the American Psychoanalytic Association*, the *Journal of Clinical Psychoanalysis*, *Contemporary Psychotherapy Review*, *Dynamic Psychotherapy*, and The Analytic Press, publisher of *Pioneers of Interpersonal Psychoanalysis* (ed. D. B. Stern, C. H. Mann, S. Kantor & G. Schlesinger, 1955) for permission to use in chapters 1 and 19 some selected content adapted from referenced articles not included as chapters.

Library of Congress Cataloging-in-Publication Data

Bromberg, Philip M.
Standing in the Spaces: Essays on Clinical Process, Trauma, and Dissociation
/ Philip M. Bromberg

           p.   cm.
Includes bibliographical references and index.
ISBN: 0-88163-356-9
  I. Psychoanalysis. 2. Psychic trauma. 3. Dissociation (Psychology).
Psychotherapist and patient. I. Title
[DNLM: 1. Psychoanalytic Therapy collected works. 2. Mental Disorders—therapy collected works. 3. Psychoanalytic Theory collected works. WM
460.6B868s 1998]
RC509.B76 1998
616.89'17—dc21
DNLM/DLC
for Library of Congress   98-29429
                     CIP

Printed in the United States of .America
10 9 8 7 6 5

For Margo

CONTENTS

ACKNOWLEDGMENTS

The primary fountainhead of nourishment for the writing of these essays has been my patients, necessarily anonymous, and it is through the give-and-take of these relationships that my contemplation of clinical process continues to draw its vitality. In each treatment I discover in some new way that my ability to facilitate a patient's growth exists to the degree that I allow his or her impact to change me in ways I had not anticipated.

My ideas have germinated in different psychoanalytic communities at different points in time. The William Alanson White Institute, home of my analytic training, remains the most significant influence that has shaped my sensibility as a therapist. There are several people from my years as a candidate and thereafter to whom my gratitude is particularly alive, foremost among them being Edgar Levenson, whose impact on my thinking is evident from the first to the final chapter. I also want to express my appreciation to Earl Witenberg, Director of the White Institute during most of my career, and to Arthur Feiner, Editor Emeritus of *Contemporary Psychoanalysis*. At a time when support of my writing efforts was most needed, each in his own way provided me with opportunities to express my ideas regardless of whether I crossed the traditional boundary of interpersonal "orthodoxy."

The evolution of my writing has further been shaped by my successive participation in three different peer groups at different phases of my professional life; the first, a study group consisting of David Schecter, Althea Horner, and myself, embodied a blend of similarities and differences in thinking that fueled each of us to write in our own way about schizoid phenomena and the vicissitudes of attachment and detachment. The second peer group, bringing me together with Lee Caligor and Jim Meltzer, began as an effort to explore the supervisory process and led to our edited book on psychoanalytic supervision in 1984. Our trio has continued to thrive as both an ever-deepening personal and professional relationship, and as a diverse, lively, and fertile exchange of ideas. The third peer group is the Editorial Board of *Psychoanalytic Dialogues* in which I have participated pleasurably since the journal's inception in 1991; my thanks to Neil Altman, Lewis Aron, Tony Bass, Jody Davies, Muriel Dimen, Emmanuel Ghent, Adrienne Harris, and Stephen Mitchell for all they have given me.

Four colleagues, Lawrence Brown, Lawrence Friedman, Karol Marshall, and Stephen Mitchell, have contributed to the writing of this book in ways that defy conventional categorization, each a unique voice, and each relationship distinctively different. For their intellectual presence and their supportive friendship I am extremely grateful.

I am also fortunate to have done a good deal of teaching during the past two decades that provided an unparalleled opportunity for broadening the scope of my clinical thinking. This has been particularly true of the seminars on psychoanalytic process I have been privileged to conduct as a faculty member of the William Alanson White Institute, the New York University Postdoctoral Program, and the Institute for Contemporary Psychotherapy. I have benefited also from lectures and workshops I have given at psychoanalytic training centers across the United States, such as those in Boston, Chicago, Dallas, Denver, Los Angeles, Pasadena, Philadelphia, San Francisco, and Seattle, but my deepest debt is to the individual supervisees and the members of the supervision groups with whom I have been meeting weekly in my office over many years. The generous, creative, and often inspirational prism of clinical wisdom they have provided has been a source of continuing revitalization for my writing efforts.

I want also to acknowledge my appreciation to Paul Stepansky, Lenni Kobrin, Nancy Liguori, Joan Riegel, and the staff of The Analytic Press for all their help, but I especially want to thank my editor, John Kerr, whose comprehension of my work and continuing encouragement and steadfastness kept my enthusiasm alive during the process of seeing this book through to completion.

Finally, and most important, I wish to express my love and gratitude to my wife, Margo, to whom this book is dedicated. Her faith enabled me to first begin writing and has allowed me to find words for what at times I was not sure was there to say.

1

INTRODUCTION

"What is the use of a book," thought Alice, "without pictures or conversations?"

—Lewis Carroll, *Alice's Adventures in Wonderland*

I've always been wary of words—a perhaps curious opening remark when one considers how many are to follow. As far back as grammar school my stubborn refusal to substitute the grownup language of "real reality" for the felt reality of my inner experience would get me into no end of trouble with the people whose job it was to educate me. My report cards, for example, invariably contained the anticipated note from my teacher: "Philip appears to be very bright but he seems to live in his own world. I never know where his mind is, and nothing I do or say seems to change that." My parents, who knew first hand what my teacher was talking about, would nod their heads with both recognition and resignation because they didn't know how to deal with it either. To the adults who were trying to help me "pay attention," my ability to disappear "inside," as if in another world, was clearly a bad habit I needed to change. I, of course, never thought about it that way and couldn't understand why it seemed so important to everyone else. So I continued to do it, and apparently to such an extent that my mother hit upon the strategy of making me repeat what she said, hoping thereby to defeat my efforts to tune her out. I can still recall the day she realized that her "technique" didn't work. Standing in front of me, hands on hips, she growled; "You never listen to me. You never hear a word I say! I'm going to tell you something right now, and I want you to repeat it to me exactly." She then told me whatever the "something" was, and I did indeed repeat it word for word, exactly as she said it. She looked at me with a strange combination of bemusement and consternation. "I don't know how you did it," she said, "but I know that even though you were listening you still didn't hear it. I don't know how you did it, but you *did* it!" She was, needless to say, absolutely right about my not processing what I was taking in while I was being "educated," but more importantly, her sense of humor about it probably contributed a great deal toward my feeling more or less comfortable with my "insideness" as I got older. As Langan (1997, p. 820) wryly put it, "What is one to do with the fractionating discovery that, as the poet Allen Ginsberg remarked, 'My mind's got a mind of its own'?" And who knows? Perhaps it was because of this that I am now able to find humor in similar moments with patients—moments that might otherwise hold a potential to become grimly adversarial as our realities collide.

I begin with this vignette from my own childhood because it touches what may be my earliest awareness of what I hold to be the heart of personality growth—the paradox of being known but still remaining private, of being in the world but still separate from it. This paradox is often as confounding to psychoanalysts as it was to the adults in my early life. The acquisition of new self-experience is a process that is not mediated by language alone. There must be communication with an "other" at a felt level of personal validity in order for linguistic content to be integrated pleasurably and safely as self-experience. The analytic situation is designed as a negotiated therapeutic relationship to bring about this integration.

The following chapters are a selection of clinical essays written over the last twenty years. They can be read simply as a book of collected papers, or they can be read, simultaneously, as the unfolding of a clinical perspective—a series of reflections on the analytic relationship with its own implicit order, its own progression of ideas, and its own internal dialectic. My hope is that most readers will find this latter approach more congenial to their taste. How a reader reads will partially depend, of course, on the extent to which the growth of his own clinical experience and the historical development of his own ideas share some common ground with the evolution of mine over the past two decades. Writers need readers. In her 1996 novel, *Hallucinating Foucault*, Patricia Duncker argues that what writers have for centuries referred to as "the Muse" is none other than the reader for whom they write. Through the voice of her protagonist she puts it this way:

> I have never needed to search for a muse. The muse is usually a piece of narcissistic nonsense in female form. . . . I would rather a democratic version of the Muse, a comrade, a friend, a traveling

companion, shoulder to shoulder, someone to share the cost of this long, painful journey. Thus the Muse functions as collaborator, sometimes as antagonist, the one who is like you, the other, over against you. . . . For me the Muse is the other voice. Through the clamoring voices every writer is forced to endure there is always a final resolution into two voices. . . . But the writer and the Muse should be able to change places, speak in both voices so that the text shifts, melts, changes hands. The voices are not owned. They are indifferent to who speaks. They are the source of writing. And yes, of course the reader is the muse [pp. 58–59].

As I now contemplate the "otherness" of my own reader-muse, I wonder whether much has changed from the years when I would say to a supervisor, "I'll tell you about the last few sessions, but you really had to have been there." I find myself once again trying to oppose the constraints of language, felt here even more keenly in the written than in the spoken word, and unwilling to accept the inevitability that the "right" words to represent the "wholeness" of this book will be inadequate to express the individual personalities of its chapters and the range of my own clinical states of consciousness that went into birthing them. I yearn to impart a taste of the multiple experiential meanings that fueled my writing of the individual chapters at the time they were originally created, each a unique event that, like an analytic session, was most meaningfully "itself" when it happened. Perhaps my attempt to introduce this volume in such a fashion embodies my hope to overcome the limitation I do not want to accept, by evoking in the reader a heightened awareness of his own inner voices as we each struggle to grasp the phenomenon of two people, patient and analyst, purposefully confronting and engaging the multiplicity of nonlinear realities (their own and each other's) that organize the relationship we call psychoanalytic treatment.

"When I was young," Mark Twain wrote, "I could remember anything, whether it happened or not." Inasmuch as we have supposedly lost this capacity in growing up, the ability to relish Twain's humor is a remarkable human achievement. As adults, we like to call it "imagination." But as analysts, we know that this kind of logical impossibility, both in our patients and in ourselves, is the stuff of conundrum and, worse, impasse. Yet on the other hand, as analysts we also grasp that just "knowing" reality is not what growing up is all about. We are all well aware from our work that "knowing" reality can be a disastrously grim experience for many people. If a child is routinely allowed comfortably to retain his subjective experience while engaging with his parents in his own way as they tell him about what is "really" happening, he stands a pretty good chance of growing into an adult who, like Mark Twain, always has a child along for the ride.

Central to the growth of psychoanalytic theory has been a continuing effort to formulate a working model of the analytic relationship that is clinically flexible and developmentally sound. All attempts, including those of Freud, have necessarily rested upon a set of explicit or implicit assumptions about the nature of reality and how human beings come to understand what is "real." These assumptions have to do with the way in which one's capacity to see things as others see them develops, stabilizes, and coexists with one's values, wishes, fantasy life, impulses, and spontaneity; in other words, these assumptions concern the conditions through which subjective experience of reality (including reality about one's self) is freed to move beyond the limits of egocentrically conceived personal "truth." In this regard, the psychoanalytic relationship is an interpersonal environment that frees patients' potential and appetite for a creative dialectic between their internal reality and the presentation of external reality as represented by the analyst as an independent center of subjectivity.

To the extent that analytic theory is not embedded in imagination, I tend to approach it mainly as an intellectual adventure, similar to my fascination with taking apart clocks during preadolescence—to see how they worked. In other words, I don't think it is necessary to have a *concrete* theory in order to work effectively, and in fact I suspect that too great a preoccupation with theory can interfere with the process of therapy in the same way that taking apart clocks can become a substitute for full involvement in the business of living. If full involvement in "living the psychoanalytic relationship" does indeed require imagination, then the soul of the process might in a certain way be seen as a return to the basics of childhood. To put it more lyrically, is there an analyst who, as a child, did not believe with Eugene Field (1883) that "Wynken, Blynken, and Nod one night sailed off in a wooden shoe," even though "some folks thought 'twas a dream they'd dreamed"?

I recall a particular session just after I had returned from summer vacation, when I was sitting, saying nothing, hoping to regain my "memory." My patient, from the couch, said: "You sound very silent today." My first internal response was "What does *that* mean?" If she had said, "You are very silent today," I could have connected to that at once. But how can I sound silent? As I started to think about what she was feeling, something happened; I "knew" what she meant. Not conceptually—I *already* knew conceptually. I knew in a different way because the words "sounding silent" no longer felt alien, just as *she* no longer felt alien to me. It's tempting to just give this a name—to say I knew "experientially" or that I made contact with her "empathically" or something of the kind. Even though I do think in exactly this kind of way, I also believe that despite the understanding contributed by these terms we have barely begun to comprehend "what makes this clock tick." Something fascinating goes on in the process of human communication which continues to be the heart of what we rely upon clinically, as well as being the one genuine subject of all analytic theory no matter whether the vocabulary we use prefers to speak of transference-countertransference, enactment, projective identification, intersubjectivity, dissociated self-states, or even the phenomenon of "imagination."

As you might anticipate, my writing is more process driven than theory driven, and you will find that the aesthetic progression of the chapters, particularly during the last decade, is configured more and more by clinical vignettes as the context for my evolving point of view as an interpersonal/relational analyst. Although I touch on existing arguments in the literature and attempt to provide, here and there, challenges and what I believe to be corrections, I am basically trying to communicate a point of view with regard to the clinical phenomena and an approach to working with them. In other words, the theoretical formulations that arise out of my contemplation of the clinical material are for the most part responsive to the phenomena rather than an inside-out attempt to theorize them ahead of time.

How is it *possible* for psychoanalysis to work? Like the bumblebee, it shouldn't be able to fly; but it does. It is the issue that always percolates slightly beneath the surface of my clinical work, sometimes conscious, sometimes not, but always informing the sense of wonder with which I participate in the process of analytic growth with a given patient. How can a therapeutic link be constructed between seemingly irreconcilable needs of the human self; stability and growth; safety and spontaneity; privacy and commonality; continuity and change; self-interest and love? Asking oneself how it is *possible* for psychoanalysis to work is not the same as asking how psychoanalysis works. The former question comes from a clinician's more querulous and unsettled state of mind—the living part of an analyst's self that swims with his patient in more or less raw clinical process and has not been *subsumed* by his self-reflective consideration of how to conceptualize it. Trying to come to grips, clinically, with how it is possible to relate to a human being in a way that will enable him to accept dismantling the protection of his hard-won character structure in order to achieve gains that may or may not be realized, is perhaps the underlying motif throughout this book.

Safety and Growth

The drastic means an individual finds to protect his sense of stability, self-continuity, and psychological integrity, compromises his later ability to grow and to be fully related to others. Thus, a person enters treatment dissatisfied with his life and wanting to change it, but as he inevitably discovers, he *is* his life, and to "change" feels, paradoxically, like being "cured" of who he is—the only self he knows. "Can I risk becoming attached to this stranger and losing myself?" "Is my analyst friend or foe, and can I be certain?" Ernest Becker (1964, p. 179) considered this paradox "the basic problem of personality change" and asked trenchantly: "How is one to relinquish his world unless he first gains a new one?" Becker's question leads inevitably to a close examination of the kind of human relationship that allows a psychoanalytic process to take place. How does a relationship between patient and analyst come to exist that gets beyond the patient's having to make the impossible choice between being himself and being attached to and thus influenced by the analyst? (See also Mitchell, 1997b.) How does the relationship ever come to transcend the patient's determination to protect his own feeling of selfhood, and what does the analyst contribute that enables this transcendence to take place?

In my view the answer lies in the therapeutic creation of a new domain of reality in which coexists a hope of the "yet to be" and a dread of the "not me." No matter how great the pain of being trapped within one's internal object world, and no matter how desperate the wish to break free, it is humanly impossible to become fully alive in the present without facing and owning all of the hated, disavowed parts of the self that have shaped and been shaped by one's earliest object attachments. "Cure me of my blindness, but do not leave me in a void while I am learning to see. If I may come to know, finally, that seeing is not illness, will I exist at all?"

No matter what we say—and we say plenty—about diagnosis, nosology, severity of pathology, and psychoanalytic technique, it could be reasonably suggested that our clinical approach to any given patient is most broadly outlined by whether that person possesses the developmental maturity to *conceive* of asking the question: "Why am I living this way?" I'm not speaking about whether he has ever thought about what "this way" means or whether he has ever seriously attempted to answer the question. Some individuals come into treatment tortured by the question, having asked it for years without feeling any closer to an answer, while others have never asked it because, for them, the concept of "why am I living my life this way?" has no personal meaning. It is as if they have been able, somehow, to disprove

Socrates' time-honored opinion (Plato/Jowett, 1986, p. 22) that "the unexamined life is not worth living," and seem to live it anyway, but invariably in great pain.

For them, the question of "why" is inherently unaskable, and no matter what we may say diagnostically about such an individual when they choose to enter treatment with us (usually in search of some relief from their pain), the initial phase of therapy either succeeds or fails depending upon whether it enables the person to reach a point where that question becomes in fact askable. Unless this point is reached, analyst and patient will have very different images of the "reality" in which they coexist and the purpose of what they are doing, and in my experience, some of the "inevitable" treatment stalemates and failures in working analytically with such patients are created by each partner trying, futilely, to force his own "treatment reality" into the mind of the other.

Dissociation and Conflict

Increasing a person's capacity to question the way in which he is living his life requires a clinical process that expands the development of self-reflectiveness. Self-reflectiveness, traditionally referred to as the presence of "an observing ego," has been the most often cited criterion of analyzability. It allows a patient fully to exist in the moment and simultaneously perceive the self that is existing. The ability of the human mind to adaptationally limit its self-reflective capacity is the hallmark of dissociation, a phenomenon that, in both its normal and pathological forms, is being taken increasingly seriously by most contemporary schools of analytic thinking. As a defense, dissociation becomes pathological to the degree that it proactively limits and often forecloses one's ability to hold and reflect upon different states of mind within a single experience of "me-ness." It is my view that this burgeoning of psychoanalytic interest in dissociation as basic to human mental functioning, and equally powerfully, in the phenomenology of mental-states, reflects an even more central shift that has been taking place with regard to our understanding of the human mind and the nature of unconscious mental processes—toward a view of the self as decentered, and the mind as a configuration of shifting, nonlinear states of consciousness[1] in an ongoing dialectic with the necessary illusion of unitary selfhood.

---

1. Mitchell (1997a), for example, notes the increasingly strong "currents within contemporary psychoanalytic thought that portray the self as . . .

In my writing over the last two decades I have been developing a clinically-based perspective increasingly focussed on the central role of dissociative processes in both normal and pathological mental functioning, and its implications for the psychoanalytic relationship. Data from many sources, both research and clinical, underline the fact that the human psyche is shaped not only by repression and intrapsychic conflict, but equally, and often more powerfully, by trauma and dissociation. My thinking evolved initially from my treatment of patients suffering from personality disorders, but I believe it to be applicable to any therapy patient regardless of diagnosis. The traditional analytic view of the therapy relationship is that of a process technically designed to facilitate the lifting of repression and the expansion of memory through the resolution of intrapsychic conflict. It is my argument that this view at best underestimates and at worst ignores the dissociative structure of the human mind and has forced us to omit from our clinical theory a central element in how personality growth occurs—an element that is present in every psychoanalytic treatment that is mutative and far reaching—the process through which the *experience* of intrapsychic conflict becomes possible. I am referring to the interpersonal process of broadening a patient's perceptual range of reality within a relational field so that the transformation from dissociation to analyzable intrapsychic conflict is able to take place.

When I first began to publish analytic papers, I wrote quite a bit about the "schizoid personality" and almost nothing about "dissociation," but I've never really surrendered my interest in the concept of "schizoid," either conceptually or clinically. I think, however, that you get a richer picture of people who are schizoid if you take into account that they also have a personality structure that is extremely dissociative yet so rigidly stable that the dissociative structure tends to be noted only when it collapses (see chapter 13). I first began to touch upon this (Bromberg, 1979) in a paper which addressed the fact that the term "schizoid" started as a concept that defined a tendency towards disintegration and was nearly synonomous with "pre-schizophrenic," but was actually much more interesting as an idea designating a stable character structure—at least it was to *me*. What intrigued me was that, apart from its dynamic origins as a mode of escape from

---

inaccessible, fluid, or discontinuous: Winnicott's incommunicado, private self; Lacan's register of the 'real,' beneath the evanescent shiftings of the 'imaginary'; Ogden's decentered subject, oscillating within dialectics between conscious and unconscious, paranoid-schizoid and depressive positions; and Hoffman's perpetually constructed and coconstructed experience" [pp. 31–32].

certain experiences including, for many individuals, annihilation anxiety, the *stability* of the personality structure is both its most cherished asset and its most painful handicap. I wrote that the mind from this vantage point is an environment—a stable, relatively secure world in which the schizoid individual lives. He is oriented towards keeping it from being rearranged by the outside, but also towards making it as personally interesting and cozy to live in as possible. Insularity, self-containment, and an avoidance of spontaneity or surprise are therefore quite important. A boundary is built between the inner world and the outer world to *prevent* a free and spontaneous interchange beyond the already known and the relatively predictable or controllable.

The mind as a stable, relatively secure world, designed to be as cozy to live in as possible, and structured so that insularity and self-containment prevent rearrangement by the outside, particularly by "surprise"! I had no idea at the time that I was writing about what I would later come to see as a dissociative defense against the "shock" of trauma and potential retraumatization. I was then describing the patholological form of what in every human being allows continuity and change to occur simultaneously and thus makes normal personality growth possible—a mental space that allows selfhood and otherness to interpenetrate, and provides the context for continuity of human relatedness *while* self-change is taking place. More recently (chapter 17) I have come to speak of it as a co-constructed mental space, uniquely relational and still uniquely individual; a space belonging to neither person alone, and yet, belonging to both and to each; a twilight space in which "the impossible" becomes possible; a space in which incompatible selves, each awake to its own "truth," can "dream" the reality of the other without risk to its own integrity. I've suggested it to be an intersubjective space which, like the "trance" state of consciousness just prior to entering sleep, allows both wakefulness and dreaming to coexist. From a more spiritual frame of reference, Roger Kamenetz (1994, p. 28) offers a similar thought in his fascinating cultural excursion to the interface of Judaism and Buddhism. He observes that "dawn and dusk are basic times to pray, because then you have daytime and nightime consciousness at the same time." I am suggesting that psychoanalysis, at its clinical best, facilitates the same interplay between seemingly incompatible states of mind.

Interestingly, there is increasing evidence that this seemingly impossible mental space that is at once uniquely relational but still uniquely individual is not only possible, but has a known neurophysiological substrate. Henry Krystal, for example (Krystal et al., 1995, p. 245), suggests that it may in fact be mediated by alterations in the activity of the thalamus that links "a spectrum of altered states of consciousness such as hypnosis, dreaming, and other conditions in which there is a combination of the features of sleep and waking states." At the level of personality growth, what Krystal is addressing here is what I call the therapeutic process of enhancing a patient's capacity to feel like one self while being many—the clinical relationship through which bridges are built between defensively unlinked islands of self-experience so that the distinction between what is "me" and what is "not-me" becomes more and more permeable (cf. Dennett, 1991; Kennedy, 1996).

Trauma and Clinical Process

Sullivan (1953) made clear that a child knows what is "me" and what is "not-me" through relational patterns of meaning established early in life. The child's experience of "me-ness," as developmental research has been convincingly demonstrating, is most sturdy when his states of mind are experienced and reflected upon by the mind of an other, particularly during moments of intense affective arousal (cf. Fonagy, 1991; Fonagy and Moran, 1991). If the other's behavior, even if it is not fully welcoming, shows that his state of mind is emotionally and cognitively responsive to what is most affectively immediate in the child's mind rather than tangential to it (Laing, 1962a), the engagement of minds constitutes an act of recognition that allows the child to accomplish the developmental achievement of taking his own state of mind as an object of reflection. He thereby becomes able to cognitively process in the here-and-now, affectively intense and affectively complex moments as states of intrapsychic conflict. Fonagy and Target (1996, p. 221) indeed put it that by the age of five or six a child should normally establish what they refer to as a reflective, or mentalizing mode of psychic reality, and that in order to do so "the child needs an adult or older child who will 'play along', so that the child sees his fantasy or idea represented in the adult's mind, reintrojects this and uses it as a representation of his own thinking."

What Fonagy and Target mean here by "play along" is of paramount importance in considering therapeutic development as well. They put it as follows:

> Our acceptance of a dialectical perspective on self-development shifts the traditional psychoanalytical emphasis from internalization of the containing object to the internalization of the thinking self from within the containing object. . . . The reflective aspect of the analytic process is understanding and not simply empathy (the accurate mirroring of mental state). It cannot simply "copy" the

internal state of the patient, but has to move beyond it and go a step further, offering a different, yet experientially appropriate re-representation [p. 231].

In other words, whether parent or analyst, the one who is "playing along" must be himself while being a usable object; that is, he must be engaged as a person in his or her own right and must be relating to the child or patient as such. It is through this that a child or patient becomes capable of retaining a more cohesive self-experience without the felt risk of traumatization leading to pathological dissociation, the failure of symbolization, and impairment of the ability to cognitively represent affectively intense or complex experience within a self-narrative of "me-ness."

Let me underline this point with an observation from another of their papers (Target and Fonagy, 1996, p. 460): "A transactional relationship exists between the child's own mental experience of himself and that of his object. His perception of the other is conditioned by his experience of his own mental state, which has in turn been conditioned developmentally by his perception of how his object conceived of his mental world." Thus, if the other systematically "*dis*confirms" (Laing, 1962a) a child's state of mind at moments of intense affective arousal by behaving as though the meaning of the event to the child is either irrelevant or is "something else," the child grows to mistrust the reality of his own experience. He is traumatically impaired in his ability to cognitively process his own emotionally charged mental states in an interpersonal context—to reflect on them, hold them as states of intrapsychic conflict, and thus own them as "me." Dissociation, the disconnection of the mind from the psyche-soma, then becomes the most adaptive solution to preserving self-continuity.

In this light, psychological trauma can broadly be defined as the precipitous disruption of self-continuity (cf. Pizer, 1996a, 1996b) through invalidation of the internalized self-other patterns of meaning that constitute the experience of "me-ness." Coates and Moore (1997, p. 287) speak of it as "an overwhelming threat to the integrity of the self that is accompanied by annihilation anxiety,"[2] a portrayal I find

---

2. With regard to annihilation anxiety in treating patients for whom dissociation and dissociative states are central issues, Fonagy and Target (1995b, pp. 163–164) hold that the aim of psychoanalytic treatment is to reduce "the intense annihilatory anxieties that have been evoked by contact in the traumatic past." The authors then go on to draw an interesting comparison between their model of therapeutic change and mine as similarly embracing the view that "the therapist must resist his inclination to correct

vividly accurate for the large number of patients one can justifiably call "trauma survivors."

Psychological trauma occurs in situations, explicitly or implicitly interpersonal, in which self-invalidation (sometimes self-*annihilation*) cannot be escaped from or prevented and from which there is no hope of protection, relief, or soothing. If the experience is either prolonged, assaultively violent, or if self-development is weak or immature, then the level of affective arousal is too great for the event to be experienced self-reflectively and given meaning through cognitive processing. Physiologically, what takes place is an autonomic hyperarousal of affect that cannot be cognitively schematized and managed by thought. At its extreme, the subjective experience is that of a chaotic and terrifying flooding of affect that threatens to overwhelm sanity and psychological survival, but to one degree or another its shadow is an inherent aspect of what to some degree shapes mental functioning in every human being.

In other words, dissociation as a defense, even in a relatively normal personality structure, limits self-reflection to what is secure or needed for survival of selfhood, while in individuals for whom trauma has been severe, self-reflection is extremely curtailed in order that the capacity to reflect does not break down completely and result in a collapse of selfhood. What we call annihilation anxiety represents the latter possibility. Thus, paradoxically, the defensive division of the self into unlinked parts preserves identity by establishing more secure boundaries between self and "not-self" through dissociative unlinking of self-states, each with its own boundaries and its own firm experience of not-self. Consequently, dissociative patterns of relating come to define personal boundaries of selfhood in a very powerful way.

What was formerly normal dissociation, the loose configuration of multiple self-states that enables a person to "feel like one self while being many," becomes rigidified into a dissociative mental structure (the most extreme form of which we know as "multiple personality" or "dissociative identity disorder"), each self now uncompromisingly boundaried within its specific pattern of interpersonal engagement that gives its self-meaning the cast of truth. Because the individual states are defensively and rigidly isolated from one another, the dissociative structure has not only been restored but now is able to protect indefinitely the subjective sense of self-consistency and continuity by locating personal identity tightly within whichever self-state has access to consciousness and cognition at a given moment. The security

---

the patient's faulty perception of reality and instead create a relationship in which previously unsymbolized experiences can find expression."

of the personality is now linked to a trauma-based view of reality whereby the person is always ready for the disaster that he is sure is around the next corner, and some dissociated aspect of self is "on-call" to deal with it. The price that is paid is that the individual can no longer afford to feel safe even when he is.

Standing in the Spaces

Part of our work as analysts facilitates the restoration of links between dissociated aspects of self so that the conditions for intrapsychic conflict and its resolution can develop. By being attuned to shifts in his own self-states as well as those of the patient, and using this awareness relationally, an analyst furthers the capacity of a patient to hear in a single interpersonal context the echo of his other selves voicing alternative realities that have been previously incompatible. I might add that it is easier for an analyst to speak to several parts of a patient's self in the same moment if he keeps in mind Harry Stack Sullivan's apocryphal though often quoted wish to be spared from a therapy that goes well—his way of dramatizing the fact that a successful treatment does not just perambulate smoothly along while you enjoy watching your patient grow. As most clinicians know, a thriving analytic therapy is frequently the opposite, seeming to move from impasse to impasse while the two participants gain increasing ability to successfully negotiate and make therapeutic use of relational collisions between different aspects of each of their selves. The form of this phenomenon with which analysts tend to be most comfortably or uncomfortably familiar is the inevitable enactment around the "treatment frame," or as I prefer to express it, the dialectic between the "personal" and the "professional" as a central configuration of the transference/countertransference field.

The opposition that patients feel toward entering a professional relationship of such intense intimacy is known to us all, but it is only because the line between "personal" and "professional" is permeable rather than hard-edged that it is possible for the therapeutic relationship we call psychoanalysis to exist in the first place. Enactment, as a phenomenon, occurs in every human relationship regardless of its nature, but it is only the psychoanalytic relationship, because of its inherent ambiguity, that allows enactment to both occur and be analyzed within the same context. When the context becomes overly personal (or insufficiently personal) it loses the paradoxical quality that makes it usable. A relationship cannot analyze itself if it has unlimited freedom to remain perpetually enacted. Enactment will of course still occur, but it will lack the analyzable collision between the personal and professional elements that creates the ongoing "analysis of the analysis"—the core process that distinguishes it from other forms of psychotherapy. A patient is given room to express himself as freely as he is able, but always within a "professional" frame of conditions established by the analyst. Which aspects of the "professional" frame are openly revealed by the analyst, which are gradually "discovered" by the patient, and which are covertly "managed" by the analyst, are themselves issues that distinguish the nature of the approach adopted by any given analyst. How the professional frame is communicated by the analyst to the patient may vary widely from clinician to clinician, but its existence is always felt as a palpable force by the patient even when genuine elements of it are denied by the analyst.

The collision between professional and personal is often the raw material of enactment. It is experienced as problematic by the analyst only when he is forced out of whatever professional context of meaning he uses to process this experience, and cannot comfortably maintain the professional frame he relies upon to understand what is going on between himself and his patient. As long as his own meaning-context feels like it is still in existence and is accepted as valid (either explicitly or implicitly) by the patient as well, personal feelings are experienced as relatively routine. They do not endanger the analyst's sense of professional identity because, no matter how "personal" they feel, they can remain framed in some manner as "material" to be looked at. It is only when the patient seriously threatens or actually manages to render the analytic situation an invalid means of examining his feelings about what is going on within it that the permeable line between personal and professional has been (at least temporarily) obliterated, and the analyst is feeling helpless in being able either to shift or regain the analytic frame he uses to give these feelings meaning.

Spruiell (1983) described what he called the "rules and frames of the analytic situation" as the analyst's way of protecting himself from the "truth" about his own deficiencies. Spruiell puts it that: "Patients who persistently broach the analytic frame are regarded as 'difficult' patients," and that "sometimes the analyst has to temporarily abandon the analytic frame in order to preserve the possibilities of work" (p. 18). In treating certain individuals, however, the point at which the analyst has to temporarily abandon the analytic frame is often not a matter of choice. Sometimes the analyst is reduced to a state of genuine helplessness and is in the grip of feelings which are experienced as out of control. If, however, he is gradually able to open himself to his full range of self-states in a context where he is no longer "possessed" by these feelings, his personal reactions to his patient—the previously dissociated quality of what he has been feeling—can then be communicated judiciously and *jointly* processed as not only material but also as "real." Analysts have always considered it a seeming paradox that certain patients start to improve characterologically only when they believe that what is going on is not part of the "treatment." I look at these examples as simply the more dramatic instances of what takes place more subtly in every analysis—an ongoing movement between impasse and repair that allows the gradual creation of a shared "potential space" by providing a patient with increased access to the reality of the "other" without surrendering his own. From my perspective, as later chapters will elaborate in more detail, it is this process through which formerly dissociated self-states begin to become integrated into a patient's configuration of "me-ness" as a cohesive human experience by becoming *relationally* consistent with his own "truth" about who he is.

For this to take place, the patient's experience must somehow or other also be consistent, at least momentarily, with the analyst's own "truth" about who *he* is. And this is not always easy or fun. The reader might guess where I am going, or rather where the last two decades have brought me. As a child I drove my mother slightly crazy by preserving my innerness. But as an analyst I find I have to let my patients drive *me* crazy, to borrow Searles's (1959) felicitious phrasing, by using my innerness as though it were their own despite the fact that at these moments my innerness does not stop being inner to me. Simply put, the patient's effort to "use" the analyst's mind as an object will be inevitably resisted by the analyst, thus allowing the patient to find himself in it by increasingly forcing his dissociated selves into the analyst's mind. The analyst will sometimes feel these as the patient's, but more often will first be in touch with them as his own feelings.

And here let me close this introduction by remarking again on the dialectic between the personal and the professional. At these critical points in treatment, the analyst must contribute to "an act of recognition," but "recognition" is not passive observation. The analyst is always a *participant* observer, and with some patients the analyst's needed participation comes about only—to use again Harold Searles's idiom—through his being made a little "crazy" by his patient. This forces him to experience dissociated aspects of his own selfhood that lead to the recognition of dissociated aspects of the patient's self, and as this oscillating cycle of projection and introjection is processed and sorted out between them, the patient reclaims what is his. Until then, neither patient nor analyst gets much rest. There's a wonderful little poem by Langston Hughes (1941) that captures it better than anything in the analytic literature:

> Seems like what drives me crazy
> Ain't got no effect on you—
> But I'm gonna keep on at it
> Till it drives you crazy too.

There is a class of personal reactions to certain patients at such times that is unlike any other countertransferential response I have. At those moments I have no doubt about the phenomenon of projective identi-fication as an interpersonal channel of communication. "Why are you shouting at me?" a patient will shout. It matters not that I am "sure" my voice level did not rise. The accusation as I feel it might more accu-rately have been, "Why are you existing at me?" My experience at such moments, once I am able to process it, is typically a powerful channel through which I know my patient, but unlike empathy (see also Ghent, 1994), the experience does not feel voluntary; it is as if the knowledge is being "forced" into me. The struggle to find words that address the gap that separates us is the most potentially powerful bridge between the patient's dissociated self-states. My ability to use this experience thera-peutically depends on my capacity to tolerate it long enough to reflect upon it. Once the words are found and negotiated between us, they then become part of the patient's growing ability to symbolize and express in language what he has had no voice to say.

What a patient is able to hold and symbolize cognitively versus what he must hold without symbolic processing and must thereby enact is the key issue. What is *there* is going to be registered in some form or other, and some unprocessed aspect of it will be enacted. The challenge for an analyst is to make what is there useful analytic mater-ial. How an analyst does this is what distinguishes the differences in "technique" between analytic schools of thought, but it is also what distinguishes individual analysts within a given school and, one may hope, the individual analyses conducted by any given analyst.

PART I

VIEWS FROM THE BRIDGE

2

ARTIST AND ANALYST[1] (1991)

Although the times have been infrequent because she doesn't like to work with an audience, there have been occasions when I've had the chance to observe my wife in her studio in the process of painting. The thought that invariably crosses my mind is how she ever came to be able to do this thing which to me seems beyond comprehension even though I'm watching it occur and can see the technical process going on in front of my eyes. I know her art background; I know with whom she studied, in which countries she was trained, what painters most influenced her, and even many of the basic principles that guide her; but the sum total of this knowledge, except at some superficial level, does not seem to account for what emerges as she works, either in the moment-to-moment process or at any phase or stage along the way. She also teaches painting, and many of her students go on to have shows of their own—but except for rare instances her students' work looks nothing like hers. What, then, can be said about the interface between what a painter does and teaches with regard to the role of what was initially taught during training?

It might be argued that the analyst-painter analogy is too thinly drawn to be usable because the analyst's efforts are directed by a continually evolving interchange with another human being, while the painter is presumably directed by his or her internal vision in a one-way

---

1. This chapter was first presented in an earlier version as part of a symposium on "Learning, Practicing, and Teaching Psychoanalysis" at the Spring Weekend Conference of the William Alanson White Psychoanalytic Society in April 1990, and was published in its present form in *Contemporary Psychoanalysis*, 1991, 27:289–300.

transformation of some internal or external reality. That is, unlike the analyst, the painter's creativity is determined largely by the blend of raw talent with what has been taught, so that the original learning has been "forgotten" as a set of rules to simply be applied while painting; what has been learned is digested into the painter's personal identity and emerges as a disciplined element of self-expression that is inseparable from the creative act itself. In other words, "technique" in a skilled artist doesn't show; the finished product, because of this, has no appearance of having been "painted by the numbers." The argument is compelling, but omits the one feature that makes the analyst-painter analogy both interesting and, I believe, valid. A painter whose internal vision renders objective reality into a representation of that vision is, no matter how gifted or experienced, limited in creative expression. Like the analyst, the painter must permit an interactive process to take place through which the painter's understanding of what he or she wants to create and how it is to be created, changes as it is expressed on canvas. In this sense, each painting is created as a new act of learning regardless of what was learned in the formal training process of becoming a painter. Each painting must be allowed to possess a changing identity of its own as it is being painted, and this identity must be free to instruct and inform the painter as to how it is to be painted in an evolving rather than a preconceived way.

In the same way, each analysis for any given analyst should be generated by an interactive learning process that occurs while the work is going on, and which shapes the analyst's vision of what is to be created (a vision the analyst must hold of the patient as "more" than he is now)[2] and how it is to be created; that is, the originally learned princi-

---

2. The paradox of the analyst as holder of the patient's potential has been eloquently developed by Friedman (1988, pp. 27–34) who states (following Loewald, 1960) "that one sort of childhood need which is not only sought in analysis, but is also fulfilled by analysis, is the need to identify with one's own growth potential as seen in the eyes of a parent. Being reacted to like that not only provides hope in general but structures reality in a relevant and promising fashion" (p. 27). But, says Friedman, "Hope can only be a present hope, in the shape given it by the patient's present psychological configuration. . . . In other words, the analyst must accept the patient on his own terms, and at the same time not settle for them. If he does not accept the patient on his own terms, it is as though he is asking him to be someone else, the patient will not have cause for hope, and he will not recognize the analyst's vision. If the analyst settles for the patient's terms, he is . . . betraying the patient's wish for greater fulfilment" (p. 34).

ples through which analysis is done are constantly being negotiated as the work is taking place with a given patient. If they are not, the analyst, like the painter, will have to fall back on a combination of whatever basic skill he or she possesses, plus whatever was initially learned as "the right way" of doing it. Certain paintings will be unpaintable, certain patients will be "unanalyzable," and the finished product in all cases will have a distinct aura of having been "painted by the numbers."

During the course of my training at the White Institute, I was fortunate to have had three supervisors (Edgar Levenson, Earl Witenberg, and David Schecter) who, in the way they interacted with me and how they listened to the work I presented, represented the kind of open-mindedness that generates creativity. These three learned as they taught and changed as they learned. This way of being, which they shared in common, had a profound impact upon me through what they said as they worked with me, despite the fact that no two of them said things in similar ways and each had different vantage points from which they viewed the nature of the treatment process. I eventually recognized that throughout my years of candidacy at the Institute, the people from whom I was learning the most were thinkers who were as different from one another as committed individualists could be, but I didn't comprehend this until some years after I had graduated. So, in terms of what I had actually "digested" from what each of my supervisors had "taught," and in what ways it was useful to me, I had very little awareness while it was taking place. However, what I did know even at the time, was that these people were not only smart, they were honest; they said what they believed and let me do with it what I would . . . and what I could. They were models for something that Lincoln Kirstein (1969) put into words in a description of the life and work of Eugene Smith, the photographer: "Honesty is not a profession. Honesty consists of what the individual brings to his work. Silence is golden, but the blank page tells no tale." Each of the people who most influenced me during the course of my training filled the blank page differently; they thought for themselves and didn't ask if what they believed was permissible. This was their legacy to me. I have taken something from what each taught and arrived at something that I believe in; something different from each, and in some ways even at odds with their views, but clearly informed by them.

I can divide the history of my thinking about psychoanalysis into two phases for the purpose of this discussion. The first is roughly defined by the time period starting with the onset of my analytic training at the White Institute in 1969, taking a path that led to the publication of my first analytic paper 10 years later, "Interpersonal

Psychoanalysis and Regression" (chapter 3). The second period, which I would say is still going on, feels in some ways like a refinement of the first, in other ways like a redefinition of the first, and in yet another way both periods feel to me as if they are temporary phases on route to something as yet unthought.

My focus from the beginning was on clinical process rather than on theory, and specifically on the treatment of severe character pathology—the so-called "difficult" or "unanalyzable" patient. It was the first period, I would say, that was most shaped by the congruence between what I was taught and what I practiced; and the second period by the interpenetration between what I practiced and what I taught and wrote.

Let me start with the first. When I look back on my years as an analytic candidate I am amazed at how long I held on to the innocent belief that, except for one or two people, there was a more or less harmonious fit between the ideas that were represented by the senior people at the Institute, and that if I smoothed out the seams and added a few stitches here or there I would end up with an approach that somehow represented the analytic thinking of all of the founders of the Institute (and all of the senior faculty), even though it required major stitching for me to manage this. Trying to get Fromm and Sullivan to sound like members of the same family is just one example. I was never very taken with Fromm as an analyst but I responded to Sullivan's ideas with passion. I even liked his quirky writing style. I read his work and tried to comprehend what was the real key to fitting his ideas into what I was being taught in classes and in supervision. What I didn't know was that I was being trained at a time when understanding Sullivan was much more difficult to achieve than it had been in the past because of a shift in philosophy that was taking place in the Institute with regard to the analyst's more open use of himself in the analytic field. It was a shift that was taking place among certain senior people at White but not among others. It's not that the new emphasis wasn't acknowledged; it was that the shift was to an analytic stance so different from Sullivan's own that depending upon whom a candidate was working with in supervision, he could be potentially unable to read Sullivan's *The Psychiatric Interview* (1954) as anything more than a technique for doing the initial history-taking and then, when that was over, he works the "other" way; that is, allows full use of himself within the transference-countertransference field rather than trying to stay out of it. While it was quietly admitted that Sullivan didn't like to work with transference and countertransference as basic to the process of analytic communication, this fact usually was presented as though it were simply an idiosyncracy of his, and that he would of course use it appropriately when it arose.

Sullivan's theory of therapy (at least the way Sullivan presented it when he wrote about it) was based on two interlocking dimensions: exploration of detail and attention by the therapist to what he called a gradient of the patient's anxiety level as the inquiry was taking place. Because some of the first-generation analysts trained by Sullivan translated this to mean that participant observation is primarily confrontational, with the ultimate goal of consensual validation being the correction of distortion,[3] it was never made clear that the very heart of Sullivan's technique was *tied* to staying out of the transference-countertransference field as far as possible. It was not idiosyncratic. It was shaped by a principle that Sullivan knew was absolutely necessary therapeutically—particularly when treating seriously disturbed patients such as the schizophrenics with whom he worked—but was a principle that Sullivan believed could be respected only by staying out of the patient's "distortions," especially during the initial phase of the work.[4] Leston Havens (1973, 1976) argued that what Sullivan (1954) was advocating came from his recognition of an intersubjective process through which an unsymbolized interpersonal field of projection and introjection underwent transformation into communicable, mentally represented thought. Havens (1973) was proposing that despite Sullivan's commitment to operationalism and staying out of the transference/countertransference field, his participant-observer approach to his patients wasn't tied simply to the *externally* observable data field, but rested on what was astutely labeled by Havens as a context of "counterprojection." In this regard, Sullivan was mapping the same experientally ambiguous interface between "internal" and "external" that Bion (1955) was beginning to examine from an object relational perspective. "In traditional psychoanalysis," Havens (1973) writes,

> the patient's attention is called to the transference distortions. The psychoanalyst wants the patient to understand what he, the patient, is doing. In short, analysis encourages rather than prevents

---

3. Clara Thompson (1953, p. 29) put it as simply as that "in Sullivanian terms, therapy consists of the gradual clarifying for the patient of the kind of things he is doing to and with other people, as a result of his distortion of them."

4. Sullivan's strongest and most direct statements addressing this issue can be found in the published proceedings of a case seminar led by Sullivan, on the "treatment of a young male schizophrenic" (Kvarnes and Parloff, 1976, pp. 122–124, 215–217).

projections . . . [In] Sullivanian technique . . . awareness of the projections may even be avoided and their rapid reduction or elimina-
tion sought. . . . At the same time that he is helping the patient gain
distance on his delusional assumptions Sullivan is disengaging
himself from those delusional assumptions. . . . Therefore, insofar
as the real current world, including the doctor, is playing into the
patient's projections, the doctor must dissociate himself from that
world if he is to help the patient gain perspective on his projections
[pp. 195–197].

I could not see this as a candidate, nor could I see it when I first
read Havens. It was too discrepant with what I had learned to believe.
It was years later on rereading Sullivan that it finally penetrated.
Reading Sullivan simply as a clinician leaves little doubt that this is
what he was doing no matter how much he chose to talk the language
of operationalism, and that this is what he meant by what he called
"an anxiety gradient." If you find yourself caught up in the patient's
projections you have made an error. He didn't use the term "empathic
failure," but in this respect Sullivan was a grandmaster of empathic
attunement long before Kohut had even thought about narcissistic
transferences.

But what about the use of the transference-countertransference field
as a creative force? What about the power that comes from addressing it
openly? Here was Sullivan's weakness, and here is where the split
occurred among Sullivanians. It was not presented as a split, nor
would I imagine that most of the people who represent this group
would even now agree that it was. At the time I was trained, analysts
like Edward Tauber, Edgar Levenson, Arthur Feiner, and Benjamin
Wolstein were already in place and influential as representing a point
of view that embraced the analyst's full use of himself with his patient.
Levenson was my first supervisor, and I think he was finishing writing
The Fallacy of Understanding (1972) while he was supervising me. His
concept of "perspectivism" as a listening stance, once I caught on to it,
changed my work totally; but it left me with the problem of how to
use this stance within an analytic field that takes into account the variability among different types of patients in their capacity to make use
of it. I knew that in one respect Sullivan was right and in another he
was wrong. I knew that there were certain patients for whom staying
out of the field and allowing a process of counterprojection to occur,
was absolutely necessary, at least for a period of time. But I also knew
that becoming caught in the field was not an error but an inevitability,
just as Tauber, Levenson, and others were proposing. Learn how to
use this inevitability creatively; this was the message I heard, but I had

to find my own path in order to implement it. Once I caught on to this I stopped "painting by the numbers" and began asking my own questions.

However, I had to put more and more stitches into the fabric in order to try and reconcile Sullivan's "stay out of the mess" approach with this (to me) transformational stance of allowing oneself to become caught up and using one's own subjective state as observable data to be explored with the patient. I began to reflect on the fact that there was a large group of my patients to whom what seemed most important was their being allowed to show who they were by being it rather than telling it. Exploring, for them, meant taking away their chance for the only authentic form of communication possible. They needed to be a mess with me, and for me to know them I had to become part of the mess in some way that I could feel internally. It couldn't be contained within a framework of perspectivistic exploration; they wouldn't, couldn't, and didn't accept that approach as anything but another technique to not have to be with them as they were; they experienced it as a violation of their very being. With these patients, during certain periods, Sullivan's counterprojective stance came closer to what was therapeutic, but it still failed to address what seemed most central to the patient; it didn't really touch their pain; it was too logical; too reasonable; too externally operational. They seemed to need attention focussed on their state of mind itself rather than on what went on between themselves and others. They needed something that approached what Sullivan advocated as an exquisite attention to detail, but where the details were experiential rather than objective events. Focussing on external events (that is, what went on between the patient and someone else in some situation) made the goal one of "understanding." Understanding is for the purpose of achieving greater clarity, for correcting distortions, for seeing things a new way, etc. These patients, at these times, did not need to be "understood"; they needed to be "known," to be "recognized." This could happen only by the analyst living in the mess with the patient, feeling all the hopelessness, negativity, and pain, and keeping focussed on the details of the patient's state of mind without trying to point out what was being missed or changing the level of discourse to something more distant from the subjective experience itself; in other words, staying away from trying to "create" consensual validation as though it took place simply at a cognitive level.

During this period of my work I became interested in British object relations theories and their interface with interpersonal thinking. It was this path that led to my writing the "regression" paper (chapter 3), or as I might have subtitled it in 1979, "Please Don't Throw Me Out of the Family for Using a Dirty Word." A recent statement representing the "independent tradition" of the British school may bring this issue into higher relief. Duncan (1989) writes about the analyst as follows:

> In the confidence of his consulting room he considers equally, without fear or favour, objectively demonstrable data and non-demonstrable, deeply subjective phenomena. This particular distinction, like any other, will in a given instance depend for its relevance or arbitrariness on the analytic context. Certainly he does not consistently place them in austerely separate compartments [p. 694].

Sullivanian operationalism, with its goal of symbolizing experience by language, focussed on what was observable ("objectively demonstrable data") as the road that led most straightforwardly to an increased ability to perceive rather than simply enact. So too, may be described most of the theories that comprise the British school. The big difference is that Sullivanian operationalism, because of Sullivan's own philosophical bent, tends to be goal-oriented while the British theories tend to be experience-oriented. Sullivan conveys an interest in the patient's experience that is largely pragmatic. It is a means to achieve consensus, to move from an autistic level of experience to a symbolized and shared context of meaning. It is the autistic context (the enactment) that I am calling "the mess," and this is indeed how Sullivan seemed to feel about it when he wrote. The "prototaxic" was the illness; the "parataxic" was a little better because at least it could be put into words; but verbal meaning was the thing. All else was a means to that end. It was pragmatic through and through.

The British group, on the other hand, valued subjective experience as a state in itself. It was not equated with "the illness," with "narcissism," with "distortion." It was, in fact, the place where what Winnicott called "the true" self was located. But more than that, it was not held to be "unobservable" simply because its meaning could not be put into language. The world of internal objects was as observable as that of real people, as long as the field of observation is defined as intersubjective rather than as interactive, and the analyst does not choose to avoid being pulled into the enactment of what is unsayable in words but exists as felt meaning. If the therapist does not avoid this, (as the British did not avoid it) then the "observable" data, as Levenson and others have shown, are coming from within the analyst's subjective state while he is with his patient. It doesn't much matter (at least to me) whether one uses the language of one theory or another; if you allow yourself to enter the field, you are knowing your patient in a way that is inescapably observable by what you feel and what you are thinking and what you find yourself doing. It is not simply a step towards something else more rational and healthier. It is itself a field that has a validity for the patient that must be felt and recognized by the therapist as an end in itself. This is what Sullivan did not convey when he wrote, although I have to believe that he must have grasped it intuitively or he could never have helped so many severely impaired patients.

The field is framed by a responsiveness between two subjectivities that are always reading one another. The analyst speaks as much through what he does not do or say as by what he does do or say. It is a stance that is as attuned as possible to the patient's need for recognition of his state of mind being valid for what it is, and no more. Sullivan's idea of the anxiety gradient touches on this, but doesn't emphasize nearly enough what the British saw immediately—the centrality of a bond based on attunement to the patient's subjective experience as an end in itself, and not simply a process based on the absence of traumatically high levels of anxiety. When Sullivan wrote of the analyst's contribution he wrote as a pragmatist; the analyst was portrayed as a skilled worker; an "expert" in human relations, untouched as far as possible by his own unprocessed feelings while with the patient, and looking at the patient's "operations" with an "objective" eye.

My interest in patients with severe character pathology—schizoid, borderline, and narcissistic conditions—developed because these people were not getting any better by simply applying the approach I had been taught. In fact, it seemed to me that when they did get better it occurred through believing that they somehow knew something about the chaotic mess we were living through that I didn't have a clue about, and that without imposing the language of "understanding," something was being created out of it that I was not to interfere with, either by "looking at what was going on between us" or by saying anything that would force a change in the level of rationality. Concepts that touched my work most deeply seemed to come from the British school at this time—ideas such as regression, projective identification, transitional space, potential space, use of the object, holding environment, part-objects, and schizoid compromise—concepts that deal with what Sullivan would have called unobservable events, but which I was coming more and more to see were "unobservable" only if the analyst defined the field simply as interactive rather than as inherently intersubjective. Then, indeed, the data that would make these experiences observable were missing—the analyst's use of his own subjective states and the changes in them, as a participant within a field that was allowed to become regressive without a stance that tries to prevent it.

Why do I see my position as inherently interpersonal rather than as simply object relational? Sandler and Sandler (1978, p. 294) have suggested that "object relationships can be regarded as role relationships. This is as true of the relationships in thought or fantasy to the various images deriving from the structures we call 'introjects' or 'internal objects' as of the relationships which obtain between the subject and persons perceived in the external environment." This formulation, which others have presented in different language, offers a conceptual link between "objectively demonstrable data and non-demonstrable deeply subjective phenomena" (Duncan, 1989) in the analytic situation, and makes the linguistic content of the external interpersonal field inseparable from the intersubjectively experienced "internal world" without words. Put somewhat differently, what is taken into the self through the analytic process is not just the verbal meaning (the "correctness" of the analyst's words), nor just a representation of the analyst as parental figure or as separate entity, nor just an experience of the analyst's parental soothing function as Kohut (1971, 1977) sees it, but a representation of the relationship itself as an evolving self-other configuration. What gets reorganized structurally by the patient are not just qualities of the analyst or functions the analyst performs, but a relational gestalt of experience that is constantly being repatterned as relative roles are being redefined.

This is the same point I made about the creative process for a painter. The growth of the painting rests upon the painter's changing relationship to the painting as the painting develops; its changing identity must change the painter's conception as he or she paints. The analyst, too, must be working with the patient in a way that, in order to be effective, facilitates the patient's immediate experience of the analytic relationship as permitting an evolving redefinition of their respective roles paralleling the patient's self growth. Only within the co-created intersubjective playground that Winnicott (1971b) called "potential space" (see also Ogden, 1985), will judicious here-and-now exploration of the analytic relationship allow genetic interpretation and historical reconstruction to aid in the integration of new self structure rather than lead to a global introjection of the analyst's "correct" interpretations. The direct connection between the interpersonal and object relational views lies in the analyst's ability to experience the intersubjective field as a process in which ambiguity, paradox, and sometimes even chaos are felt to be relationally valid elements in the growth of self.

Questioning seems to be part of my basic nature. I can't read anything I've written without wishing I could take it back and say it in the way I think about it currently. It's the same with teaching; I seem to naturally raise questions about everything and focus on what the student or writer seems to be struggling with rather than on the rightness or wrongness of their solutions. I also question what I myself do and I don't in fact believe I understand how this thing we call psychoanalysis really works. And in a certain way, I'm always more excited by what I consider my failures than by what appear to be my successes. My failures are the evidence that, just as I suspected, there's more to it than the current self-satisfied view I am holding as my "truth." I have something real to take apart and look at. The failures force me to do it; with the successes, the effort is more optional, and sometimes I'm too lazy to say "Why was it good? Was it really? What if . . . ?" When I think my questioning has led me somewhere new, sometimes I will write a paper. And even though it enriches my interactions with students, supervisees, and patients, another voice is saying, "If before you die or retire, you are doing even 50 percent of what you tell your students and supervisees they should do, then maybe I'll leave you alone." And that seems to be how it is with me.

3

INTERPERSONAL PSYCHOANALYSIS AND REGRESSION[1] (1979)

Psychoanalysts have long been aware that in the day-to-day practice of their somewhat subjective art they can become seduced by their own explanatory constructs. As in any developing discipline there is an intrinsic pressure to accept the empirical success of one's own technique as objective validation for a particular theory of psychological functioning and growth, and refuting those concepts which seem to oppose it. Thus ideational systems become "fact," and "truth" is discovered. Levenson (1972) has developed some general implications of this phenomenon in what he calls "the time-bound nature of psychoanalytic truth." More specifically, a relatively experienced and successful therapist, trying to formulate what he does, *must* derive his conceptual position, at least in part, from a fundamental need to maintain cognitive consistency.[2] His relative dependence upon

---

1. An earlier version of this chapter was first presented at a symposium held at the Institute for Contemporary Psychotherapy, New York City, in December 1977, and was published in its present form in *Contemporary Psychoanalysis*, 1979, 15:647–655.

2. See Festinger (1957) for the development of this idea, and R. Brown (1965) for a lucid review of the empirical concept of cognitive consistency and its implications for theories of personality development and attitude formation.

data coming from within his consulting room fosters the rigidifying of a shared belief system which makes sense of the evidence that his own technique is effective in some consistent way. Commitment to a particular version of psychoanalytic "truth" is therefore not only *time* bound; it is also bound to the cognitive demand to give structural meaning to the basic dimensions of one's effectiveness at any given point in time while keeping the door open to reconceptualization and change.

Witenberg (1976), among others, has argued that "schools" of psychoanalysis have become overly dedicated to objectifying their collective "truths." Although interpersonal psychoanalysis has been less prone to this practice than has the orthodox Freudian school, it too has developed pockets of quasi-sacred dogma, some of which are now beginning to be reexamined.

For example, it has been pointed out by a number of authors (e.g., Wolstein, 1971; Crowley, 1973) that the concept of unique individuality need not be barred from interpersonal theory, and that it may in fact be necessary (Klenbort, 1978) for the continued development of Sullivan's most central contributions. Klenbort asserts that Sullivan's singular adherence to consensual validation is not primarily a methodological overemphasis, as Crowley (1973) sees it, but rather an idiosyncratic overreaction to the potential in psychoanalytic theory for the aggrandizement of personal uniqueness. She advances the position that although Sullivan "has rejected half of the dialectic of human being . . . the unique self whose aims are individuation and experience of the other" (p. 133), there is room within the theory for the gap to be bridged just as it is inevitably bridged clinically "in every unique psychoanalytic experience that is genuinely far-reaching and mutative in nature" (p. 135).

This paper will attempt to extend this reexamination by suggesting that the concept of therapeutic *regression* has, in a parallel way, been systematically excluded from interpersonal theory and needs to find its place within this framework. By therapeutic regression I refer to the "raw" state of mind of the patient most closely connected with the development of insight which leads to change in the self-representation.

Stanton (1978), while not using the term "regression," suggests that this is already built into Sullivan's viewpoint but that many of his followers do not take it seriously enough; "these essential states for proper communication are, in fact, underrecognized, underanalyzed, and capable of much fuller understanding by both patient and therapist, economically, and with considerable benefit" (p. 134). Stanton makes the point that this is one aspect of interpersonal psychoanalysis in which attention must be focused on the state of mind of the patient, *not the interpersonal situation*. Furthermore, Stanton states that it is during a regressed period when he is functioning best as a psychoanalytic patient.

Sullivan (1940) formulated the process of growth in psychotherapy as dependent upon the expansion of the self by increasing insight and awareness of interpersonal relations through consensual validation. The curative factor in psychoanalysis thereby emphasizes that which maximizes accuracy of mutually shared perceptions, and minimizes those conditions in the psychoanalytic situation which are considered as working against rational inquiry. Regression, like unique individuality, has consequently been viewed primarily in the negative context of its insularity, irrationality, and relative inaccessibility to "correction" through a shared interpersonal field. In other words, it has tended to be associated only with illness and not with "cure."

The problem which this has created for interpersonal theory is that Sullivanians have often sidestepped the issue of what constitutes the optimal psychological state in the patient which leads the inquiry to have its greatest impact on the self-representation. And this in turn has permitted a blurring of the distinction between interpersonal and interactional. It therefore fails to provide a safeguard against the interactional process of consensual validation replacing rather than enriching the immediacy of the interpersonal experience itself.

For several years I believed that regression was not necessary in interpersonal psychoanalysis, and that it in fact more often interfered with growth than enhanced it. And it seemed "true." For the way in which I worked, regression, the use of the couch, and the development of the transference neurosis fit as comfortably as socks on a rooster. Sullivan never systematized a technique. He presented an *approach*-participant observation. Consequently, the way in which an individual therapist interpreted this concept could make quite a difference; one man's participation is often another man's observation.

I believed that regression was unecessary because my patients seemed to do better face to face than on the couch. Yet I kept the couch and used it with a few patients. In retrospect I think, in part, that I hoped someday I might discover why some analysts considered it useful. Over time, changes began to take place in my interests. One major one was an increased fascination with more severe psychopathology and how to work with it within an interpersonal psychoanalytic model. I found myself becoming more and more drawn towards object relations theory, thinking to account for what I began to see emerging in my work. The theory not only permitted regression, it positively revered it. For a period of time it became my new "truth." Regression was no longer "bad"; it was now "good." And it was not simply naiveté which possessed me. In many ways I was not happy with the British school. However, their concepts allowed me to make greater sense of the new depth and richness in my work, which did indeed involve regression and a more natural use of the couch. Was I still an interpersonal analyst? It seemed to me that despite Sullivan's repudiation of regression as therapeutically useless, and of the fundamental structure of classical psychoanalysis in general, his overall approach was not incompatible with it.

A central key to the effectiveness of the interpersonal model is consistency. An interpersonal analyst is as much bound by this as any other analyst, or the analytic experience will not make sense to the patient. A highly interactional Sullivanian who suddenly withdraws to let a transference neurosis develop is simply being mystifying. But it would in no way be a technical error for any analyst, including an interpersonal analyst, to encourage regression if it is not out of context with his natural stance. If inconsistent, however, it will indeed get in the way and will only confirm the "truth" that it is a pathological *rather* than therapeutic state.

It has become more and more clinically evident to me that it is unnecessary to take an a priori position on whether regression is or is not therapeutically useful, and equally unnecessary to conceptualize it as something one induces, even though it is technically possible to do so. It is something which will in and of itself occur under certain conditions, a primary one being that one allows it to happen. With many patients, in fact, I began to observe that the only way regression did not occur during the course of therapy was if I consciously or unconsciously prevented it by becoming increasingly interactional. It was at this point I realized that over the years my posture had become less *interactional*, but my approach and my commitment was no less *interpersonal*. The two are not synonymous. Therapeutic regression can often be as inconsistent with the former as it can facilitate the latter.

The issue is whether one's own view of interpersonal psychoanalysis and one's understanding of how psychotherapeutic change occurs, makes it more consistent to allow regression or to inhibit it. Interpersonal theory does not come packaged with a predetermined technique. Depending upon how interactional one tends to be, certain dimensions of technique will follow in a natural way. If it doesn't fit with one's overall perspective of psychological growth and with one's basic therapeutic stance then regression *is* useless just as any consequence of a technical maneuver can become nontherapeutic when it is felt as an alien force in the natural flow of the process. Moore and Fine (1968) spell out the centrality of the concept of regression in classical Freudian theory, within the context of the definition of transference. They write:

> The demonstration, interpretation, and resolution of transference in the analytic situation constitutes the core of analytic therapy. Thus the technical procedures of psychoanalysis are in part designed to encourage and facilitate regression with the concommitant unfolding of the transference. [Transference] achieves a major impact in treatment from the fact that these feelings and attitudes are directed toward the person of the analyst, and eventually develop into the transference neurosis. . . . The transference neurosis is an indispensible therapeutic tool since the feelings experienced by the patient in the transference have a unique vividness in the present which make their interpretation and the sense of conviction about them especially effective [pp. 92–93].

I believe that this is an empirically accurate description of how analytic growth occurs, and is acceptable to all analysts regardless of point of view, providing one's technique is not highly interactional. I define interpersonal in terms of its basic commitment to a contextual view of personality development and growth of self. What is emphasized by Moore and Fine are the feelings experienced by the patient (his states of mind) while he is in the process of being a patient. This is precisely what Stanton (1978) has argued as being underemphasized by many of the students and followers of Sullivan.

The kind of change we try to facilitate in psychoanalysis is not simply a change in behavior or even a change in cognitive understanding. It is a change in the self-representation out of which behavior will organically and naturally reflect reorganization of the self at increasingly higher levels of interpersonal maturation. This is the most difficult kind of change to achieve because one of the two central qualities of the self is to protect and maintain its own internal consistency; that is, to preserve its stability.

This quality of the self as the guardian of its own internal integrity protects us from madness, as Sullivan points out, because if it fails too substantially it leads to what is usually called "losing one's mind"—a "*dis*-integration" of one's experience of being a self. Sullivan (1940, p. 184) referred to this process of guardianship as the operation of the self-system, which functions by the regulation of anxiety, "excluding from awareness all the data which would expand the self at the cost of insecurity." This, of course, is the aspect of the self towards which

Sullivan's focus was almost exclusively directed, and has been developed with such theoretical brilliance that an empirically oriented ego theoretician like Loevinger (1973, p. 87) has called Sullivan's conception of the self-system the definitive theory of ego stability.

Stability, however, is only one of the two central qualities of the self. The other is growth (whether it is called maturation, mastery, actualization, effectance, etc.). This second dimension was more problematic for Sullivan to develop theoretically as it has been for *all* personality theorists who have not chosen to rely on Freud's concept of libido as the energy source which runs the psychic machinery. Sullivan's (1940) position does take into account that the self-system is not conceptually sufficient in itself to replace libido theory. Some construct was needed to explain why stability should not always be preserved at the expense of growth. His way of dealing with this issue was to postulate that the personality inherently tends towards interpersonal adjustive success. "The basic direction of the organism is forward" (p. 97). What this means, of course, is that the self is not only trying to insure its stability by keeping out overly discrepant data, but is also trying to find room for these data in order to satisfy its inherent need for interpersonal growth—to move forward. Thus, at any given moment there is a balance of forces reflecting the concurrent needs both to *stay the same and to grow* (see chapters 12 and 18).

It is a view of ego growth which rests on structuralistic principles; an organization whose course of development is governed by its own dialectic or inner logic. It may be conceptualized as a self-regulated struggle to maintain the present state of structural equilibrium by means of selective inattention to facts inconsistent with the current level of development, and a simultaneous attempt to allow *some* disequilibrium as a necessary condition of assimilating discordant experience. Psychological development, however, whether in a natural setting or in psychoanalysis, does not maintain an organized course. It is defined by uneven growth spurts marked by periods of reorganization interwoven with periods of stability. Most importantly, the individual is always engaged in the integrated process of breaking down the old and rebuilding into more highly differentiated and complex patterns. The weakness in Sullivan's theory has always been its failure to make this explicit, and by so doing to safeguard against the one-sided overemphasis on "building up" being perpetuated and even dogmatized by his followers.

What, therefore, are the conditions which facilitate growth rather than stability, in the absence of an energy concept such as libido? In general terms the answer has to be an interpersonal one. Through the process of psychoanalytic inquiry new experience tends to be assimi-lated just as Sullivan argues, but the intrinsic operation of the self-sys-tem is always trying to produce the least amount of structural reorganization. What is needed, therefore, is an analytic environment which encourages the emergence of discordant experience in a vivid way, but where the ongoing self-representation feels sufficiently safe so that it does not have to protect its stability at the expense of devel-opment. The vividness and immediacy thus become the core of a posi-tive reorganization of the interpersonal self at a higher and more differentiated developmental level rather than an anxiety-cueing sig-nal to protect the old organization from "force feeding" and lowered self-esteem.

One aspect of the analytic situation may be looked at as the cre-ation of just such an interpersonal environment, which permits rather than induces the ego to regress; that is, to become relatively disequili-brated or "raw." By this I mean that it allows itself to give up to a cer-tain degree the function of protecting its own stability because the person feels safe enough to turn this role partially over to the analyst. Winnicott (1955–1956) addresses this point, stating that "this is a time of great dependence and true risk, and the patient is naturally in a deeply regressed state" (p. 297). But regardless of how "deep" the regression is, I am suggesting that regression, in the sense I am using it here, is not a concept limited in analytic work to patients having severe ego impairment, but is a fundamental component of psycho-analysis in general, and the interpersonal approach in particular. The ego (or self), in order to grow, must voluntarily allow itself to become less than intact—to regress. Empirically this is one way of defining regression in the service of the ego.

There is room for this concept in Sullivan's theory as Stanton (1978) demonstrates when referring to "being a patient as an ego interpretive state" (p. 138). He carefully makes the distinction that this type of experience is not equivalent to the regressive state in schizophrenia, and is in fact incompatible with it. By partially relinquishing the func-tion of protecting his own ego stability, the patient allows the emer-gence of regressed states of experience along with the intense reenactment of early and sometimes primitive modes of thinking, feel-ing, and behaving. Within Sullivan's frame of reference it is called parataxis, but I suggest that it is a necessary condition for movement towards optimal syntaxis. The deeper the regression that can be safely allowed by the patient, the richer the experience and the greater its reverberation on the total organization of the self. Psychoanalytic change is not simply a matter of a new piece of information being added to an otherwise intact and well-organized data bank. For the deepest analytic growth to occur, the new experience must require that the existing pattern of self-representation reorganize in order to make room for it.[3] In terms of the epistemology of human growth this is certainly not a new idea. At the level of self-schematization it is a restatement of Piaget's (1936) principles of accommodation and assimilation, and of Merleau-Ponty's (1942) idea of development as a progressive, self-perpetuating process of restructuring. Sandler (1975), in an excellent paper on Piaget and psychoanalysis, specifically emphasizes that in normal cognitive development, growth is always marked by movement from structural disequilibrium to structural equilibrium, and that "the period of structural disequilibrium which marks the entry into a new cognitive stage is often accompanied by a heightened emotional vulnerability" (p. 366). The implication for interpersonal psychoanalysis is not that the analyst must thereby become less interactional, but that conditions which facilitate regression must be balanced with those that facilitate inquiry within the total analytic climate for any given patient, and that this must be built into the theory itself.

The heart of the matter is the management of the interpersonal climate while conducting an analytic inquiry, and this is where our individual personalities determine what we see as our personal "truths." What one therapist feels is the "right" analytic atmosphere for a particular patient to safely regress but still work within an interpersonal field, will be experienced by another therapist as too stifling of his own more active style, and perhaps by yet a third as too intrusive into the natural unfolding of the transference. Winnicott (1962, p. 166) stated that his motto was to ask how little need be done rather than how much can one be *allowed* to do. In practice, participant observation contains a large element of individual style. Our skill, and sometimes our luck, determines to what extent our work leads to growth. It is rarely our "truth" which does it. Regression, I believe, is a part of interpersonal psychoanalysis, and it must be allowed to find its place as a concept which has for too long been discordant.

---

3. For an illuminating and well-documented psychoanalytic perspective of the ego and ego growth from a structuralistic vantage point see L. Friedman (1973).

4

EMPATHY, ANXIETY, AND REALITY: A VIEW FROM THE BRIDGE[1] (1980)

Sullivan's notion of "personification" implies that the way a person relates to other people is a reflection of how "people" are represented mentally, how the "self" is represented mentally, and at what developmental level the concept of "relationship" is represented mentally. Further, and perhaps more important, it is the maturational level of the patient's representational world which determines the degree to which Sullivan's concept of consensual validation is possible as a therapeutic process, and thereby shapes one's analytic approach to any given patient. It is, in other words, the bridge which links developmental theory to the interpersonal method of participant observation.

In another paper (Bromberg, 1980) I presented a structuralistic perspective of consensual validation which I suggested might allow the concept greater theoretical scope in accounting for therapeutic regression and the depth of change that we observe clinically in the process of psychoanalysis. I offered the view that as a necessary step, the developmental continuum of mental representation in interpersonal theory needs to progress beyond Sullivan's personifications of

1. This chapter was originally published in *Contemporary Psychoanalysis*, 1980, 16:223–236.

"good-me," "bad-me," and "not-me," and that the groundwork had already been prepared by Sullivan (1950a) for subsequent elaboration, despite his own reluctance to take these ideas farther.

It has been suggested (e.g., Klenbort, 1978) that a possible reason for Sullivan's hesitancy in doing so is that it would have required him to make a clearer distinction between the concepts of *self*, and *self-system*—a distinction which was implied in his early formulation of self-dynamism (Sullivan, 1940, pp. 18–29)—and would thus have opened the door to the idea of unique individuality, a notion which he vigorously challenged (see Crowley, 1973, 1975, 1978). The problem, however, is that unless the concept of self-dynamism is revived and synthesized with a developmental evolution of "personifications" which is broader in scope, it will be extremely difficult to develop interpersonal theory beyond the point of seeing the "self" simply as an "anxiety-gating" mechanism (Loevinger and Wessler, 1970, p. 7) with only ambiguous theoretical linkage to how it undergoes representational change in psychoanalysis.

Mental Representation of the Interpersonal Field

Piagetian "Conservation" and Consensual Validation

Like Piaget, Sullivan (1953) was captured by the dramatic qualitative shift in mental organization that occurs between the first and second years of life—the shift to representational thought—and by the further shift in later childhood to conceptual thought.

> [T]he first instances of experience in the syntaxic mode appear between, let us say, the twelfth and eighteenth month of extrauterine life[2] when verbal signs—words, symbols—are organized which are actually communicative. . . . Of course, a vast deal of what goes on during this period of life is not in the syntaxic mode [p. 184].

Sullivan, in more global language, is here making the same observation as made by Piaget, that the development of representational thought goes through a period of communicative, but egocentric

---

2. It is also at about the eighteenth month of life that Piaget (1969) places the transition out of the sensory-motor stage of mental development, and Mahler et al. (1975) places the beginning of psychological awareness of separateness.

(presyntaxic) organization—what Piaget referred to as preoperational thought—prior to the stage of objective verbal conceptualization. Like Piaget, he viewed the development of mental processes as both continuous and discontinuous; continuous in its natural evolution of sequential stages, but discontinuous in the categorical and irreversible leap that is ultimately made in the ability to reason conceptually—that is, by logical necessity rather than by egocentrism.

Piaget's emphasis was on the internal development of conceptual mental representation (genetic epistemology); he refers to this achievement empirically as "conservation," and structurally as "operational thought." Sullivan (1972 pp. 34–35) emphasized the interpersonal field in which it occurs, and refers to "a fundamental schematic distinction between implicit mental processes on the basis of their potential consensual validity." But basically, Piaget and Sullivan are describing the same thing; the awesome potential for the ability to see things as other people see them through the capacity for conceptual (and thereby objectively modifiable) organization of experience. Both theoreticians attributed a central role to the development of language and interpersonal communication as the mediating context for the transition from autistic to objective thought. Piaget (1932) states that

> intelligence, just because it undergoes a gradual process of socialization, is enabled through the bond established by language between thoughts and words to make an increasing use of concepts; whereas autism, just because it remains individual is still tied to imagery [p. 64].

The parallel between this statement and Sullivan's (1953) formulation of consensual validation is striking:

> I should stress that syntaxic symbols are best illustrated by words that have been consensually validated. A consensus has been reached when the infant or child has learned the precisely right word for a situation, a word which means not only what it is thought to mean by the mothering one, but also means that to the infant [pp. 183–184].
>
> It is probable that up to the age of—let us say—three or four,[3] words, mostly still of the child's special language, are used very

---

3. In Piaget's observations it is closer to age seven or eight that the shift from imagery to verbal conceptualization is most manifest (Piaget, 1969, p. 97), but Sullivan may be describing the earlier and equally dramatic shift in how words are used, at the point when "libidinal object constancy" is normally attained at about age three to four (see Fraiberg, 1969).

much as pictures might be used in a book; they decorate, concentrate, or illuminate referential processes which are not verbal but which are the manifestations of experience in the parataxic mode organized at various times earlier [p. 185].

The Conception of "Tenderness" as "Personification"

I think it is fair to state that despite his emphasis on the external, observable field, Sullivan is clearly anchoring the development of syntaxic thought through consensual validation, to the progressive restructuralization of mental representation. On the other hand, it is also a fair hypothesis that he was never too comfortable with the idea if it went beyond the anxiety-organized personifications of "good-me," "bad-me," and "not-me." He did, however, make one significant attempt at further developmental elaboration (Sullivan, 1950a), but far outside of the main body of his theoretical writing where it has remained, unintegrated, and available for "internalization" by object relational theorists. Sandler and Sandler (1978), for example, write the following:

> As we have tried to emphasize, object relationships can be regarded as role relationships. This is as true of the relationship in thought or fantasy to the various images deriving from the structures we call "introjects" or "internal objects" as of the relationships which obtain between the subjects and persons perceived in his external environment [p. 294].

It is time for the theory of interpersonal psychoanalysis to begin to reconceptualize and broaden its own developmental bridge between the inner world and the external environment. The most immediate need is to extend the concept of "interpersonal" to experience which has its roots prior to structuralization by the presence or absence of anxiety. I refer to personifications which are organized by a feeling of deep "communion," and have their developmental origin within the relatively undifferentiated mental representation of self and other, which Sullivan states is associated with "need satisfaction" in infancy. This global matrix of what Sullivan (1953, pp. 37–41) refers to as "tenderness" is the first domain of human dialogue.[4] It is the mental struc-

---

4. Sullivan (1953, pp. 186–187) also acknowledges his recognition that satisfaction as well as anxiety is an organizer of experience that has to be dealt with in the analytic situation. "[F]or the purposes of psychiatric theory I am

ture from which the anxiety-organized personifications later emerge, and is what I have suggested (Bromberg, 1980) provides the pre-syntaxic bridge that allows clinical psychoanalysis to become genuine restructuralization of the self.

Sullivan (1950a), in what may be his only developmentally elaborated statement which places this early personification in perspective, puts it as follows:

> [E]veryone has come along a developmental course that began in the region of personifications that are truly nebulously cosmic in proportions, vested with the most extreme "felt" aspects of comfort and discomfort and essentially without relationships other than temporal coincidence and succession. These figures moved without anything approaching rhyme or reason in the growing framework of a center of awareness of vague but impelling recurrent needs which as it were, stood out against a background of euphoria, a "state of empty bliss." There was in the cosmic center of events a . . . frequently successful tool, the cry. It gradually appeared that this magic was effective only in the presence of the Good-Mother— who could suddenly be replaced by the Bad-Mother with her aura of anxiety. . . . Still later, Bad-Me was differentiated as that of the center of which often evoked the Bad-Mother. . . . From such a beginning . . . a gradual refinement in differentiating experience has progressed up to the present [pp. 310–311].

Sullivan is here saying that: (a) there is a developmental continuum of mental representation that parallels the field processes; (b) the representational world moves from a relatively undifferentiated "interpersonal" organization structured around need satisfaction (the "felt aspects of comfort and discomfort"), through a socialized process of gradually differentiated but egocentric (parataxic) organization based on avoidance of anxiety, and culminates in conceptual representation (syntaxic experience) based more and more on the process of consensual validation.

Why has it taken so long for the significance of the preverbal stage to be given full theoretical stature, developmentally and therapeutically, in interpersonal theory, whereas object relations theory is becoming more and more "Sullivanized"? Settlage (1977), for example, retranslates Mahler's (Mahler et al., 1975) conception of the stages of the "separation-individuation" process into a form descriptively

---

concerned exclusively with covert and overt symbolic activity—that is, with activity influenced by the organization into signs of previous experience *in terms of satisfaction, or in terms of avoiding or minimizing anxiety*" (italics added).

parallel to the complete continuum presented by Sullivan above. Settlage writes:

> The first need is reaffirmation, through interaction with the mother, of the precognitive or preverbal sense of core identity. Also, as the child proceeds through this subphase, an increasing differentiation of self- and object representations normally takes place. . . . As these differentiations take place, the sense of well-being character- istic of the preverbal period becomes, in effect, the nucleus for the sense of self-esteem. As is true of his sense of identity, the child's self-esteem is also tied to his mother's continued acceptance and approval of him. . . . The internalized representation of the love object, initially the mother, continues to be libidinally cathected in the face of both absence of the object and anger towards the object. The intrapsychic representation of the love object includes images of the object as both loving and disapproving and as both loved and hated, as good and bad. . . . It is during the rapprochement subphase that the earlier and developmentally normal tendency to avoid anxiety by separating the good from the bad representations of the love object . . . is replaced by repression [pp. 814–816].

Whether it is called "the rapprochement subphase of separation- individuation" or the beginning of the "preoperational stage of mental representation," Piaget, Mahler, and Sullivan each see the fourteenth to eighteenth month of life as ushering in the transition from the pre- verbal world of illusion to the verbal world of external reality. It is the stage at which another human being first performs the function of pro- viding the bridge between two levels of mental organization, and is the first instance in which an anxiety-organized personification under- goes restructuralization through interpersonal mediation.

Reality as a Creative Process

Since it is only with the arrival of the time of Piagetian "conservation" that Sullivan saw genuine syntaxic communication possible, and though he wrote about the nature of less differentiated mental struc- ture, he chose to present his theory of the therapeutic growth of reality (consensual validation) as an observable analog to the anxiety-orga- nized changes that occur after age three to four. This is the age (see footnote 3) at which "libidinal object constancy" is normally achieved; that is, the ability that allows a child to experience the mother as the same person regardless of whether she is meeting his needs at the moment. From this achievement gradually emerges the socialized capacity to "represent" the "other person" as a "personality"—what Sullivan (1953, p. 111) defines as the "relatively enduring pattern of recurrent interpersonal situations"—that is, as a concept rather than as a stimulus-bound "image." As Blatt (1974, p. 150) put it, "conceptual representations are based on abstract enduring qualities of the object . . . they transcend time and are independent of the physical properties or presence of the object." Inasmuch as it is this shift that we attempt to bring about in psychoanalysis, it is easy to see why Sullivan, viewing pre-syntaxic experience as noncommunicative, tried to avoid participating in any form of transferential enactment that was not directly accessible to intervention and why this emphasis has continued to adhere to his formulation of consensual validation.

Sullivan tended to feel that the earliest organization of experience was therapeutically inaccessible because it remained at an autistic, and therefore uncommunicable level. In his thinking, it was more associated with "that which needs to be treated" than with the process of treatment itself. This earliest mode of mental structure in severe psychopathology does indeed find unmodified expression as pathological symbiosis, but in a therapeutic milieu it is enlisted in transitional form in the service of maturation. Bird (1972, p. 297) in fact asserts that it is an ego function in itself, and goes as far as to suggest that the regressive experience of "transference in analysis, may be seen, as the power which in a general sense endows the ego with its crucial capacity to evoke, maintain, and put to use the past-in-the-present."

Empathy, Anxiety, and Reality

The Developmental Bridge

Sullivan's therapeutic analog to early development is accurate but not well balanced. To profitably reconceptualize it, the interrelationships among empathy, anxiety, and "reality" during the first three years of life must be scrutinized. The earliest interpersonal experience of "felt discomfort" takes place before self-other differentiation. Sullivan is careful not to speak of it as "anxiety," because in his scheme anxiety requires some registration of self-other differences for the infant to first receive it by "contagion" from the mother. It is more accurate, I think, to look at the earlier predifferentiated discomfort as reflecting the momentary disruptions of symbiotic bliss; that is, as a drop from the state of empathic one-ness, rather than as the induction of something external, at least at this stage. This may in fact be what develops a little later into "separation anxiety."

At about eight months of age the normal infant has just achieved the capacity to sustain an image of the mother as long as she is in his presence. This capacity for "object permanence" or "recognition memory" now allows the organization of discomfort to become part of the emerging structural configuration of "other," and the further continuing restructuralization into self and other. It is only at this point that Sullivan's anxiety-organized personifications of "good," "bad," and "not" come into existence, and if all goes well, participate in the normal shaping of self-other differentiation and the emergence of external "reality." It is the age at which the experience of "discomfort" can be accurately called "anxiety," and begins to become less associated solely with the disruption of "blissful oneness," and more connected with the painful growing awareness of the differences between "motherness" and "otherness"; for example, seven to eight month "stranger anxiety."

Then at about 18 months of age the capacity develops for genuine representational thought—an image of the mother is sustained even in her absence. But because this "evocative memory" is still organized around her role as a need-satisfier, this stage of new and exciting growth brings with it the full and devastating impact of psychological awareness of separateness, and the fuller restructuralization of experience into "good" and "bad" aspects of self-other representations organized around anxiety. It is what Mahler calls a "crisis of rapprochement," and its successful negotiation by the mother and child becomes the anlage for the process by which highly discordant self-experience can get "assimilated" as self-awareness; that is, it becomes the template through which at all subsequent stages of life, "not-me" is able to be restructured as "me"; and "bad-me" is restructured as "good-me." The role of the "rapprochement mother" (18 mos. to 3 yrs) is to sensitively utilize empathic verbal communication as a transition from the preverbal symbiotic matrix, so as to "mirror" verbally the child's inner world while slowly introducing external reality. She thus serves as the bridge between pre-syntaxic and syntaxic experience until the attainment of genuine conservation of the self and the other (libidinal object constancy) at age three to four.[5]

---

5. Steingart (1969) has developed a well-documented and thoughtfully reasoned paper on the subject of "conservation of the self" as the cognitive base for the psychoanalytic understanding of character development.

The Psychoanalytic Bridge

In interpersonal psychoanalytic theory, the same phenomenon can be encompassed by Sullivan's largely undeveloped "Tenderness Theorem" (1953, p. 39), as the therapeutically pre-syntaxic bridge that allows the concept of consensual validation to include the elements of empathy and regression as clinical variables. The need to expand Sullivan's concept of tenderness has already been alluded to by Chrzanowski (1977, pp. 25–26), and will take in what Stanton (1978, p. 134) calls the "ego-interpretive state" when the patient is functioning best as an analytic patient. It is not a regression to symbiosis. It is a me-you experience which, as Settlage (1977) has described, reaffirms the precognitive or preverbal sense of core identity, and leads to the feeling of "being understood" as a cognitive bridge to being able to understand the analyst. It is an ego-regulated derivative of exactly what Sullivan describes in his "Tenderness Theorem"—a synchronicity between the need tension level in the infant and the mother's responsiveness to it, which is the first affirmation of core identity. It is, above all else, interpersonal, but not in the sense that "interpersonal" is most typically associated with the single aspect of "clarification" in consensual validation.

Once the self has been "conserved" (its separate existence experienced as an invariant "fact"), consensual validation takes place in psychoanalysis pretty much as Sullivan conceived it—as a shared process in a communicative field that moves representational thought from egocentric (parataxic) organization to objective (syntaxic) organization. It depends, however, for some patients more than others, on the felt existence of the preverbal empathic bond as a transitional form of mental representation. It is this preverbal bond that the self-dynamism enlists throughout the life cycle as part of the "regressive" interpersonal matrix of communion that mediates the deepest and most profound experiences of self-other restructuralization, including that of psychoanalysis. Leonard Friedman (1975) writes:

> We know that when we are working well with any patient in a good hour we are in a state of free-floating attention. States of deep rapport develop in which we are open to the totality of our patient's communication in a way which allows us to oscillate between empathic contact with our patient and the capacity for being ourselves responding to his experience. We grasp his allusions and we can expand his metaphors. We sense both his affect and our tendencies to respond to it without being caught up in it. We communicate our sense of where the patient is with a terseness

which intimacy allows. The experience is a vivid one for both participants and both have a sense of creative interplay. Each builds on
the other's communication. The analyst's understanding of his
patient functions implicitly and largely preconsciously at such
times. He can offer his responses without deliberation [p. 143].

Representational Change and Clinical Approach

The Concept of an Empathy Gradient

Clinically, what has been described by Friedman is familiar and self-
evident to most analysts regardless of theoretical persuasion. But how
do we use this description in trying to further develop the theoretical
bridge to the representational constructs of interpersonal psychoanalysis?

My first suggestion is concretely to introduce the conception that
syntaxic reorganization within the analytic field depends upon the
interpenetration of inquiry with two major modes of pre-syntaxic representation. The first of these modes (Sullivan's interpersonal matrix of
tenderness) constitutes the preverbal empathic bond that allows analytic inquiry to become restructuralization. The second of these modes
(Sullivan's interpersonal matrix of anxiety) organizes the illusory
(transferential) experience that becomes the content of analytic inquiry.

The next step is to speculate on the possible advantage of viewing
the interpersonal approach as a process of analytic inquiry mediated
by maximal responsiveness to the interplay between a gradient of anxiety and a gradient of empathy. This conception has a distinct advantage over that of the "therapeutic alliance" or the "working alliance."
Both of these latter formulations depend on the notion of an extra-ana-
lytic bond (either global or specific) which is somehow more "real"
than the transferential bond, and has continued to remain a thorn in
the side of analytic theory. Furthermore, the conception of an empathy
gradient is a variable rather than a static element, and can thus deal
with a much broader spectrum of psychopathology and personality
structure without having to modify the definition of psychoanalysis. It
encompasses the fluctuating need for the analytic relationship to be
more or less "personal"; for the level of empathic contact to be more or
less "deep"; and it encompasses the capacity of the patient to be more
or less "suitable" for psychoanalysis. Finally, it removes the need to
introduce another "parameter" such as an analytic "holding environ-

ment" (Winnicott, 1955–1956; Modell, 1978) so as to conceptualize the fact that patients with more severe ego pathology require greater adaptational responsiveness from the therapist in the earlier stages of analytic treatment.

The Clinical Process of Restructuralization

Words used cognitively as communicative speech are higher order signifiers of previously unsymbolized (sometimes developmentally preconceptual) experience. For the interpersonal matrix of communication to be an analytic matrix of self-other restructuralization, it is not simply a matter of getting the patient to "confront" the unconscious, repressed, dissociated, or unattended-to data. To do so may or may not create useful behavioral change but it will not in itself lead to representational restructuralization. What keeps preconceptual or unsymbolized experience so rigidly unyielding is that the "me-you" representation is organized around elements which are more powerful than the evidence of reason. Thus, with regard to the use of the transference, a transferential inquiry will always fail if its primary appeal is to reason; it must try to contact the experience out of which reason can ultimately emerge. A genuine transferential inquiry does not address the question: "Why do you see me as your father at this moment?" At a rational level reasons always exist that make "sense." It instead addresses the totality of the experience that leads a patient to *only* see me as his father at that moment—the experience of me which overrides every other aspect of our relationship. In terms of meta-theory, the general transferential question might be formulated as: "What is the nature of the powerful preconceptual illusion that is interfering with a patient's potential to represent his analyst as an enduring personality?" To change the me-you organization of experience in this sense requires the direct emergence of the parataxic representation in the most vivid and immediate form possible. Then, and only then, does the term "validation" have analytic meaning, because only then are the pre-syntaxic elements which overpower reason available for communication with the process of consensus. They are then, and only then, amenable to restructuralization through language.

I am suggesting that what is "validated" is better conceptualized as the emergence of a new reality rather than the clarification or correction of a previously perceived distortion. Looked at in this way, the process of analytic inquiry operates at varying levels of power, ranging from the exploration of events in the person's life per se, to exploration of the patient-analyst relationship per se. Many analysts (e.g., Bird, 1972; Gill, 1979) feel that it is only through the surfacing of the direct transferential experience that structural (mutative) change occurs. One of Sullivan's contributions was to show that participant observation is a more effective conception than "free association" in the identification and symbolization of parataxic distortion, but it brings with it an important corollary: do not assume that the "real-life" material which is being explored is in itself the analytic "content." The patient may indeed "see" in a practical way, aspects of his functioning that he did not see before, but this is analytic content only as a bridge to the anxiety-organized experience contained in the process of the inquiry itself. This latter experience can become most fully available for exploration only if the focus on the external content doesn't become so sharp, or the inquiry so interactional, that the patient is not permitted the opportunity for therapeutic regression.

I am not advocating that interpersonal theory limit the concept of consensual validation only to "regressed" experience or to transferential material. What I am suggesting, in fact, makes it unnecessary to even think of it as an either-or decision. Sullivan's field theory, because it lends itself so well to a structuralistic perspective, allows all elements within the analytic field to be defined in terms of the role each plays in the overall process of restructuralization, rather than in terms of which are "analytic" and which are not.

Verbal Mirroring

When I write of the interplay between a gradient of empathy and a gradient of anxiety, I am referring to the sensitivity of the analyst in being able to therapeutically vary his use of communication in the process of inquiry, so as to respond to its dual function of expressing empathic contact and of increasing verbal clarification of meaning. It is his ability to do this which allows the patient more and more access to the less differentiated levels of "not-me" and "bad-me" experience that would otherwise remain dissociated. In terms of character pathology this includes the level at which the object relations theorists refer to the "unassimilated bad object."

To get to the therapeutically optimal level, regression does not have to be induced (see chapter 3). It will occur with most patients eventually (if not interfered with) simply by the analyst's ability to stay in communication at the presymbolic level and not pull the patient away from that mode of experience by overclarification of meaning outside of the matrix of empathy, or by being systematically "conversational."

For some patients characterologically, but for all patients at certain points, the process of restructuralization begins with the patient requiring a communication field in which the analyst is providing a more or less high level of what might be called "verbal mirroring."[6] During these periods the process of inquiry is mediated, to a relatively greater extent, by communication expressive of particularly close attention to the empathy gradient. The analyst is primarily using language to maintain preverbal-verbal contact rather than to expand meaning; he is "mirroring" what the patient is experiencing but in verbal terms that are *his own*.

I would wonder if the above might not be the very heart of analytic technique, and although the patient's need for verbal mirroring decreases as the analytic work progresses, it is only the relative significance of each gradient that shifts as an element in the communication field. One avenue for future study might in fact be the clinical examination of how an interpersonal approach to working at the interface of anxiety and empathy is most effectively translated therapeutically within a broad spectrum of psychopathology and at various stages of treatment.

6. I am grateful to Dr. Althea Horner and to Dr. David Schecter for the give-and-take of ideas out of which the term "verbal mirroring" emerged as applicable to interpersonal theory.

5

GETTING INTO ONESELF AND OUT OF ONE'S SELF

On Schizoid Processes[1] (1984)

The word "primitive," applied to a society or to the mental state of an individual, is linked to a context defined by the role of language. With regard to a society, a primitive culture is one that has not developed a written language. Written language is necessary when the members of a culture require a means of communicating their group identity as an objective social reality which extends beyond the here and now, and presupposes the ability to frame social reality by a process of consensual validation, as Harry Stack Sullivan (1950b, p. 214) termed it. It is taken as a sign that the individual members of the society have achieved a level of consensually defined self- and object-representation needed to schematize social reality beyond their own subjective needs, and that the process of communication uses language not only as a tool to get what one wants but also as a means of expressing who one is.[2]

---

1. This chapter was originally published in *Contemporary Psychoanalysis*, 1984, 20:439–448.

2. G. H. Mead, the social psychologist whose work profoundly informed the work of Sullivan, deals with the idea as central in the relationship between mind, self, and society. He writes (Mead, 1934): The human individual who

When the term "primitive" is used psychoanalytically (i.e., in relation to the psychological state of a person) the meaning is more
ambiguous, but equally embedded in the context of language and how
it is used. Freud (1913a) suggested that primitivity reflects a state of
mind which is dominated by an unquestioning belief in the power of
thought; a phenomenon which he also held to be the foundation of
magic. The link between magical thinking and the obsessive quality of
one's private inner world has been always a subject of great fascination to psychoanalysts. Freud proposed the idea that magic is nothing
more than the imposing of the laws governing mental life upon real
things, rather than allowing the world of real things to shape one's
mental life. This same point was developed systematically, and at
length, in the novels of Carlos Castaneda (1968, 1971, 1972, 1974, 1977,
1981), and was the cornerstone of Castaneda's apprenticeship to his
sorcerer-teacher Don Juan as they journeyed through the interface of
shamanism and science, as illustrated in the following excerpts from
the ongoing dialogue between them:

> "Whenever you are alone, what do you do?"
> "I talk to myself."
> "What do you talk to yourself about?"
> "I don't know; anything, I suppose."
> "I'll tell you what we talk to ourselves about. We talk about our
> world. In fact we maintain our world with our internal talk."
> "How do we do that?"
> "Whenever we finish talking to ourselves the world is always as it
> should be. We renew it, we kindle it with life, we uphold it with
> our internal talk. Not only that, but we also choose our paths as we
> talk to ourselves. Thus we repeat the same choices over and over
> until the day we die, because we keep on repeating the same inter-
> nal talk over and over until the day we die" [Castaneda, 1971,
> pp. 262–263].
> "We are complacently caught in our particular view of the world,
> which compels us to feel and act as if we knew everything about

---

possesses a self is always a member of a larger social community, a more
extensive social group, than that in which he immediately and directly finds
himself, or to which he immediately and directly belongs. . . . And their
awareness of that reference is a consequence of their being sentient or conscious beings, or of their having minds, and of the activities of reasoning
which they hence carry on. . . . This wider reference or relational implication
of the general behavior pattern of any given human social group or community is least evident in the case of primitive man, and is most apparent in the
case of highly civilized modern man [pp. 272–273].

the world. A teacher from the very first act he performs, aims at stopping that view. Sorcerers call it stopping the internal dialogue. . . . In order to stop the view of the world which one has held since the cradle, it is not enough to just wish or make a resolution. One needs a practical task" [Castaneda, 1974, p. 236].

Sullivan (1953, 1954) postulated as the impetus behind human personality development that the power invested in thought must be superseded by the ability to see things as other people see them through the capacity for conceptual, objectively modifiable organization of experience. In other words, magical thinking must give way to shared rules (usually totally out of awareness) through which reality is constructed and judged. In a relatively well-functioning individual these rules are not conscious; they simply serve as the organizing mental structures which shape immediate experience into broad patterns of meaning. Focal involvement is normally not with the rules governing reality but is centered on whatever current, ongoing aspect of the world is commanding attention. To put it another way, *reality is normally generated as we participate in it*, rather than it being simply an internal template which we apply to the outside world in our biological need to adapt. In a given social situation we "know" which rules frame ongoing reality without knowing that we know, because we are creating "new" rules at any specific moment within the context of applying the shared internalized ones. It is this ability that gives spontaneity to our lives and a sense of continuity to feeling "real" in the real world, and it is this ability which in the primitive mental state of chronic schizoid detachment is wholly or partially lacking (Bromberg, 1979, and chapter 6).

The schizoid individual is empathically cut off from adequate interpersonal involvement in the external world and generates a single concrete reality. Full emotional access to the multiple realities created by genuine social interaction is severely limited, and the individual lives in a relatively stable but sterile world of facts and rules. He cannot reframe the concreteness of the past through his direct empathic experience of the moment. He cannot, in effect, get out of his inner world. In some cases the difficulty approaches the point of incapacity or at least feels like that to the person himself. It is characterized by a state of pathological character detachment—living in the inner world and manipulating the perception of external reality without the experience of actually participating in it. For these individuals a personality structure has developed which is extremely difficult to change in analytic treatment because they use the outside environment (including the analytic environment) mainly as a source of material to control and orchestrate the internal environment (see chapter 13). The psychoanalytic situation therefore poses a particular dilemma. How might it best be structured so that it will feel real to the patient . . . how to best prevent it from being interminably transformed into simply one more stage set in his inner world? To what degree and in what way does an analyst need to modify his basic treatment model so that the patient is required to directly engage the immediacy of the analytic situation, thus allowing the analyst the best chance of having a genuine and analyzable impact? Should the treatment be face to face rather than on the couch? Should the analyst be unusually lively and interactional? Is it necessary for him in any way to *try* to be more of a "real" person? In my view the basic treatment model of participant observation is not only sufficient, it is preferable, because the real issue is not how to reach the patient but to help the patient become reachable on his own.

Henry James (1875, p. 27), in a novel entitled *Roderick Hudson*, wrote the following: "True happiness, we are told, consists in getting out of one's self; but the point is not only to get out—you must stay out; and to stay out you must have some absorbing errand." Ideally, the errand is, of course, simply the act of being absorbed in the living of life with full emotional involvement, but this is precisely what the schizoid individual is unable to do. One of the tasks of the analysis, therefore, is to embody within its own structure an "errand" which is so absorbing that the patient is required to "get out of his self" while he is "getting into himself."

The "Absorbing Errand"

Regardless of whether an analyst holds the view that the core ingredients in the schizoid process represent, as Guntrip (1961b) suggests, a basic element in the human condition, the importance of "getting out of one's self" through full involvement in the real world, and the achievement of the ability to *stay* out, is a view of self-actualization expressed not only by Henry James. It is also reflected, for example, in the words of the Zen master to his disciple who asks for the way of wisdom: "When you are hungry you eat; when you are tired you lie down."

Freud (1911, 1913a, 1914) writing on the developmental shift from narcissism to object relatedness, and Sullivan (1953) writing on the psychoanalytic method of participant observation, have each arrived at a different variation of the same insight as the mediating factor in personality growth, social evolution in human culture, the perception of reality, and the therapeutic action of psychoanalysis.

Psychoanalysis is traditionally conceived as an opportunity for a motivated person to "get into himself"; it is launched by the patient's agreement to follow Freud's basic rule of the free association method (Freud, 1913b). The patient agrees to try and report everything he is feeling and thinking without editing or censoring. But "getting into oneself" is psychoanalytically productive only if it is part of the larger process of getting out of the solipsistic strait-jacket that is used to maintain a fixed image of who we are in our own eyes and what we are thus willing or able to perceive as "reality." What we refer to as a "primitive mental state" is usually the outcome of having been "into oneself" for too long a time, or not having adequate ego structure to get out of one's "self" in an enduring way with regard to significant aspects of external reality and human relationships.

Classically, Freud's basic rule has been read so as to emphasize the "getting into" more than the "getting out of" experience; most specifically, it focuses upon that which is gotten into—that is, the "content"—the conscious derivatives of unconscious fantasy. Becoming aware of the unconscious linkages and "resistances" as they are interpreted by the analyst leads the patient more deeply "into himself" via the free association method, bringing to the surface more and more derivatives of unconscious content which become accessible to the patient's integrative capacity and effort. Sullivan's method of participant observation regards the "getting into" and "getting out of" as inseparable parts of the interpersonal analytic field. It has led to a process of clinical psychoanalysis that works with transference and resistance from a theoretical rationale that has *inherently* permitted the analytic treatment of severe ego pathology and primitive mental states. It views content as an aspect of process rather than seeing process as a means of uncovering content. Human development is seen as mediated not by the increasing ability to manage and integrate instincts and unconscious wishes, but by a progressive capacity to symbolize and communicate to another person through the use of language, "who you are" rather than simply what you want or need. The therapeutic action of psychoanalysis is predicated, therefore, on the capacity of the analytic situation to require the patient, as a continuing task, to symbolize progressively in an interpersonal context, previously unformulated aspects of self as they emerge (chapter 4; also Bromberg, 1980). In this light, Freud's basic rule of free association—the patient's stated commitment to try and fully reveal himself and the meaning of his words and behavior—is not simply the doorway to the "real" material, but, in the context of participant observation, is part of the continuing "task" built into the analytic structure. If it is used by the analyst with sensitivity and judgment it can become a significant aspect of the "absorbing errand" that Henry James referred to. It keeps the analytic process from becoming solipsistic by making it inherently interpersonal through its demand quality, and thus particularly valuable in the treatment of schizoid pathology. The patient, by agreeing to try to follow the rule, cannot easily divest himself of the analyst's presence as part of his ongoing subjective experience while free associating, without his state of detachment itself becoming the content which is revealed. In other words, the basic rule permits the exploration to be focused upon the fact of the detachment and the transferential operation through which it is being played out at that moment in the room, rather than simply upon the content of what the patient might be wishing to hide by his reverie state or somnolence. The patient, at such a moment, is required in a direct way to "get out of his self" as part of the process of looking at his wish not to, and cannot as easily engage in a "pseudo-exploration" of the reasons for his detachment while simultaneously continuing to remain cut off and hidden behind the very content he is "into."

With schizoid patients the analytic situation runs a constant risk of being a dialogue *about* the patient rather than an analysis *of* the patient; the reported contents of his life, without immediacy, can too concretely become the frame that shapes his reality during the sessions. Because he cannot easily retain the analyst's presence in the room as part of the ongoing associative context, he has great trouble hearing his own words as process and not simply as external content. "There's nothing new to talk about today" is a statement the schizoid individual typically feels unconflicted in making *about* the analysis rather than a statement *within* the analysis. It is experienced, in effect, as a license either to enter a reverie state or to "look" for something to talk about. As long as the patient has agreed to try to follow the basic rule and report "marginal" thoughts and feelings, then he has implicitly agreed that this type of statement is in itself material for further association and is aware at some level that the analyst knows this. This frees the analyst to work in a more flexible way with transference and resistance, by gradually creating with the patient an analytic reality that defines the *absence* of external content as no different in terms of the patient's ongoing task as the *presence* of external content. In other words, the basic rule slowly becomes the patient's "absorbing errand" which he can't easily escape, and the analyst is thus able to maintain a relationship with a schizoid patient that preserves the analytic stance of participant observation, allows the patient's defenses to be respected, but requires the patient to more and more directly engage external reality as a voluntary act. The patient's stated commitment to the basic rule remains the same regardless of his initial degree of ego capacity to adhere to it, but in order for such an analytic stance to be productive *the analyst must be constantly working with the ongoing effects of this situation upon the patient, as a primary source of transferential material.*

The process of analytic work with a schizoid patient is in a certain way a paradox. The schizoid mental state is not simply a state of split emotional investment. It is a chronic state of hopelessness about feeling "real" in the world of the "here and now." The individual's frame of reference is his internal dialogue. This is where he lives and looks out at the world from behind his eyes, as if peeking at a motion picture in which he is playing a role. In analysis, he does not report the inner dialogue. It is not reportable as formulated experience. It is the private rehearsal studio that structures the form and content of his role as patient, and is not part of the interpersonal world of communication. It appears in dreams of schizoid patients in various metaphorical guises—living in a room within a room; serving a life term in prison but being let out each day as a trustee; driving along in a car with the view from the windshield being a framed Renaissance landscape painting. The inside room, the prison, the interior of the car; they are inherently inside and cannot be directly contacted by the analyst. The outer room, the trustee, and the framed painting *can* be engaged, but they are all "not-me." The only hope of bridging inside and outside is to provide an analytic structure which will get the patient voluntarily, albeit reluctantly, to make the outside interpersonally authentic. Any attempt by the analyst to pull the patient into an exploration of his internal dialogue is inevitably artificial because it occurs in a setting which is interpersonally artificial to *him* and to which he has learned to adapt as a "trustee." He will therefore either adapt his patient role to this new environmental demand and watch himself talking about himself, or will retreat into an even deeper state of detachment. This is why the analytic situation must include some "absorbing errand" that he has voluntarily agreed to undertake, which requires that he go beyond his ability to temporarily adapt to the real world—something which requires him to transcend his role as patient and his role as "trustee." He must have a task which he is obliged to take with him into his inner world, that will require him to inch his way gradually out of that world on his own. The basic rule of free association becomes that task because he has agreed to it, and the analyst reminds him of that fact by his stance as participant observer.

Let me conclude with a brief example to illustrate this point, using two statements made by one patient at different stages of treatment.

The first occurred during the course of an hour in his third month of analysis. It followed a session during which, in the face of his protests that he didn't know what I meant, I had been gently confronting him with the fact that he was not reporting all of his ongoing experience, since he made no mention of the lengthy silence that began the hour. He opened the next session by saying with great sincerity that he did realize what I was talking about once he got home and that I was right in what I was saying, and that he is like that everywhere. "Life," he said, "feels like a classroom, and I'm just auditing the course." As a descriptive statement in itself, his comment was, of course, incisively accurate and wonderfully charming. At another level, that was just what he intended it to be—wonderful and disarming "material." His primary source of security at this point was his inner world, just as his witticism implied, and his "accurate statement" was a means of presenting me with a piece of witty, accurate, and transferentially enticing content—like throwing a piece of meat to a lion, as he later put it—so I would "chew" on that and allow him to go back inside in peace. At this stage in treatment his core dynamics and conflicts were, except for fragmented glimpses, sealed off by his character armor. There was almost no access to his unconscious: no parapraxes, no dreams, nothing but "role playing" the good patient. His wish to disarm me was not yet—as it was later in treatment—a defense against internalized conflict involving power, sadism, and disavowed oedipal rage. At this point his wish was simply to satisfy me—to meet the environmental demand—so that he could return to the comfort of his detached state.

The second statement was made during a session about two years later. He was much more out in the open and much more critical of me, particularly with regard to what he perceived as my failure to provide him with the kind of unconditional trust and acceptance he claimed to have always received from his mother. He was quite angry at this moment, knowing that he was hiding transferential feelings and knowing that I knew he was aware of his dilemma and that I needed to do nothing but remain silent. He suddenly blurted out: "Why can't you be like my mother—someone who *doubts* on me!" It was the kind of slip he could never have made in the past, and led to the core of the avoided transferential feeling with a depth of richness that encompassed both a new level of reality with regard to his past and a newly created reality in the room with me. Our mutual enjoyment of the humor in the slip was genuine on both our parts, as compared with his earlier use of wit as an artful piece of "magic" designed to deflect attention away from himself.

It is the *freedom* to be interactional within an analytic framework that defines the interpersonal approach, and it is, in my opinion, the internalization of the basic rule in a gradually evolving way that gives the patient his "absorbing errand." Without that commitment from the patient, the analyst is in the continued position of trying to extract the detached patient from his inner world and bring him into the room, without the patient ever having to surrender his ego passivity as a voluntary act that is gradually able to become integrated into his self-representation as initiative and autonomy. It is this combination of the two ingredients which, in my view, allows the analyst to most productively use himself in helping the schizoid patient to get out of his self and stay out.

6

THE USE OF DETACHMENT IN NARCISSISTIC AND BORDERLINE CONDITIONS[1] (1979)

One aspect of the current developmental emphasis in psychoanalysis is that the concept of ego defense has become more broadly conceptualized so as to take into consideration the evolution of certain defenses prior to the full development of the ego and of intrapsychic conflict. The writings of Fairbairn (1944), Anna Freud (1946), Guntrip (1961a), Kernberg (1966, 1975), Mahler (1968, 1975), Sullivan (1940, 1953), and Winnicott (1960a, 1963b) have been particularly influential in shaping this perspective. Detachment, for example, is seen at the early stage of human growth as guardian of the integrity of the ego itself, arising to protect a fragile, growing sense of differentiated self from the threat of potential annihilation by internal and external stimuli that the ego is not yet strong enough to integrate. The role that detachment plays in character formation and in ego functioning during later stages of development has received notably less theoretical attention, although its adaptive as well as its more pathological manifestations are commonly acknowledged.

1. An earlier version of this chapter was presented at the 22nd Annual Meeting of the American Academy of Psychoanalysis, Atlanta, Georgia, in May 1978, and was published in its present form in *The Journal of the American Academy of Psychoanalysis*, 1979, 7:593–600.

As I have elaborated more fully elsewhere (Bromberg, 1979), one reason for this conceptual gap is that the immense contribution of the British school has tended to make detachment synonomous with "schizoid," and patients are described as though detachment were a monolithic, undifferentiated state. Its developmental function is thus difficult to relate to the great differences in personality structure in which it appears or to its use in the same personality structure as different developmental changes occur in treatment over time.

Detachment as an ego defense is in some ways a singular phenomenon although it shares attributes in common with other defenses. It operates directly upon the external world—that is, upon the real object itself—rather than upon its internal representation as does repression and its related mechanisms, such as isolation of affect. The real object becomes *in fact* less important, less valued, and less desired. But for any given patient we also need to know what purpose the detachment is serving at that phase, and whether its function has changed.

It is of special importance in psychoanalytic therapy to assess the operant quality of detachment in an ongoing way so as not to misperceive the predominant level of self and object representation, and the capacity for relatedness. In the initial stage of treatment the functional significance of detachment may be quite different, for example, in narcissistic and in borderline patients, and quite different in each from their later stages of treatment. These differences are sometimes minimized or even bypassed in an effort to head directly for the deepest common element—the original anxiety surrounding abandonment and early object loss. This sometimes leads to seeing the patient prematurely as though he were in the grip of a dynamic conflict from which he is actually several degrees removed, and thus failing to respond to him as he experiences himself at the moment. In borderline and narcissistic patients this of course serves to activate even further the already severe character pathology.

Detachment in Borderline Conditions

Traditionally, detachment is viewed in its function as a protection against painful affects that are associated with attachment, such as separation anxiety, loss of love, and yearning without hope. Detachment, however, does not follow an inner dialectic of its own, and its purpose is thereby inseparable from the level of personality integration at any given point in the growth process. For example, there exists a source of anxiety which is not *directly* associated with attachment in the above sense, but which plays a major role in the use of detachment as seen in borderline patients. I am referring to the deep, often projected fear of the destructiveness of one's love that plays such a central role in the need-fear dilemma in schizophrenia, and in the rigidity of the splitting processes in borderline conditions. Winnicott (1963b) describes this vividly when he writes of the failure to develop a capacity for concern, and of the ruthless quality of the infant's attachment to the breast.

As Buie and Adler (1973, p. 130) state, the patient may attempt to save the object from his destructive urges by withdrawal. But that too "threatens intolerable aloneness. Projection can be called upon to deal with his rage. But projecting it on to his object now makes the object a dreaded source of danger; self-protection is once again sought by distancing, and by withdrawal—again the state of aloneness is faced."

Thus, although the fear of abandonment and of inner chaos may indeed be the ultimate source of anxiety in these patients, what we first see when the detachment begins to peel away is not the beginning of genuine object relatedness, but an insatiable, possessive, demanding hunger, along with an intense fear of both destroying and using up the other person, who is also perceived as having a retaliative need to similarly devour *them*.

This, in fact, may be what accounts for the long periods of hate in the initial stage of work with certain borderline patients, that precedes the emergence of the primitive "love" and its attendant need-fear dilemma. It may be a way of saying: "If you can survive what I do to you while I am hating you, without retaliating, then perhaps we can *both* survive what I do to you while I am loving you."

Clinical Vignette 1

Mr. L, a 40-year-old playwright, entered therapy in a state of intense agitation, unable to write, and bristling with barely suppressed vindictive rage. The woman with whom he had been living for several years had just moved out, and he was filled with hate towards the world, towards her, towards being in therapy, and for the first three months of treatment, towards me. Nothing I did or said was right; the treatment was a waste of the little money he was earning; any indication of concern or involvement on my part was met with either icy contempt or increased complaints; efforts to inquire into his life or his feelings, past or present, were experienced by him as treating him "like a specimen under a microscope."

At the beginning of the fourth month he informed me that he had decided to stop treatment because "it wasn't giving him anything." It was only at this moment, in his decision to leave, that he obliquely allowed that there was something that he wanted. I acknowledged that it indeed did not seem to be giving him anything, and that although I wasn't sure why this was true, I hoped he would stay a while longer and that perhaps we could figure it out. He agreed to give it a little more time and left the session with his usual remark, "I suppose I'll see you next week." While the tone of this comment contained its usual virulence and sarcasm, it sounded strangely artificial and forced. Moreover, there was just the hint of feeling that it *mattered*. He appeared the next session with the following dream:

> He was living in a strange town which had been occupied by Nazis, from whom he had finally decided to escape. In order to make this journey he needed to assure that he had enough food, and was trying to get some juice from a local storekeeper who he thought was probably not a Nazi collaborator. But he was becoming anxious because the two containers of juice which the storekeeper had were too large for him to carry off, and anything smaller would not be enough to sustain him on his journey. He therefore realized that he would have to drink part of the contents in the store, but was afraid that if he stayed too long he would be discovered and destroyed by the Nazis, as would the storekeeper for sheltering a criminal.

It was at this point in treatment that his persecutory feelings began to diminish, and his detached, Nazi-like hate gave way to the layer beneath—the greedy, possessive quality of his hunger and the fear of its destructive consequences, along with the detachment to keep it under control.

If the earliest function of detachment as an ego defense is to prevent severe damage to the emerging experience of self, then the quality of hate in this patient is particularly interesting. It was above all, detached. It was cold, remote, unambivalent, and determined. It contained a strong wish to hurt . . . to *get* to me. I suggest that it is because there is no attachment to the object in that kind of hate, that the experience of successfully hurting the other person affirms the existence of the fragmented sense of self. Hate feels real—and when the self is threatened in its own ability to exist, if there is only minimal object constancy as with borderline patients, then detachment is vital. It expresses and insures the patient's "entitlement to survive" (Buie and Adler, 1973). The unencumbered ability to validate the self by having an impact is preserved through hurting, without the fear of loss of love or abandonment. The turning point for Mr. L was when he was able to have an impact on me by threatening to leave therapy. I had survived his hate, and acknowledged *his reality* that the therapy had not been giving him anything, without retaliating by "accepting" his wish to leave.

Mr. L, like many borderline patients, fiercely protected his right to hate as an expression of his right to survive. He could not let me be anything but bad until there was some trust in his own ability to have an impact on me other than by hate. He could only then gradually begin to risk attachment and the release of the primitive "love" which when not fully and immediately acknowledged led to the more deeply buried fear related to loss.[2] It was at this point that detachment became directly related to attachment and to the fear of abandonment accompanying it.

Detachment in Pathological Narcissism

In general, the detachment defense attempts to convert the fear of being abandoned, an ego-passive fear, to an active movement away from relationship. The consequence, as Schecter (1978a) points out, is that the greater the depth of detachment, the greater will be the sense of futility; that is, no hope for a "good relationship."

I think that this is accurate for the most part, with at least one exception that is worth distinguishing—that of pathological narcissism. It is, in fact, the *absence* of this particular experience of futility that is one of the hallmarks of the disorder, and which makes severe cases so resistant to analytic therapy and often such an ordeal for the therapist. Unlike psychoneuroses, schizoid personalities, and borderline conditions, in which detachment does function primarily to protect the ego against the painful affects associated with attachment, in narcissistic personality disorders it functions to preserve the integrity of the pathological grandiose-self structure (see chapter 7). So, until that structure begins to lose its sovereignty, the dysphoria and futility that exist do not come from the lack of hope for a good relationship,

---

2. For an interesting comparison of this idea with that of Sullivan's concept of malevolent transformation, see Chrzanowski, Schecter, and Kovar (1978).

but from any sense of needing a relationship at all; that is, from the experience of inadequacy that accompanies any evidence that the patient lacks anything he cannot give to himself.

As the grandiose-self structure does begin to diminish in scope, a congruent shift in the operant function of detachment is often revealed. One place this frequently shows up as a manifestation of change is in the use of language, especially language which relates to the concept of one's own limitations. Take for example, the distinction between the words *choice* and *decision*.

Clinical Vignette 2

Miss R, a patient of many years, whose character pathology was fundamentally narcissistic, had reached a major crisis point in her life. She was faced with the irreconcilable alternatives of immediate marriage or a highly desired career appointment which required extended business trips for undetermined lengths of time. She was quite involved with her boyfriend and had grown to care deeply for him, but also saw this career opportunity as a long awaited challenge. She ultimately took the job and lost the boyfriend, but for her the broader issue was the level of interpersonal maturity she was able to sustain during the process of inner struggle, agony, joy, loss, and gain.

It was a telling moment in her analysis for her to recognize that unlike similar situations in the past, she had made a choice rather than a decision, and was able to feel sorrow and loss without loss of self or self-esteem. Her characteristic pattern had always been to protect her grandiose-self representation by detaching herself from any relationship that was not felt to be totally under her control. The ending of a relationship had always been experienced as her *decision*. The term "decision" implies mastery—a command of the facts and an awareness of the options that lead to selecting the *right one*. The term "choice" conveys a difficult selection process in which something of value is gained only by losing something else of value. It involves a capacity to acknowledge the ambivalence that is felt when one's own mastery of situations is imperfect, and this is a touchstone of the extent of narcissistic vulnerability.

Faced with such a difficult trade-off in the past, Miss R typically would detach from one of the options and "decide" on the other. The detachment was not directly a defense against the experience of object loss, but a means of preserving the illusion of perfect mastery attached to the grandiose-self. She was fond of quoting a line from one of her favorite popular songs: "Freedom is another word for nothing left to lose." To have nothing to lose is of course the sine qua non of narcissistic self-containment. To have felt the reality of a genuine *choice* would have formerly produced not grief or mourning, but the loss of self-esteem that follows severe narcissistic injury, which for her at times approached actual loss of self.

This is not to say that there was no detachment as part of the choice process in this instance, but it was of a different quality and reflected the shift in her level of ego integration. It did not rob her of the experience of loss, but enabled her to preserve her full sense of self while loosening the emotional bond enough for a choice to be possible.

In summary, looking at some of the ways in which detachment issues are organized and expressed in the psychoanalytic treatment of differing character structures makes the need for a finely tuned interpersonal environment in analysis particularly compelling. Finding the appropriate spot to occupy in the dimension of distance and closeness with a detached patient depends heavily on the ability to maintain an empathic "feel" for the aspect of self that is closest to the surface of the detachment, and cannot easily be dealt with by broad rules of thumb or diagnostic conceptualizations of detachment as simply a global entity.

PART II

SAFETY, REGRESSION, AND TRAUMA

7

THE MIRROR AND THE MASK

On Narcissism and Psychoanalytic Growth[1] (1983)

Trying to extract some coherent view of narcissism from the ongoing controversy in the current psychoanalytic literature is somewhat like trying to chill Russian vodka by adding ice cubes; it is possible to do it, but the soul of the experience is diluted. Levenson's (1978, p. 16) suggestion that "it may not be the truth arrived at as much as the manner of arriving at the truth which is the essence of therapy" leads me to wonder if it may likewise be said that it is not the definition of narcissism arrived at as much as the struggle to arrive at one, which is the essence of recent progress in psychoanalytic thought. The struggle contains within it, an emerging shift in perspective that has begun to influence our conceptions of clinical diagnosis, the nature of human development, psychoanalytic metatheory, and the parameters of psychoanalytic treatment itself.

---

1. The central theme of this chapter draws upon ideas from an earlier unpublished paper, "Current Psychological Concepts of Narcissism," presented in 1978 at a symposium sponsored jointly by the Brooklyn College School of Social Science and the William Alanson White Psychoanalytic Institute. The present version of this essay was originally published in *Contemporary Psychoanalysis*, 1983, 19:359–387, and then as a chapter in *Essential Papers on Narcissism*, edited by A. P. Morrison (New York: New York University Press, 1986, pp. 438–466).

During the past two decades there has been a gradual but consistent movement of the mainstream of psychoanalysis in the direction of field theory, and toward the interpersonal context as the medium of both normal maturation and therapeutic change (see chapter 3). This has brought the developmental models of psychopathology and analytic technique into closer harmony than ever before, and has focused attention on the growth of "self" as inseparable from the interrelationship of "self and other," whether in the parental environment or the therapeutic environment.

Analysts have been studying how the interpersonal field mediates the process by which self and object representations are born and internally structured; how inadequacy of interpersonal experience during various phases of maturation can lead to structural pathology of the representational world itself; how this structural pathology can lead to specific forms of character disorders traditionally considered untreatable by psychoanalysis; and how a psychoanalytic relationship with such patients might indeed be possible from a field theory orientation.

As one outcome of this paradigm shift, the subject of narcissism has become as currently fascinating and humanly real as it had formerly been wooden and artificial. The metapsychological "puppet," like Pinocchio, has come alive and gained a "self." In so doing it has become more interesting to psychoanalysts as an issue of treatment approach and as a clinical data base supplementing hysteria, than as the original construct shaped by Freud (1914) to account for certain aspects of theory.

The narcissistic personality has become accessible, as a live human being, to psychoanalytic treatment; but the term "narcissism" is now more vague and ambiguous as a hypothetical construct and as a nosological entity—"the narcissistic personality disorder." It has in fact become almost a kind of operational watershed which is used to describe those individuals whose object relations are characteristic of the developmental level of mental representation that Anna Freud (1969) calls "need satisfying," that Mahler (1972) describes as "magical omnipotence," and that Immanuel Kant might consider a systematic violation of his categorical imperative; individuals who experience other people as a means to an end rather than as an end in themselves. The defining qualities are most often described in the psychoanalytic literature as a triad of vanity, exhibitionism, and arrogant ingratitude, which for better or worse (Lasch, 1979, p. 33), is what the word "narcissism" has come to mean in popular usage.

Bach (1977, p. 209) describes what it feels like from behind the analyst's couch as "talking into the wind or writing on the sand, only to have one's words effaced moments later by the waves. The patient either welcomes or resents the analyst's words [and] frequently does not even register the actual content. A session which seems to have led to a certain understanding or experience of some kind may, 24 hours later, be totally forgotten."

It is a quality of unrelatedness which represents the failure in development of a spontaneous, stable, taken-for-granted self-experience. The individual tends not to feel himself at the center of his own life. He is prevented from full involvement in living because he is developmentally stuck between "the mirror and the mask"—a reflected appraisal of himself, or a disguised search for one, through which the self finds or seeks affirmation of its own significance. Living becomes a process of controlling the environment and other people from behind a mask. When successful it is exhilirating; when unsuccessful there is boredom, anxiety, resentment, and emptiness. But the critical fact is that an ongoing sense of full involvement in life is missing, often without awareness. The intrinsic experience of accomplishment is transformed into one of manipulation, exploitation, and a vague feeling of fooling people. A state of well-being becomes the goal of living rather than its characteristic quality, and the moment to moment sense of being has little relevance other than as a preparation for the next moment. Existence becomes either a search or a waiting period for that moment not yet here when real life and true love will begin. The present is always imperfect in and of itself.

What keeps the person going, and often able to manage the external appearance of a relatively well-functioning life, is an internal structure referred to in the psychoanalytic literature as a "grandiose self" (Kernberg, 1975; Kohut, 1971, 1972, 1977). Its main job is to be perfect (see Rothstein, 1980); that is, to achieve approbation, to never be dependent, and to never feel lacking in any way. Although there is theoretical disagreement as to how this "grandiose self" is established, most analysts pretty much concur that it conceals beneath it a self-image described by Kernberg (1975) as

> a hungry, enraged, empty self, full of impotent anger at being frustrated, and fearful of a world which seems as hateful and revengeful as the patient himself (p. 233). . . . The greatest fear of these patients is to be dependent on anybody else because to depend means to hate, envy, and expose themselves to the danger of being exploited, mistreated, and frustrated [p. 235].

Consequently, any confrontation with this self-image of perfection evokes an immediate need to protect it, and the other person is typically greeted with either an increased dose of disdainful aloofness or with self-righteous rage. This often poses a bit of a problem for mates, lovers, employers, friends, and analysts, should they tend to be more than a "need-satisfying object."

The picture I have been presenting is that of pathological narcissism. Whether such a thing as "normal narcissism" can be said to exist as a distinct entity is currently a controversial issue. Ernest Becker (1973) has presented a particularly compelling sociological position which examines and recasts the psychoanalytic theory of neurosis in the context of man's need to cope with existential anxiety. "In man," Becker states,

> a working level of narcissism is inseparable from self-esteem, from a basic sense of self-worth . . . it is all too absorbing and relentless to be an aberration; it expresses the heart of the creature: the desire to stand out, to be *the* one in creation. When you combine natural narcissism with the basic need for self-esteem, you create a creature who has to feel himself an object of primary value: first in the universe, representing in himself all of life [pp. 3–6].

Becker here argues that man is hopelessly absorbed with himself, and "if everyone honestly admitted his urge to be a hero it would be a devastating release of truth" (p. 5). But the truth about one's need for a sense of personal heroism is not easy to admit, and thus, "to become conscious of what one is doing to earn his feelings of heroism is the main self-analytic problem of life" (p. 6). He is not taking a position that narcissism is psychiatrically healthy; rather that it is an inevitable and essential form of madness which protects us from the greater clinical madness of having to apprehend fully our own mortality in an ongoing way. As Becker sees it, our normal narcissism spares us from having "to live a whole lifetime with the fate of death haunting one's dreams" (p. 27), a truth which if fully faced would literally drive man insane. What psychoanalysis has done, Becker asserts, is to reveal to us the complex intrapsychic and interpersonal penalties of denying the truth of man's condition. The psychological and social costs of pretending to be other than what we are is called "neurosis."

Pathological narcissism, in this framework, is one of the particular characterological tolls that is increasingly being paid by man in contemporary society as he tries to deny his apprehension of non-being. At its core, it describes a sense of self lacking sufficient inner resources to give meaning to life simply through living it fully. Man's relentless need to validate the "self" as the goal of living may be the form of personality disorder that most fascinates psychoanalysts in our time because the experience of meaninglessness may be the context in which the feeling of non-being most typically expresses itself in our time. Peter Marin (1975, p. 6) in fact believes that in current society "the self replaces community, relation, neighbor, chance, or God," and sees the culturally prevailing psychological character organization as what he labels "the new narcissism."

Psychoanalytically, it can be argued that in line with Becker's perspective on the nature of the human condition, the potential for normal as well as pathological narcissism is coexistent with birth. Mahler for a separation-individua- that

ıd the psychological birth
me. The former is a dra-
scribed event; the latter, a
r the more or less normal
in" and at the same time
ɛre" is among the givens

with birth and regardless
nent, the human being is

l isolation. One could
more or less successful
n of the lost symbiotic
fantasied "ideal state of
tic fusion with the "all
me part of the self in a

ner animals, our psycho-
ɔirth and outside of the
maturation is inherently
the "self" is never fully
ɪgy—difficulty in being
ally separate from "the
th but need not develop
"self" in adulthood.
ıich the pleasure princi-
rnal world is excluded

l
u
tı
sː
b
w
ir

pl

wᴀs a bird s egg with its food supply enclosed in its shell. Ferenczi (1913) expanded on Freud's statement that the prototype of the pleasure principle was in this self-contained existence where no stimuli from the outside can impinge, and he asserted that it is in fact the period of life spent in the womb which, as a stage of human development, totally represents Freud's example. It is this stage, Ferenczi argued, which truly defines omnipotence. It is not the state of having all of one's needs met, but a state in which one doesn't even need to need. It is the state of total self-sufficiency. Glatzer and Evans (1977) formulate Ferenczi's view as follows:

> The clear implication of this first stage . . . this period of unconditional omnipotence . . . is that growing up is painful quite apart from the nature of the environment. The unconscious fiction of the frustrating "outside" is ineluctable and universal. It is the inevitable consequence of being born. The cardinal importance of Ferenczi's contribution is this: The reactive rage of the child to not being fed is not due merely to the fact that he is hungry; he is more likely to be depressed. The main cause of his anger is that his illusion of self-sufficiency is constantly being shattered [pp. 89–90].

The parallel is striking between Ferenczi's idea of traumatic loss of omnipotence, and an existential view of narcissism in man (Becker, 1973, p. 30) as "the toll that his pretense of sanity takes as he tries to deny his true condition." From the vantage point of this parallel, what is called the "grandiose self" structure might reasonably be seen as a core patterning of self-other representation designed to protect the illusion of self-sufficiency at all costs, because in pathological narcissism the structure is also disguising the individual's lack of a fully individuated identity. The way in which such patients use detachment as an ego defense is illustrative. Schecter (1978a, p. 82) points out that in most character structures the detachment defense attempts to convert the fear of being abandoned, an ego-passive fear, to an active movement away from relationship; the consequence is that "the greater the depth of detachment, the greater will be the sense of futility; that is, no hope for a "good relationship." It is my belief, however, that in the case of pathological narcissism, as I've stated in chapter 6, the emptiness and futility that accompany detachment do not come from the lack of hope for a good relationship, but as a functional consequence of dimly recognizing a need for any relationship at all. The futility is most directly an experience of "ego depletion." It is a felt "inadequacy" of the grandiose self elicited in these individuals by evidence that they lack anything that is not contained in themselves; it is, in effect, a temporary unmasking of the illusion of self-sufficiency.

Whether we accept Becker's premise that the basis of narcissism is man's need to deny mortality by an illusion of total self-sufficiency (which he calls "heroism"), his viewpoint is paradigmatically consistent with that of Sullivan (1948, 1950b, 1953) and Fromm (1947, 1956, 1964), and follows the direction in which interpersonal psychoanalysis and object relations theory seems to be moving; namely, toward the concept that all narcissistic pathology is, fundamentally, mental activity designed by a grandiose interpersonal self representation to preserve its structural stability and to maintain, protect, or restore its experience of well-being (see Schafer, 1968, pp. 191–193; Stolorow, 1975, p. 179; Sandler and Sandler, 1978, pp. 291–295; Horner, 1979, p. 32). Becker's formulation also resonates in an equally notable, although conceptually distinct way, with Kohut's (1971, 1972) position that narcissism and narcissistic rage are developmentally normal, and given the proper early environment should lead to healthy assertiveness, to a firm sense of self-esteem, and to a relatively well-integrated balance between feeling both in the world and separate from it. Becker (1973) writes:

> The child who is well nourished and loved develops, as we said, a sense of magical omnipotence, a sense of his own indestructibility, a feeling of proven power and secure support. He can imagine himself, deep down, to be eternal. We might say that his repression of the idea of his own death is made easy for him because he is fortified against it in his very narcissistic vitality [p. 22].

The clinical problem confronting contemporary psychoanalysis, however, is not metaphysical and is no myth, even though it allegedly all started with one.

The Problem of Analyzability

It has been written that the nymph Echo had fallen in love with a handsome youth named Narcissus, who unfortunately loved nobody but himself. Echo, however, had her own problems. She had been previously punished by a jealous goddess and had lost the gift of forming her own words, so that she could from then on only repeat the words of others. As Narcissus bent to drink one day in a quiet pool, he noticed in the mirroring surface of the water, the handsomest face he had ever seen. "I love you," said Narcissus to the handsome face. "I love *you*," repeated Echo eagerly as she stood behind him. But Narcissus neither saw nor heard her, being spellbound by the reflection in the water. He sat smiling at himself, forgetting to eat or drink, until he wasted away and died. This, by one account (D'Aulaire and D'Aulaire, 1962) may be the first recorded instance of premature termination due to an unresolved mirror transference.

The descendants of Narcissus now lie upon an analytic couch, as self-absorbed as ever, while behind them, as in the myth, sit the determined but still frustrated counterparts of Echo, trying to be heard. Old narcissism or "new narcissism," it's still not easy. In some ways, though, we have progressed since that fatal day at the pool. Psychoanalysts have begun to recognize that the solution to the problem is not located solely in the patient, and that perhaps Echo and Narcissus were less than an ideal match. One might even go as far as to suggest that Echo was working under an unnecessary handicap of her own.

Psychoanalysts, in order to practice psychoanalysis as defined by its agreed upon parameters, are bound by a particular stance which, like Echo's, may have handicapped them in facilitating structural growth in narcissistic patients. Echo's burden was not just that she could only repeat what she heard, but that in so doing, she too was unable to exist as a person in her own right and thereby unable to know whether Narcissus could be reached by a different approach.

Analysts have more or less agreed that narcissistic disorders are difficult to treat and that the so-called "unmodified psychoanalytic situation" doesn't do the job. Gedo (1977, p. 792), for example, states that "In effect, no consensus has yet been reached about the appropriate analytic response to the transference manifestations of the grandiose self. Everyone is in agreement, however, about the absolute necessity of responding to these infantile claims with maximal tact and empathy . . . any failure in this regard is inevitably followed by humiliation and outrage."

In discussing the analyzability of narcissistic personality disorders, Rothstein (1982) accurately observes that certain of these patients lack the ego assets to enable them to participate in an analytic process that is relatively independent of what the analyst contributes through his own personality and approach to the patient. Because, however, these ego assets are in his view "essential prerequisites" for a genuine analytic experience, their core psychopathology is inaccessible to interpretation and these patients are deemed unanalyzable inasmuch as their pre-existing personality structure requires more than the unmodified psychoanalytic situation. "Interpretive attempts to facilitate a working through process can evoke psychotic regressions (and) serious acting-out, sometimes including rapid disruption of the working relationship" (p. 178). This emphasis, Rothstein argues, is important because there are subjects who can accommodate to an analytic situation but whose analytic processes rarely develop past the regressive internationalization of the analyst as a reparative narcissistically invested introject characteristic of mid-phase process. These subjects may experience significant therapeutic benefit from such a relationship. However, where reparative or "transmuting" internalization gained in the non-verbal "mirroring," "holding" or "containing" ambiance is the primary mode of therapeutic action, a therapeutic rather than analytic result had been achieved [pp. 177–178].

In other words, the prognosis for a successful analytic outcome is tied directly to a model of treatment in which the primary mode of therapeutic action is held to be that of interpretation. The patients Rothstein describes are considered unanalyzable because he feels them to be characterologically unable to utilize verbal interpretation, and able to benefit therapeutically only from "mirroring"—from "swallowing whole" the analyst's nonverbal positive attitude and unconditional acceptance.

Perhaps so. But once again, might not the problem as well as the solution be located in the nature of the relationship between Echo and Narcissus, rather than in Narcissus alone? The issue of whether interpretation or internalization of the analyst is the "genuine" agent of analytic growth may not only be irrelevant (see Strachey, 1934; Friedman, 1978), but may itself lead the analyst, like Echo, to a technique which fulfills its own prophesy of analytic failure.

The patient's sovereign need to control the object from behind a mask often precludes an ability to "work" in the transference; that is, to directly experience and report, as material, ongoing thoughts and feelings about the analyst and the process itself. The need to protect the stability of the grandiose self requires that he ward off any experience that leads to relinquishing his narcissistically invested representation of the analyst and the analytic situation. Right from the start, therefore, there is a frequent challenge to the conditions and formal structure of the analysis itself, in order to prevent direct experience of the transference. By the establishment of narcissistic transference configurations, the patient limits the analyst's ability to create an analytic setting which might lead to transference regression and any experience of needing more from the analyst than he is getting. The patient's only initial hope of success in treatment is that which unconsciously guides the rest of his life—to perform for the analyst and be rewarded by "cure." The analyst is therefore typically under pressure to bend his analytic structure and his approach regarding such issues as frequency of sessions, use of the couch, payment of bills, and his own characteristic level of responsiveness.

If the analyst holds a strong commitment to the concept of a classical "unmodified psychoanalytic situation," then any compromises he may make out of "therapeutic necessity" are simultaneously processed by him as "resistances" to a "genuine" analysis that has not yet begun, and which must be interpreted when the timing seems right. For certain types of patients this perspective is suitable and often will lead to a relatively successful outcome, but for others—narcissistic disorders in particular—it easily may work against its own intent and can potentially become a significant factor in either treatment impasses or a premature diagnosis of unanalyzability.

The goal of getting a patient to experience and acknowledge an ongoing transference process and to work with it analytically, is indeed the central issue. But the heart of the pathology in these patients focuses upon that being their most fundamental inability; to be both "in the world" and "separate from it" at the same time, without endangering the internal structure they most depend upon for a sense of identity—the grandiose self. The wish for the patient to enter into a "real" analysis is not in itself untherapeutic, inappropriate, or even "countertransferential" in the narrow use of the term; but in treating narcissistic disorders it is a perspective which, if too important to the analyst, may subtly become, for the patient, the unconscious focal point that allows him to remain safely stuck between the mirror and the mask. As long as interpretations, no matter how tactfully administered, are directed towards the patient's transference resistance, the patient will process the experience as though the analyst were another version of a self-interested, narcissistic parental figure who is more involved with getting the patient to meet his own needs than in helping the patient. In order to ward off this perception of the analyst, the narcissistic transference configurations will become even more impenetrable or more brittle. The patient will, in other words, respond with either increased idealization of the analyst, with increased detachment, or with a marginal transference psychosis.

The clinical dilemma is genuine. There are indeed patients who, at least for long periods of time, react to interpretations only as personal feelings held by the analyst, and from the unmodified analytic stance are unanalyzable when they seem to have a serious potential for ego-disorganization or acting-out in response to this stance. If for the moment we reduce the priority of whether what we are doing conforms to the more orthodox definition of psychoanalysis, then much of the apparent disagreement becomes secondary to an approach which is potentially reconcilable with the majority of analytic viewpoints, though it most directly reflects the influence of the interpersonal position and object relations theory. It is based upon looking at the analytic situation as an open, empathic, interpersonal matrix within which the patient's representational world has maximal opportunity to become systematically repatterned and restructured at increasingly higher development levels. It is a perspective which has its deepest roots in the pioneer work of many different analysts at different points in the history of psychoanalysis, and represents a common thread linking the otherwise diverse schools of thought represented by such seminal authors as Ferenczi (1909, 1930b); Strachey (1934); Fairbairn (1952); Sullivan (1953); Thompson (1956); Guntrip (1961a, 1969); Gitelson (1962); Winnicott (1965); and Balint (1968).

Ernest Becker's (1964) treatise on what he views as the post-scientistic "revolution in psychiatry" captures this orientation particularly vividly and without recourse to the theoretical constructs of any one school of psychoanalysis. He writes:

> The patient is not struggling against himself, against forces deep within his animal nature. He is struggling rather against the loss of his world, of the whole range of action and objects that he so laboriously fashioned during his early training. He is fighting, in sum, against the subversion of himself in the only world that he knows. Each object is as much a part of him as is the built-in behavior pattern for transacting with the object. Each action is as much within his nature as the self-feeling he derives from initiating or contemplating that action. Each rule for behavior is as much as part of him as is his metabolism, the forward momentum of his life processes [p. 170].
>
> The individual would have an easy time changing his early "inauthentic" style if he would somehow disengage his own commitment to it. But rules, objects, and self-feeling are fused—taken together they constitute one's "world." How is one to relinquish his world unless he first gains a new one? This is the basic problem of personality change [p. 179].

Becker then addresses an issue which encapsulates the dilemma faced by analysts in attempting to treat narcissistic disorders; the patient's lack of an observing ego which can disembed itself sufficiently from its own world to allow the patient to examine with the analyst the structure he is most in danger of losing should he become too clearly aware of it. "Some individuals," Becker (1964) observes (p. 179), "are fortunate in their early training."

The result is that they have their own feeling of value pretty much in hand, so to speak. . . . Hence they can "back off" from any *particular* object and examine it critically; they are not bound to narrow action needs. To be able to withdraw from any action-commitment long enough to appraise it critically needs the secure possession of one's own positive self-feeling. . . . The self-image does not depend hopelessly on any one object, or on any unquestionable rule. . . . Obviously this strength will be absent where . . . the rules are uncritically and inextricably fused with a particular concrete object [pp. 179–180].

Here in this final sentence is the kernel of the issue of analyzability. Individuals for whom interpersonal rules are rigidly fused with a particular concrete object representation, bring to the analytic situation a core representation of "self" which is fused equally concretely to the same interpersonal unit. Such individuals do not possess a core identity which is stable enough in its own right and flexible enough for them to "back off" and observe themselves in the analytic process while still being immersed in it. They cannot "work" in the transference until they free themselves, at least to some degree, from the particular concrete object or part-object (Fairbairn, 1952) representation which defines their basic feeling of self-value.

For patients suffering from pathological narcissism, the "grandiose self" representation is developmentally fused to the "need satisfying object" by a set of interpersonal operations designed to prevent the object from being little more than a mirror, and to keep the true nature of those operations "masked." The analyst and the analytic situation are primarily external versions of that concrete mental representation, and it is thus extremely difficult to help such patients mobilize their own power of critical observation to examine their narcissistic transference configurations objectively. They cannot, in Becker's terms, genuinely work on "relinquishing their old world" without a "new one" being felt as at least within their grasp. From this orientation, one aspect of the analytic process is to facilitate the patient's development of the necessary mental structure to utilize it most fully. The analytic relationship is thus the most potentially powerful and subtle instrument in the treatment process. It represents a therapeutic environment which can be flexibly adapted to the patient's developmental level and its variability, rather than a fixed set of roles to which a patient must be able to accommodate or the analyst must "modify" if the patient does not possess the "prerequisite ego assets."

The analyst is committed to an approach rather than being bound to a technique. He does not need to make a choice, independent of any particular patient, between interpretation as mutative and mirroring as reparative. The therapeutic action of the analytic process is seen as containing for all patients both elements as necessary and intrinsic parts of the interpersonal field which mediates it. For any given patient, however, the relative significance of each element in the overall field will initially depend upon the developmental level of mental structure that defines his core identity. For some patients the ability to utilize fully the analytic situation will then depend upon how much growth has occurred in the establishment of a stable sense of separate identity, while for others (the traditional "good analytic patient") it is less of an issue.

Pine (1979, p. 93) makes the distinction between affects which are transformed from earlier affects (such as traumatic anxiety into signal anxiety), and affects which are created when the inner psychological structure is right for it. He refers most specifically to affect states that "crystallize around the child's acquisition of self-other differentiation" and are "first born at later stages in the developmental process when the psychological conditions for their emergence are met. These psychological conditions involve new learnings—new acquisitions of mental life." In my view this is equally pertinent as a treatment issue where a sufficient sense of separate core identity is not present to begin with in the analysis. It implies the developmental necessity of an initial period in treatment that allows the creation of the "right inner psychological structure" upon which later acquisitions can be built. By being able to utilize the presence and emotional availability of the analyst, the patient is given a setting in which he can begin to build this "prerequisite" structure and slowly "heal" the developmentally fixated source of anxiety associated with the insufficient maturation of autonomous tension-reducing patterns of self and object representations; that is, a core identity whose stability is relatively independent of external nourishment. In the case of pathological narcissism, before the patient can develop a genuine working alliance and the ability to value and conceptually utilize new experience of himself conveyed through another person, he must first modify the sovereignty of the grandiose self enough to permit another person to exist as a separate entity in his representational world. Without this, he is, as Rothstein (1982) argues, primarily dependent upon mirroring as a means of mediating anxiety, and will continue to ward off any experience discrepant with his self-image of needing nothing beyond what is already part of him or within his perfect ability to control in the narcissistically invested "other."

For such patients the growth of anxiety-tolerance is central to the analytic process. It moves hand-in-hand with the development of "self" and self-structuring, and is one of the key variables which determines the initial capacity of these individuals to work in the transference. It is also an ego function which should show dramatic improvement if the analytic work is accomplishing its main task. The goal of the work, as in any analysis, is for personality growth to be self-perpetuating; that is, for the patient to internalize the analyst's analytic function as an aspect of his ego autonomy (Loewald, 1960). This achievement depends upon the ability of the analysis to free the patient from the grip of the narcissistic transference as the primary source of ego-sustenance, and from the fear of ego-depletion (or "non-being") as the most powerful developmental line of anxiety.

The Question of Anxiety and the Development of "Self"

In light of the above, it is of interest to consider the possibility that the development of anxiety-tolerance and higher level "self-other" mental representation during treatment may have a parallel in normal cognitive-emotional maturation in early life that is especially relevant for these patients. Schecter (1980) presents the view that we can concieve of each form of infantile anxiety—anxiety by contagion, separation anxiety, stranger anxiety, anxiety through loss of love, castration anxiety, and superego anxiety—as constituting the beginning of a developmental line which runs through childhood into adulthood. He suggests, as Pine has, that the quality of the original form of each type of anxiety is related to the developmental level of psychic structure that exists at that time, and that although each earlier line of anxiety is modified or "healed" by the subsequent development of new structure or maturation of older structure, the particular quality of the original experience continues to resonate throughout the life cycle to varying degrees for any given individual.

This orientation is particularly useful in differentiating the analytic treatment approach most suited to patients for whom an individuated core identity is taken for granted, from the approach most facilitating to patients such as narcissistic disorders, for whom it is a task to be completed through the work of the analysis itself. In this latter group of patients, the most profound source of anxiety at the onset of treatment has its origin prior to the full development of the ego and of intrapsychic conflict, and prior to the evolution of higher level ego defenses. It arises from a need to protect the fragile, poorly differentiated "self" from the threat of potential annihilation by internal and external experience that it is not yet autonomous enough to integrate, and which is thus felt as impinging, or "strange." Schecter, in fact, considers the most powerful line of anxiety that emerges in analysis—what he calls "strangeness anxiety"—to be a derivative of the early experience of stranger anxiety. It seems clinically clear, writes Schecter (1980, p. 551), "that much of what we call resistance in psychoanalytic therapy has to do with anxiety connected with the conscious discovery of strange, new, ego-alien aspects of the self, of significant object-persons, and of their relationship."

"Strangeness anxiety" as a developmental line of affect has not fit easily into Freud's theory of anxiety until now; that is, until the recent new respect being paid to the structural aspects of the separation-individuation process, and to the interpersonal context which mediates the normal healing of more primitive sources of anxiety as later structure develops. In this sense it helps to bridge a conceptual gap between Freud's theory of anxiety as an affect derived from motivational conflict, and Sullivan's theory of anxiety as an affect derived from structural disequilibrium of the "self."

Stranger anxiety, when it does occur overtly, is normally seen in infants of about seven to eight months of age, which is approximately the point in cognitive development at which there is the first evidence that an object concept has begun to develop. Fraiberg (1969) calls it the beginning of "recognition memory." Even though the infant at that point cannot be said to have a true internalized mental representation of the object since its image cannot be evoked when the object is absent, it is the beginning of the process through which the gradual loss of omnipotence becomes attached to the outside world which the infant gradually comes to accept and call "reality." It begins here because here is where the cognitive structure is first born that allows an outside and an inside to be created. The existence of this new mental structure therefore becomes in and of itself a potential source of a new line of anxiety associated with threat to "self" because "self" now begins to have a representation which organizes experience vis-à-vis an object. In other words, as the process of separation-individuation continues, the source of anxiety shifts slowly (or sometimes abruptly) from separation to individuation; that is, to the "self" and its own ego defenses or security operations. The greater the development of an interpersonally differentiated self and object, the more the experience of individuation and its higher level ego defenses, rather than the illusion of non-separateness, mediates the integrity of the "self." What we see as eight-month stranger anxiety may be the most observable instance of failure of the interpersonal matrix to smoothly mediate the infant's rudimentary transition to a differentiated experience of "self"; it may occur in those infants for whom the birth of this new mental structure precipitates a fall from perfection which is too abrupt and thereby too discordant with previous mental organization. In this light, it would tend to be traumatic if, as Sandler (1977) suggests, the perception of "other" evokes a too discrete recognition of a nongratifying constellation of images as "not mother"; "strangeness" and "the stranger" thus become an intolerable threat to the integrity of the newly hatching self. External reality, which is too discrepant with the experience of self-contained gratification (omnipotence), reinforces the need to retain the security of omnipotent self-containment by controlling rather than internalizing reality. It is the beginning, one might say, of Narcissus and Echo at the pool; the incapacity to "take in" anything that isn't an extension of the grandiose self. It may also be the beginning of the difficulty which inhibits the normal development of more mature modes of anxiety mediation, interpersonal relatedness, and self-growth. It occurs at a time during the separation-individuation process that optimal development of self and object representation is, according to Mahler (1968, p. 20), dependent upon "the child's achievement of separate functioning in the presence and emotional availability of the mother." "Even in this situation," Mahler here states, "this process by its very nature continually confronts the toddler with minimal threats of object loss." Trauma during this "early practising subphase" (seven to ten months of age) interferes with what Mahler describes (1972, p. 336) as the infant's later capacity for "exchanging some of his magical omnipotence for autonomy and developing self-esteem." As an adult he will thus tend to retain this early vulnerability to anxiety from a developmental source which has never "healed"; and if the developmental arrest is severe enough, his "inflated, omnipotent self-object representation is the nucleus of the grandiose self which obtains in cases of pathological narcissism" (Horner, 1979, p. 32).

What, then, is the most useful analytic approach in treating these individuals suffering from pathological narcissism? How does such a patient ever reach the point where there is enough genuine relatedness to the analyst to form what is usually called an analyzable transference neurosis? Or to put it more operationally, how does the analysis enable the patient to assimilate anything from the analyst that he hears as less than flattering, without the grandiose self organizing the experience?

Treatment: The Integration of Mirroring and the Dissolution of the Mask

Before addressing the above question in the context of pathological narcissism, it might be useful to first consider my approach to the same question as it pertains to the general interpersonal model of psychoanalytic treatment (see also chapters 3 and 4). What makes the patient "trust" the analyst sufficiently to engage in a joint dismantling of his protective system with the same person who transferentially is the source of most immediate danger? Sullivan's answer (1953, pp. 152–154; 1954, pp. 217–239) was that the analyst works much like a sensitive musician; responsive to where the patient is on a gradient of anxiety, and trying to maintain it at an optimally minimal level—low enough so that the patient's defenses do not foreclose analytic inquiry, but high enough so that the defensive structure itself can be identified and explored.

In my experience, this description of keeping a finger on the pulse of the patient's level of self-esteem is accurate and valuable, but incomplete; it does not address the overall quality of the patient-analyst bond, which unlike that of other relationships of minimal anxiety, allows an extraordinary degree of growth to be possible. I have suggested (chapter 4) that the nature of this bond involves a controlled but consuming immersion by the patient in something positive, as much as it does a responsiveness to the absence of something negative. This aspect can be looked at, in my view, as a shared empathic matrix between patient and analyst which, as Settlage (1977) has described, reaffirms the patient's precognitive or preverbal sense of core identity, and leads to the feeling of being "understood" as a potential cognitive bridge to being able to understand the analyst even with regard to things he experiences as too threatening to "understand." It is an ego-regulated derivative of what Sullivan (1953, pp. 37–41) depicts as the first interpersonal affirmation of core identity in the life cycle—a synchronicity between the need-tension level in the infant and the mother's responsiveness to it.

In conjunction with an appropriate working level of anxiety, it is this empathic matrix which, in my opinion, allows an analysis to take place. Tolpin (1971) puts it as follows: "By re-creating the merger and the maternal functions on which it depends, the psyche establishes an auxiliary pathway for the acquisition of tension-reducing mental structure" (p. 347). The important issue to recognize with regard to the analytic situation is that it is not a return to symbiosis, but the re-creation in the analysis of the transitional mental structure through which communication with the analyst includes the patient's growing ability to become to himself what he experiences the analyst is to him. In a skillfully conducted analysis, the patient's "self" does not use this experience as a crutch, but, as Tolpin puts it, is enabled by its existence to "perform soothing operations for itself, but now without the need for an illusory external soother" (p. 329). It is only as part of the ability to internalize the soothing function that the patient is able to utilize the analysis in its fullest sense as Rangell (1979, p. 102) describes it: "a constant series of microidentifications . . . with the analyzing function of the analyst." In this light I have proposed in chapter 4 the possible advantage of viewing the interpersonal approach to analytic treatment as a process of inquiry mediated by responsiveness to the interplay between a gradient of anxiety and a gradient of empathy. In my view this conception has a distinct advantage over the concepts of a "therapeutic alliance" or a "working alliance" in that it encompasses the variability between different analyses and within each analysis for (a) the analytic relationship to be more or less "personal," (b) the level of empathic contact to be more or less "deep," (c) adapting to the "analyzability" of the patient, and (c) working with the fact that patients with more severe ego pathology require greater adaptational responsiveness from the therapist particularly in the earlier stages of analytic treatment.

It is my position, in other words, that regardless of who the patient is, ego growth and the ability to mature through mastering internal conflict and frustration, require an analytic setting which meets the ego's earlier and more basic need for affirmation. The need for such a setting is obviously greater in patients who begin with greater ego impairment. Ego pathology such as severe pathological narcissism does not, in this view, require a different form of treatment; it requires a greater sophistication and personal maturity on the part of the analyst in adapting to the patient's shifting need for affirmation in a way which enriches rather than contaminates the analytic field.

Affirmation, or mirroring, as ingredients in the analytic process, do not preclude interpretation as long as one accepts the idea that what needs to be interpreted can extend beyond the orthodox meaning of the term and need not focus only upon transference and resistance. When Winnicott (1971a, p. 141), for example, states that "psychoanalysis has been developed as a highly specialized form of playing in the service of communication with oneself and others," he is offering "playing" as a metaphor, not as a substitute for interpretation. It is a climate in which the timely and creative use of interpretation can flourish so as to maximize the patient's own creative use of the analytic experience.

There are those narcissistic patients for whom traditional interpretation at certain stages in their analysis cannot be distinguished by them from acts of negative attribution by parental figures. The act of interpretation is indistinguishable from an attempt by the "all-knowing" parent to disqualify their reality and leave them with nothing but whatever selfishness and failure is being attributed to their behavior at that moment. These are individuals for whom the content of an interpretation directed towards a resistance will be processed as a sign of the *analyst's* narcissism; an instance of nonresponsiveness to them, and a failure to appreciate or value them simply for who they are. The ability of these patients to work eventually in the transference is an inch-by-inch process, the final stage of which is the capacity to perceive a transference resistance as a transference resistance.

For certain of these patients more than others, analytic success depends upon being able to participate in an initial period of undefinable length, in which the analysis partially protects them from stark reality which they cannot integrate, while performing its broader function of mediating their transition to a more mature and differentiated level of self- and object representation (see Winnicott, 1951) capable of mediating and changing its own "reality." During this period, what Schecter (1980) calls "strangeness anxiety" stems more from the threat of failure to control the analyst and the analytic situation—failure of the grandiose self—than from having to deal with material which evokes specific areas of intrapsychic conflict. *"Resistance" during this transitional period is better understood as a global defense against precipitous undermining of the "old world" rather than as an effort to ward off new insight.*

It is a period in which the patient's fantasy is that there is no need for him to work; no need for him to obtain anything for himself, and that in spite of this the analyst has the power to make the analysis succeed. The proper balance between empathy and anxiety during this period is, as I see it, an analytic approach which begins subtly to challenge this fantasy without seriously threatening the patient's ability to use it to the degree he needs it transferentially. I do not share Modell's (1976) view that during this phase the patient's "cocoon" fantasy must remain unchallenged and that he will simply hatch out of it organically, nor do I agree with Kohut's (1971) similar position that narcissistic transference configurations will undergo a natural developmental evolution if the empathic "ambiance" is right. Both of these perspective, in my view, underemphasize the fact that the patient is an adult whose ego functions are underdeveloped within a human relationship, and that he is not simply an infant in disguise. Interpretive work of a certain kind can and must be attempted right from the beginning if "empathy" is to have any meaning beyond a quasi-artificial technical maneuver designed hopefully to recapitulate infancy and repair what was originally lacking.

With patients suffering from notable narcissistic pathology, the empathy-anxiety balance during the initial period of the analysis is optimally weighted on the side of empathy. Interpretations made during this phase are of two types which tend to overlap; neither is directed towards transference resistance or analytic resistance in general, but are not thereby valueless. Their therapeutic action is simply of a different order but to my way of thinking is every bit as "analytic" as interpretations aimed at promoting insight. At this stage, however, their analytic value has less to do with their accuracy than with the patient's feeling understood. The first form of interpretation is one which Horner (1979) refers to as "structuralizing interpretation"; that is, responding to the issue of the patient's valid need for the existing self and object structure, rather than responding to the content through which the need for that structure is being expressed at that moment. In the early phase of treatment this helps to introduce the patient to his character structure as a functional part of his personality and not simply as a piece of "illness" for which he is being blamed under the pretense of being "helped." For example, highlighting the use of detachment or self-containment as a means of avoiding the experience of inadequacy when he needs more than he can get, is a formulation that the patient can often accept and even begin to work with on a surface level without it threatening the narcissistic base of the transference itself. The general purpose of this form of interpretation is to accustom the patient to looking at himself from outside as part of an interpersonal process, but without any threat to the "mask" which he still needs in order to work at all. The second type of interpretation does address content and looks at the patient's behavior, but tries to avoid bringing the issues prematurely into the transference. Attempting to get the patient to report the minute details of specific external events and interactions, although often an ordeal for patient and analyst, is frequently a source of important movement during this phase of treatment. The goal at this stage is not to examine his transference resistance as manifested in trying to avoid the details, but to try and provide enough mirroring and understanding of his discomfort in pushing himself, that he is secure enough to take the risk. The more details he discloses, the more he becomes the agent of his own self-awareness. Through revealing details he would otherwise have omitted in order to maintain control over his self-image from behind his mask, aspects of his personality emerge which he can sometimes pick up on his own, and which can sometimes even be underscored by the analyst without the patient having to accept the analyst's reality before he is ready. Overall, the analytic approach during this early phase of treatment is one of helping a patient to accept a tolerable level of frustration through providing an especially high level of verbal and nonverbal responsiveness to his need to be accepted and understood on his own terms.[2] It is a stage of maximum empathy and minimum confrontation, but with sufficient anxiety to get most of the core issues out on the table.

As the patient's regressive experience deepens through the analyst's ability to protect the core fantasy of entitlement from precipitous empathic disruption in the transference, the yearnings that had been initially warded off by the illusion of self-sufficiency and idealization of the analyst gradually become more manifest in the treatment situation itself, and the balance between the gradients of empathy and anxiety begins to tilt in the opposite direction. This ushers in what might be considered the beginning of a new phase which is more confrontational but also more "real." The issue of what factors will most productively lead to this new phase is one which evokes serious differences of opinion among the various psychoanalytic schools of thought.

While for certain less seriously impaired individuals the relatively smooth evolution described by Kohut does seemingly occur, my own view is that for the larger group of narcissistic patients it is less a smooth transition than a genuinely new phase which is initiated by a certain amount of "pushing." The "pushing," which is confrontational in form, is not only needed but is developmentally facilitating in itself. It enables these patients to inch themselves out of their core fantasy of entitlement by mobilizing their newborn observing ego and focusing it not simply upon their external life, but upon the narcissistic transference itself. It is at this point that the patient's integration of mirroring is allowed to work in its own behalf. Its therapeutic value is no longer simply an aid to the acquisition of new mental structure, but is now aiding the patient's ability to use this new structure in the dissolution of the mask. It is here where I agree with Rothstein (1982, p. 177) that "it is not the ability to establish stable narcissistic transference configurations that renders a subject analyzable. Rather it is the analysand's

---

2. Lawrence Friedman (personal communication) has wryly referred to the process as "smuggling interpretations across narcissistic lines."

ability to work these through." The onset of this shift, in my experience, doesn't depend simply on how long the analyst can personally tolerate the patient's unrelatedness and self-centeredness. As the patient's narcissistic demands become more manifest in the treatment situation, the analyst will become more confronting because not only is there more to confront, but also because a bridge to this new level of "reality" (see chapter 4) has been laid by having addressed these same issues nontransferentially that now begin to be experienced and identified in the here-and-now of the patient-analyst relationship. Little by little this permits a gradual and systematic interpretation of the underlying feelings of entitlement, and the emergence of genuine affect and a new sense of personal authenticity. The rage, emptiness, and despair that have been warded off by the grandiose self now start to be felt and mastered.

This phase marks what some schools of thought would call the *genuine* analytic work. Most prominent, especially at its onset, is intense rage in the transference. With some patients there is also concurrent movement into and out of the thin area between transference neurosis and transference psychosis, often accompanied by periods of acting-out. On the surface it may seem that at this juncture we are simply back at the pool with Echo and Narcissus. Why should one hope for an analytic outcome rather than a transference psychosis or termination? The patient is being confronted and is enraged. What makes it therapeutic simply because it is being done by an analyst? The answer, in my view, is that the analyst, unlike Echo, is not out for his own self-interest, and that at this point the patient knows it at least dimly. Because of the initial phase, the patient has a beginning capacity to feel another person as a separate entity and has already started to look at himself in an interpersonal context with some objectivity. They have a history together which Echo and Narcissus did not have, and if the confrontations and interpretations are being introduced gradually and empathically, the rage itself should support the individuation process, the analysis of the underlying fantasy of entitlement, and the dissolution of the mask. The rage, and often the envy, that have been attendant upon the denied yearnings, become gradually integrated as normal assertiveness and self-regard[3] as a growing sense of separateness, a therapeutic collaboration, and a communicable and analyzable transference experience begin to develop. There is more and more a sense of two people being present as the patient gradually begins to accept and even enjoy the fact that he has a responsibility for the ana-

---

3. See Winnicott (1950, pp. 204–218; 1971, pp. 86–94) and Kohut (1972, pp. 378–397) for a fuller theoretical elaboration of this issue.

lytic work. There is less fear of losing the mask and consequently less dread of working in the transference. Interpretation and the active taking in of ideas from a perspective other than one's own becomes less a source of "strangeness anxiety." It becomes more a part of the patient's total affective thrill in his own growth rather than an impinging threat to be warded off.

This approach is independent of the analyst's personal metapsychology. It does not demand that the analyst hold the view that there are separate categories of patients: the transferences neuroses, for whom unmodified psychoanalysis resolves intrapsychic conflict, and those patients with preoedipal ego impairment (narcissistic, borderline, schizoid, and character disorders) for whom modified psychoanalysis repairs damaged structure. It can accommodate, for example, Kernberg's (1975) view of narcissistic transferences as defenses against an almost inborn infantile rage, as well as Kohut's (1971, 1972, 1977) position that they are interferences or fixation points in a normal developmental process. The value of this approach is that it is exactly that . . . an approach. It does not predetermine technique. It does not require the analyst to feel he is being nonanalytic if he allows a transference configuration to remain uninterpreted during a particular phase of treatment for a particular patient, nor does it require that he should allow it to do so, simply because his own analytic metatheory demands it. What it does demand is that the analyst have an ego-development rationale from which he works, within which he can flexibly conceptualize the various stages of growth during the analytic process, including psychosexual growth, if this is a metaphor he uses.

I am suggesting that many difficult narcissistic patients might be analyzable if the treatment begins with a stage of analysis managed without the imposition of a classical interpretive stance or the belief that it is only this stance which truly defines psychoanalysis. Such patients may then gradually become more accessible and available to hearing what they do not want to hear without the narcissistic wound having to be prevented at all costs. I do not, however, believe that all individuals suffering from pathological narcissism are analyzable. In my experience there are patients who would be deemed unanalyzable regardless of approach, and others whose particular impairment in ego development will limit how far they may be able to go in analysis. Early psychopathology is a major factor as is the potential for psychotic transference, but I prefer to use these data in determining the approach to the analytic work rather than as a diagnostic criterion of analyzability.

As to the question of how effective psychoanalysis can be at its best, in treating narcissistic disorders, I don't think we really know. I believe there is little question that we are in part fighting against cultural forces as well as intrapsychic ones, although I do not feel that culture creates pathological narcissism. I tend to agree with Kernberg (1975) that it is pretty much a developmental outcome related to parenting, but I suspect that its increased incidence culturally (Marin, 1975; Lasch, 1979) and part of the difficulty in treating it in therapy, are influenced by our socioeconomic milieu in the following way.

Talking about psychopathology is just one metaphor among other possible metaphors to describe the same phenomenon. What we call pathological narcissism someone else might not feel is an illness at all, but rather that the person just needs to "grow up." In one way, of course, it is quite true. "Narcissistic psychopathology" is a way of saying that an individual is stuck at a particular level of emotional and interpersonal development, and manages to maintain his self-esteem only at the expense of further growth. Growth can come about only under conditions that will allow a person to experience himself in some way that is different. It requires an environment which tends to facilitate the acceptance and integration of unpleasant but accurate experience of oneself that would otherwise be discarded because it is too discordant with one's interpersonal self-representation. Psychoanalysis is an attempt to create a controlled environment which will accomplish this systematically. It is clearly not the only way that people who have been stuck at early levels of development can grow. Religion, an important friendship at a crucial moment, in fact any important relationship if it is the right one at the right time, can often get the process moving again. Narcissistic personalities are no different from any other personality organization in this regard. A positive change in the natural environment at critical times can create influences that will foster concern, tenderness, relatedness, and appreciation. But in a social climate where the opposite characteristics tend to be almost institutionalized politically and economically, the grandiose self has a natural ally to support its already powerful claim to sovereignty. Thus, a relationship, including an analytic one, which might in a different cultural atmosphere help a person with severe narcissistic pathology see himself objectively, will tend to have less impact if in the larger scheme of things he can secretly say to himself: "We are all out for ourselves anyway." In spite of this, however, I believe that the new psychoanalytic emphasis on the whole person in an interpersonal context, is a vitalizing force which can only make psychoanalysis more open to its own continuing development, and its potential for treating serious character pathology increasingly broader.

8

ON THE OCCURRENCE OF THE ISAKOWER PHENOMENON IN A SCHIZOID PATIENT[1] (1984)

In a now classic paper, Isakower (1938) described a relatively rare but intriguing complex of sensory phenomena recalled and reported by certain of his patients as occurring in the twilight state of consciousness just prior to their entering sleep. These phenomena, taken together, appeared so closely to recapitulate precognitive elements of nursing at the breast that they were considered by Isakower, and thereafter, as parts of a single experience. The predominant theme in the subsequent psychoanalytic literature on the subject has been an effort to establish more precisely the psychodynamic nature and etiology of this hypnogogic event by examining the personality structure of those patients who, during the course of an analysis, either report it as a childhood memory or reexperience the event itself.

The Isakower phenomenon, as it is referred to, is characteristically remembered or reexperienced by the individual as the visual sensation

---

1. An early version of this chapter was presented to the William Alanson White Psychoanalytic Society as the Presidential Address, May 1984. It was published in *Contemporary Psychoanalysis*, 1984, 20:600–624, and then revised (in the form presented here) as a chapter in *Relational Perspectives in Psychoanalysis*, edited by N. J. Skolnick and S. C. Warshaw (Hillsdale, NJ: The Analytic Press, 1992, pp. 257–279).

of a large, doughy, shadowy mass, usually round. As it comes nearer and nearer to his face, it grows larger, swelling to a gigantic size and threatening to crush him; it then gradually becomes smaller and moves farther away. Often there is an indistinct perception of a purplish shape like the nipple area of the breast. The approaching mass slowly seems to become a part of the person, obscuring the boundaries between his body and the outside world and blurring more and more his sense of self. All this is typically accompanied by sensations of tactile roughness on the skin and inside the mouth, and a milky or salty taste in the back of the throat. Often there are feelings of floating or loss of equilibrium. In some people there is, interestingly, a memory of voluntarily producing the experience or prolonging it.

Lewin (1946, 1948, 1953) and Rycroft (1951) believe there are several modified manifestations of this event and that the Isakower phenomenon, the "dream screen," and "blank dreams" are essentially equivalent experiences; whereas Stern (1961) holds the view that all these should be considered variations of a more inclusive category of perceptual disturbances, which he calls "blank hallucinations."

Case histories and reviews of the literature have described the phenomenon from a variety of clinical and theoretical perspectives—oral hunger, oral frustration, a defense against unmet oral needs, a defense against primal scene memories, a character manifestation of passive aims, an early representation of the mother's face rather than the breast (Garma, 1955; Sperling, 1957, 1961; Stern, 1961; Dickes, 1965; Fink, 1967; Easson, 1973; Blaustein, 1975). It has also been reported as occurring in people whose development seemed to be normal (Heilbrunn, 1953); it does not, then, appear to be in itself a pathological phenomenon.

Each of the interpretations of the phenomenon, informative within its own metaphor, reduces its context to a circumscribed developmental crisis or trauma, a defense against such trauma, or an expression of a particular level of psychosexual conflict or interaction between levels. From a review of reports of the phenomenon, however, what appears quite conspicuous is that although it has a clear core of consistency across individuals (which is the aspect that different authors have been attempting to explain), it also has a large idiosyncratic component that tends to be discarded as random "noise" in the system. Some people, for example, report it as a benign, even pleasant experience. Some describe it as terrifying. Some report instances of both. Certain experience it passively, while others make a determined effort to control it.

I am going to discuss these issues in the context of my work with an anxiety-ridden, schizoid man, whose seven-year analysis began with a recollection of the Isakower phenomenon as a memory from early childhood and was marked at about its midpoint by the direct occurrence of this event during the course of a session. It is my view that, at least in his case, the appearance of the Isakower phenomenon did indeed relate to oral conflict, to passive aims, to a defense against primal scene experience, and to a characterological vulnerability to traumatic anxiety—but not to any one of these as the defining concept for best understanding it. All those perspectives are framed by something more comprehensive. I believe the appearance of this event signaled the reemergence of an early, unsuccessful struggle to deal creatively and adaptively with potentially catastrophic interpersonal experience prior to the development of an impenetrable character structure (see chapter 13) that shielded him from the complexity of human relatedness. I hope to demonstrate that, for this man, the significance of the Isakower phenomenon can best be understood by looking at it not simply as a libidinally derived symptom, but as a map of his capacity for human relatedness, reflecting, as did his dreams, daydreams, and schizoid life style, his unique patterning of interpersonal mental representation at a given point in time.

The schizoid character structure is a tightly regulated balance between relatedness and detachment. As a personality disorder it embodies a mode of living that I have described elsewhere (Bromberg, 1979) as a "psychopathology of stability," allowing the person to manipulate fantasy in the service of securing a sense of control over his inner world, his place of primary residence. Guntrip (1969) views this cramping of the self into itself as enabling the person to live his life by establishing what he calls "the schizoid compromise" in the struggle to maintain an ego:

> The schizoid person, because of his fears, cannot give *himself* fully or permanently to anyone or anything with feeling. . . . This makes life extremely difficult, so we find that a *marked schizoid tendency is to effect a compromise in a half-way-house position, neither in nor out.* . . . Yet in this compromise position people live far below their real potentialities and life seems dull and unsatisfying [pp. 59–62].

The issue of a "schizoid compromise" is particularly relevant to how one manages the treatment process with such a patient because it really goes beyond what would typically be called a character resistance. It becomes the fundamental quality of the working alliance itself. At one level it can be seen as a chronically blocked analysis or therapeutic stalemate. At another level it expresses the schizoid patient's sense of stability and security and is thus the only pathway to growth. The analysis itself, in other words, often serves the purpose of an ideal schizoid compromise—a way of retaining the security of a relationship that does not involve a full emotional response even while this very issue may be the subject of verbal exploration in the content of the sessions (see chapter 5). For both the analysis and the patient to emerge ultimately as alive and real, the analyst must work toward engaging the immediate moment as content and process simultaneously, while taking into account that this can happen only if the overall ambiance of the treatment generates sufficient anxiety to allow the patient an increasing sense of mastery in regulating it, but not so much anxiety that it evokes a sustained reliance on character detachment as the primary mode of defense. In this regard, how one conceptualizes the interrelationship between earlier and later phases of ego development is particularly significant for schizoid patients in whose history traumatic anxiety appears to have been a central issue.

Let us say that somewhere in the domain of prelogical experience in infancy—before the development of language and higher order symbolic processes—serious psychic trauma occurred consistently. The memory traces laid down by the prevailing sensorimotor organization of experience will tend to remain symbolized in precognitive form as body sensations and as global apprehensions that become phobically linked to aspects of the real world. Regardless of one's theory of personality development, I think it can be postulated that this state of affairs will influence and reverberate with subsequent developmental phases and will contribute to the shaping of adult character. I believe it is also reasonable to hypothesize that it will become a particularly difficult problem when interpersonal experiences with significant figures during later stages of development do not lead to identifications which facilitate the structuring of a sense of self that is cohesive and active enough to "heal" the earlier precognitive wound. In such cases, derivatives of the early trauma would tend to be avoided at all costs, and the individual will learn to structure his life so as to minimize the possibility of such encounters. The shame and anxiety surrounding this course of behavior will gradually lead to the motivation behind his life style becoming unconscious and will further reduce the likelihood of his engaging in interpersonal experience that might successfully promote maturation and an ability to feel fully in the world with a sense of mastery. Often the best that is achieved is an increasing withdrawal into his inner world and a futile, counterphobic struggle to behave "as-if" he felt autonomous, but that masks a perpetual longing for the moment when he is released from the demands of living and is permitted to be at peace.

For the most part, the person has no way of dealing with the entirety of this situation in a human relationship that could potentially lead to a synthesis of his ego functioning with interpersonal security. Despite his forays into the real world, he always feels alone inside himself. The external world—ordinary day-to-day life and its routine pressures—remains represented as a potential preverbal horror that continues to haunt him in dreams, physical derivatives, and sometimes hypnogogic states, appearing in its most threatening form in those contexts where there is the least verbal and cognitive structuring.

The phenomenological experience for the person is, in daily life, that of being endangered by something that cannot be handled, and may cover a broad range of derivatives. "A party I give may be dull, and I will feel humiliated; I may not know the answers on a test; I may step on someone's feet if I have to go the bathroom while in a theater, so I'd better make sure to sit on the aisle; I may have nightmares if I go to sleep; I may not be able to perform sexually if someone is willing to go to bed with me; I may go into a panic on the subway and might not be able to get out."

It seems to me that to comprehend most fully a person in such a state and to work most usefully with him in a psychoanalytic setting, no single theoretical perspective should be applied as an attempt to encompass all levels of meaning. There are issues of self-esteem to be considered, precisely in the way that Sullivan (1953) viewed the interpersonal nature of anxiety; but with patients such as the man I discuss here (who will be referred to as Mr. C), raw feelings are frequently felt as sources of anxiety in the way Freud conceived of it, because their potential expression is not under the command of the cognitive patterning of the self-representation. In such people, the feelings are global, undifferentiated, and "not-me." They thus remain as alien forces and potential sources of anxiety in their own right.

The Case of Mr. C

For Mr. C, any internal or external experience with the potential to lead to a situation that could not be regulated in a predictably secure manner was felt as a threat not only to his self-esteem but to the stability of his core identity. Something as innocuous as the ticking of a clock, the sound of his own heartbeat, or the falling of raindrops upon him when he did not have an umbrella would produce enough anxiety to resomatize the precognitive channels and snowball into either a panic or a state of mild depersonalization.

The force acting against the threat that these states might unexpectedly occur was the security of feeling able to prevent them or escape from them. Thus, passivity was his hallmark. In reality, it was a caricature of passivity that served as an active and ever-present screening device against the imperatives of both the external world and his inner life—work demands, sexual demands, sleep demands, intense affect, and so on. His life-style was "passive" interpersonally because initiative and assertiveness failed to develop as a dimension of his self-representation linked to his functioning in the real world. Initiative and assertiveness are also *unlikely* to have developed because he then would have had to commit himself wholeheartedly to a person, duty, responsibility, or goal from which he was then not free to escape without reproach. Inasmuch as full emotional involvement meant turning some control over to the outside, it evoked, in a variety of forms, feelings of potential helplessness, enslavement, and burial by the crushing force of a sadistically perceived other.

Thus, character detachment became a primary means of avoiding panic states and acute anxiety symptoms associated with his felt inability to regulate self-esteem in everyday life. He clung to a self-generated reality of weakness and ineptness that no encounter with the external world could disprove. Passive behavior became a security operation designed to maintain the "schizoid compromise." That is, it became a means of avoiding the state of normal ego passivity that involves a certain degree of regression through which partial ego control can be trustingly surrendered to both the outside world and to one's own feelings, and in which mutuality, love, a sense of being fully alive, and the ability to enjoy peaceful sleep can all find their place.

If a feeling of one's own humanness in a human world has not fully developed, then any situation in which regression occurs or is anticipated is potentially fraught with anxiety. In the regressed state of Stage IV sleep, for example, Mr. C was particularly vulnerable. He had a childhood history of enuresis, sleepwalking, and pavor nocturnus—those cataclysmic eruptions of somatized anxiety into terrifying dreams which continue to be felt as real even after one is fully awake and which the mind and body cannot shake off for a long while.[2] In the process of falling asleep, when control is normally surrendered gradually, there was an elaborate presleep ritual as well as the partially structured event of the Isakower phenomenon that allowed some

---

2. The studies of Fisher et al. (1970, 1974) and Broughton (1968) present an informative and conceptually thoughtful treatment of the psychoanalytic and psychophysiological aspects of Stage IV sleep phenomena and their associated pathologies.

degree of ego participation. In waking situations, where surrender of control was voluntary but was felt as unavoidable—such as being a passenger in a car—the anticipation of the event would elicit heart palpitations that could themselves threaten to generate into a full-blown panic state.

Mr. C, a verbally gifted, unmarried man of middle-class, Protestant background, entered treatment in his late 30s. He was unusually tall and, despite an insatiable appetite, was slender to the point of looking undernourished. Thick hornrimmed eyeglasses he had worn since childhood partly masked the tenseness in his face while giving the impression of his peering down at you through binoculars. He worked as a free-lance speechwriter at the local political level. As is often true of extremely bright people with severe character pathology, he was in many ways quite astute at looking at himself while feeling hopeless that his insights would ever lead to change. He was well aware, for example, that his choice of career was somehow tied to his difficulty in finding a voice of his own and that speaking through another person was a comfortable compromise.

He had been claustrophobic and an insomniac and for most of his life had suffered from various manifestations of anxiety ranging from somatic symptoms to panic attacks. His relationships felt unreal and always stressful; he had a constant expectation that they would end at any moment. He felt very little hope of any of this changing. The one positive relationship that felt genuine and stable was with his only sibling, a married sister six years younger than he. He entered analysis to try to cure the problem that was for him the most immediately real and inescapable: sexual impotency with a woman he had begun to care for. Treatment was established on the basis of three sessions a week with Mr. C on the couch, a combination of conditions that was for him as initially frightening and then rendered as unreal as the rest of his life.

As an infant, hungry or not, he had been breast-fed on a rigid schedule for the first six months of his life. Between ages one and two he was unable to sleep through the night and cried inconsolably. His parents disagreed on how to respond to this behavior, and a pattern emerged in which he was allowed to cry to the point of hysteria, at which juncture, depending on which parent prevailed, either his mother would take him from the crib and carry him around, or his father would come to the side of the crib and shout. If neither procedure stopped his crying, they would take him into their own bed where he would eventually fall asleep between them. He slept in his parents' bedroom until age six, a situation structured around the same power struggle between the parents as to whether he should be forced to grow up and sleep alone in another room or should be allowed to feel "comfortable" and be permitted to sleep in their room until he grew up.

This pattern of relating to him was consistent throughout his history with his parents and was replayed in different forms and in different situations at different times in his life. His parents fought constantly over how to rear him and showed little more respect for one another's identity than they showed for his. Unable to relate to peers in any way other than as either a pampered child or a bullied victim, he became a loner, hiding his envy and isolation behind a mask of congeniality, false humility, and verbal manipulation of reality. The one aspect of his life that was mutually respectful and mutually supportive was his closeness to his sister, the person whose birth demanded that he finally leave the parental bedroom.

The broad objective during the early part of Mr. C's analysis was the development of more fully individuated self- and object representations and their integration into those areas of his ego functioning that were either mechanical and dehumanized or were filled with dread. The goal was to enable him gradually to surrender his attachment to his inner world as the embodiment of reality and to engage the external human environment in new ways experienced as genuine, if not always pleasant. *His ability to relate to me was limited mainly to my role as a potential bridge between one of his various disconnected experiences of himself and another,* and depended on my own ability to have a direct impact that would increase over time. In the back of my mind was always the question of whether I was making my presence felt in a way that increased his ability to sustain the representation of a reliable external figure who was not simply supportive, or whether the analytic situation remained at its core just another schizoid compromise— an ongoing test of his facility in writing verbal cadenzas to his analyst's compositions. For the most part, although my feelings about my impact were mixed, I did not have a sustained conviction that anything palpably changed between us during the first three years. My deepest experience was that the impact of my presence was an illusion I had created to keep from feeling hopelessly helpless, but it was only by my ability to accept this experience and communicate it that any genuine impact was possible at all.[3] It was primarily through my own helplessness that I was able to convey my experience in the context of

---

3. Feiner (1979) has creatively developed this same point from a theoretical base that places the *countertransferential* issue into clinical and historical perspective.

his own feelings of helplessness and convey my own sense of "false-ness" as part of the overall "falseness" that framed the ongoing inter-action. For brief periods of time he was able to respond in a way that seemed to be more immediate, credible, and involved, but I was sel-dom sure how my words were being processed in the deeper domain of trauma and trust.

The "Isakower Session"

We were just starting our fourth year of work when something quite unexpected occurred. While on the analytic couch, Mr. C directly expe-rienced the Isakower phenomenon, which he had reported early in treatment as a childhood memory from ages three to six and which had not been mentioned since. It occurred at about the halfway point of the second of his three weekly sessions, following a rambling, unin-volved discourse on the previous day's events; he then fell silent. He had of late been indulging in long periods of silence with even greater determination than usual, as a transferential affirmation of his right to retain his use of detachment as an ego-syntonic character trait and in secret defiance of my efforts to make him aware of it on his own. I had not perceived that anything out of the ordinary was going on during the silence because it appeared to be simply another of his routine phases of somnolent reverie. In reality, his mental state had changed while he was lying silently, and he had let himself drift into the twi-light state of consciousness that precedes sleep. It was at this point that he experienced the Isakower phenomenon and continued to remain silently in this hypnogogic state, eyes almost completely closed as he actively engaged it. After what he later estimated to be two or three minutes of this experience, he brought himself out of it and reported it. His description of the sensory aspects was, except for one addition, identical to his early memory, but his affective experience was totally different.[4] It was not frightening nor did it feel like something com-pletely outside of his self-experience. He was not helplessly at its mercy, as he had remembered it from his past. He described the reexperience

---

4. His childhood memory reported during the initial interview had been of lying in bed and seeing a large, "soft" grey shape (sometimes round and sometimes amorphous) with a blurry protuberance in the center, slowly descending upon him while he tried to hold it away; he recalled also grow-ing more and more panic stricken until he opened his eyes and sat up, usu-ally in a state of dizziness.

as pleasurable: pushing the mass away, letting it approach, pushing it away again, and continuing this push and pull as though playfully wrestling a ghost from his past—a ghost he no longer experienced as an enemy, but not yet as a friend.

His early memory of the event had been of visual and kinesthetic phenomena only, with no mention of any sensation referring to the skin, mouth, or sense of taste. In the reexperience, the one addition he reported was of a rough and tingling feeling on the left side of his face, a sensation he had no recollection of from childhood. (No tactile sensations in the mouth or unusual tastes were mentioned.) That the description of this addition was volunteered (not elicited by questioning) made highly unlikely any possibility that Mr. C was either consciously or unconsciously "putting on a performance" for me by creating an event, the details of which he already knew would interest me. His earlier description of the event, which he reported as a childhood memory during the initial interview, had evoked no special interest on my part and very little on his, other than his listing it along with his many other symptoms and jokingly referring to it as "a big tit that came to me in the night." I had never questioned him regarding the unreported aspects associated with the phenomenon, so until the session in which it was reexperienced he had no reason to view it as anything other than idiosyncratic and possessing no greater significance than any of his other dramatic symptoms. In other words, the addition of the skin sensation during the reexperience was a manifestation that was, to the best of his recollection, completely new and a total surprise. It was, however, immediately associated by him with the fact that he could fall asleep only if he was lying on his left side with his own arm cradling the left side of his face.

The event can be conceptualized theoretically from a number of vantage points, but the overriding quality, as Mr. C described it, was that of a very young child using a newly discovered physical capability and seeing how far he could safely and creatively go with it. In one sense, it was reminiscent of Silberer's (1909) experiments in producing and observing hypnogogic hallucinations in himself as an act of scientific discovery. Winnicott's (1971a) notion of "playing" as a bridge between fantasy and reality and Mahler's (1968) description of the "practicing" subphase of the separation-individuation process capture further aspects of it in overlapping but different ways. In the context of Mr. C's specific life experience, it could be conjectured that he was at that moment, with a feeling of relative security, allowing himself to regress to an interpersonal position he had attempted to master as a young child but lacked sufficient ego strength to utilize in the service of his own growth. In the act of "playing" with the Isakower phenomenon during his session, he let himself reencounter a direct facsimile of an early interpersonally traumatic situation and play with it hypnogogically while "playing" with the previously frightening analytic situation itself in a simultaneously identical manner. In other words, what frames this event conceptually is not simply its intrapsychic locale, but that it took place in the context of a relationship that felt secure enough at that point to enable him both to let the event occur and to use himself that way in my presence—to "play" with it and with me at the same time.

He later stated that as part of his background experience he had been aware that he had to make a choice between reporting it and letting it happen and that he chose to keep it going until he had had enough. He further stated that unlike previous sessions, in which he was afraid I might become angry if he fell asleep, he was not focused on what my response might be and just "let himself go."[5] Interestingly, the event was in this regard more important to me than it was to him. He was actually a bit amused by my excitement, in part because I had never witnessed it before whereas he had, but mainly, I think, because he was starting to become interested in something other than his own ability to be an object of adulation. I am referring to something more fundamental emerging in him, of which this experience was a symbolic, albeit dramatic, expression: his growing sense of feeling real in the real world and the existence of a state of mind in which he could acknowledge my presence without loss of his own. It was as if at this moment his precognitive and cognitive domains of experience were being given one more chance to synthesize under the umbrella of a newly emerging sense of self that he knew about but that I felt as only illusory.

Twilight Consciousness and "Coming Awake"

In the next session, this "half-dead" man with his history of lively symptoms revealed that when watching television he always turned

---

5. Tauber and Green (1959), expanding on Silberer's (1909) position that hypnogogic phenomena occur at the point of tension between drowsiness (a passive condition) and the effort to think (an active condition manipulated by the will), state: "It is thus a struggle between these two antagonistic conditions that elicits what Silberer calls the autosymbolic phenomenon. . . . It is essential, he asserts, that neither of these two conditions outweigh the other. . . . The prevailing of the first condition would lead to sleep, the prevailing of the second to ordered normal thinking" (p. 42).

away when people kissed and would simultaneously remove his eyeglasses. He had, however, become aware the night following the "Isakower session" that he was not performing those two acts at a moment when they would usually have been automatic, and he reported that this awareness felt somehow important to him. Not a very dramatic piece of material for someone whose calling card was inscribed with chronic insomnia, depression, night terrors, and claustrophobia, and who just the previous session had captured my intense interest with a dramatic hypnogogic phenomenon. Unlike in the preceding phase of his analysis, his self-experience in response to the "Isakower session" was organized not simply in terms of what he had exhibited or "shown"—his ability to exist through making an impression—but also in terms of what he "gave"—his having determined on his own when and how he relinquished total control over the experience and "gave" it to me through the reporting of it.[6] In other words, it was an event (his television-watching behavior) that had significance in its own right and engendered curiosity in himself from a vantage point other than having given an interesting performance.

His associations to this change in his television-watching behavior, and the analytic work that followed, centered on his recalling and working through vivid primal scene material that had appeared in derivative form throughout his treatment in dreams and symptoms, but that had been hollow and intellectualized or overly dramatized by him whenever it was addressed by me. This aspect of his early life and the issue of its impact on his personality development was now alive and real to him and interlocked with the parallel appearance in his character of a greater degree of forthrightness in his manner of relating both to me and to people in his outside life. This new "directness" included the disappearance of the sexual impotency problem that had originally brought him to treatment. His ability to recall the act of turning his eyes away from the television while removing his eyeglasses, and to engage this issue actively on his own while in my presence, had a greater impact on him than his ability to impress me with the Isakower phenomenon.

It is important to note, however, that the sexual issue itself had significance only in the context of his level of psychological individuation

6. I refer here to Fairbairn's (1940, pp. 19–20) view that the inner uncertainty of self-experience in schizoid persons leads to an interpersonal stance in which "showing" rather than "giving" is the dominant mode of relatedness, because giving feels too much like self-emptying. In Mr. C's dream that concludes this paper, this issue will surface once more as a self-image in the process of accommodating a wish to prepare a satisfying meal for his friends while poignantly mourning his diminishing exhibitionistic power.

and interpersonal relatedness. Although Mr. C's sexual conflict was profound, for the largest part of his treatment it was only tangential as a point of leverage in my making contact with him. Until this pivotal point in his development, it was in my ability to understand the act of turning away—not what he turned away from—that the therapeutic action of psychoanalysis existed. Only now did his impulse life, erotic and otherwise—as well as his fear of its traumatic potential—become real enough as part of his self to be genuine analytic material. He had indeed been "tuning out" to kissing on television for many years. But he also tuned out to nonsexual aspects of real life; for example, when in conversations with friends the topic turned from politics to something "real" like how to invest one's money, or interesting restaurants to try, he would stare vacantly into space. The common denominator was not the content of what he was trying to hide from, but the act of hiding itself. It was this investment in ego detachment that shaped his personality structure and the variety of archaic mental states that were a lifelong part of it. *The process of chronically and automatically "turning away" from full emotional involvement with the external world in order to preempt the triggering of potentially overwhelming affect, led to a pathology of both his internal world and his perception of real life.* The act of averting his eyes and removing his glasses had been until now simply one of many expressions of his failure to integrate the two worlds. In this sense it paralleled his wish to stay asleep in the relative security of his fantasy life and to avoid being pulled too sharply awake by some aspect of reality perceived as a harsh voice demanding that he face an interpersonal setting that he felt as totally alien, and once again play-act participation while concealing his ever present hopelessness and dread.

The session of the Isakower phenomenon was special to me because it was such an unusual mental state to witness for the first time. From a broader vantage point, the session was special because his behavior during his twilight state of consciousness was structured by the manner in which he was interacting with me as it was going on. By his own self-authorization, he had actively pushed me away until he had "had enough" on his own terms and reported this act of self-assertion without deference or anxiety. This was the significance to *him* and from that perspective might be viewed as both a verbal and a preverbal beginning of a working-through process. In this context his behavior during the "Isakower session" could be seen as a creative act, much as proposed by Tauber and Green's (1959, p. 42) suggestion that hypnogogic phenomena demonstrate the creative function of imagery.

But how did it happen? What combination of factors permitted him to have this experience during a session at this particular instant in time, to grasp the moment and take it as his own, and to then use the experience as a transition point in his growth? Although I can say little that might qualify as an answer to these questions, two issues are relevant as speculations. For one thing, it had already become increasingly difficult for him to use his inner world as a secure hiding place. Our ongoing struggle over his detachment during sessions was becoming an internalized experience from which he could not escape but had not yet fully addressed with me. My approach of underlining his moments of greatest detachment had already begun to accomplish its aim, leaving him no longer able to retreat into a reverie state and remain peacefully unconflicted with regard to his silence.[7] At this point he had already begun to process his own silences as violations of his stated agreement to try to disclose all his experience as it occurred, regardless of its nature, and he could not free himself from the *internal* imperative of this task by using my silence as tacit permission to avoid experiencing his own. In other words, because he was now unable to dissociate; that is, to detach from my presence emotionally when he needed to avoid anxiety, he was "awake" to my existence as a real person within his inner world and thereby awake to his own experience of feeling violated and diminished—an inner drama in which one of us had to submit to the will of the other.

This scenario of forced submission followed by self-righteous indignation had recently been a powerful theme through which our relationship was represented in his unconscious fantasy life but until now had been played out only in dissociated form (through his dreams). More recently, however, it had emerged directly in the transferential relationship itself as a consequence of the diminishing effectiveness of his detached state as a means of avoiding the here-and-now. He had stated his own view of the matter a short time earlier as follows: "I resent the fact that you can just sit there knowing that I can't stay silent, and that I now have to think about the fact that I'm not saying anything. Anything I can think of to say is so trivial it's embarrassing, but it's now also embarrassing not to say anything. I even resent saying *this*." In this light, the Isakower session might justifiably be seen as a continued working-through of the same issue, but at a level that reactivated and integrated some of the earliest and most deeply buried aspects of its mental representation.

---

7. The approach to which I refer here is taken up at length in chapter 5 where I discuss the relation between schizoid processes and the value of Freud's basic rule of free association as the patient's "absorbing errand." The "basic rule," seen in this light, is really a dyadic process that requires a patient gradually but increasingly to engage the immediate transferential context as a voluntary act, rather than being "pulled" into it as a continued schizoid compromise maintained by a pseudoexploration of content.

Why, then, did it play itself out in a manner that freed him to exist as a person in his own right, instead of taking the form of an act of rebelliousness or subtle exhibitionism? Looking back on that session, I suspect that a gradual shift in the transference had already occurred of which I was unaware at the time and that this shift enabled him to trust both me and my genuine regard for his autonomy despite my "tough" analytic stance. The relationship providing the wellspring for this transition that comes most readily to mind is the one with his younger sister and even raises the possibility that something as seemingly minor as my own "innocence" during the Isakower session might have played a major role in shaping its meaning for him as a turning point. On that occasion I was the wide-eyed, naive child, and he the sophisticated expert, helpful and playfully amused by my genuine amazement. It was one night later that he noticed he was no longer behaving like the innocent child, averting his eyes from the television screen. If this element of my "innocence" was indeed significant, perhaps it reaffirms not only the importance of maintaining a consistent attitude of curiosity, but also that the most genuine definition of analytic technique may be what I have called "hindsight in the service of the ego."

Dreams, Daydreams, and Reality

During the remainder of Mr. C's analysis, much of what had been worked on in the earlier phase of treatment surfaced again in a richer, more integrated context and as an active, analyzable aspect of the transference. He was a prolific dreamer and had flooded the analysis with dreams for a long time. The self-protective function of the deluge-like quality in his dreaming had been much explored, as had the expressive function, but the work in this area typically felt as unalive and as unconvincing as the man himself. The dreams, in contrast, were alive to the point of bursting, filled with shimmering meaning and begging to be analyzed. Early in treatment they seemed to be the only channel Mr. C could use to structure his unformulated experience of our relationship in an ongoing way. What we did with each other as we dealt with his dreams in one session became the latent content of his dream life in the next session, with never a direct or overt sign that he consciously registered an interaction going on between us other than in his dutiful responses when I would probe for one. During this period of work, the dreams seemed more a source of raw material through which reality was to be constructed than a channel through which it was revealed.

His earliest dreams in treatment were traumatic, chaotic, archaic, and often bizarre, filled with images of his severely damaged sense of self and his terrifying vulnerability to the world as embodied in the strange situation called psychoanalysis. There were dreams of gouged-out eyeballs speeding past his field of vision, calves whose throats had been cut out by the milkmaid but who were unaware of what had happened to them, and radio programs that suddenly became real, leaving him nowhere to hide. Night terrors were not infrequent—all too real dreams of being devoured by cats, which had been peaceful house pets on a beautiful tropical island but without warning became creatures out of hell. In one ghastly metaphor after another, the voice of the dreamer screamed in terror as it received sadistic, talionic self-punishment for attempting to reveal the existence of dissociated reality in Mr. C's past and personality. It was as if the dreamer were signaling: "To preserve my sanity and emotional survival, the dangerous organs of seeing, knowing, and speaking shall be once again torn away." In fact, that is precisely what began to take place.

As this phase of treatment progressed, Mr. C's schizoid defenses against his dissociated sadistic rage became more pronounced. It was then that the analysis began to take the form of what Guntrip (1969) has described as a "schizoid compromise." The nature of his character structure, not the uncontrollable and traumatically sadistic quality of his reality, became the core of his dream imagery. Dreams of watching movies abounded. Dreams of prisons and concentration camps were frequent, but always created with guards who looked the other way while he briefly escaped. As he put it: "It didn't matter that I would eventually have to go back; the fact that I got out *at all* was rubbing their noses in it, and that was the real freedom." During this period of the analysis, it was difficult for me to manage my continued feeling of helplessness in response to his somnolent state of consciousness without becoming overly active in order to feel alert and productive. My words were taken in by him readily and hungrily, but they entered only his "false mouth"—an invisible anatomical lining within his real mouth, created in one of his dreams. His mouth was actually "false" in both meanings of the word; it was false both in what it emitted and in what it appeared to receive.

It was the reexperience of the Isakower phenomenon that seemed to usher in a new stage of the analysis. Even his dreams took on a different character. They were clearly recognizable as belonging to no one but Mr. C, but now *he* was alive as well as the dream content. He spoke openly and spontaneously of his wish to remain "asleep" on the analytic couch so as to avoid direct contact with me, and of his fear of revealing his anger (not yet brought into sessions) at having to follow my rules in such matters as the use of the couch and payment for missed hours.

His wish to be able to return to his formerly schizoid state of half-deadness and his inability to do so were represented by a dream in which he decided it was time to die, but when he lay down in his grave he did not feel as if he were dying. In the dream he became afraid that the cemetery caretaker (a figure resembling me) might cover him with dirt while he was still alive, so he got up out of the grave and began to walk toward a distant town. I had no difficulty in empathizing with either my own role as the caretaker who heaps words on his passive body or with his role of wishing he could deaden himself when he wanted to—particularly when he mentioned that the date of his death inscribed on the tombstone was April 15, the date income taxes are due.

As in his real life, Mr. C's progress in the analytic process was characterized at this point not by a sudden or dramatic shift from a state of half-sleep to a state of full engagement, but by a lengthy transitional period during which he did with me what he did with the Isakower phenomenon: lying on the couch in a half-awake state; playing with my potentially smothering ideas as they approached him, pushing them away, looking at them from different perspectives, challenging them with ideas of his own; and gradually using the total interpersonal context in a creative act that more and more felt as if it belonged to both of us. In this manner the analysis approached what could be considered the final phase, in which the "false mouth" and his use of detachment to avoid life were felt by him as ego alien. In his outside life, his relationships both personally and professionally had become richer and more fulfilling, and he anticipated marriage to a woman with whom he had been living for more than a year. With regard to the analytic process, he had reached the point where he could not only take in my words without anxiety, but also no longer attributed any magical power to them. His own use of language was therefore employed less as a shield to neutralize the other person's potentially traumatic impact (cf. Sullivan, 1956, pp. 229–283) and became more available as a genuine expression of his own personality in the context of full emotional involvement in the external world.

His daydreams, for example, became alive to him and a subject of his own curiosity. "I became aware over the weekend, while taking a walk," he said, "that my daydreams really prevent me from seeing what's around me, and I realized that I don't daydream when I'm at home. It struck me that my daydreams perform the function of screening out the outside world in the same way that reading or watching TV does it when I'm home. The reason I don't need the daydreams when I'm there is that I'm already in my apartment with the blinds down. In my daydreams I'm usually exploding at some situation in the real world that I might get into, and I'm full of righteous anger at being taken advantage of, and I'm telling them off. It's like walking down the street writing somebody's political speech except that the speech is in me. I also thought that my daydreams might have the same purpose as my dreams at night. I can deal with the real world in my head but still stay asleep to it out there and not have to really get involved with anybody."

This insight was achieved and articulated by Mr. C while, with my active participation, he was in the midst of recovering some very early primal scene memories and disclosing some vivid fantasies associated with them. It struck me shortly thereafter that what Mr. C was attempting to deal with there in bits and pieces resonated closely with Lewin's (1950, 1952, 1953) conceptualization and description of the function of dreaming and the relationship between the primal scene and what he refers to as the "oral triad"—the wish to eat, to be eaten, and to sleep. In claustrophobia, Lewin (1950) suggests, "the fantasy of being within the mother's body, there to eat and sleep, is a displacement downward and inward of the wish to eat and sleep at the breast." He states:

> I propose an additional, and perhaps essential factor: namely the wish to sleep is a repetition of nursing and a defense against the disturbance of the primal scene. . . . Because the primal scene interferes with the course of sleep, it reactivates the whole oral triad. This may be studied in certain insomnias. The sleeplessness can be traced back to the primal scene experiences, but the problem of going to sleep is expressed in oral terms. The patient manifests a continual hunger of one sort or another . . . and the insomnia of the primal scene is equated unconsciously to the sleeplessness of an unfed baby. The patient wishes to eat so that he may sleep, and the insomnia of the primal scene gets put into the terminology of the nursing process. . . . The first line of defense against the primal scene stimuli at their origin is sound sleep, a complete repetitive success of the oral procedure of nursing. The secondary defense, after some penetration of the stimuli, would be a dream, a guarding of sleep by the oneiric neutralization of the intruders [pp. 120–121].

Mr. C's bedtime pattern had been to eat until he felt bloated—he was unable to sleep if he felt the least bit empty—and then enter his bed and fixate on the television screen until he was totally exhausted. At other times he would fight sleep with obsessive rumination until he finally succumbed to overwhelming fatigue. The transitional period between the waking state and sleep had always been harnessed with the tightest rein possible and until this point in his life was designed as an experience in which looking without seeing would lead to sleeping without falling asleep.

The Primal Scene and the Terminal Scene

For Mr. C, the "seeing" issue was the last to be resolved during the course of a stormy and confrontational termination phase. The question of termination had emerged in a way he perceived as overly authoritarian on my part because the subject had been overtly initiated by me rather than by him. He felt that for me to raise the issue first was equivalent to a "command" that impinged on his right to leave when "he felt ready." At about this same time he had paid several visits to an optometrist to replace his thick eyeglasses with new, more flattering contact lenses. He had come to view the old glasses as a kind of prosthesis—an artificial addition to his body, similar to his metaphorical "false mouth"—which made him look harmless and thus served the function of protecting him from potentially harmful people whom he could not clearly see. The contact lenses, however, were quite another matter. They were openly associated with the wish to see as a statement of potency, sexual attractiveness, and manifest sexual initiative.[8] It was in the context of having the lenses made that the wish to see, to be seen, and to act became, in his sense of self, compatible with the developmentally earlier triad—the wish to eat, to be eaten, and to sleep. He experienced, for the first time while in treatment, intense anger toward a male figure of authority while in that person's presence. Mr. C felt that there was something wrong with the lenses and with my raising the issue of termination, and that in both cases he was being prevented from "seeing" as well as he potentially could. His

---

8. Fink (1967), reporting on one of her own patients who experienced the Isakower phenomenon five times during analytic sessions, mentions the striking fact that "the first two reports of the phenomenon came in two consecutive sessions in which the patient wore his contact lenses in the session, something he rarely did, and which he associated with potency and sexual looking" (p. 238). Like Mr. C, the patient described by Fink subsequently elaborated a rich associative context of primal scene fantasies and memories.

anger was directed simultaneously toward the optometrist and toward me, and, in this final phase of the work, its previously uncontrollable and sadistic quality was gradually worked through and integrated as normally assertive, authoritative self-expression. He was able, in each relationship, to feel his own impact on resolving the issue with the other person to a conclusion that he was able to accept even though he felt it as less than "perfect."

Transferentially, the same elements were operating here that had been at issue all along—oral conflict, erotic wishes, and fear of parental authority—but now there was a sense of self that was sufficiently individuated to enlist his anger in the service of his own growth. It was even possible now to see the interplay between the various levels of conflict as expressed through his relationships with each parent and with his sister. At the level of oral deprivation, he was the infant who experienced his whole being as in the control of a maternal figure who was unresponsive to it, not an ungiving maternal figure, but one who disregarded his unique identity and gave when she decided something was needed. It is in this sense that the Isakower phenomenon is, of course, the breast, but it is also an interpersonal phenomenon, as in Mr. C's symbolic and creative effort to overcome the ego passivity of his early precognitive experience with his mother around the act of feeding. His lifelong hopelessness paralleled his chronic feeling of impotency in his interchanges with the external world. At the oral level, the world embodied a mother who, if he was not self-protected and self-fed, would suffocate him when he was already full because she felt he *should* be hungry or would starve him when he was empty because she felt he should not *still* be hungry. This level of experience was vivid in his perception of me around the issue of termination and in his perception of the optometrist around the issue of whether the lenses still needed further correction.

At the level of oedipal experience and primal scene fantasy, the two male figures were seen by him as replicating the way in which he had felt treated by his autocratic, insecure, competitive father. "I know what's best for you" was the communication he heard again, but at this level he heard it as a retaliation for the way he was using his new visual clarity. He was using it both sexually and aggressively and had started to look at me and say what he saw, in the same way he perceived me using my own vision. What had made the primal scene so singularly terrifying for Mr. C was not simply that he had slept in his parents' bedroom for the first six years of his life; it was that he could organize what he saw and what he fantasied, only into a rigid interpersonal frame of reference that had nothing to do with two people doing something together that was fun, exciting, and mutually satisfying. Nothing in Mr. C's relationship to either parent would have led him to believe that something mutually respectful of one another's identity was going on. Since in his experience one person had to be submitting to the will of another, his oedipal fantasies would be inevitably terrifying because he already felt "preoedipally castrated" as a person. Trauma was built upon trauma, with no developmentally secure interpersonal context except the relationship with his younger sister, whose birth had probably provided the nexus for therapeutic hope.

Regardless of the inviting developmental smorgasbord that was always available in the content of the sessions, the crucial dimensions of meaning were, during the early phase of the analysis, structural rather than dynamic. What mattered most in Mr. C's personality growth had not been determined simply by phase-specific psychosexual conflict defined by unmet oral needs or oedipal castration anxiety. What most influenced his early development as well as the course of his analytic treatment was the issue of whether the structural level of mental representation that existed at a given point in time, was able to engage and use new phase-appropriate interpersonal experience. For a long time the instability in his representational world framed the degree to which he could process and own a full range of human emotions without burying himself in the only source of security he trusted—his inner stage and the dyadically structured scenario it provided (cf. M. Balint, 1968).

The end of Mr. C's treatment can be summarized by a dream he reported three months prior to the agreed-upon date of termination. Like the analysis itself, the dream did not tie up all the loose ends but conveyed his new sense of hope, potency, and security in the outside world, as well as his resentment that he had to surrender his old sources of self-aggrandizement in order to achieve it. It also conveyed a genuine feeling of sadness at the loss of our relationship.

> He was being visited in his apartment by some important childhood friends whom he wanted to both impress and cook dinner for, but his apartment was too dimly lit. Accompanied by his friends, he went out in search of a brighter light bulb and encountered a variety of obstacles, which they, as a group, were able to deal with successfully and aggressively. At last, dirty but exhilarated, they returned with the bulb. He replaced it, and the apartment was filled with light and looked lovely. But by this time the friends had run out of time and could not stay for dinner. They were happy to have seen him and to have gone on this adventure

with him but were now ready to go about their own business. ("There was this terrible frustration," he commented in session, "that they were going to leave and couldn't stay for dinner. I wanted so much for them to be there longer. I went through all this stuff to let more light in, but when I finally did it, it was too late. By that time the people from my past were beyond being impressed.")

During these final three months, each of the "old" themes resurfaced with an uncanny realness, as though we were living out a shadowy replica of the same uncertainty that had characterized his parents' conflict about how to do the "right thing." Was the termination perhaps premature? Was I, like his friends in the dream, "leaving too soon," perhaps to preserve my role as the analyst who, except for rare and dramatic occasions, is "beyond being impressed"? If so, was I unwittingly enacting the father's unconscious wish to "throw him out" of the bedroom just as he was becoming old enough to see me clearly and challenge me? Or was I perhaps playing out the role of the mother who wished to keep him around only as long as he validated her significance as his ego support; and once I had helped him achieve a full sense of separate identity was I then ready to receive a "new baby" to take his place? Should this uncertainty have been resolved before termination? Could it have been? By my own standards as well as his, the analysis had been a success. Why, then did his termination process recapitulate the past with such vividness?

Levenson (1976a), from the vantage point of what he calls "the aesthetics of termination," proposes that

> one might expect that a patient would terminate more or less in the configurational style within which he operates. One would hope that the improvement would be evident in that the configuration would be markedly extended and modulated. . . . I would say that it makes no more sense to ask when to terminate than to ask when to die. It is a natural event in the course of therapy [p. 341].

In Mr. C's case, this metaphor is, I think, both apt and ironic. For most of Mr. C's life, asking when to die had indeed made perfect sense to him. Death had always been unconsciously experienced as under his control through his ability to remain detached from life and thus to feel that "living" had not in itself yet begun. As in the dream in which he entered his grave to await his death, it was only in the act of climbing out and seeking the real world, that death, like the eventual culmination of his analysis, could become for better or for worse, part of the natural configuration of life.

9

THE DIFFICULT PATIENT OR
THE DIFFICULT DYAD?[1] (1992)

In a paper entitled "The Unreasonable Patient," Giovacchini (1985) refers to the general situation in which a patient's psychopathology clashes with the treatment process, as a psychoanalytic paradox. He puts it that "transference repetition is essential for analytic resolution but with some patients, its very nature seems to preclude analysis" (p. 8). Taking as an example patients who seem to enact their right to be unreasonable during the course of treatment, he sees their need for enactment dominating the analytic situation, and the patient's ego as having lost its self-observing function. Clinically, this frequently results in a situation where the therapist, because he feels helpless and unable to maintain his analytic role, experiences the patient as "difficult." The paradox to which he refers is in the fact that a central part of the analytic process is for the patient to be able to experience his "primitive" affects and mental states in the treatment itself, and that insight formulations always contain the potential of depriving the patient of fully experiencing an affective state to its ultimate resolution. "To some extent every interpretation is potentially premature, since it is impossible to determine how long an affect has to be experienced before it can be resolved" (p. 6).

---

1. An early form of this chapter was presented at a William Alanson White Institute clinical symposium, "Interpersonal Frontiers in Psychoanalytic Practice," in November 1990. The present version was originally published in *Contemporary Psychoanalysis*, 1992, 28:495–502.

What is an analyst to do? How is he to work with the "unreason-able" need of certain patients to transferentially enact unsymbolized experience in a way that makes the traditional analytic situation itself experienced by these patients as incompatible with being understood?

With tongue slightly in cheek, I will present a few excerpts from one of the earliest known clinical vignettes (Carroll, 1871) of an initial interview with an "unreasonable patient," a young lady (probably a passive-aggressive personality) who had suffered a traumatic fall and was currently entertaining the fantasy of having entered a world that existed in her mirror. The patient (Alice), in an obviously unreceptive state of mind, has arrived at the office of Dr. H. Dumpty. Her first response (as with many such patients) is to devalue the apparent inequality of the seating and the analyst's professionally neutral atti-tude. She notes to herself that Dr. Dumpty is sitting on top of such a high wall that she "wondered how he could keep his balance—and as his eyes were steadily fixed in the opposite direction, and he didn't take the least notice of her, she thought he must be a stuffed figure" (p. 251). The interview begins with the analyst's immediate recogni-tion that the patient has a serious character problem and that her defensive use of naiveté calls for a "no-nonsense" approach. It was important to get her to recognize as quickly as possible that she suf-fered a severe impairment in seeing reality clearly, and to accept that she may in fact not even possess an adequate awareness of her own identity.

> "Don't stand there chattering to yourself like that," Humpty Dumpty said, looking at her for the first time, "but tell me your name and your business."
> "My *name* is Alice, but—"
> "It's a stupid name enough!" Humpty Dumpty interrupted impa-tiently. "What does it mean?"
> *"Must* a name mean something?" Alice asked doubtfully.
> "Of course it must," Humpty Dumpty said with a short laugh: "*my* name means the shape I am. . . . With a name like yours, you might be any shape, almost" [p. 263].

The issue of Alice's marginal sense of self having been clarified, the analyst moves on to the next order of business, the establishment of respective role definitions. In the next segment an effort is made to structure the analytic frame while incorporating the appropriate amount of early "limit setting" necessary with such patients. The issue of distinguishing between healthy and impaired reality judgment con-tinues to be emphasized, and the efficacy of this approach is clearly illustrated by Alice's increased reasonableness as a prospective patient.

"When *I* use a word," Humpty Dumpty said, in a rather scornful tone, "it means just what I choose it to mean—neither more nor less."

"The question is," said Alice, "whether you *can* make words mean so many different things."

"The question is," said Humpty Dumpty, "which is to be master— that's all."

Alice was much too puzzled to say anything; so after a minute Humpty Dumpty began again. . . . "*I* can manage the whole lot of them! Impenetrability! That's what *I* say!"

"Would you tell me please," said Alice, "what that means?"

"Now you talk like a reasonable child," said Humpty Dumpty, looking very much pleased. "I meant by 'impenetrability' that we've had enough of that subject, and it would be just as well if you'd mention what you mean to do next, as I suppose you don't mean to stop here all the rest of your life" [p. 269].[2]

The interview concludes with Dr. Dumpty again introducing Alice to the experience of analytic abstinence, and in his concluding statement letting her know that he is aware of her narcissistic yearning for mirroring, but that it will not be gratified.

There was a long pause. "Is that all?" Alice timidly asked.

"That's all," said Humpty Dumpty. "Good-bye."

This was rather sudden, Alice thought: but, after such a *very* strong hint that she ought to be going, she felt that it would hardly be civil to stay. So she got up, and held out her hand. "Good-bye, till we meet again!" she said as cheerfully as she could.

"I shouldn't know you again if we *did* meet," Humpty Dumpty replied in a discontented tone, giving her one of his fingers to shake: "you're so exactly like other people" [pp. 275–276].

During the early years of our profession's existence, the working psychoanalyst could be relatively secure in maintaining the comforting illusion that, when necessary, his periods of confusion, lapses in concentration, gaps in memory, failures in comprehension, and even his ignorance, could be discreetly shielded behind his analytic role; a stance of technically permissible nonresponsiveness that was at least tolerated by most patients even if covertly (and sometimes overtly)

---

2. Here we have the suggestion of a possible countertransferential issue (the analyst's unconscious dread of being swallowed up by an interminable analysis), a fear not infrequently evoked by difficult patients such as Alice (individuals who don't know the rules of analysis and couldn't care less about the "frame").

mistrusted and resented. It was an era in history when the analytic situation, from the vantage point of the "difficult patient," could well have been caricatured as the "difficult process." For a variety of reasons, including the dramatic shift in our cultural attitude towards paternalistic authority, during the last thirty years the prototypical analytic patient has more and more claimed the right to a verbally visible, relationally responsive, and thereby more personally vulnerable partner. To paraphrase an old joke, "it is no longer enough for an analyst to know absolutely nothing; it is now also important to be able to express it." The day of the nonresponsive analyst is largely a memory; the day of the "difficult patient" has arrived. It is thus only fitting that in a period when psychoanalysis has become the "impossible profession" and its practitioners are said to run the constant risk of "burnout," analysts are allowed some small cathartic relief through the opportunity to publicly discuss their "difficult patients."

Writing about difficult patients within a psychoanalytic context, however, also has tended historically to reflect the author's theoretical position or sensibility with regard to other more basic issues. One thing that is often revealed, for example, is the extent of an analyst's embeddedness within one of two opposing and sometimes passionately held conceptual frames of reference. The first might be said to represent the view that the bond which exists between patient and analyst is simply a catalytic agent that allows the one genuine mutative ingredient—insight—to structurally rebalance the psychic apparatus. The other vantage point represents some variation of the view that an aspect of this bond, whether it is called attachment, relatedness, holding, empathic attunement, or some other term, is a developmentally-linked ingredient in the process of structural change and thus an agent of therapeutic action. Analysts whose thinking has been strongly shaped by the first perspective have tended to write about the difficult patient as the "unanalyzable patient"; unanalyzable with regard to what has been called by traditional metatheory the "unmodified psychoanalytic situation." Within this frame of reference, the guiding principle in treating the "difficult patient" has been to preserve the concept of a basic treatment model consistent with the classical definition of what does and what does not constitute psychoanalysis, while expanding clinical horizons as far as the boundaries of Freud's thinking has seemed to permit at that time. The effort has been largely one of how to make difficult patients fit on the couch without lengthening or shortening the couch or the patient. The historical solution, with which we are all familiar, has been the introduction of additional permissible elements in the analyst's technical repertoire, called parameters, that can ultimately be analyzed. The idea of a "difficult" analytic patient is defined in this context, at least implicitly, in relation to the patient's ability to utilize a model of the analytic situation that depends upon his bringing to it ego assets that will enable him to participate in an analytic process that is relatively independent of what the analyst contributes through his own personality or approach to the patient.[3]

At the other extreme have been writers such as Haley (1969), for example, who have used the term "difficult" ironically, so as to caricature what was felt to be the absurdity (and even presumptuousness) of the idea of a "basic" treatment model defining the state of a patient's mental health by his ability to survive for years in a relationship without requiring that it be modified in an ongoing way by his own impact upon it, and not simply by that of his partner. The main way in which difficult patients are "difficult," Haley asserted, "is their insistence on dealing directly with the analyst once they begin to feel some confidence" (p. 18). Haley, in effect, turned the other position on its head and argued (I think, unfortunately shrilly) that the difficult patient who is too "crazy" to be analyzed is simply expressing openly what the analyzable patient puts up with passively. I say "unfortunately shrilly" because I feel that Haley has weakened an otherwise valuable point that not only needed to be made but has been made by many others, more evenhandedly, more circumspectly, and is now almost commonplace, including among many classical analysts. Haley was asserting through caricature what Stone (1961), for example, has argued with tact and compassion; that there has been an unnecessary rigidity in analytic procedure that has forced certain patients to accept being "tailored" to the process rather than vice versa. If the patient cannot (or as Haley claims, *will* not) adapt, he has been defined as "unanalyzable" and a "modified" psychoanalytic technique may be introduced to work with him, thereby preserving rather than questioning the concept of a basic treatment model.

At this point in psychoanalytic history when we are all more or less familiar with and more or less weary of and wary of analytic politics, the topic of the "difficult patient" is particularly fascinating. It is an expression with which no one is satisfied, about which almost everyone has an opinion, and with regard to which the fact of not liking it may be one of the few things with which most every school of analytic thought can agree. Even in writing about it, authors often criticize the term as soon as it leaves their pen. Feiner (1982, p. 397), for example, in a paper entitled "Comments on the Difficult Patient," starts off by

---

3. See chapter 7 for a fuller development of this point.

saying that "perhaps it isn't the word 'difficult' that we ought to consider but the word 'the.'" "*The* difficult patient," Feiner states, implies that we are looking at the problem as located solely in some attribute of the patient (such as unreasonableness, concreteness, contentiousness, etc.), and looking at the patient solely as a separate entity. In other words, as soon as we attach the word "the" to a descriptive category or group of people, we limit our ability to know any particular person, and reveal as much about ourselves in the labeling as we do about the patient. He suggests that if we shift the emphasis away from global categorization, we can then use the term "difficult" not as an attribute but as a behavior that occurs in a context, and can frame the field in a way that respects the patient's unique qualities, but as part of a dyadic field that makes understanding and treating him more possible within an analytic setting. In any event, the concept of the "difficult patient" is like a bad itch that scratching doesn't relieve; it remains with us regardless of analytic politics, and it seems to me that its refusal to die is based more upon its clinical vitality than on theoretical necessity. As we are quite well aware, the term is in no way a formal diagnosis nor does it suggest, even as an impressionistic label, the existence of a consensually derived body of data to which it adheres. I think this is equally accurate for the concept of the "difficult *dyad*." Both phrases, I would suggest, arise imperatively from the need of the individual analyst to symbolize his personal, private distress with certain of his patients—as much from an analyst's soul as from his brain.

What makes a patient difficult clinically is the issue. How do we reconcile the diagnostic, characterological, and individual psychodynamics of the patient with each unique patient/analyst configuration? Is "difficulty" simply in the pain of the beholder? I doubt that anyone seriously believes this to be true, but if it is false—if one analyst's difficult patient is not simply another analyst's routine patient—then what are we actually talking about when we use the term "difficult"? If patient and analyst do indeed comprise an inseparable, interpenetrating dyadic unit, then in one way or another every patient should be experienced, at least for some period of time, as a difficult patient; in other words, if all goes well in an analysis, there is something very wrong with the analysis. The question then becomes, "difficult in what way"? For what analyst, in what here-and-now context, and with reference to what psychodynamic issues, historical enactments, transference/countertransference configurations, and basic personality structure, can the patient in a particular "difficult dyad" be most usefully comprehended while the treatment is taking place?

For instance, in an initial interview with a prospective patient, what actually goes into the choice the analyst makes in deciding how willing he is to bend the frame in order to provide the conditions necessary for a given patient to form a therapeutic alliance? Perhaps the initial consultation with certain patients might in fact be largely a negotiation around the issue of adaptation versus interpretation. Some therapists are more willing than others to bend the frame. Is this simply idiosyncratic to the particular analyst or is there something about certain patients that make certain analysts more willing to adapt for personal reasons, and others less so? Equally to the point, how does an analyst come to understand the reasons behind his choices, and what criteria does he apply with a given patient as to how far he is willing to bend the frame? How much of this should be discussed openly with a patient right from the beginning? What about those analysts who see the frame itself as a product of ongoing negotiation rather than a "basic" structure to be either preserved or "bent?" What criteria do they use, and to what extent does their conscious or unconscious experience of the patient as "difficult" enter into the matter? The line between adaptation and countertransference is sometimes rather thin, and in various instances one's so-called "easy" patient may in fact be a "difficult patient" that the analyst, in some central way, has avoided engaging so as to prevent being a difficult patient. One example of this is those individuals whose characteristically easy-going manner and reliability are so congenial to the analyst's feeling of well-being that the analyst doesn't notice his own complicity in failing to address a stalemated treatment. An analyst's personal responses to his patient in such instances are often useful sources of data if given appropriate attention. At times it may be something as subtle as noticing one's tendency to exploit unconsciously specific patients by thinking of them before other patients when needing someone to switch an hour because of a scheduling problem; less subtle, and more potentially harmful to the patient is an analyst's willingness to allow certain patients' unchanging life issues to remain unexamined longer than he would with other patients because the patient seems to be working hard in treatment and "these other things will change in their own time." With some individuals this is, of course, accurate, but for others it is a rationalization to maintain the illusion that a "difficult" patient is in fact an "easy" patient.

All this being said, the most solace that an analyst can take when he feels himself locked into an impasse with a "difficult patient" is that it comes with the territory. It is my view that when he looks around and tries to understand what is going on, he will more often than not find himself back on solid ground if he addresses what is going on between himself and his patient rather than looking for the difficulty in the patient alone.

10

ON KNOWING ONE'S PATIENT INSIDE OUT

The Aesthetics of Unconscious Communication[1] (1991)

When I had been a small boy someone told me that the blood in your veins was blue, the way it looked through the skin, and that it only turned red when you exposed it to air. What I felt was one thing when I kept it in. It changed color entirely when I exposed it.

—Robert B. Parker, *The Widening Gyre*

It is in the nature of the human condition that the experience of "insideness" helps to protect the self from excessive external impingement, while the act of interpersonal communication releases it from excessive internal isolation. The "illusion of personal individuality" (Sullivan, 1950b), in this light, is a paradoxical state of mind that can be reasonably portrayed as a continuing negotiation between the two subjective realities of creative interiority and social relatedness or, from a slightly different standpoint, between imagination and adaptation.

---

1. An early draft of this essay was presented in March 1989 at a symposium sponsored by the Institute of Contemporary Psychotherapy, New York City, and was published in its present version in *Psychoanalytic Dialogues*, 1991, 1:399–422.

As a patient gradually reveals himself through the give-and-take of the analytic relationship, the analyst correspondingly acquires an increasing sense of knowing his patient. It is the ever-changing configuration of this experience that an analyst attempts to put into language through the interchanges of the clinical process and the interpretive formulations he offers as the work goes on. As any analyst knows, it is never really that simple. The verbal picture he paints of his patient at any given moment—sometimes even as the words leave his lips— is wrong, and the analyst will frequently register its wrongness consciously. By "wrong," I do not simply mean incomplete, not to the point, or out of tune with the patient's picture of himself. I mean wrong with regard to the analyst's own experience of the patient; wrong in the way an antique dealer uses the word in rejecting an object he senses is not the "real" thing; wrong as in "not right." Language, by its inherent nature, is unavoidably drained of much of the color, texture, and vitality held by the subjective experience of one's patient, and particularly so when words begin to *substitute* for experience (see chapter 1). No matter how evocative the language, words are but symbols for the experiential "thing" as a felt truth (thus the power of the phrase *"true self"*). But if an analyst is able to listen, his words will sometimes echo back to him and by their very hollowness will help, paradoxically, to restore relatedness by creating a mutual bond of human understanding through a shared but unspoken secret: "There's more inside of me than I can put into words, more than meets the eye." Most people take their own subjective states of interiority for granted and can routinely accept the feeling that there is more to them than meets the eye, as a mental state that joins them to the rest of mankind without intrinsic emotional isolation. They can be both in the world and separate from it as a unitary experience that blends selfhood and relatedness. Others, more developmentally fragmented, protect their subjective interiors as a lifelong task of emotional survival while paying the price of never-ending efforts at self-validation or desperate aloneness. For them, being known inside out is their most dreaded nightmare and their most fervent wish. "There's more to me than meets the eye" is as much a battle cry and a cry for help as it is a statement of subjective reality.

In chapter 11 I present a brief clinical illustration that I would like to introduce preemptively into the present context. The vignette is about a patient who had used a dream as an unconscious communication to her analyst to inform him in this transferential mode that the clinical stance through which he was relating to her while "conducting" the analysis was unendurable to her and that his belief in the rightness of his technique made him so unattuned to its effect on her that there was no way for her to negotiate being herself while being his patient.[2] The use of a dream for this purpose provided a creative channel to enact a message she could not consciously formulate as a sayable thought because such a thought could not be processed within the present structure of their relationship. In the dream imagery, she portrayed the fact that she was starting to feel hopeless about his potential to recognize that the act of "doing" analysis was making her less able to show him who she was. "I am someone for whom relationships feel artificial and oppressive," the dream signals; "I can't respond to what you are doing in the way that you think I will. I must be allowed to exist with you in whatever way I can, and perhaps then you will start to know me." If the analyst hears this message in the dream, what is he to "do" in response to it? The communication, after all, does not come with instructions about "doing," only about "not doing." Furthermore, if he is capable of recognizing the negative impact of the certainty in his stance, he will have to start by accepting that the "message" he hears in the dream is only a possibility, not a fact. My position, in brief, was to suggest that he should listen as carefully as possible to the moment-by-moment effect that his existence appeared to be having on her and respond with this in mind. That is, he should try to allow his felt experience of her state of mind to inform his stance vis-à-vis the dream because his stance will constitute the interpretive context through which the content of his words will generate meaning. He will be, in effect, communicating his understanding of the dream through the degree to which his "doing" embodies visibly increased attunement to what the dreamer seems to mean by "not doing," that is, what he (the analyst) shows he does not expect or require of the relationship independent of their intersubjective negotiation. Furthermore, to the extent that what he is hearing in this dream is felt by the patient as inaccurate or only partially accurate, he must be ready to listen for this possibility with equal receptivity and involvement. What this patient appeared to need at that moment was her analyst's recognition that overinvestment in his own approach was depriving her of her opportunity to regress to a level of self-experience that, interpersonally, could only be shown, not said—and shown only

---

2. In the dream, the analyst, undisguised and with an earnest manner and a genuinely warm smile, throws into the patient's lap a bag containing a two-headed monster. The patient is terrified because she knows she is expected to open the bag, but she cannot tell the analyst how frightened she is because the monster will just get larger.

to someone attuned enough to it to participate at that level without requiring that it be prematurely surrendered and replaced by a dissociated exercise in adaptational pseudomaturity.

Is it justifiable to portray the analyst's participation in such transferential enactments as an aspect of unconscious communication? I believe so, in the sense that it embodies an act of interpersonal recognition that communicates an analyst's willingness to know his patient inside out in the only way possible—directly and personally. The potential usefulness of this metaphor, however, lies not in the persuasiveness of its logic but in whatever concrete clinical value is derived from framing the analytic process through this image. I am therefore going to try to explore in the following pages some of the therapeutic implications of looking at unconscious communication in this way, particularly with certain patients. Because the concept of dissociation plays such a major role, I would like to start by examining its clinical characteristics in a somewhat broader analytic perspective.

Dissociation

It has been stated by Rycroft (1962, p. 113) that "the aim of psychoanalytic treatment is not primarily to make the unconscious conscious . . . but to re-establish the connexion between dissociated psychic functions so that the patient ceases to feel that there is an inherent antagonism between his imaginative and adaptive capacities." Rycroft is suggesting here that if all goes reasonably well developmentally, an adult should not experience a fundamental discontinuity between internal and external reality, and a choice need not be routinely made between creative self-affirmation and adaptive human relatedness. In other words, there should develop the natural ability to let oneself be known inside out through an intimate relationship without the fear of surrendering one's interiority as an act of soul murder. To examine in any detail how this state of affairs is effectively brought about in the analytic treatment of individuals for whom things did not go well enough in their early development makes its intrinsically relational nature fairly clear. From birth on, human beings need to structure their experience through the medium of relationships with other human beings. To the extent that an individual's early object relationships were reasonably adaptive to this need, the process of consensually symbolizing subjective experience through the use of communicative speech is a relatively nontraumatic process and, apart from exposure to extraordinary traumatic events, continues to be so throughout adult life.

As with any other way of knowing one's patient, however, developmental diagnosis is never black or white, and as Edel (1980, p. 9) has cogently observed, "Insecurity and anxiety breed a quest for other selves. Sometimes this becomes schizoid and troublesome; sometimes it creates nerves of steel." When dissociation is typically seen in a relatively cohesive personality, the various aspects of self-experience are bound together by a core sense of common quality and sameness of existence over time. Each dissociated aspect of self has its own degree of access to the various levels of psychic functioning, such as capacity to feel and tolerate the pressure of one's needs and wishes, capacity to judge what is adaptive social behavior, capacity to act from a sense of one's values as well as from a sense of purpose, and capacity to maintain object constancy. This is what we are accustomed to working with clinically in the routine treatment of character neuroses when we are dealing with dissociative phenomena. We count on the existence in the patient of a cohesive core personality that feels to us and to the patient more or less like the same person regardless of moment-to-moment shifts in self-state, alterations in mental functioning, or even the unanticipated emergence of dissociated phenomena that Sullivan (1953) calls "not-me" experience. And yet, even with such patients, the analyst must be careful to retain his capacity for viewing each individual through the lens implied in the question asked by Enid Balint (1987, p. 480): "If the ability to perceive is lacking because it is too traumatic or too alien, can one think of an individual as being truly conscious?"

For example, a 30-year-old female patient, the youngest of four sisters, had sought analysis with me because of paralyzing dissociative states that left her feeling "unreal" and "empty" when she attempted to assert herself among strangers. In her growing up, her characteristic experience of trying to negotiate the nonfamilial environment had been terror. Attempts to communicate about these feelings within the family were met by responses that either ignored her subjective reality or dismissed it in favor of the parental and sibling fantasy of who she "really" was. As she was consistently left alone with these painful feelings, ashamed, and unable actively to take them into her socially defined self-representation, her adult personality became shaped by a dissociative process to the extent that any nonfamilial act of self-expression that she initiated triggered a self-state she referred to as "the watcher," who observed her "not-me" projection engaging in a meaningless, mechanical performance. Three years into her treatment, she relived with me, through an intense transferential enactment, the following memory, which she came to call "the birth of the watcher":

> I was in my second-grade class, and we were all playing a game where we would send letters to other kids, and they would write back. I sent a letter to Meg asking for a date. She didn't answer. I wrote another letter, and she wrote back and said no. I felt strange, totally and completely alone. It was the first time I was ever aware there was a "me." I became self-conscious—conscious of having a self, and that there was something wrong with it. I was so ashamed. I was ashamed of what happened; I was ashamed of asking; and I was ashamed of being so sensitive. My mother didn't understand. When I tried to tell her about it, she told me not to worry because there were plenty of other kids to play with.

This woman, despite her dissociative symptom, had a fairly cohesive core sense of self and was someone whom Edel might well have characterized as having developed "nerves of steel." There are, however, other patients for whom the process of dissociation occurs not just between domains of self-experience but almost (and sometimes actually) between aspects of self-existence. For these individuals, inadequacy of early object relationships has so seriously impaired the normal development of tension-reducing mental structure that certain constellations of presymbolized experience too intense to be cognitively processed by the forming self were forced to be retained as traumatically unbearable mental states that were then dissociated to whatever degree possible to preserve other areas of adaptive functioning and sometimes sanity itself. Freud, despite his eventual shift from the position taken in his early writings with Breuer in "Studies on Hysteria" (Breuer and Freud, 1893–1895), continued to be fascinated by the issue of dissociation even while developing his structural theory, and he implicitly retained the concept in his formulation that contradictory identifications in the ego could lead to pathological outcomes. In *The Ego and the Id* (1923), Freud states that if the ego's object identifications

> become too numerous, *unduly powerful and incompatible with one another*, a pathological outcome will not be far off. It may come to a disruption of the ego in consequence of the different identifications becoming cut off from one another by resistances; perhaps the secret of the cases of what is described as "multiple personality" is that the different identifications seize hold of consciousness in turn. Even when things do not go so far as this, there remains the question of conflicts between the various identifications into which the

ego comes apart, conflicts which cannot after all be described as entirely pathological [pp. 30–31, italics added].

Sullivan (1956, p. 203) speaks of "the magnificence of the apparatus . . . which is required for the maintenance of dissociation" and of "how the dissociated personality has to prepare for almost any conceivable emergency that would startle one into becoming aware of the dissociated system." Dissociated experience thus tends to remain unsymbolized by thought and language, exists as a separate reality outside of self-expression, and is cut off from authentic human relatedness and deadened to full participation in the life of the rest of the personality. To the extent that a traumatized child has the capacity and opportunity to use dissociation as a means of coping, he will typically do so, but the cost of shaping the personality in this direction is, for some people, an enduring experience of something being "wrong"—something the adult patient cannot put into words—and a consuming determination to put it right. Meaningful existence in the present is preempted by the repetitive, timeless, traumatic past, and the present is little more than a medium through which this unprocessed past may be known, actively engaged, and, in this sense, "cured." The use that such patients make of their analytic hours sometimes makes them seem as if they are "rehearsin' for a nervous breakdown" (to quote an old Charlie Shavers jazz tune). Winnicott's (1974) concept of "fear of a breakdown that has already been experienced" speaks to this pathological state of timelessness:

> It must be asked here: why does the patient go on being worried by this that belongs to the past? The answer must be that *the original experience of primitive agony cannot get into the past tense unless the ego can first gather it into its own present time experience* and into omnipotent control now [p. 105, italics added].

By way of illustrating the effect on personality structure of failed efforts to master dissociated experience, I would like to return to a psychic event (see chapter 8) that occurred in the treatment of a male patient for whom the terror of unstructured experience virtually shaped his personality and his life and whose need to master this state was represented in the rare but fascinating Isakower phenomenon (Isakower, 1938). Briefly, the symptom is a complex of sensory experiences recalled and reported by certain patients as occurring in the twilight state of consciousness just prior to entering sleep. It is a hypnogogic phenomenon, characteristically experienced as the visual (and often physical) sensation of a large, doughy, shadowy mass, swelling larger as it comes toward the face and threatening either to crush or envelop the person. As it approaches, it slowly seems to become part of the person, obscures the boundaries between his body and the outside world, and blurs his sense of self. It has been conceptualized by the use of terms such as "the dream screen" (Lewin, 1946, 1948, 1953) or "blank hallucinations" (Stern, 1961), and the literature describes different individuals reporting having coped with it in creatively different styles.

I recently reencountered this phenomenon in a second male patient who, in the first year of his analysis, reported an early childhood history of the event. It is not, however, the occurrence of the phenomenon itself as much as his powerful and unique way of having attempted to master it that I believe is worth considering. The patient remembered having first experienced it between ages four and five as a soft, white bubble taking him inside of it as he was falling asleep, and he recalled trying to control his panic by attempting to write into it. His memory was not of writing words, just the *act* of writing. The feeling he described was of needing desperately to communicate through the act of writing, but, he said, "The bubble was soft and mushy so my hand went into it and left no impression." He remembered this event happening at about the time he was just starting to learn to write and recalled that in later years he was consistently praised for his penmanship. "I could make letters exactly the way I was taught . . . with perfect control . . . exactly the way the teachers wanted me to do it."

Aside from vividly capturing the human need for active engagement with one's environment in order to construct reality, this illustration also speaks directly to the need for a firm relational context to structure the dialectic between imagination and adaptation. If this context is not available or is perhaps too "soft and mushy," the need for mastery over one's state of helpless "possession" becomes desperate, compulsively enacted, and the child cannot pleasurably link his imaginative and adaptive capacities. For this patient, what might have led to pleasure in creative writing was transmuted into a self-protective counterfeit: satisfaction derived from impressing teachers through penmanship, and the development of a character armor that prevented his existence from becoming much more than a painfully masked exercise in "penmanship."

Life becomes a search for some way of processing demonic internal reality through a human relationship, but there are no thoughts that bridge past and present so as to link the intersubjective world of trauma with the subjective world of another person. The patient is, in one respect, an island of tortured affect, and this experience, along with its felt hopelessness of verbal expression, becomes the patient's essential "truth," while words and ideas become empty "lies." The appearance is of a *dis*-integration of the affective state associated with the trauma, so that the experiences linked with that state of mind have no self-authorized "voice" with which they can be communicated. What could not originally be said could not come to be thought, and what cannot now be thought cannot come to be said. In Winnicott's terms (1963a, p. 186), what cannot be said needs to be "found," but how? What is the process through which this thing that Winnicott calls "a game of hide-and-seek" can be successfully addressed in treating a person for whom the risk of traumatization is always a felt reality? Finding a voice for what may drive the self mad if it speaks is no easy matter to negotiate. But unless it is found, the patient will die without having lived, and only the patient can fully appreciate the agony of this struggle. C. S. Lewis (1956) poignantly addresses this experience through the voice of one of the characters in his novel *Till We Have Faces*:

> To say the very thing you really mean, the whole of it, nothing more or less or other than what you really mean; that's the whole art and joy of words. A glib saying. When the time comes to you at which you will be forced at last to utter the speech which has lain at the center of your soul for years, which you have, all that time, idiot-like, been saying over and over, you'll not talk about joy of words. I saw well why the Gods do not speak to us openly, nor let us answer. Till that word can be dug out of us, why should they hear the babble that we think we mean? How can they meet us face to face till we have faces? [p. 294].

The Analytic Relationship

How is one to describe the position of an analyst attempting to enable someone who has fought all his life to keep traumatic aspects of self-experience from being thought, to find a voice for these self-states? Lerner (1990) writes:

> If there is an affirmative side to the fact of pain and illness, it consists in our having to cope with them by calling on the perverse humanity of our sheer creatureliness, which is rarely elegant and almost always messy. "Inter urinam et faeces nascimir," Freud used to remind his associates. Between urine and faeces are we born [pp. 65–66].

If psychoanalytic treatment can be in any way considered an opportunity for individuals in psychological pain to experience a "rebirth," then this description might be worth reflecting on as a metaphor for the context in which patient and analyst must, at least for some period of time, coexist. It is an image that is less unpleasant when said in Latin than when said in English, but that is precisely the point. In our ability to abide with our patients in the experiential "mess" of the analytic work without escaping prematurely into the language of conflict and defense, we most feel Freud's metaphor as applicable and the analytic process as, above all else, human. Khan (1971) has eloquently expressed a similar view:

> There is more to human experience and psychic functioning than conflict, defence and repression. It is here that I believe the concept of dissociation can help us recognize certain types of clinical material and subjective experiences of the patient more fruitfully. What is repressed is always sensible to us through its absence and the countercathexis against it (i.e., defence mechanisms). In the case of dissociations no such evidence is available to us clinically. The person *is* all the elements of his dissociated states and lives them as such. It is for the analyst operating as an auxiliary ego . . . to register these dissociations and help the patient to integrate them into a coherent totality of experience [p. 245].

Beginning with Freud's own clinical sensibility in this direction, there has been remarkable resiliency over time and across diverse schools of analytic thought with regard to the idea that because dissociation is a response to trauma, the quality of the analytic relationship takes on special significance. Ferenczi (1928, 1930b, 1931, 1933), M. Balint (1935, 1937, 1952, 1968), Sullivan (1940, 1953, 1956), Fairbairn (1941, 1952), Bion (1957), and Kohut (1971, 1977) all saw the etiology of severe dissociation as linked to an early history of psychological trauma and leading to personality development designed to protect against its recall at almost any cost. Each was struggling, in his own way, with the question of how dissociation shapes the analytic relationship and its effectiveness. Ferenczi, for example, pioneered the contemporary analytic view that regressive reliving of early traumatic experience in the analytic transference is, to some degree, curative in itself because it encourages active mastery of the traumatic "past" through use of the here-and-now analytic relationship (cf. Weiss and Sampson, 1986). Ferenczi (1930b) writes:

> In every case of neurotic amnesia . . . it seems likely that a *psychotic splitting off* of a part of the personality occurs under the influence of

shock. The dissociated part, however, lives on, hidden, ceaselessly endeavoring to make itself felt. . . . Sometimes, as I said, we achieve direct contact with the repressed part of the personality and persuade it to engage in what I might almost call an infantile conversation[3] [pp. 121–122].

Clinically, I would see the term "persuade" as defining a process of ongoing negotiation between the analyst and the varying self-states of the patient. But how is analytic work to be negotiated with patients for whom negotiation is an art that has never been learned, and what is the nature of the interpersonal field in which it is to take place? Or, to paraphrase Ferenczi (1930b, p. 122) (and Johnson, 1977, fn. 3): What are the key elements in the process by which "the repressed part of the personality" is "persuaded" to engage in direct conversation without the "trauma of interpretation" being, once again, an "intolerable situation?" Metaphorically, there is an inside, there is an outside, and there is an analyst trying in his own individual style to keep one foot in each without losing his balance or his mind. It is the ability of the analyst to create and sustain such a frame—to maintain dual citizenship in two domains of reality, with passports to multiple self-states of the patient—that Winnicott (1951) describes as the use of "transitional space"—an undisturbed, intermediate area of communication through illusion.[4] The analytic task is particularly complex because it is within this special field of communication that the patient is most vulnerable to traumatization by the analytic process itself, and as Winnicott states (1963a), "If we fail to behave in a way that is facilitating the patient's analytic process . . . we suddenly become not-me for the patient, and

---

3. It is interesting to compare this early relational perspective with, for example, the currently popular deconstructionist view of psychoanalysis as summarized by Johnson's (1977) following statement: "Psychoanalysis is not itself the *interpretation* of repetition; it is the repetition of a *trauma of interpretation* . . . the traumatic deferred interpretation not *of* an event, but as an event which never took place as such. The 'primal scene' is not a scene but an *interpretive infelicity* whose result was to situate the interpreter in an intolerable position. And psychoanalysis is the reconstruction of that interpretive infelicity not as its interpretation, but as its first and last *act*. Psychoanalysis has content only insofar as it repeats the *dis*-content of what never took place" (p. 499).

4. With regard to the subjective experience of reality that is created in this idiom, Bollas (1989) presents a persuasive argument for substituting the term "intermediate object" for Winnicott's "transitional object" because it "respects the fact that it derives from the contribution of two subjectivities" (p. 109) through continued patient and analyst interplay.

then we know too much, and we are dangerous" (p. 189). With certain patients this phenomenon is sometimes so consuming that it seems to turn the traditional analytic situation on its head. The act of trying to know the patient—the ordinary verbal context of the work—is itself forced to become the primary "material" through the powerful enactment of the patient's message that it is his tormented state of mind that is crying to be heard, rather than its contents needing to be understood. In one way, it is as if the patient is communicating that the analyst must somehow "lose" his mind in order to know the patient's. The analyst's ability to make creative use of this disorganized state of relatedness, while keeping his own center of subjectivity without inflicting it on the patient, is the heart of this part of the work. "Inter urinam et faeces nascimir," but where is the analyst to anchor his own "professional" reality? There must be some valid "outside" in which to place his second foot, some conceptual frame into which he can analytically incorporate the experientially idiosyncratic world he has agreed to help create and sustain as an intermediate reality. The problem, of course, is that any such conceptual frame must be detailed enough to serve the analyst as a reliable and credible treatment context but cannot be "packaged" or codified into a clinical technique without being perceived by such patients as what Winnicott calls "dangerous" and thus failing in its own purpose!

Regression as a Relational Construct

Each major school of analytic thought speaks to the above issue in its own language, but the most persuasive descriptions have always come from analysts whose thinking was shaped primarily by their clinical astuteness rather than by their theoretical allegiances. Historically, there have been relatively few major figures who have been able to bridge the domains of experiential and observable reality as clinicians and were also able to translate the analytic process into written language that itself has one foot "inside" and the other "outside." Those who have been able to accomplish this task have left a priceless and unique legacy to our understanding of unconscious communication as a relational configuration. Along with the work of analytic writers such as Ferenczi, Sullivan, Bion, Winnicott, Fromm-Reichmann, Fairbairn, Searles, and Kohut, the writing of Michael Balint represents a core contribution to this legacy. Balint, like Sullivan, was an original thinker and creative clinician, with a commitment to understanding and treating regressed states of mind in a psychoanalytic milieu. His belief in the centrality of the human relationship as the locus of both developmental and therapeutic personality growth, as well as his skepticism with regard to the unalloyed efficacy of verbal interpretation, positioned him, as it did Sullivan, as a controversial figure within mainstream psychoanalysis. Ultimately, both writers have had a profound and far-reaching impact on succeeding generations of analysts, but in each case, an impact that is only now beginning to receive appropriate acknowledgment.

Each held a view of personality development organized by a relational matrix that both shaped and was shaped by representational mental structure. Inasmuch, however, as their respective ideas evolved from different cultural, analytic, and philosophical backgrounds, there was a difference in the figure-ground configuration that each created to portray the interface between inside and outside reality; what was figure for one was ground for the other. Historically, Sullivan's formulations have been described primarily in terms of the operational emphasis in his writing, particularly in terms of his careful explication of what occurs between people that leads to the formation of unadaptive representational mental structure. Balint's work, conversely, has tended to be identified mainly with the experiential emphasis in his writing and with his profound understanding of what goes on inside people (the self-states associated with the faulty mental structure) as a result of inadequate or traumatic interpersonal experience early in life. In the balance of the paper I would like to create an area of "transitional reality" that bridges their individual emphases, within which the aesthetics of unconscious communication might be usefully considered as a relational configuration that bridges inside and outside through the process of regression. To develop this perspective as clearly as possible, I will first outline in a more general way the essential thrust of Balint's developmental and clinical contribution.

Along with Fairbairn (1952), who postulated that libido was intrinsically object-seeking, and Sullivan (1940, 1953), who held that the essential nature of human personality development was relational, Michael Balint (1965, 1968) conceived of the infant as inherently engaged interpersonally from the very start of life. Acknowledging the ambiguous and unstable quality of self-other differentiation prior to the attainment of communicative speech, he vividly and sensitively portrayed the subsequent development of the core sense of self that normally takes place when the baby and mother are able to participate in a relatively harmonious attunement to one another that allows preconceptual self-experience to become organized interpersonally by thought and language. Bacal (1987) summarizes Balint's conceptualization of this process as follows:

> Balint (Balint, 1968, pp. 16–17) proposed that pre-oedipal configurations have sufficient, significant identifiable characteristics in common to justify a name of their own. The term he suggested was the level, or area of the *basic fault*. . . . Here, conflict is not the essential dynamic force; experiences occur within a two-person relationship, and *"adult language is often useless or misleading in describing events . . . because words have not always an agreed or conventional meaning"* [p. 91, italics added].[5]

Like Winnicott (1960a,b), Balint was struck by the facilitation of self-development that takes place through the mother's active recognition of the infant's needs as an interpersonal process that transcends issues of gratification and frustration. As the child's subjective awareness of himself as a self-reflective, independent entity begins to form out of his preconceptual experience that was engaged and confirmed within the mutuality of the mother-infant dyad, Balint characterizes the emergence of two distinct interpersonal stances toward life that develop to varying degrees as the child individuates. Balint sees these as the fundamental dimensions around which future personality growth is shaped: ocnophilia and philobatism, the first a tendency to feel safety in bonding, and the second a tendency to feel security in being on one's own. Within the normal range of everyday living, the two tendencies are usually working relatively harmoniously and are not felt as opposing forces except for those moments—some voluntary, some less so—when one's subjective sense of reality is less organized by verbal and conceptual modes of structuring. The worst that is typically felt is the kind of existential anxiety that Becker (1964, p. 176) calls "the dizziness of freedom," experienced when "the symbolic ani-

---

5. Balint's statement that words do not always have "an agreed or conventional meaning" is dramatically parallel to Sullivan's (1942, 1953) formulations of human personality development as based on the process of consensual validation. Sullivan wrote: "In principle, that which appears in one's mind is subjective to comparison with past experience in which others have agreed as to what was the case" (1942, p. 163). "A consensus has been reached," Sullivan stated, "when the infant or child has learned precisely the right word for a situation; a word which means not only what it is thought to mean by the mothering one, but also means that to the infant. . . . And if a word evokes in the hearer something quite different from that which it was expected to evoke, communication was not a success" (1953, pp. 183–184).

mal looks out from his closed world and dizzies himself with the realization that he can become something different than he was made" (cf. Fromm, 1941).

Some individuals are less fortunate. Like the others, they look out from their closed worlds, but, unlike the others, they feel trapped within them—symbolic animals desperate for symbolic release. To the degree that either the ocnophilic or philobatic tendency overly dominates the personality, the individual suffers from the effects of his characteristic modes of compensating for the insufficiency of its opposite. The experience is not one of life being lived in a state of conflict; it is rather that of a pretense of life, with the one genuine experience being that of something "wrong" inside that language is useless to describe. Balint saw this situation occurring at the level of the basic fault and considered it to result from serious failure in relatedness on the part of primary objects prior to the conceptual structuring of experience. He believed that the infantile trauma caused by this failure in proper relatedness is all too often repeated in the analytic situation because of what he labels "the ocnophilic bias" of classical analysis—the overvaluation of language and verbal interpretation as the sole medium of the relationship. He offered the view that the patient's anxiety that his analyst will fail him is not based solely on early life experience but is also based on what really takes place between patient and analyst (1968, pp. 101–107). The patient's feeling that someone in his life has failed or "defaulted" on him is thus as much a matter of here-and-now experience as interpreting the past. Nowhere is this complex interface between the here-and-now of the therapeutic dyad and the there-and-then of a patient's dissociated mental states more evocatively presented than in Balint's development of his concept of benign regression.

Like most of Balint's formulations, his metaphor of benign regression does not tell the analyst what to "do" in terms of the specifics of his therapeutic stance because his emphasis, like Sullivan's, was always on the uniqueness of the patient-analyst dyad. Consider, for example, the following three excerpts from *The Basic Fault* (Balint, 1968), which were drawn from slightly different contexts but which, when taken together, convey the difficulty of putting the analyst's role into language that translates into a relational "procedure" for working with dissociated states. There are here, as with interpersonal psychoanalysis, an approach and a set of principles that guide the analyst, but above all else there is a participating therapist who is genuinely curious to know and relate to *that self actually in the room with him at that moment.*

Regression is not only an intrapsychic phenomenon, but also an interpersonal one; *for its therapeutic usefulness, its interpersonal aspects are decisive.* The form in which the regression is expressed . . . must be considered as one symptom of the interaction between the patient and his analyst. This interaction has at least three aspects: the way in which regression is recognized by the object, in which it is accepted by the object, and in which it is responded to by the object [pp. 147–148, italics added]. . . . All this means consent, participation, and involvement, but not necessarily action; only understanding and tolerance [p. 145]. . . . He should be willing to carry the patient, not actively, but like water carries the swimmer or the earth carries the walker, that is, to be there for the patient to be used without too much resistance against being used. True, some resistance is not only permissible but essential [p. 167].

Balint is clearly struggling to find language that evokes an image of receptivity without intrusiveness while making his interpersonal stance explicit.[6] But in trying to capture this aesthetic of unconscious communication, he arrives at a metaphor that suffers a handicap similar to my own when I speak of knowing one's patient "inside out." To someone more traditionally interpersonal, it might seem preferable had I described knowing one's patient "outside in" and thereby emphasized the relational field as the medium through which internalization occurs. Because I choose otherwise, my terminology, like Balint's "water and earth" description of the analyst, may make the concept of participant observation appear to be overbalanced on the side of observation. With regard to Michael Balint's environmental imagery, it is all too easy to interpret his statement, "but not necessarily action," as implying passivity rather than attuned responsiveness. Obviously, there is always action on the analyst's part, and that includes his state of receptivity; the analyst cannot choose not to be active as a participating center of subjectivity. In this sense, understanding and tolerance are not qualities inherent to an analyst's being, as buoyancy is a quality of water. The analyst, unlike the earth or water that "sustains and carries a man who entrusts his weight to them" (p. 145), is a thinking human being who *chooses* to put attune-

---

6. Enid Balint (1968), writing from her own perspective, engages here in a similar struggle and attempts to expand Freud's "mirror metaphor" so as to encompass the perspective of participant observation. "We have come to the conclusion," she writes, "that the implications of Freud's metaphor about the mirror are more far reaching than one would think at first glance. . . . The mirror model presupposed not a detached, but a participating observer, where participation, however, is strictly limited" [p. 348].

ment to the patient's state of mind ahead of all else at certain times. It is an active choice, and the patient, at one level, always feels it and knows it to be that. It is a different order of "safety" than entrusting oneself to a "mindless" primary substance from which no subjective action independent of the patient's usage of it is anticipated because it is not conceivable. Trust given by an adult patient (including a regressed patient) is based on an ability to depend on the analyst despite an awareness of the analyst's capacity for self-interest, and this fact is why the concept of benign regression does not simply imply a redoing of the past in a better way or the right way. How, then, might the construct be viewed from a contemporary relational perspective?

The Aesthetics of Unconscious Communication

From my own vantage point, more fully elaborated in chapter 3, therapeutic regression refers to the "raw" state of cognitive disequilibrium allowed by an analytic patient as part of the progressive, self-perpetuating restructuring of self and object representations. The vividness and immediacy of regressed states of experience become the core of an active reorganization of the interpersonal self, and one aspect of the analytic situation is the creation of a relational environment that permits, rather than induces, therapeutic regression. This environment allows the individual partially to surrender the role of protecting his own ego stability because he feels safe enough to share the responsibility with the analyst. By so doing, the patient permits the emergence of regressed states of experience, along with the intense reenactment in the transference of early and sometimes developmentally fragmented modes of thinking, feeling, and behaving. The deeper the regression that can be safely allowed by the patient, the richer the experience and the greater its reverberation on the total organization of the self. In cases of severe dissociation, the person is blocked from full selfhood and is unable to feel real or to achieve creative use of himself in the world with a sense of authenticity until those aspects of self-experience that have been dissociated are recontacted and bridged. This process can be seen as a regression to the level of object relating where the dissociation occurred, but in a now reliable environment through which the internal world is being restructured by interpersonal communication in a safe atmosphere.

Looking at regression in this light has advantages and disadvantages. Many analysts working from a relational perspective prefer to abandon the concept completely rather than adapt it to contemporary thinking. I find the construct far too useful to give up, particularly when dealing with clinical issues such as those discussed in the present chapter. In using the concept, however, there is an important issue with regard to one's listening stance that should be emphasized. As I stated earlier, psychoanalysis might reasonably be seen as an opportunity for psychological "rebirth," but it is not literally a redoing of the past. The "child" in the patient is a complex creature; he is never simply the original child come to life again, but always an aspect of an aware and knowing adult. In this respect it is fair to portray the relationship between analyst and "child" as simultaneously real and metaphorical. Regression in one respect is a metaphor, but not *only* a metaphor. It is also a real state of mind of the patient, and it is only by respecting Ferenczi's (1930b, p. 122) brilliant observation on the importance of relating directly to the self-state that is the real child (rather than talking about it to the less-regressed self) that we can achieve direct contact with the dissociated parts of the personality and "persuade" them to engage in what he called "infantile conversations."[7]

The act of "recognition," as Balint uses the term, is in fact the means through which the patient is "persuaded" (in Ferenczi's language) to allow what is inside to interact with the outside. It might be described as the analyst's efforts to create an area of illusion that goes beyond his image of reality that is based on the parental fantasy (or delusion) of who the patient "really" is, and beyond the unformulated "privacy" of the dissociated, "inside" self-experience. Transference, from this perspective, involves an enactment in which these two ele-

---

7. Mitchell (1988, pp. 141–143, 153–155) argues that Balint's concept of benign regression underplays the fact that the "baby" is a metaphor and thus risks infantilizing the patient. My belief is that while Mitchell is accurate in pointing out the danger of infantilization by failing to relate fully to the adult, there is equal (and with many individuals, greater) danger of "adult-erating" the patient if the baby is seen *only* as a metaphor. Certain patients will benefit from treatment only when they are allowed to reconnect with the "baby" as a reality that is lived with the therapist. An analyst who believes only in the baby as metaphor will tend to form a secret (and sometimes traumatizing) collusion with that part of the patient's self that is geared more toward protection than toward growth. My clinical experience, similar to that of Ferenczi, is that speaking directly with the dissociated aspects of self (including, often, the preverbal aspects), is important for most patients but *vital* for some. For the latter, I have observed that if it does not take place, the therapy is simply one more exercise in pseudo-adulthood in the patient's life.

ments are bridged by the patient and analyst as intersubjective communication. The analyst facilitates conditions that allow this process to occur and him (the analyst) to participate in it. He is thus able to experience the patient's inner world directly as a relational act—not to correct it, but to know it with the patient so that the patient can make the most use of it imaginatively.

The analyst's role, however—his ability to bridge therapeutically the nonverbal and verbal domains of experience—is created not simply by his natural empathic giftedness with regressed patients but by his use of the patient's ongoing enacted interchange with him. If he pays attention, this often unsettling feedback will teach him how to be the "primary object" in an ever-evolving way *that allows him to be emphatic as well as empathic.* As Balint states (1968, p. 181), recognition "is only a part, not the whole of the task. . . . The analyst must be also a 'need-understanding' object who, in addition, must be able to communicate his understanding to his patient." The latter, of course, involves the existence of the analyst as a separate and distinct entity, with his own subjective reality. The emphasis here, however, is not, as in classical ego psychology, on the accuracy of the understanding but on the importance of the analyst's ability to communicate his own subjective survival as a real object in order to be available as a usable primary object for the patient. It is the act of communicating his understanding to the patient, not simply the correctness of that understanding, that matters. In fact, it is in part the poverty (i.e., the "wrongness") of the analyst's communications that allows the patient to correct him and thus re-create him as part of the evolving process of self re-creation that constitutes the core of the patient's growth. Through this interpersonal process of recognition, therapeutic regression, confrontation, and understanding, an integrated adult begins to emerge, an adult who can ultimately accept his own impulse life, feel authentic, and behave with concern for himself and others, rather than relating through what Balint (1959) refers to as a "shell." He writes (1968, p. 135) about his own analytic work that when it has reached the area of the basic fault, his patients "sought satisfaction from objects, and experienced in the transference an ability to shed all sorts of character and defensive armors and to feel that life had become simpler and truer." Balint's emphasis was not on whether the shell feels false or "is" false (as with Winnicott's [1960a] concept), but on the fact that because the shell has become rigid in order to manage intolerable degrees of early anxiety, it prevents a full range of experiencing, relating, and creative living. If one views the shell as a rigidified character structure, in the same way Sullivan (1953) conceived of what he called the self-system, then "inside" of the shell are dissociated aspects of self, each in its own way limited in its social development and, in one way or another, a "child" needing self-expression through interpersonal existence. If these aspects of self and the needs, affect states, and ways of relating they embody can be recognized through the medium of the analytic relationship itself, then the shell becomes more and more flexible, while the person relates more and more authentically as reflected by the changing structure of his mental map of external reality.

Simply put, the patient is seen not as someone in need of "insight" that will correct faulty reality but as someone in need of a relationship with another person through which words can be found for that which has no verbal language. As the patient finds words with which to represent his experience, he "knows" himself. The return of memories from a genuine past and an interpretive process that includes historical reconstruction will then find their natural place. As Sullivan (1937, p. 17) has stated, "Information can arise only from explicit or implicit attempts toward communication with other persons. One has information only to the extent that one has tended to communicate one's states of being, one's experience." In the symbolization of one's situation, one's past as well as one's present comes to be understood, and this process is what insight and self-understanding fundamentally mean when working within this perspective. Newly constructed meaning that is created out of here-and-now experience is the goal. A patient's analytic progress is estimated on the basis of his movement toward a point where his states of mind are explored in detail and his deepest levels of experience serve as the reservoir for self-understanding. The interpersonal field of patient and analyst is the external context that shapes the process, but it is the patient's subjective reality, affectively laden with immediacy, that gives "new meaning" its structural resonance within the growth of self. The analyst provides a usable therapeutic matrix for the work to take place; the patient provides the active hunger for a "new beginning"; together they create their own unique intersubjective aesthetic of unconscious communication. If things go reasonably well, the experience of being known "inside out" will become the natural process of human relatedness through which the patient leads his life.

11

INTERPERSONAL PSYCHOANALYSIS AND SELF PSYCHOLOGY

A Clinical Comparison[1] (1989)

"I dance naked in my apartment," she confessed. "Sometimes I even do it with abandon." My air conditioner slightly muffled the last hesitant syllable as she spoke, turning what my patient had just said into an image so unexpectedly comic that I, equally unexpectedly, heard myself responding with a laugh, "You do it with a band? Are *they* naked too?" This was a woman who until that moment seemed to possess no available sense of identity other than that of a grimly pitiful misfit, without humor but ever ready to be laughed at, and ostensibly incapable of experiencing a difference between being seen as zany and being seen as ridiculous.

In fact, she burst into laughter so deep and so "abandoned" that tears rolled "nakedly" down her cheeks. Had I first thought about my response and weighed the risk, I doubt if I would have (or could have)

---

1. This essay was originally published as a chapter in *Self Psychology: Comparisons and Contrasts*, edited by D. W. Detrick and S. P. Detrick (Hillsdale, NJ: The Analytic Press, 1989, pp. 275–291).

chosen that path. Was it a "technical error" that luckily turned out well? A merciful rescue from a serious breach in empathy? Or was I perhaps more empathically attuned than I recognized? Was I allowing my unconscious to guide me to an aspect of her that could emerge only in response to an authentic reaction to it? Or was it just counter-transference, plain and simple? Perhaps I was unconsciously disguis-ing with humor my disclaimed reciprocation of her emerging sexual transference, and if so, might not her "abandoned" laughter have been the laughter of relief at having been spared the technically more "gen-uine" analytic response she anticipated? For an interpersonal analyst the answers to questions like these are not derived a priori from one's theoretical assumptions or metapsychology. They are arrived at with the patient in a mutual exploration of the event as it was enacted on both sides, and it is through this process of exploration that interpreta-tions can find a context in which to be formulated, and the work progresses.

In making an evaluative assessment of an alternative school of ana-lytic thought, it is always heartening to discover some support from within that school itself. I can imagine no more eloquent or candid a summation of the main theme of my critique than the following state-ment made, not by an interpersonalist, but by Schwaber (1983), and it is with her observation that I would like to begin. Kohut, she asserts, has in his later work

> betrayed the position that it is the correctness of the theory rather
> than how we use our theory which was of the foremost impor-
> tance. In assigning this status to theory and arguing for a more
> "correct" view of man, by implication, he placed the analyst in the
> position of arbiter of which is the more "correct" and which the
> more "distorted" view [p. 381].

It is no secret that the primary reader to whom Kohut (1971, 1977) addressed his most powerful and persuasive arguments is the "classi-cal" psychoanalyst—the analyst who systematically interprets into the patient's pathological narcissism and unmasks its disregard of reality and of others. Amazingly little effort has been expended by self psy-chologists in surveying the broader landscape of analytic thought to discover and acknowledge those who advanced similar ideas before Kohut, so as to distinguish those areas where Kohut's formulations are indeed original from those in which his departure from Freudian metapsychology echoes and often draws upon similar revisions that preceded them. In this regard, interpersonal psychoanalysis (and object relational theories) have tended to be ignored by Kohut rather than credited and challenged. In his seminal work on narcissism, Kohut (1966) in one broad stroke of the brush rejects the assumption that narcissism is basically pathological, postulates a developmental line of mature narcissism, and exiles object relational theories (and, by implication, interpersonal theory) to "social psychology." He here establishes the importance of the *function* of the object in contrast to its representational qualities, paving the way for his 1971 monograph, in which he makes the sharp distinction between a selfobject and a real object. In the invention of the idea of a selfobject, Kohut hit upon a brilliant strategy that, as Ghent (1989) puts it, "played down the focus on the real object, . . . retained the focus of psychoanalysis as a one-person psychology[2] [and] avoided the taint of in any way being associated with interpersonal theory " (p. 190). In contrasting interpersonal psychoanalysis with self psychology, it must therefore be kept in mind that for Kohut, the "selfobject" is also a "strategic" object.

The Interpersonal Listening Stance

In a 1986 dialogue between Arnold Goldberg and me, a pair of contrasting statements were made that I hope might place the basic distinction between the interpersonal and self-psychological positions into high relief and set the stage for its exploration in greater detail:

> An interpersonal position takes as axiomatic that growth of self occurs through dyadic interchange rather than through what the patient receives in some "correct" way. . . . For an interpersonal analyst, the empathic mode of observing is *not* designed to discourage an observational stance in the patient nor are confrontations systematically avoided as "failures" in empathy. . . . For characterological growth to occur the patient must be able to see himself through the eyes of the analyst as an ongoing aspect of feeling himself validated and understood in the terms he sees himself [Bromberg, 1986a, p. 382].

Self psychology struggles hard not to be an interpersonal psychology not only because it wishes to avoid the social psychological connotations of the phrase but also because it wishes to minimize

---

2. Gill (1984) presents a thoughtful and lucid argument for taking the two-person view seriously in the context of the classical view of analytic technique and for reconceptualizing the nature of the interpersonal interaction between patient and analyst.

the input of the analyst into the mix. . . . It is not minimized merely to keep the field pure so much as to allow a thwarted development to unfold. Since self psychology is so pre-eminently a developmental psychology, it is based on the idea of a developmental program (one that may be innate or pre-wired if you wish) that will reconstitute itself under certain conditions [Goldberg, 1986, p. 387].

Different analysts not only conceptualize differently, they also listen differently. Although an analyst's theoretical allegiance certainly plays some role in the latter, I believe there is much more to it than that. Once we have settled into our "normal" stance with someone, how do we frame what we hear as going on? Is it going on in the patient's life? In the patient's psyche? Is it going on between ourselves and the patient? Do we see these kinds of distinctions as clinically relevant? If so, do we see them as blending, as shifting from one to the other, or as one always framing the rest? If the latter, which one frames our most basic listening stance? Finally, how does the way we listen to process versus content inform what we personally believe is a "legitimate" analytic situation and what we think is therapeutic?

In an article on the journals of Princess Marie Bonaparte (Goleman, 1985), a number of excerpts were quoted in which Bonaparte records comments allegedly made by Freud, among which is the following parable:

A European comes to Japan and sends for a Japanese tree expert to have a garden planted. On the first day, the gardener sat on a bench all day long and did not do anything. On the second day, it was the same. And the same on the third, fourth, and fifth day—all week long. Then the European asked: When are you going to get started on the garden? "When I have taken in the scenery." It is the same with analysis. One first has to take in the scenery of every new psyche [p. C2].

Freud (1912) described the appropriate stance for the analyst "taking in the scenery" as one that

consists simply in not directing one's notice to anything in particular and in maintaining the same "evenly suspended attention" . . . in the face of all one hears. . . . Or to put it purely in terms of technique: "He should simply listen and not bother about whether he is keeping anything in mind" [pp. 111–112].

Translated into our everyday work with patients, Freud's definition remains a one-word guideline, as valid now as it was then, that directs everything we do. The word is *listen*. But what do we listen to? What constitutes the "scenery" that we are taking in? Historically, the conception of the analyst listening to the patient as if the analyst were observing scenery has made two important shifts, the second of which is still in progress. The first, which was more or less initiated in 1923 with Freud's publication of *The Ego and the Id*, became the foundation of analytic technique based on Freud's structural theory—the shift from observing a descriptive unconscious (that is, static "scenery") to observing a dynamic unconscious whereby the analyst is listening to an implied (but one-sided) interaction between the patient's psyche and the analyst's presence as a fantasy object of projected imagery.

The second shift ultimately led to the development of different camps within the Freudian model and to the revision or abandonment of the classical model by others. Probably the single most powerful set of ideas that has shaped this frame of reference has been the work of the interpersonal school of psychoanalysis and the influence of Harry Stack Sullivan (1940, 1953, 1954) in particular. The model is of a field of observation framed by the *real* (not implied) interaction between the two participants. It rejects the idea of an analytic situation divided into two components; "how to listen" and "what to do" (that is, "technique"). *The analyst's participation is seen as an ongoing element in the field of observation and inseparable from it.* What the analyst must be trying to listen to in his basic stance includes the immediate and residual effects of his own participation.

From this perspective, transference is not simply something that *has* happened, which the analyst then interprets to the patient. In its most vivid form, transference is what is *still* being enacted *while* the analyst concentrates on making the transference interpretation. The interpersonal analyst's frame of reference is optimally structured to hear these here-and-now moments and make clinically appropriate use of them. In this regard, technique is something the analytic candidate learns not from a supervisor, but from his patient. Countertransference, therefore, is, in its broadest meaning, "the natural, role-responsive, necessary *complement or counterpart* to the transference of the patient, or to his style of relatedness" (Epstein and Feiner, 1979, p. 12). The awareness and use of it requires that the analyst disembed himself from the immediate context that is framing his experience and broaden his perspective to one that now includes observing his own participation as well as the patient's. It requires, in other words, a shift from the stance of full participation to that of participant observer. By full participation I mean whatever was commanding focal involvement; it could be an involvement with one's own interpretive efforts, or with the details of the patient's life, or with one's empathic related-ness—or it could even be an involvement in exploring some aspect of the analytic interaction. Regardless of which it may be, it is the shift to observing oneself as part of the immediate field that is the critical ele-ment and is what permits participant observation its exquisitely refined use of the here-and-now as the flexible frame of reference for a multilevel listening stance. Its therapeutic benefit is fundamentally a characterological enrichment of *perceptiveness*, which then enhances self-understanding, self-acceptance, and human relatedness.

Let me give an example of what I mean by drawing upon a paper from the classical analytic literature, entitled *"China" as a Symbol for Vagina* (Gray, 1985). This is a brief report of an analytic turning point that was achieved through understanding a specific dream in the treat-ment of a female scientist who was unable to achieve vaginal orgasm in her marriage, and who was unable to publish her research under her own name but permitted her immediate supervisor to present it as if it were his own. The dream was as follows: "I was preparing to give a dinner party with my husband. I was setting the table and I went to the cabinet where my party dishes are stored. I found they were all broken. It was frightening. I woke up and I found my period had begun. I was bleeding profusely" (p. 620).

The author traces the patient's associations to the dream and states that

> the dream confirmed to the patient her continuing, unconsciously held belief that her female organ, which was represented by the highly condensed symbol of her wedding china, had been perma-nently damaged. . . . Through the analysis of the dream, we discov-ered a path that led to the source of the patient's neurosis. . . . Eventually, over the long course of the psychoanalysis, we were able to reconstruct an early experience which formed a basis for the patient's symptoms. . . . She became the docile, compliant, helpful, and definitely asexual little girl who was content to wait for per-mission to be a woman at some later time. This was symbolized by her hope of receiving some family china as a gift. The feminine oedipal nature of the core neurotic conflict was unequivocally com-municated in the symbolic equation, china = vagina [pp. 622–623].

What is of interest here is the nature of the listening stance and to what in the work the author attributes the cure, not whether I agree with the metapsychology. Gray's explanation for the cure is that the analytic work led to a reconstruction of the early experience that resulted in the neurosis, and that it was *the integration of the reconstruc-*

tion that led to the conflict resolution and to analytic growth. The here-and-now relational process, the act of psychoanalysis itself, is seen by the author as simply the medium through which the "genuine" analytic material—the symbolic equation, "china = vagina"—could emerge from the buried past and is thus framed by and listened to for its derivative content.

My point, also made by Levenson (1983), is "not to say that the traditionalists are not interested in the present or that interpersonalists are not interested in the past; but for the former, the past is impacted on the present. For the latter, the past and present lie on an experiential continuum" (p. 68). What is going on must coexist with what has gone on. For an interpersonal analyst, the first must frame the field of perception for the second to make its contribution.

As an interpersonal analyst, I am no more able to listen to a session the way Gray does than I was able to read her paper from that frame of reference. It is simply built into my listening stance to widen my perspective to include the ongoing participation of the analyst, regardless of what the analyst may be doing at the moment (including writing a paper). So as I read Gray's paper, my thoughts went as follows:

Observing customary procedure, Gray would have undoubtedly obtained permission from the patient to publish this material and, I would guess, would have waited until the analysis was terminated successfully. If so, that would make the finding, "china = vagina," itself a piece of "successful research" that the patient and analyst did together, and was then published under the analyst's name. The patient, however, would no longer be the same "docile, compliant, helpful little girl" who formerly granted the permission (to her supervisor) out of neurosis, but someone who could now grant it maturely, with free choice. My reading of the paper was thus framed by my observation of what seemed to me a remarkable posttermination scenario between patient and analyst that embodies the same issues that brought the patient into treatment in the first place. What particularly caught my attention was that the termination occurred without being commented upon by the author even if only as evidence supporting a successful analytic outcome, citing a significant difference in the way the patient had dealt with the analyst's request as compared to the way she formerly dealt with her supervisor. Why, as an interpersonalist, would I find this omission so noteworthy? Because it is only through the act of living that a person comes to be understood. In a psychoanalysis, patients do not reveal their unconscious fantasies to the analyst. They *are* their unconscious fantasies and live them with the analyst through the *act* of psychoanalysis. A symbolic equation such as "china = vagina" is not located in the patient's psyche as "content." It is lived by the patient as process within the space framed by the interrelated acts of two people.

The interpersonal listening stance, however, no more reveals the ultimate truth than does any other. Analysts of all persuasions have historically embraced schools of thought that turn useful formulations into "truths" that then limit their own natural evolution. The most obvious case in point, the classical Freudian school, has found itself entrenched in this position largely because of its militant insistence on enshrining *psychic reality* as the one source of clinical truth. With regard to interpersonal psychoanalysis, Sullivan's opposite emphasis on *observable reality* is itself vulnerable to the same fault, but nevertheless has remained remarkably flexible because the intrapsychic has always been an intrinsic aspect of the interpersonal perspective. But in the midst of the debate between the proponents of reality as framed by the patient's intrapsychic world and those who frame it by the interpersonal field, a new perspective has emerged out of the former tradition, with its own reality that defines the analytic situation: the *empathic/introspective* listening stance of self psychology. Since the defining element of this stance is its dedication to full empathic responsiveness to the patient's subjective experience, I think it appropriate to turn now to the issue of empathy and empathic communication.

The Interpersonal Nature of Empathic Communication

It seems to me that the most critical clinical difference between the interpersonal and the self-psychological models is in an attitude toward the process of analytic treatment that has always distinguished the interpersonal tradition from all others. I refer to its fundamental commitment to the process being shaped by who the specific individual is as a human being rather than by its theoretical assumptions, thus making it an approach rather than a technique.[3] It would therefore be antithetical to interpersonal analysis to consider any analytic stance—including the empathic/introspective stance of self psychology—as facilitative to all patients. We see human personality development and change as located within a relational context and not as

---

3. See chapter 7 for an elaboration of the "approach" versus "technique" distinction with specific regard to the treatment of narcissistic disorders.

Goldberg (1986) put it, "prewired." To an interpersonalist, the latter conception misses the crucial point of what is analytic—the need to find out who the patient is rather than believing you know in advance what he needs, be it conflict resolution or reconnection to his selfobjects. The interpersonal approach by its very nature engages in an ongoing struggle, or dialectic, with the very issue that self psychology sees as resolved by the "correct" analytic stance. We see this ongoing struggle as the heart of the work itself and as the act that embodies the very growth that we are hoping to bring about in the patient.

Barrett-Lennard (1981), in an empirical study on the interactive nature of empathy, points out that the effects of the therapist's empathy depend on characteristics of both patient and therapist and may be a function of unique differences in perceptual, cognitive, and even personality styles. For different patients, what feels empathic involves components that might be predominantly cognitive or affective, or sharing, or supportive, and so on. Kohut's (1971) original findings were derived from a relatively homogeneous patient sample possessing a certain personality configuration (which he called narcissistic personality disorder) that was highly responsive to the stance he described. But then to generalize the "truth" of this stance to all patients and build a developmental theory upon it is, in my view, precisely the same error made by the classical analysts. It casts the process of therapeutic relatedness into a mold that is mechanistic and causal. "In this view, intentions to direct the experience in advance, that is in prescribed roles—if unexplored—however well intentioned, whether to correct, inform, repair, or restore, will only lead to obfuscation and falsification of the analytic process" (Held-Weiss, 1984, p. 355).

Interpersonal psychoanalysis is based on a field theory paradigm. Each person is shaping the responsiveness of the other, including empathic responsiveness. There is no suggestion of an empathic therapist operating on a patient in need of empathy. Rather, the model is of an open system, changing, developing, enriching itself through a process of interpenetration. Barrett-Lennard (1981, p. 84) reports something very close to this in his empirical description of the cyclical stages of empathy. The patient's perception of the therapist's empathy is followed not only by the patient's further capacity for self-expression (Kohut's, 1977, "self as independent center of initiative"), but by an interpersonal process in which this increased self-expression includes feedback by the patient that signals the extent to which he feels understood. This, in turn, has an impact on the therapist's affective state, mood, and frame of reference, which then shape the quality of his further efforts (and limitations) in empathically communicating with his patient. Thus, depending on the individual empathic style of a given patient, the manner in which empathy is communicated by a given therapist will be differentially effective.

For example, a patient reports a dream in which she has asked me to serve her breakfast and I willingly agree. She expected "natural-grain" health food but got something that was too sweet, as if it were sugar coated. The dream followed a session in which I had acknowledged that her difficulty in feeling comfortable about revealing her current state of panic and loneliness was increased by my having responded to a previous panic without realizing the shame she was experiencing in showing those feelings to me. She left that session saying that she felt better in one way by my having said this but also felt "weird" in another way. Her associations to the dream led to an image of me in the previous session as not wanting to see how angry she was at me underneath her panic and of my trying, as her father had, to cajole her away from her anger by giving her a "sugar-coated" gift. Further exploration of our respective experiences during the previous hour (as well as in the current moment), confirmed some degree of accuracy to her perception of me, which I acknowledged. This allowed her to become vividly aware of how attached she was to her unconscious fear that I, like her father, could not tolerate seeing myself as I really was and that if she had revealed her perception that my "empathic response" was partly self-serving, it would have destroyed the security of mutual protectiveness upon which her core identity had long been based.

Sullivan's manner of communicating his empathic understanding was built into the process of analytic inquiry. It was not contained in a prescribed mode of interacting designed to convey empathic contact. The interpersonal method of participant observation is, consequently, more intrinsically flexible in adapting to the individual empathic styles of a broad range of patients than is *any* one-person psychology, including self psychology. Empathy is inherently interpersonal. In psychoanalysis, its cyclical nature is built into participation observation. As part of the pursuit of an analytic inquiry, the analyst is monitoring (resonating with) the patient's experience of feeling understood or not feeling understood, resulting in a progressive development of intersubjective attunement that is the heart of the growth process referred to by Sullivan (1940, 1953) as *consensual validation*.[4] "Do I understand

---

4. For a more detailed exploration of Sullivan's concept of "consensual validation" as it relates to empathy and intersubjective attunement, see Bromberg (1980).

correctly that . . . ?" "How do you mean that?" "Am I to understand that . . . ?" Analytic inquiry is not simply a means of obtaining factual information; it is not data collection in the obvious meaning of the phrase. It is an interpenetrating involvement with both the there-and-then (the obscure details of the patient's narrative and history) and the here-and-now (the analysis of the analysis). Is inquiry into unreported details, for example, evoking shame and making the patient feel empathically abandoned? Does he experience the analyst's need for more—the analyst's need to question—as equivalent to being robbed of his own experience and meaning? Is he becoming increasingly anxious, ashamed, or depressed? These kinds of questions are continually alive in the interpersonal multilevel listening stance. There is no need for a concept such as optimal failure in empathy because the analytic process is an ongoing dialectic between empathy and anxiety (see chapter 4) and between responsiveness to the patient's state of mind and the elucidation of external events. It is this dialectic that I find most lacking in the clinical technique of self psychology and that I hold to be its most serious limitation. Consider, in this light, a statement made by Ricoeur (1986) in a paper otherwise highly supportive of Kohut's major contribution to psychoanalysis:

> For a mature narcissism to emerge from an archaic one, the self has to discover, at the price of inevitable blows, that it is not the omnipotent self that is reactivated by mirroring transference. . . . We have already seen that the self always needs the support of a selfobject that helps it to maintain its cohesion. . . . What needs to be added now is that a certain degree of disillusionment about oneself, *of deception as regards others*, needs to be integrated into the self's education [pp. 446–447, italics added].

Exploration and Interpretation

To add the dimension pointed out by Ricoeur, self psychology faces a barrier that is quite substantial, though not necessarily insurmountable. The trouble, as I see it, is that the empathic/introspective stance is in its own but opposite way as unnecessarily one dimensional as that of the school of thought it departed from—the classical inferential stance that positions the analyst *outside* of the patient's subjective world. The self-psychological stance focuses in the opposing direction, only on what the patient needs from the analyst, or, how it feels to be the subject *rather* than the target of the patient's needs and demands.

From an interpersonal standpoint, a self psychologist is thus required to function as if he were an interpersonal analyst who is deaf in one ear. This same limitation is I think what Modell (1986) had in mind when he said that "there is a dark side of empathy which Kohut does not adequately acknowledge. The analyst who is constantly empathic may seriously inhibit the patient's own creative powers" (p. 375). The analyst is locked into the closed-ended position of attributing his "failures in empathy" to a presumed (but unstated) deficiency in himself, as though he himself should require nothing from the patient other than what he gets, in order to use his own capacity for empathy, and should be able continually to meet the patient's need for empathic responsiveness regardless of what the patient himself brings to the relationship. The analyst is implying (without saying it) that unlike the patient, he, for better or for worse, in effect exists as a real person in a real relationship *now*, while the patient can only hope to exist *later* through the analyst's humanly imperfect ability to relate empathically to him.

So the most an analyst is allowed to reveal of himself from the empathic/introspective stance is a kind of quasi-apology for having failed to be sufficiently empathic, and a rectification of the "imperfection" by admitting it (even if the admission is only by implication). The patient thus has little opportunity to deal with his feelings about his analyst's empathic stance as ongoing analytic material without breaching the analyst's own interpretive context of meaning. Ornstein and Ornstein (1980), for example, report a clinical vignette in which the turning point hinged on the fact that the analyst

> finally said [to the patient] on further reflection that his earlier attempt . . . rightly created the feeling in her that he was by-passing or minimizing the patient's current reactions. . . . It was important to her—the analyst was now able to say—that this time someone should understand *exactly how she felt*; only then could her feelings be validated and made acceptable and thereby real for her [p. 209, italics added].

Is not the process through which the analyst "failed" in his earlier attempt richer than simply the fact of the failure itself? Did the failure have nothing to do with the patient, as she existed, that is worth considering as part of the interpretive context? Reflect on what Friedman (1986) has to say about this issue:

> If the analyst could see only maturational inevitabilities, he would lose the ordinary social sense of what the patient is *doing* to him. If

a patient is mean, envious, degrading, competitive, angry, or seductive, the analyst must be able to feel the act as mean, envious, competing, degrading, etc., in order to *recognize* it as such, before he considers its use to the patient's equilibrium. How is one to perceive the particulars of interaction if not by the ordinary, only semi-empathic sensitivities of everyday life? We may approach a holistic view in composing a eulogy. But in the live moment, we think of people as attracted and attracting, lustful, fantasying, envious, appeasing, flattering, combative, scornful, dangerous, evil, as well as admiring, admirable, useful, and using, etc. These ordinary perceptions and attributions must be felt by an analyst as well [p. 346].

What Friedman is saying is not simply that a self psychologist overlooks who the patient is as a real person. He is saying that the stance interferes with the patient's ability to exist fully as he is, with the analyst. Self psychology remains embedded in a mode of intervention that it inherited from classical analysis, the unalloyed process of interpretation. The difference is that what is interpreted is focused on an explication of the selfobject transferences rather than on an explication of the patient's unconscious motives. In both cases, however, some aspect of the patient must be sacrificed to the interpretive context of meaning and is lost to the living act of the analytic process itself. In the Ornstein and Ornstein (1980) clinical vignette, for example, the actual transaction between patient and analyst that led to the analyst's earlier "failure" is interpreted away, and along with it, the potential for empathically shared use of the analyst's "ordinary social sense" of what the patient is doing to him.

An interpersonal analyst's mode of listening allows him optimally to widen his perspective so that both his own countertransferential response and his empathic sensitivity to the patient's state of mind are incorporated by him as inseparable elements in a single relational matrix. As a participant observer, he is free to use himself within this field to explore with the patient their respective experiences of whatever transaction has occurred (or is occurring) rather than having to make a choice as to the "correct" stance from which to interpret it. It is not that an interpretation might not be offered. It is simply that there is no great investment in its power per se or a conception of it as being mutative in and of itself. An interpretation is not seen as containing a "reality" that is more accurate than the patient's own, but rather as a formulation coming from the analyst's experience of the patient, to which the patient will have some response that becomes, in turn, more grist for the mill. The content of an interpretation is a moment in an analytic process; the analytic process is not the raw material for a "correct" formulation of content or the cause of an "optimal failure in empathy."

The interpersonal stance is an empathically implemented, two-sided look at both participant's roles; it inherently allows the analyst to make statements about what he sees in the patient that the classically derived, interpretive stance of self psychology cannot accommodate. The focus is not on what a person lacks internally (a developmental deficit), but on what he does with that which he already has and on what sorts of fixed, concrete patterns constitute his world of interpersonal mental representation. Past parental failures in empathy are indeed explicated where relevant, but always in the context of elucidating how the patient's resulting character development has led to ways of being in which he manages to evoke those same types of responses in others (including the analyst), and how he has become "geared" to the familiarity and security of these fixed patterns of relatedness even though he desperately wants to be released from them.

For the patient to be able to look into his own nature through the analytic process, the context must permit him not to feel continually blamed for being who he is. It is not easy, however, to maintain a "nonadversarial approach to character analysis" (Schafer, 1983, p. 152) from an interpretive analytic posture; and interpretations made *outside* of the nonadversarial context are always experienced by the patient as parental acts of attribution and fail in their purpose. Participant observation inherently provides the needed context. It allows the patient to look at himself and at what he is doing to the analyst without having to surrender his own perspective. The context of *exploration*, unlike that of interpretation, is not trying to get the patient to "own" the analyst's construction of reality. It is not an attempt to get the patient to accept the analyst's image of him, but rather to let him know how the analyst is experiencing him. Because the patient's own "truth" is less at risk in this approach he is able to live more fully who he is in the analysis and allow most aspects of himself to find their place in a broader configuration of interpersonal reality that was shaped by the perspectives of both parties.

Nonetheless, it is undeniable that self psychology has made an outstanding contribution to clinical psychoanalysis. Its listening stance, focused on the patient's subjective experience and state of mind as the primary data base, came out of Kohut's work with patients he called narcissistic disorders and out of his recognition that something in his stance allowed these people to grow beyond where they were stuck developmentally. Showing them what they were "really like" only made them worse. The accuracy of these observations and the power with which he formulated them has left an indelible impression on analysts of all theoretical persuasions. So whether or not an analyst adopts the self psychology paradigm as his "truth," there must be a central dimension of this same element in whatever model informs his clinical work, including, of course, the interpersonal.

Levenson (1983), speaking from an interpersonal position, accurately asserts that "the cardinal question for the patient may not be "what does it mean?" but "what's going on around here?" (p. ix). With certain patients, however, this stance can prove to be as unadaptive as any other if simply applied as a technique. Its ongoing effects must be scrutinized by the analyst in order to monitor how any particular patient is experiencing it and is able or unable to make use of it. In an earlier disscusion of interpersonal psychoanalysis as an approach rather than a technique (chapter 7), I presented the view that there are patients who need to *not* see "what's going on around here" for a long initial period of an analysis. They need the analyst to adapt his own interpersonal style to their inability to work in the here-and-now of the transference without their feeling lost, artificial, shame-ridden, or abandoned empathically. Consider, for example, the following situation:

A patient has a dream in which the analyst, undisguised, and with an earnest manner and a genuinely warm smile, throws into the patient's lap a plastic bag containing a small, two-headed monster. The patient is terrified because she knows she is expected to open the bag, but she can't tell the analyst how frightened she is because the monster will just get larger. As an interpersonal analyst I would (if I were aware enough at the moment) hear the dream at several levels: first, as an expression of the current state of the patient's internal object world; second, as a statement of her more characterological level of self-development. Third, I would hear the dream in its expressive function as a channel of communication to the analyst about something he is doing with the patient that the patient is not benefiting from (to say the least), but that the analyst believes is good for the patient. The patient cannot consciously formulate any of this, much less communicate it, without the likelihood (probably accurate) that telling the analyst will just make the problem grow larger. How is it possible for the analyst to go anywhere near the dream in his usual style without enacting it?

I do not know what I would do. I would probably just have to see how it felt *not* to do what I might typically do and see what comes out of that. I hear one level of the dream as a message that the approach of "exploring what is happening between us" is being experienced by the patient as empathically unadaptive and is gradually changing an otherwise positive (though perhaps overly intense) analytic stance into a monstrosity, without the analyst's being aware of it. At the level of technique, I would try to use the dream as if it were supervision and would try to modify my natural stance in some way that would not feel like a sudden retaliative withdrawal, but without trying to communicate what I think is going on or asking the patient what *she* thinks is going on. The likelihood, however, is that none of this would "work." I would probably end up mystifying the patient, and consequently another dream might be produced in which I appear equally naive but in which further information is communicated as to what I was failing to perceive the last time. I suspect that gradually, being led by the patient, things would become clearer for both of us, and the analytic work would move along. As Witenberg (1987) has aptly put it, "A theory which is devised to explain clinical phenomena should also be a source of questions for clinical experience. Hopefully, relevant questions will eventually give us relevant answers" (p. 194).

PART III

DISSOCIATION AND CLINICAL PROCESS

12

SHADOW AND SUBSTANCE

A Relational Perspective on Clinical Process[1] (1993)

B rigid, a young female servant to an archbishop—a girl loving and lovable, unworldly and selfless—is tormented by a secret: She receives visitations, advice, and instructions from her name-saint, Saint Brigid, with whom she converses regularly. The archbishop, her employer, is a cynical and domineering man, certain of his wisdom. Except for the uncharacteristic tenderness he feels for his servant, he is privately tormented by his own secret: his inner isolation and absence of authentic spiritual or human feeling despite his uncompromising adherence to accurate interpretation of church doctrine. His genuine wish to help the young girl is framed by his conviction that her experience is simply a symptom of the illness from which she must be rescued, because true religious experience cannot take such a personal form. In the course of his efforts to help her, he finds

1. An earlier draft of this essay, sponsored by Division 39 of the American Psychological Association, was presented as an invited address at the "Centennial Conference of the American Psychological Association" in Washington, DC, in August 1992, and published in *Psychoanalytic Psychology*, 1993, 10:147–168. The author acknowledges with gratitude the invaluable personal support and intellectual input of Dr. Leopold Caligor during all phases of the evolution of the manuscript.

that Brigid's resistance slowly leads him to encounter painful aspects of his own nature; Brigid cannot claim her perceptions of him as her own, however, and can confront the canon only as a conduit for the words of Saint Brigid, who commands her to speak them. He tries to dismiss her perceptions as further evidence of her illness, but (to parody Samuel Johnson) a diagnosis of psychotic transference is the last refuge of a beleaguered analyst. His insistence on the priority of his own truth only makes her more and more desperate to reach him personally. Ultimately, but too late to save her from death, he is able to allow her humanness to directly reach his, where the absolute rightness of his own truth gives way to a shared reality and to his ability to experience the world through her eyes as well as his own.

What I have just summarized is, of course, one of the masterpieces of Irish playwriting, *Shadow and Substance*, a work written by Paul Vincent Carroll (1937) and first performed at the Abbey Theatre in Dublin. The play has meanings at many levels, including historical, sociopolitical, religious, and spiritual. But what is most relevant to my topic is the level of meaning that overrides differences in sex, social class, and role definition. It is a nakedly honest portrayal of the painful struggle in simply being human; a nonjudgmental recognition of the inevitable and lifelong collision of selfhood and empathy. It is an encounter, both glorious and ignoble, between the self-preservative power of one's subjective truth and the self-transformational power of human relatedness, between personal reality and interpersonally negotiated reality, between self-aggrandizement and love.

My choice of title for this article was influenced not only by the play, however. I also wished to convey in a single phrase my view of the unconscious as a reality that is "inside," "outside," and simultaneously both—a phenomenon that an analyst, at certain moments, subjectively senses as a shadowy presence peeking out from the unsymbolized and unshared reaches behind his patient's eyes; that he at other moments objectively observes in his patient's associations, dreams, parapraxes, and transferential behavior; and that he, most powerfully of all, experiences as a manifest presence living in the shared world of intersubjective reality jointly constructed by himself and his patient as they coexist in the analytic process.

As psychoanalysts, we hope to succeed where the archbishop could not; we hope that the process of psychoanalysis and our use of interpretation will not become an act of indoctrination (either failed or successful) and that a consensually constructed reality will begin to develop before the patient "terminates." But on what do we base this hope? What do we believe is the relation between the human personality in its capability for change and the unique role of the psychoanalyst that allows us to entertain such a hope even though other efforts have failed? In the face of the strong adaptational value that resides in the stability of an individual's sense of personal identity, why should anyone agree to go through an internally disorganizing process that systematically tampers with stability? In other words, it might reasonably be asked why self-equilibrium is not always preserved at the expense of growth. Why should anyone ever change? The answer is self-evident but thought provoking: The human personality possesses the extraordinary capacity to negotiate stability and change simultaneously, and it will do so under the right relational conditions. This attribute is, in fact, the basis of what we rely on to make clinical psychoanalysis possible. How we understand this remarkable capability of the mind, how we conceptualize it structurally and psychodynamically, and what we see as its clinical implications (i.e., the optimal conditions for it to occur) are the questions that shape psychoanalytic theory and practice.

Much has happened to the psychoanalytic conception of the human mind and to its notions of consciousness and unconsciousness since Freud, in his case history of Katharina (Breuer and Freud, 1893–1895), stated that he "should like at this point to express a doubt as to whether a splitting of consciousness due to ignorance is really different from one due to conscious rejection" (p. 134). Since then, there have been quite a few "changes of mind," including, several times, Freud's own. I was trained in interpersonal psychoanalysis and paid particular attention to the thinking of Harry Stack Sullivan (1953, 1954), whose pragmatic conception of the mind emphasized dissociation, observable reality, and the field of interpersonally communicable data. Although there have been scattered appearances throughout history, the term *relational* as applied to psychoanalysis entered our vernacular approximately 10 years ago through the contemporary classic, written by Greenberg and Mitchell (1983), that distinguished between a *drive/structure* and a *relational/structure* model of psychoanalysis, further elaborated by Mitchell (1988) into a *drive/conflict* and *relational/conflict* distinction. Partly as a result of the unprecedented and continuing dialogue among the major postclassical schools of analytic thought— Freudian, interpersonal, self-psychological, and British object-relational—the boundary between what psychoanalysts consider psychic reality and what they conceptualize as observable reality has become increasingly permeable. "Within the mind" and "between people" no longer delimits two discrete and unambiguous domains of experience (intrapsychic and interpersonal). What is meant by fantasy and reality, and by unconscious and conscious, has thus become more interesting and complex.

Freud's view of consciousness and unconsciousness is embedded in the idea of a self or psyche that is inherently unitary and structured archeologically in terms of a particular layer's degree of access to awareness; thus, we find his topographical conceptions of unconscious, preconscious, and conscious. I do not suggest that these distinctions have been lost or that they are not worthwhile. My argument, rather, is that we are moving increasingly in the direction of a model in which our view of what is conscious and what is unconscious is informed by a conception of the mind as a nonlinear, dialectical process of meaning construction, organized by the equilibrium between stability and growth of one's self-representation—the balance between the need to preserve self-meaning (the ongoing experience of safely "feeling like oneself") and the need to construct new meaning in the service of relational adaptation that Sullivan (1940) called *interpersonal adjustive success* (p. 97).

Further, I suggest that the way analysts conceptualize reality in terms of past and present is also changing. The clinical focus is not as much on discovering past roots of current problems—as though past experience and present experience are discretely stratified in the memory bank of a unitary "self"—as on exploring the way in which the self-states comprising a patient's personal identity are linked to each other, to the external world, and to the past, present, and future. In a seminal article on the experience of temporality, Loewald (1972) wrote:

> When we consider time as psychoanalysts, the concept of time as duration, objectively observed or subjectively experienced, loses much of its relevance. We encounter time in psychic life primarily as a linking activity in which what we call past, present, and future are woven into a nexus. . . . The individual not only *has* a history which an observer may unravel and describe, but he *is* history and makes his history by virtue of his memorial activity in which past-present-future are created as mutually interacting modes of time [pp. 407–409].

From this perspective, the "contents" of a patient's mind and what constitutes memory and time at any given moment are psychoanalytically contained not in an image of memory retrieval from an archive of historically organized information, but by what Bach (1985) called the ability to maintain "state constancy" (p. 187)—that is, in the interplay between an individual's capacity to access and cognitively process dissociated perceptual experience (past and present) and his felt vulnerability to potential traumatic disruption of his ongoing feeling of self-hood. One consequence of this shift in thinking is that postclassical analytic theory is now giving broadly based reconsideration to the phenomena of trauma and dissociation and their effect on both normal personality development and the process of clinical psychoanalysis.

In what is probably the most famous literary soliloquy ever written (Shakespeare, 1599–1601), Hamlet ruminates on the pain that accompanies being alive and wonders whether death will end what he calls "the thousand natural shocks that flesh is heir to" (pp. 1066–1067). Shakespeare's choice of the word *shock* has always intrigued me. Why *shock*? Why is that word so particularly evocative? Why is it able to unmask the essential quality of human vulnerability that allows us to know what Hamlet feels at that moment—to know in our own souls the enemy that we are all helpless to oppose and possibly unable to escape even through death? Reik (1936), in *Surprise and the Psycho-Analyst*, a work considerably ahead of its time, stated:

> *The root problem of neurosis is not fear, but shock.* In my opinion, *that problem remains insoluble until fear is brought into connection with the emotion of shock.* . . . Shock is the prime emotion, the first thing that the little living creature feels. . . . I hold that shock is in general a characteristic of a traumatic situation, fear one of danger. *Shock is the emotional reaction to something that bursts in upon us, fear the reaction to something that comes with a menace.* Fear is itself a signal preceding shock, it anticipates the emotion of shock in miniature, and so protects us from it and from its profound and harmful effects [pp. 267–268].

Recall that Freud (1926) made the distinction between a danger situation and a situation that actually becomes traumatic, stating that the essence and meaning of the traumatic situation *consists in the subject's estimation of his own strength compared to the magnitude of the danger and in his admission of helplessness in the face of it"* (p. 166, italics added). He emphasized that it is not the source of the danger that is primary, but whether the affect is subjectively experienced as overwhelming. The person is psychologically over-stimulated such that he loses the capability of perceiving, and instead experiences a generalized flooding of affect—what Reik (1936) called *shock*. This idea may be our greatest unacknowledged debt to Freud—that what a person perceives in front of his eyes (so-called objective reality) is a construction that is partially shaped by his state of mind, not simply vice versa. "Psychic" reality, the world "behind" one's eyes, is thus in a continuing dialectic with perception, and our success as clinicians with any patient depends on our ability to work at the boundary between unconscious fantasy and perception (most particularly, perception of the analytic relationship itself). That is, what we call psychic reality and observable reality—past experience and "here-and-now" experience, unconsciousness and consciousness—are subjective constructions that comprise the complex relational matrix that organizes human experience. Each, in its own way, is both "shadow" and "substance."

Dissociation, Enactment, and Clinical Process

It has long been recognized that every patient enters psychoanalysis with the same "illogical" wish—*the wish to stay the same while changing*. Traditionally, this recognition has been handled simply by the classical definition of "resistance"—the clinical phenomenon that "encompasses all of a patient's defensive efforts to avoid self-knowledge" (Moore and Fine, 1990, p. 168). Most postclassical theory, however, tends to subsume the "defense" component more and more into the broader context of a complex reality, a necessary illusion that configures and sustains the analytic situation as a playground for self-development that Winnicott (1967) called the use of "potential space." Within this context, a primary task of the analyst's therapeutic role is to contribute to the viability of the patient's illusion that he can stay the same while changing. The analyst accomplishes this task by not attempting, through interpretation, to force a conceptual distinction among levels of reality in the patient's ambiguous self-experience, and by not insisting that the boundary between conscious and unconscious and between reality and fantasy be defined other than through a relational process of consensual negotiation (see also Ghent, 1992; Pizer, 1992). The goal is to enable the *experience* of self-growth—not simply its result or outcome—to be rewarding, to be one of transition rather than of traumatic "force feeding."

The transference-countertransference field, if looked at through this lens, is a dramatization of the patient's illusion, an externalization of the patient's internal communication with his own subjective phenomena in the form of an enactment with his analyst's reality. One dimension of the analyst's role is to create a therapeutic environment that allows this enactment to occur, and for him (the analyst) to participate in it and thus experience the illusion implicitly, not simply explicitly, as through language. His job is not to correct the illusion but to *know* it with the patient so that the patient can make the most use of it creatively and imaginatively. The desired analytic outcome is not a surrender of the illusion as a distortion of reality, but the patient's pleasurable construction of a more inclusive reality that emerges from his illusory experience and becomes linguistically symbolized by the consensual construction of new narrative meaning. *The heart of the process depends on the ability of the analyst to avoid imposing meaning, so that the patient can feel free to enact new ways of being without fear of traumatically losing the continuity of "who he is."* As Friedman (1983) so evocatively put it: "Insight is the score that the patient learns while practicing on a well-tuned therapist" (p. 348).

From a relational standpoint, enactment defies categorization as either pathological or normal. Levi (1971, p. 184) described it from an interpersonal perspective as "the product of not just one, but two forces, contradictory and opposed; the one attempting to maintain the delimited self-system intact with its established boundaries and dissociations, and the other attempting to break down this organization . . . a powerful though perverted attempt at self cure."

The process of enactment, in analysis, often occurs in a dissociated self-state that is designed to communicate the existence of a "truth" that the patient is experiencing about the analyst, and that cannot be thought or said within the context of the self-other representation that the relationship is based on at the moment.

Consider, for example, the puzzling, unsettling, and multidetermined phenomenon referred to in the clinical literature as "delicate self-cutting." Some patients threaten to hurt themselves physically but do not, whereas others may or may not threaten and really do it. Apart from a patient's past history, and even apart from the details of the patient's immediate life, an analyst often intuitively "knows" with a remarkably high degree of accuracy, which patient is likely to hurt himself and which is not. It has been my experience that, notwithstanding the multiplicity of factors that may be operating at a given moment in patients who do hurt themselves, such acts occur with impressively lower frequency in patients whose core personalities could be considered organized more conflictually than dissociatively, and that an analyst will tend intuitively to worry less about the former than about the latter (patients who enact rather than think about their feelings toward themselves and toward significant objects, including the analyst). Patients who really *do it* are typically those who fluctuate among dissociated domains of reality, each with its own imperative truth.

In this connection, I am also reminded of certain patients who seem unable to tolerate analysts' holidays or vacation breaks. Analysts have sometimes discovered that giving a patient a phone number where, "if

172 ■ CHAPTER 12

necessary," the analyst can be reached during the break provides a transitional object linkage that reduces abandonment anxiety. But . . . the more interesting issue arises not when this linkage "works" but when it does not. With the vast majority of patients, the result is that the patient does not call and does not feel any great sense of urgency to do so, despite a certain amount of anxiety. The link is experienced as enough because the capacity exists for the person to both feel the need and evaluate the relative balance among permission, necessity, and concern for the other person's needs. But with some patients, calls are indeed made, sometimes many calls, often to the analyst's surprise and even consternation (because this was not supposed to happen). In such instances the concept of "acting-out" is applied, in my view often inaccurately (even when it is not used retaliatively by a grouchy analyst). It tends to presume avoidance (through "acting-out") of a state of internal conflict, and it misses what is more frequently the revelation of a personality organization not yet sufficiently cohesive to hold simultaneously the need to make contact, the experience of having been given permission to do so, and the ability to empathize with the analyst's own legitimate limits, particularly when they have not been made explicit (usually because the analyst was less than candid about them). The reason that the analyst may not have chosen to spell out the fact that his offer was not equivalent to a continuously open telephone line varies from situation to situation, but certain patients are expert at spotting the inconsistencies between what someone says and the unverbalized aspect of what they "mean." These individuals have a nose for the slightest scent of hypocrisy, no matter how "well-meaning" the motive. The patient who does phone without "good" reason (from the analyst's perspective) is often in a dissociated self-state that permits access only to the need for contact and to the memory of having been given permission to call if necessary; in such a state, the felt need and the concept of "necessity" are experientially equivalent. The phone call is thus an enactment, much like certain forms of self-cutting, that is designed to make an impact on the object. To what end? It is not an easy question to answer with any degree of confidence. My strongest hunch is that it is an example of what Levi (1971) called "a powerful though perverted attempt at self cure" (p. 184). It involves a need to be known in the only way possible—intersubjectively— through playing out with the analyst, in some mutually creative way that is different from the old and fixed patterning of self-other interactions, a version of the situation that led to the original need for dissociation. Through this relational act of sameness and difference, an opportunity is provided to construct jointly an act of meaning (Bruner,

1990) that allows the dissociated threat of potential trauma to be cognitively processed.

Putnam (1992) called dissociation "the escape when there is no escape" (p. 104). It is a defense against trauma, which, unlike defenses against internal conflict, does not simply deny the self access to potentially threatening feelings, thoughts, and memories; it effectively obliterates, at least temporarily, the *existence* of that self to whom the trauma could occur, and it is in that sense like a "quasi-death." The rebuilding of linkages, the reentry into life, involves pain not unlike that of mourning. The return to life means the recognition and facing of death; not simply the death of one's early objects as real people, but the death of those aspects of self with which those objects have been united. At the point the patient begins to abandon the instant and absolute "truth" of dissociative reality in favor of internal conflict and human relatedness, the patient discovers that there is no path without pain. Russell (1993, p. 518) speaks to the experience of the patient's recognition and processing of trauma as requiring the capacity for a particular kind of grief. "We have to presume," he writes, "that the pain accompanying this grief is extreme, among the most painful of life's experiences. We make this assumption because of the enormous psychological price that is paid to continue to avoid it."

A brief clinical vignette may help to illustrate this more vividly. A man in his late 30s had been seeing me three times a week for about two years and had lived since early adolescence in a state of timeless, purposeless, and concrete reality, marked by the ritual performance of daily activities that anchored him to what little sense of meaning life imparted. For many years he had been structuring his life by time spent in an apartment in New York and time spent in a weekend house in Vermont, each experience disconnected from the other, as if being lived by separate people. The regularity of this schedule and the regularity of his three visits each week to my office were each protected by him as a matter of life or death. If a session had to be canceled by either of us (including for holidays), it had to be replaced at almost any cost. One Monday morning, after returning from Vermont as usual, he arrived for his session even more unfocused and disconnected than he ordinarily was upon leaving one place and entering another. But there was a strange sadness to his voice that felt unfamiliar to me, and something additional that I could not quite put my finger on—there was almost what seemed like a hint of fright. He reported that he could not even remember why he was at my office other than that he was supposed to be, and then he quietly said, "Vermont is dead." There was something about his state of mind at that moment that was both so poignant and so unusual that I felt as if I were meeting him for the first time. "I am never going to have it again," he said. "It's not that I don't remember it. I do, but that just makes it worse. And right now, *I* am dead too; I have to look for something to do in order to know why I'm here." "Where does that feel like it leaves you?" I asked. "It's just me and the world," he replied, continuing:

> I can't find a way to put all my other images of myself in the middle. This is all there is. I suppose it's liberating, but what I'm liberated into is a life that has death as a part of it. Maybe you can give me two weeks' worth of sessions as a single event, so they are linked, so they don't die, like Vermont died. When I leave Vermont, it dies, because it can never be there again in the same way. The memory only makes me sad.

Perception, Language, and Selfhood

Almost any human being, even in the most primitive of mental states, is able to use language as communicative speech—that is, to communicate his personal identity as an objective and enduring social reality that transcends the here and now. He is able to use his linguistic capacity not only to illuminate vocally what he feels and wants but to express through linguistic interaction who he believes he is, who he believes others are, and how accessible these self-other mental representations are to negotiated modification in the face of contradictory perceptions arising from social interchange—a process that Sullivan (1950b) termed "consensual validation" (p. 214). No matter how idiosyncratic or impaired an individual's manner of interpersonal self-expression happens to be, it almost invariably conveys that it was shaped, for better or for worse, in an environment recognizably human regardless of its degree of dehumanization (see also chapter 5). The capacity to express linguistically one's experience of personal identity—"who one is"—is so fundamental to the essence of being human that in those rare instances when it is lost or altered in a central way, the experience is almost incomprehensible to others.

In the March 26, 1992, *New York Review*, Oliver Sacks wrote a piece called "The Last Hippie" about a patient he had treated. Sacks's patient, Greg, because of an unusually placed brain tumor that damaged both temporal and frontal lobe functioning, developed both episodic amnesia (an inability to transfer perceptual memory into permanent memory) and an incapacity to retain a sense of personal, unique identity, tending to "shallow" him, to remove genuine feeling and meaning, to replace these with a sort of indifference or frivolity . . . Greg knew only presence, not absence. He seemed incapable of registering any loss—loss of function in himself, or of an object, or a person [pp. 59–60].

This man, by most standards of prognostic evaluation, was hopeless, except for Sacks's perception that, although his frontal lobe damage had taken away his experience of personal identity,

it had also given him a sort of identity or personality, albeit of an odd and perhaps primitive sort . . . by his relationship to and participation in an act of meaning, an organic unity, which overrode or bypassed the disconnections of his amnesia. . . . Music, songs, seemed to bring to Greg what, apparently, he lacked, to evoke in him a depth to which he otherwise had no access. Music was a door to a world of feeling, of meaning, a world in which Greg could, if only for a while, recover himself [pp. 58–59].

It could be argued that the nature of the "organic unity" to which Sacks referred as "at once dynamic and semantic" (p. 59) is the heart of the interpretive process in psychoanalysis, what is often called "the words and music" of the analytic relationship. Sacks stated:

It is typical of such flowing dynamic-semantic structures that each part leads on to the next, that every part has reference to the rest. Such structures cannot be perceived or remembered in part—they are perceived and remembered, if at all, as wholes [p. 59].

Sacks concluded his essay with a question that I think has interesting implications for what I have called the shadow and substance of clinical process in psychoanalysis and its relation to dissociation, memory, and the interface between perception and self-narrative. He wrote the following:

It is easy to show that simple information can be embedded in songs . . . but what does it mean to say, "This is December the 19th, 1991," when one is sunk in the profoundest amnesia, when one has lost one's sense of time and history, when one is existing from moment to moment in a sequenceless limbo?" "Knowing the date" means nothing in these circumstances. Could one, however, through the evocativeness and power of music, perhaps using *songs with specially written lyrics*—songs which relate something valuable about himself or the current world—accomplish something more lasting, deeper? [p. 62, italics added].

"Songs with specially written lyrics!" Perhaps not a bad way to conceive of analytic process: songs that bridge the space between a patient's inner reality (his preestablished view of who he is) and his perception of external reality as constructed through the analytic relationship: a harmonic joining of seeing and saying as an affectively organized flow of experience.

In brief, I am arguing that personal narrative cannot be edited simply by more accurate verbal input. Psychoanalysis must provide an experience that is perceivably (not just conceptually) different from the patient's narrative memory. Sullivan (1954, pp. 94–112), recognizing that self-discordant perceptual data must have an opportunity to structurally reorganize internal narrative for psychoanalysis to be a genuine "talking cure," emphasized the powerful relation between personality change and what he called "the detailed inquiry" by the analyst. This latter phrase refers to the clinical reconstruction of perceptual detail, the recall of affects, areas of perception, and interpersonal data that are excluded from the narrative memory of the event as reported to the analyst. A central aspect of this process is that the patient-analyst relationship itself is inevitably drawn into the telling of the narrative and experienced by both parties as a living entity that must be continually renegotiated as the analysis proceeds. The core of the negotiation is that the *meaning* of the relationship is intersubjectively, though asymmetrically constructed out of the patient's self-narrative and the differences from it (see Aron, 1991; Hoffman, 1991). It is in this sense that psychoanalytic inquiry breaks down the old narrative frame (the patient's "story") by evoking, through enactment, perceptual experience that doesn't fit it, thus allowing narrative change to take place. Alternative, consensually validated narratives that contain events and experience of self-other configurations formerly excluded, begin to be constructed and *symbolized not by words themselves but by the new relational context that the words come to represent*.

This view has implications that affect our concepts of neutrality, interpretation, anonymity, self-revelation, and many other dimensions of what we believe to be an acceptable analytic posture. For a patient in analysis to look into his own nature with perceptiveness, and to utilize creatively what is being enacted, there must exist a simultaneous opportunity for the patient to look into the *analyst's* nature with an equivalent sense of freedom and security. For one thing, an analyst can no longer technically attempt to maintain an image of opaque neutrality without recognizing that it will be perceived by many patients as an injunction to see the analyst not as he really is and only to see him as different from the "other" (e.g., father, mother) except for transferential "distortions." Some patients, particularly those with personality disorders, will inevitably respond to this stance simply as an attempted extraction of their perceptual reality and either enter a prolonged analytic stalemate or learn to be "better" patients as part of their preexisting self-narratives (see Franklin, 1990; Greenberg, 1986, 1991a).

In chapter 5 I quoted from the work of Carlos Castaneda (1971, 1974) brief passages in which the shaman/sorcerer Don Juan was trying (once again, unsuccessfully) to "explain" to Carlos why people remain stuck in their own limited versions of reality:

> Whenever we finish talking to ourselves the world is always as it should be. We renew it, we kindle it with life, we uphold it with our internal talk. Not only that, but we also choose our paths as we talk to ourselves. Thus we repeat the same choices over and over until the day we die, because we keep on repeating the same internal talk over and over until the day we die [Castaneda, 1971, p. 263].

> [W]e are complacently caught in our particular view of the world, which compels us to feel and act as if we knew everything about the world. *A teacher from the very first act he performs, aims at stopping that view.* Sorcerers call it stopping the internal dialogue. . . . In order to stop the view of the world which one has held since the cradle, it is not enough to just wish or make a resolution. One needs a practical task [Castaneda, 1974, p. 236].

This was Castaneda writing 20 years ago about the stubborn power of self-narrative to preserve itself, and about what he wryly described as its ability to change only through negotiation with a "sorcerer" whose goal it is to facilitate commitment to a "practical task"—perhaps what Bruner (1990, p. xii) called an "act of meaning"—that will rewrite the internal dialogue. Judging from the number of times the words "hermeneutic" and "narrative" appear in the contemporary analytic literature, the therapeutic process of altering the internal dialogue is no longer simply the domain of sorcerers. It has been discovered by psychoanalysis, and the "practical task" in this context is the negotiation of the analytic situation. Schafer (1983) stated that, when you help the patient rewrite his story "in a way that makes change conceivable and attainable" (p. 227), you have done your job as an analyst. I tend to agree, but how does this model of analytic growth (if it is a model) speak to the *act* of what we do with our patients? Don Juan's explanation did not change Carlos's own story of reality despite the accuracy of what the shaman said. One's personal meanings do not change simply through the power of reason or convincing verbal explanation. Carlos became able to expand his vision of reality only when his relationship with his mentor led to actions within it that began to free him from the self-imposed reality that had defined its limits. In other words, he had to find a way to escape a relationship from which there was no escape other than through interpersonal action that changed its self-imposed story. The fact that Carlos later came to feel that he was "tricked" into these "acts of meaning" suggests an interesting comparison with certain aspects of the analytic relationship, but to develop this idea would take me too far from the present topic.

During my first year of graduate school, the instructor of our diagnostics class illustrated a point with a "psychoanalyst/patient joke" that I've never forgotten. It may serve equally well in the present context to vividly get at what self-narrative is not: it is neither a patient's spoken version of who he is, as when we conduct a formal "interview," nor something that can be changed or rewritten by the introduction (whether gently or abruptly) of a more "accurate" version of who he is. The joke is as follows:

> "Doctor, I came to see you because I have a humiliating sexual problem that I have to talk about, but no one believes me."
> "Don't worry, sir, this is my specialty; I promise I will take you seriously."
> "Well, all right, but it really is very embarrassing. My problem is that my penis fell off." (Long pause while doctor thinks about how to respond.)
> "I can tell, sir, that you are convinced this is what happened, and I am certain that your reasons for believing it are very important for us to talk about. I want to hear more about it, but I first want to assure you that it can't literally be true; penises don't just fall off."
> "I knew you would say that; this is what makes it so hard to talk about. But this time I came prepared: Here! Look!" (Patient reaches into his jacket pocket and shows doctor what he is holding in his hand.)
> "But that's not your penis; that's a cigar!"
> "Oh, my God! I smoked my penis!"

It is my view that the essential quality of what Bruner (1990) calls an act of meaning lies in its being a relational act—an act mediated not by indoctrination (no matter how tactfully administered) but by consensually constructed interchange between the timelessness of one's internal "self-truth" and the immediacy of a discrepant, external perception of oneself as seen by an other. Only then can new meaning be cognitively conserved—that is, accommodated into one's internal dialogue, self-narrative, or unconscious fantasy, whichever phrase one chooses. To put it a bit more simply, the power of a relational act to alter self-truth is in the opportunity it presents to *perceive* an alternative version of reality rather than struggling to believe an alternative version that makes sense but has minimum interchange with self-narrative. Thus, if we conceive of perception as involving an interactive process of responsiveness to the world that operates on behalf of the motivation and behavior of the perceiver (Bruner, 1990), then the information we perceive is given meaning by these very actions. It is a view of perception as a dynamic process, that in the world of human relatedness includes the dynamic interplay between two subjectivities that are always reading each other but are not always immediately aware of what they read. One might therefore suggest that *psychoanalysis is a process that is designed to enhance perception as its first act.*

But if this is so, then why do we laugh knowingly at "Oh, my God! I smoked my penis!"? There's the cigar, right in front of the patient's eyes. Why doesn't that perception lead the patient to consider the possibility that his reality might be worth questioning? Why does he instead create a logically possible but highly implausible crutch to support his self-truth? One answer, I think, is that new relational conditions were not yet present for his perception of the cigar to become part of a discrepant self-perception. By this I don't mean that the patient was looking at an inanimate object (the cigar) rather than at himself. The ability of an individual to allow his self-truth to be altered by the impact of an "other" (whether the other is an analyst or a sorcerer) depends on the existence of a relationship in which the other can be experienced as someone who, paradoxically, both accepts the validity of the patient's inner reality and participates in the here-and-now act of constructing a negotiated reality discrepant with it. Clinically, of course, the critical issue for any given person is the power held by the subjective truth of early self-other representations and the degree to which they are anchored in place by the dread of psychic trauma.

In the interchanges between Castaneda and Don Juan, and between the patient and doctor in the joke,[2] the power of self-truth to remain unchanged was as yet unchallenged by perception. A relational

---

2. Granted, there is the not insignificant issue of paranoia to be considered in this joke. Could it not be reasonably argued, however, that paranoia may be a special case of self-narrative that is highly—sometimes intractably—resistant to change even through relational negotiation, but that is no different in structure from any other? Perhaps it is the extremely dissociative isolation of the self-state that holds paranoid self-narrative, that makes what we call a "delusional" story virtually immune to perceptions

context, an act of meaning, had not been constructed that could include the realities of both self and other. In both cases, the immediate perceptual context was an enactment of the patient's fixed, internal self-narrative of some "other" trying helpfully and logically to extract the person's own reality and replace it with theirs (albeit a "better" one). In both relationships, because the "patients" acted in ways consistent only with internal truth, their self-narratives remained unchanged even in the face of convincing perceptual data (the cigar) and persuasive logic (Don Juan's attempt at Socratic dialogue). In Piaget's (1936) terminology, perceptual and cognitive experience was simply assimilated into the ongoing self-schema rather than the internal patterning of self-other representation having to accommodate discrepant data and to undergo structural reorganization. In other words, it is only when perception, in a relational mode, demands narrative accommodation, that language, logic, and what we typically call "insight" become effective.

All this being said, isn't the entity we call *narrative* then somewhat elusive as a concept? Where is self-narrative located? It obviously is not to be found simply in the linguistic content of a patient's story, for example, in the words, "my penis fell off." Patients, in fact, do not reveal their unconscious fantasies *to* the analyst: They *are* their unconscious fantasies (see chapter 11) and live them with the analyst through the *act* of psychoanalysis, which includes the analyst's subjectivity as well as the patient's. In this sense, the patient's self-narrative is always in the interface between shadow and substance, and it is through the relational act of psychoanalysis that the patient, as the embodiment of his own narrative, comes to be known through enactment while telling his story. The shadow and substance of unconscious fantasy are thus captured and reconstructed in a new domain of reality; a chaotic intersubjective field where the collision between narrative memory and immediate perception contains the simultaneous existence of multiple realities and disjunctive self-other representations.

---

inconsistent with it. It would therefore follow that as disjunctive perceptions become so powerful that the internal logic of the self-narrative cannot be reasonably maintained, the individual's efforts to hold his dissociated self-state intact by shoring up the narrative become more and more "irrational." As in the example of the cigar joke, the shoring up of narrative can include what Shapiro (1965) called the propensity of a paranoid person to "make brilliantly perceptive mistakes . . . [and to] be absolutely right in his perception and absolutely wrong in his judgment" (pp. 60–61). The dissociation must be preserved, sometimes at any cost, to prevent the return of unbearably traumatic self-experience.

The chaotic nature of the intersubjective field at such times is well portrayed, for example, by McDougall's (1987) evocative discussion of a case presentation in which she frames the description of her initial reaction to the case within her metaphor of the "psychoanalytic stage." She writes:

> Much of the confused impression at first reading stems from the fact that these contradictory people in . . . [the patient's] psychic world are both talking at the same time. (When this occurs, whether within the analytic situation or in everyday life, it is difficult to hear what is being said!) [p. 224].

Dissociation and Conflict

I propose that structural personality growth in psychoanalysis is not simply a process of helping a patient change a unified, unadaptive self-representation to an equally plausible but more adaptive one, but rather a process of addressing individual subnarratives, each on its own terms, and enabling negotiation to take place between them (see also chapter 10). What do I mean by "subnarratives?" Simply that every person has a set of discrete, more or less overlapping schemata of who he is, and that each is organized around a particular self-other configuration that is held together by a uniquely powerful affective state. There is increasingly strong evidence supporting the idea that the psyche does not start as an integrated whole that then becomes fragmented as a pathological process, but is nonunitary in origin; it is a structure that originates and continues as a multiplicity of self-other configurations or "behavioral states" (as Wolff, 1987, called them) that maturationally develop a coherence and continuity that comes to be experienced as a cohesive sense of personal identity—an overarching feeling of "being a self." Osborne and Baldwin (1982), for example, considered the fact that consciousness is discontinuous to be the most serious and overriding problem for all systems of psychotherapy. The data, they argued, are too powerful to be ignored any longer:

> We excerpt features of our experience rather than the whole and tend to conciliate parts into a compatible whole. Our consciousness is essentially a state of illusion embroidered by these processes upon a series of discontinuous moments of consciousness from our experience [pp. 268–269].

In most people, the adaptive illusion of one's "sameness" is taken for granted. In other individuals, the experience of continuity and integrity of the sense of self is never taken for granted; it is absent either partially or totally, and it often involves a lifelong struggle to deal with the existence of relatively or totally dissociated self-states. Am I thereby implying that we are all, in one way or another, multiple personalities? No, I am not. I am suggesting that what we call the unconscious might usefully include the suspension or deterioration of linkages between self-states, preventing certain aspects of self—along with their respective constellations of affects, memories, values, and cognitive capacities—from achieving access to the personality within the same state of consciousness. The extent to which one's individual self-states are simultaneously accessible to awareness (what has been called the *observing ego*) is the criterion that analysts have traditionally used in determining whether a patient is "analyzable." The difference between patients who have classically been defined as analyzable and those who have been seen as unsuitable for analysis is from this perspective a matter of the degree to which the self-states are dissociated from one another.

Paradoxically, the goal of dissociation is to maintain personal continuity, coherence, and integrity of the sense of self and to avoid the traumatic dissolution of selfhood. How can this be? How can the division of self-experience into relatively unlinked parts be in the service of self-integrity? The most plausible answer has already been discussed: Self-experience originates in relatively unlinked self-states, each coherent in its own right, and the experience of being a unitary self (cf. Hermans, Kempen, and van Loon, 1992, pp. 29–30; Mitchell, 1991, pp. 127–139) is an acquired, developmentally adaptive illusion. It is when this illusion of unity is traumatically threatened with unavoidable, precipitous disruption that it becomes in itself a liability because it is in jeopardy of being overwhelmed by input it cannot process symbolically and deal with as a state of conflict.

When the illusion of unity is too dangerous to be maintained, what we call compulsivity and obsessional thinking may often serve primarily to bolster the dissociative process by filling in the "spaces" and denying that they even exist. There is then a return to the simplicity of concreteness. Personality disorders of whatever type might, in this light, be considered the characterological outcome of inordinate use of dissociation in the schematization of self-other mental representation; that is, an identity organized, in part, as a proactive, defensive response to the potential repetition of early trauma. A centrally defining hallmark of such a patient would be the dominance of a concrete state of mind in which the experience of internal conflict is only remotely and briefly possible (if at all), in the presence of data that require looking at himself through someone else's eyes. As a result of the subjective isolation of discretely organized realms of self-experience, data that are incompatible with the ongoing self-state are denied simultaneous access to consciousness. Thus, unlike less dissociated personality organizations in which the experience of conflict is structurally possible but psychodynamically avoided, in a personality disorder the individual cannot hold conflicting ways of seeing himself vis-à-vis his objects within a single experiential state long enough to feel the subjective pull of opposing affects and dissonant self-perceptions as a valid state of mind that is worth taking as an object of self-reflection. Inharmonious contents of the mind (affects, wishes, beliefs, and so on) are not readily accessible to self-observation; the individual tends to experience his immediate subjective experience as truth, and any response to it by an "other" that contains the existence of data implying an alternative perspective, as disconfirming and thereby unthinkable.

Where there is little or no capacity for self-reflection, the analyst's experience of the patient, if incompatible with the patient's present state of mind, cannot be talked about as an object because the patient cannot conceive of the analyst's perspective as an object even potentially belonging to the self, much less as something potentially observable. The one vehicle for the expression of the patient's dissociated "data of experience" (see also Boris, 1986) is through enactment in the analytic relationship where the presence of these data is revealed in the co-created intersubjective world of the transference/countertransference gestalt and never in the mind of the patient alone. The phenomenon is not *intra*psychic and can be observed only through living it with the patient in the joint creation of an intermediate reality that bridges the experiential void between the patient's self-states and helps meet his essential experiential need "to stay the same while changing." In the proper analytic setting, there is a chance, with the analyst, for the dissociated domains of self to play out aspects of unsymbolized experience that will allow motoric, affective, imagistic, and verbal elements to coalesce with relevant narrative memory in the context of something formerly unthinkable: a perceptual experience of the patient-analyst relationship as a dyadically constructed illusion, linking internal truth with a new, self-consistent, more flexible version of external reality. A basic dimension of analytic technique might then be conceptualized in terms of how the therapist negotiates the transition from relating to self-states that are dissociated, to relating to the same patient when internal linkages begin to exist as part of an experientially consistent human alliance and analytic process.

What about the act of interpretation? Greenberg (1991b) stated that "an interpretation—complete or incomplete, exact or inexact, correct or incorrect—is as interactive as a handshake or a silence or a forgotten session." In the same vein, Bass (1992) felicitously noted:

> The analyst responds directly to what he perceives or believes to be that patient's needs, and in this sense his response is based on his interpretation of the patient's experience, even if he does not articulate an explicit interpretation with the patient [p. 128].

I would certainly agree that interpretation as an event is given meaning that does not depend simply on the accuracy or exactness of the verbal content. Because any verbal interpretation is (inevitably) the analyst's own conceptual construction of reality, it is only containable within the patient's perceptual reality if it is consistent with the patient's experience of the analyst's attitude toward him while making it, and consistent with the "felt" meaning of the behavior of both parties. Ogden (1991) referred to this idea as "an interpretation-in-action" and stated:

> I have on occasion allowed patients in states of near panic to make use of my waiting room as a place to spend time as they choose. I have later discussed with them the meaning of the experience of spending that time in my waiting room as well as the meaning of my allowing them to make use of me in that way [p. 366].

Dissociation, as an ego function, is distinguished by the presence of a selectively amnesic mental state. As a global defense against ongoing trauma or the fear of potential trauma, it represents as adaptive hypnoidal capacity of the personality. It serves to protect against what Reik (1936) called *shock*: the real or perceived threat of being overwhelmingly incapacitated by aspects of reality that cannot be processed by existing cognitive schemata without doing violence to one's experience of selfhood and sometimes to sanity itself. If we take seriously the growing body of research reviewed by Bonanno (1990), the relation between dissociation and memory becomes clear, as does one of the primary features of dissociation—"the fallibility of memory for discrete and emotionally charged events" (p. 176). Bonnano here demonstrates the validity of Bartlett's (1932) proposal 61 years ago that memory cannot be conceived as an expanding library comprised of records of discrete events, but rather as a *process* involving bits and pieces of information that are continually interpreted and reconstructed during the course of remembering . . . and that the contents of what is recalled are dependent on the manner in which the memories are accessed [Bonanno, 1990, pp. 175–176].

In the presence of new linguistic schemata that are experienced as fitting the perceptual event, symbolic consolidation is optimally possible; cognitive reorganization of narrative memory (what we call *insight*) will more and more integrally link the patient's potential for unitary self-experience to his ongoing perception of external reality. With highly charged emotional experiences, whether past or present, this is particularly difficult to accomplish because, in the interest of preserving ego stability, discrete, affectively intense events that are inconsistent with narrative memory are largely deprived of a self-context into which they can be accessed and cognitively processed.

As Laub and Auerhahn (1989, p. 392) succinctly expressed it, "because the traumatic state cannot be represented, it is unmodifiable by interpretation . . . [and] what is required initially in the therapy is not elucidation of psychic conflict but . . . [that] the link between self and other must be rebuilt." The course of a successful analytic process thus involves periods of transition from the patient's primary use of dissociation and enactment in the transference-countertransference field to an increasing capacity to sustain the experience of internal conflict and to a growing commitment to taking the functioning of his mind as an analytic object in its own right. These periods, prior to a patient's full ability to experience without trauma the pull between opposing frames of self-reference, are often captured particularly vividly through patients' dreams[3] as they enter this transitional configuration of self-experience. The analytic process during such a transition typically involves a decrease in the patient's use of externalization, projective identification, and extractive introjection (Bollas, 1987) as primary modes of securing his dissociative bound-

---

3. Marcuse (submitted) advanced a similar view that the meaning created from patients' reported dreams during analytic work is inherently relational in nature and demands that the distinction between what we have called latent (unconscious) content and manifest (conscious) content be reexamined: "I believe we need a model that frees us from the insistence on a radical distinction between manifest and latent content in dream analysis . . . [and] that the dichotomy tends to disappear in actual practice because the analyst's participation has a role in shaping what appears to be manifest or latent."

aries, and a corresponding increase in recognition of the dissociative process and the fear of surrendering it. Because this recognition (except through dreams) may not be openly acknowledged by a patient for long periods of time, it is important that the analyst not lag too far behind in his own ability to process change, but it is equally critical that the analyst not impose his view of what he believes is going on with his patient.

The psychoanalytic transition from dissociation to the subjective experience of internal conflict is not one that has a linear beginning and end. In some patients, the initial shift is dramatic and involves a major personality reorganization, but the basic configuration is there in every analysis and is part of every treatment process during all phases. To put it as simply as possible, I argue that there is no such thing as an integrated self—a "real you." Self-expression and human relatedness will inevitably collide, just as they did in both Brigid and the archbishop, but *health is not integration. Health is the ability to stand in the spaces between realities without losing any of them. This is what I believe self-acceptance means and what creativity is really all about—the capacity to feel like one self while being many.*

I would like to conclude with a dream presented by a 45-year-old woman in her sixth year of treatment. For most of her life, she had virtually no perspective from which she could see herself except in the self-state that existed at the moment. This meant that she was unable to access either memory or imagination of herself in any context that was inconsistent with her ongoing state of mind. To say that she lacked an observing ego would be a more than fair statement. Her elaborately contrived modes of relating in order to disguise what was really a functional amnesia for many of her own actions, had become her means of surviving in the real world. As she so often put it, "It's as if I can't *watch* myself. If only I was able to *watch* myself." The dream, which we both recognized was a powerful communication about the shift taking place in her current self-experience, came to be called by us, the dream of the "good watch":

> I was on the beach with my family and I could see a wave coming. I knew it was going to be a tidal wave and was scared, but not terrified. The tidal wave hit and my family disappeared. I was hit too, but I was picked up and put down a long way from where I was standing. I didn't know where I was. Then the scene shifted. I was in my apartment, and many people from my past were there. I had put a good watch on the table. When the people left, the good watch was gone and there was cheap jewelry in its place. I was very upset—because I trusted them. Later, I discovered the good

watch. But it was in a different place than I thought I had put it.[4]
Then I woke up.

As she was about to tell me the dream, she "forgot" it. She then "remembered" it, "forgot" it again, and finally "remembered" it enough to report it, but with obvious conflict. When she finished, she said, "I'm not sure now if I did find the good watch or if I'm just making it up." But for the first time there was a hint of playfulness in her eyes.

---

4. It is of interest to note the uncanny similarity between this dream and that of another patient, Mr. C, described in chapter 8. Both patients were in the process of surrendering their reliance on dissociation and were simultaneously accepting and mourning the loss. Each dream spoke to the bittersweet pain of losing the familiar presence of unlinked, unbridgeable, "separate" selves, as if they were "friends" or "family members" with whom they had shared an existence but who would now be lost because they were no longer what they had been.

13

PSYCHOANALYSIS, DISSOCIATION, AND PERSONALITY ORGANIZATION[1] (1995)

If one wished to read the contemporary psychoanalytic literature as a serialized Gothic romance, it is not hard to envision the restless ghost of Pierre Janet, banished from the castle by Sigmund Freud a century ago, returning for an overdue haunting of Freud's current descendants. With uncanny commonality, most major schools of analytic thought have become appropriately more responsive to the phenomenon of dissociation, and each in its own way is attempting actively to accommodate it within its model of the mind and its approach to clinical process. A pivotal concept in the birth and development of interpersonal psychoanalysis (Sullivan, 1940, 1953) and "independent" British object relational theories (Fairbairn, 1944, 1952; Winnicott, 1945, 1949, 1960a, 1971d), dissociation continues to receive its most active clinical and theoretical attention from contemporary analysts whose sensibilities most directly represent one or both of these schools of thought (e.g., Bromberg, chapters 5, 8, 10, 12–19; D. B. Stern, 1983, 1996, 1997; Smith, 1989; Mitchell, 1991, 1993; Davies, 1992; Davies and Frawley, 1994; Harris, 1992, 1994; Reis 1993; Schwartz, 1994; Grand, 1997). It has also found its way into the work of analysts

1. This chapter revises and expands the original version of the essay published in *Psychoanalytic Dialogues*, 1995, 5:511–528.

writing from a self-psychological orientation, particularly those interested in the phenomenology of self-states (e.g., Stolorow, Brandchaft,
and Atwood, 1987; Ferguson, 1990) and has gained stature among
Freudian analysts, both classical (e.g., I. Brenner, 1994, 1996; Kernberg,
1991; Shengold, 1989, 1992) and postclassical (e.g., Marmer, 1980, 1991;
Goldberg, 1987, 1995; Gabbard, 1992; Lyon, 1992; Roth, 1992; Gottlieb,
1997). Cutting across the range of analytic persuasions, what is probably the most broadly accepted current understanding of dissociation
has been well stated by Schwartz (1994, p. 191), who proposed that it
"can be most simply understood as a self-hypnotic process that
attempts to anaesthetize and isolate pain." "The mind," he wrote, "is
essentially . . . fleeing its own subjectivity to evacuate pain."

Peter Goldberg (1995) has recently enriched the literature in this
area with a challenging paper that in particular draws attention to the
impact of dissociative processes upon the experience of psychosomatic
unity. Goldberg maintains that where dissociative processes are in the
ascendency the patient's experience of his body and of the immediate
sensory world come to be inauthentic in specific ways, and that these
inauthentic uses of the body and of the sensory experience in turn
become part of the patient's overall personality integration. One can
almost see adhering to his depiction the presence of a classical libido-
theory remnant, in that ultimately he sees the body, or rather the experience of the body, as providing vitality to the self. This leads to his
discussing personality organization when it is dominated by dissociative mechanisms in terms of what he calls "pseudovitality" resulting
from the disturbance in psychosomatic unity. In connection with this
last point, further, it interests Goldberg to point out that the phenomena he describes are not characterized by repression, in which bodily
experiences might simply drop out, but by a kind of "de-repression,"
in which bodily and sensory experiences enter consciousness, but in
an "inauthentic" way.

Notwithstanding this libidinized emphasis on the body, Goldberg's
view of dissociation as a fundamental organizer of personality structure is a view that is relational in every real sense of the term: between
individuals, between the individual and society, and within the individual's representational world. He presents the process of dissociation as a distancing of the mind from the sensory apparatus that
manifests itself both symptomatically and as a defensive organization
of mental structure; what he calls a "pseudointegration" of personality
that embodies, when it is "successful," an absence of dialectic between
thinking and perception that prevents symbolization of experience
and robs selfhood of authenticity. Fundamentally, it is a model of how

dissociation leads people to use the field of mind-body relations (I/it relations) to enact conflicts that might otherwise be expressed as symbolized wishes and object relations. In the absence of symbolization, he argues, dissociated experience forces one's body and one's feelings to become "things" that "commoditize" the mind and damage its capacity for perception rather than, as Winnicott (1949) has expressed it, allowing "the psyche and the soma aspects of the growing person [to] become involved in a process of mutual interrelation" (p. 244) whereby the psyche-soma, rather than the head, comes to be the residence of the self.

Goldberg (1995) speaks of the phenomenon he labels "de-repression," as stemming from the "exploitative relation of mind to sensory experience" (p. 503) through which dissociation frees the libido without "censorship" from internalized social restraint. De-repression has relation to the libido opposite to that of repression and turns the libido into an instrument of "pseudovitality" whereby the psyche-soma becomes its slave and uses its aliveness as an antidote to depersonalization and deadness. The libido now has "user value" in that we use it and manipulate it without resolving or diminishing the "universal anguish of psychical conflict" (p. 508); we simply find new forms of gratification to stay alive. Goldberg's contribution is particularly important in this regard because it accelerates our delayed recognition that within the psychoanalytic process the enhancement of perception is the gateway to structural personality growth, a fact also recognized by Enid Balint (1993), who, in describing artists losing their capacity for perception, commented that "if their ability to perceive gets cut-off then they are finished; they can only repeat themselves. But their perceiving is terribly painful; don't let us forget that" (p. 235).

As a case in point, Goldberg (1995) presents a vignette about a complex clinical enactment between a patient and therapist, evocatively capturing the impact of dissociative processes upon the perceptual field and states of mind of both partners within an abruptly shifting interactional field:

> A patient with a family background of cruelty and abuse begins a session with an unusual tone of relaxed spontaneity, reciprocated in the therapist's own relaxed state of mind. Then, quickly, the patient falls anxiously silent, and a deadening and withdrawal in her state of mind becomes palpable to the therapist. Presently, the patient begins to report the circumstances of a perceived slight she felt at the hands of a supervisor at work, a man she hardly knows but admires from a distance. This was a very slight slight, mind you—he reportedly failed to acknowledge her enthusiastically. She

goes on to describe what followed: she became instantly dejected, and swamped with feelings of self-loathing and worthlessness; she felt physically unwell. To the therapist she catalogues the blows to her self-esteem occasioned by this slight. The sensations preoccupy her. She says she is wrapped around with the feeling and sensation of rejection. All the while, she is wringing her hands, pulling at her fingers. The therapist finds himself asking many questions that convey interest and even concern, but he is at the same time vaguely distracted by street noise and glare and a tiny spider spinning its web against a window pane [p. 494].

In his comments Goldberg succinctly portrays how the patient's emotionality has become a kind of cocoon that, among other things, denies the therapist the kind of access to her that he felt at the outset of the session. This results, in turn, in a change in the therapist's state of consciousness and compromises his ability to retain his perceptual focus on what is taking place between them in the here-and-now. In his portrayal of the event, Goldberg's relational sensibility asserts itself. He clearly recognizes that the therapist's response is contributing to an ongoing interaction that both recapitulates the patient's past experience and establishes a new form of experience at the same time.

Speaking as an interpersonal/relational analyst, I feel that this perspective describes accurately the basic interpersonal model of the psychoanalytic situation as a process of participant observation (Sullivan, 1954) in which the analyst's role is negotiated through a real relationship between two people. Because, however, the "self" is an interpersonal entity relationally structured as a multiplicity of self/other configurations that are developmentally "integrated" by an illusion of unity, the "real relationship" in any given analysis is, inevitably, an ever-shifting configuration of *multiple real relationships* in which dissociation plays a role in both the normality and pathology of the patient's original self-configuration and in the process of its therapeutic repatterning between patient and analyst. My own current thinking about the specific nature of these "multiple real relationships" in analysis has led me toward a detailed examination of the process of dissociation, an effort that has been fueled by my belief that its powerful clinical presence must be more directly engaged in a consciously consistent way for any given analysis to be far reaching and enduring. It is my perception that, within the clinical stance of participant observation, an analyst is in fact always relating to a diverse range of discrete and discontinuous self-states, regardless of whether he is aware of it, and that the next natural step in the evolution of our therapeutic efficacy entails thinking in these terms consciously and systematically (see chapter 12). By so doing, an analyst will more easily recognize the moments of opportunity for access to direct relationships with otherwise dissociated self-states, thus building into the analytic process a fuller use of the transitional space through which connections may be intersubjectively negotiated between unlinked domains of self. Goodman (1992) has vividly captured this relational aesthetic in his statement that "what seems most effective is the ability to move freely between different complementary positions in response to a fast-moving interpersonal field" (p. 645). Once the concept of dissociation becomes entrenched within a therapist's clinical imagery, the hermeneutic process of analysis is shaped neither by interpretation nor by interaction per se, but by the analyst's effort to maintain dual citizenship in two domains of reality, with passports to multiple self-states of the patient (see chapter 10).

Consider again Goldberg's (1995) clinical illustration. He writes that immediately following the unusual tone of friendly spontaneity with which the patient began the session, the therapist perceived a subtle deadening of affect, a "ghostly" withdrawal, and an abrupt switch in her demeanor, her state of mind, and the content of her thought processes, as if she were suddenly "wrapped around with the feeling and sensation of rejection" (p. 494). Typically, this sequence of events is more "felt" than observed by a therapist because the therapist's own immediate self-state almost invariably switches when the patient's does. Inasmuch as they are sharing an event that belongs equally to both of them—the intersubjective field that shapes their immediate reality and the way they are experiencing themselves and each other—any unsignaled withdrawal from that field by either person will disrupt the other's state of mind. Goldberg in fact addresses this point when he speculates as to whether "the therapist's distracted mild preoccupation with sensory experiences of his own, reflects the countertransference analogue of the patient's withdrawal" (p. 495). (See also Ogden, 1994.)

Goldberg (1995) conceptualizes this sequence of events as the patient's retreat into an "invisible sensory cocoon" that functions smoothly in creating a "narcissistic world . . . that makes intercourse with other people both redundant and impossible" (p. 495). The cocoon, regardless of what personality style it embodies, is, I feel, an inevitability as soon as dissociation becomes necessary, because *consciousness will become inherently a cocoon unless it has access to a sufficient range of self-states to allow authentic interchange with the subjectivity of others. Without this flexibility, other people are simply actors in whichever mental representation of reality defines the self-state that exists at the moment.*

Whatever the patient's state of dissociated reality may be, the person to whom the patient is relating will be interpersonally "tailored" to fit the image of the necessary internal object. As a patient recently put it, "If all you have is a hammer, everything else has to become a nail."

In my view, the essential paradox in what Goldberg calls the seemingly "smooth functioning" of the "cocoon" is that the very nature of this form of "smoothness" is in the success of its disruptiveness. No matter how walled-off from intimate contact with others, the cocoon is a *dynamic* configuration. It is geared not only to deal with actual danger but also to disrupt any perception of life as a "safe harbor" by disrupting the potential growth of attachment, thus preserving the patient's vigilant readiness for disaster. This is why the experience of hope is felt as an enemy to such patients; hope compromises the vigilance a patient relies on to maintain control over the dissociative system.

The apparent smoothness of the cocoon as seen externally can, in some patients, be accompanied internally by a cacophony of accusatory voices, alarums, and the like. Or it can also be accompanied by an eruption of obsessive rumination, by a retreat or flight into confusion, by an outbreak of contentiousness, by the discovery of perceptual distractions, or whatever. But regardless of whether the appearance of a somato-sensory cocoon is accompanied by an array of internal voices or other phenomena usually associated with character pathology, the primary reason behind a patient's sudden shift in self-state (such as took place in Goldberg's clinical vignette) is to prevent the potential growth of hope that the possibility of a good relationship is actually an attainable reality (cf. Schecter, 1978a, b, 1980). If such a patient forgets, even briefly, that feeling secure and connected to her analyst can lead to unforeseen betrayal and the terror of self-dissolution, she betrays her own hard-won coterie of protective inner voices. Thus, an abrupt shift in the interactional field at the very moment she starts to feel close, announces a switch to a state of consciousness in which she will find or evoke something she can use as a danger signal associated with the potential for hope of continued closeness. Put another way, a patient's greatest vulnerability is not to the analyst's "interpretive" efforts, but to the hope of sustained and satisfying intersubjective contact.

Let me reiterate this last point. I see the "cocoon" as a *dynamic* state of consciousness designed to anticipate trauma, but sufficiently permeable to be a potential doorway to therapeutic growth (see also chapter 7). Its insularity reflects the necessity to remain ready for danger at all times so it can never—as with the original traumatic experiences—

arrive unanticipated; the cocoon's permeability reflects a capacity for authentic but highly regulated exchange with the outside world and similarly regulated spontaneity of self-experience. Its key quality is its ability to retain the adaptational protection afforded by the separateness of self-states, so that each can continue to play its own role. As an outcome of dissociation, it functions to induce life into a moribund psyche while attempting to disrupt any experience of extended human relatedness that could lead to a positive shift in perceived reality.

Integration, Authenticity, and Potential Space

The type of solution just described helps the individual to function more adaptively by providing relative stability in the face of chronic potential for severe dissociative symptomatology. Here I would resist the temptation to characterize such patients as exhibiting or suffering from what Goldberg (1995) terms "pseudointegration." I believe that personality integration as a human quality is too complex a concept to be adequately captured by the prefix "pseudo." It is, in essence, no different from any other personality attribute—an interpersonal construction jointly shaped by the individual and the eye of the beholder. The "beholder" is frequently another person but is always, simultaneously, a dissociated voice of the self. "Integration" is thus relative to the context of external reality as well as to the shifting of the multiplicity of self—other representations that define the experience of selfhood at a given time. I have argued in chapter 12 that there is no such thing as an integrated self—a "real you." Self-expression and human relatedness will inevitably collide, and emotional health is not integration. It is what I have called the ability to stand in the spaces between realities without losing any of them—the capacity to feel like one self while being many. I thus equally believe, as Mitchell (1993) has commented, that "the sense of authenticity is always a construction and as a construction, it is always relative to other possible self-constructions at any particular time" (p. 131).

When one's normal illusion of "integration" is disrupted by trauma, the basic dissociative structure of personality is adaptationally restored and psychodynamically maintained in its original developmental discontinuity (Wolff, 1987; Putnam, 1988; Barton, 1994). This preserves both sanity and the most socially developed areas of ego functioning but renders the latter into relatively mechanical instrumentalities of survival. Whichever self-state is experienced as "me" has little simultaneous access to other domains of personal experience or memory, but the presence of other self-states holding incompatible experiences is felt experientially, and often concretely, as oppositional voices undermining the "me" that is existing in the here-and-now. (See also Fairbairn's [1944, pp. 102–111] description of what he calls the "internal saboteur.") The person's inner life is a guerilla war that Schwartz (1994) describes as "an internal paradigm of domination, disparagement and repudiation" (p. 208) in which he is the target of a variety of direct or subversive activities and accusations, including stupidity, cowardice, sadism, insanity, treachery, and, worst of all, naiveté. To combat these voices and the "noise" they produce in the sensorium, each individual will develop measures (within his own personality style) to continue functioning in spite of them and will try desperately both to silence and to "mask" their existence. As a result of these measures, a dissociative personality structure can become highly routinized and unrelentingly stable.

I have found this to be the case, for instance, in narcissistic personality disorders (see chapter 7) where living becomes a process of controlling the environment and other people from behind a mask in order to find and seek affirmation for a self robbed of life and meaning by its own dissociative protection system. But it is not only with narcissistic disorders in the formal use of the term that this phenomenon can be discerned clinically. Indeed in my work with a broad range of patients I am often aware of the powerful impact created by what Bion (1970, pp. 6–25) has called the "no-thing," the presence of an absence. The primitive, almost somatic state of mind through which it announces its existence, if it can be borne and processed, necessarily draws one's attention away from the content of communication to the medium itself. It is at those moments that the issue of authenticity can most readily force its way, uninvited, to the threshold of consciousness, bringing with it questions such as that asked by Boris (1986): "Is the analysis being done an analysis or is it *like* an analysis?" (p. 176).

As a supervisor, for example, I sometimes listen to audiotapes of an ongoing analytic treatment (see Bromberg, 1984, p. 41), and as I listen I may react to certain moments in the process during which I "sense" something that feels indefineably "off-key." I sense it not only by what I hear but also by what I *don't* hear—by the visceral experience of absence as much as the cognitive processing of presence. Sometimes it embodies for me the image of two solitary people in a large, empty ballroom, each trying to move as if dancing with the other, apparently oblivious to the absence of shared "music." At those moments I can hear, loudly, the presence of the absent music—the palpable absence of the sound that Khan (1971) writes is "heard with the eyes," the recognizable melody of authentic self-experience that stems from the relational wholeness of what Winnicott (1949) calls psyche-soma. When this melody is missing, both the analytic "lyrics" and the interpersonal context in which they are spoken feel "off," because each partner in his own way has become more of a visitor than an inhabitant of his own psychosomatic existence. If and when the melody is restored, it becomes the music of intersubjectivity—"dance music"—and infuses the lyrics of a deadened analytic relationship with life.

To some degree, interruptions in the "dance music" are an expectable and indeed necessary part of any analytic process, and so too are fluctuations in the sense of personal authenticity felt by both patient and analyst. There are some patients, however, who will *chronically* feel as if the self that is being seen is a fraud—not real—and that his "real" self is some part of him that other people cannot see, do not want to see, or should not see and that is "inside" fearing discovery but clamoring to be found. When the pressure to be recognized is warded off for too long, the voice of a dissociated self-state is then often strong enough to take over. "'It's as if a voice rises up in me,' reported one patient described by Davies and Frawley, 1994, p. 69: 'I know it's my voice . . . I recognize the sound of it . . . but it's so odd. I have no idea what the voice is going to say. All I know is that usually it says something to get me in trouble.'"

The experience of inauthenticity is based in part on the fact that, as long as there is an aspect of the self that is being shut out, what is relationally accessible to others is felt by its author as inherently false and inauthentic simply because it lacks the modulation that would ordinarily be provided by other self-perspectives. In other words, one dimension of inauthenticity resides in the absence of a full range of interpersonally organized self-experience. What is visible to others is not thereby a lie, but is, from one perspective, inauthentic because it is tailored to exclude as much as it reveals—a partial truth. The nature of dissociative experience is that the self the world sees at any given time is doomed to be less than "true" in Winnicott's (1960a) sense and to feel subjectively inauthentic at any given moment. *The experientially authentic self is always felt to be the one knocking at the door*—the oppositional inner voice that is heard but not "thought" (Bollas, 1987). This voice is inevitably felt by the person as more subjectively true simply in that it holds a separate but unformulated "truth" of its own—an alternative vision of reality that is denied to whatever aspect of the self may be then dealing with the world, thus rendering the latter relationally limited and inherently compromised in its felt authenticity. As Mitchell (1993) has put it, "what may seem authentic in the context of one version of self may be quite inauthentic with respect to other versions" (p. 131).

Worth mentioning in this context is a particular configuration of "successful" dissociation organized around a form of "pseudomaturity," a highly adaptive, dissociated caricature of adulthood that makes it very difficult for the therapist to engage other individual self-states directly. As a mode of relating, it holds a narcissistically invested history of interpersonal "success" with caretakers that is frequently so seductive it can easily lead to a collusive integration with the analyst and what Goldberg (1995, p. 500) has called "false knowing" in the psychoanalytic situation. It is this form of "successful dissociation" that led me to emphasize, in chapter 10, the importance of the analyst's recognizing when he may be unwittingly robbing his patient of authentic self-experience by requiring that other "less mature" self-states be prematurely surrendered and replaced by a dissociated exercise in adaptational pseudomaturity which can, in some patients, perpetuate what Sullivan (1953, p. 251) has called "the patient's remarkable capacity for deceiving and misleading," to the point that the result (Bromberg, 1993, p. 100) "is a genuine analysis of a pseudo-patient."

I do not, however, see the issue of inauthenticity as related to the "pseudoness" of personality integration itself. A person with a dissociative personality structure is fated to suffer from feelings of inauthenticity, but only as the result of an inevitable combination of certain relational factors: (a) a dissociated self-state is intrinsically self-serving—it functions in terms of its "user value" to the personality—and thereby "masks" its basic goal; (b) each self-state is forced to compensate for its incompleteness by exaggerating its own "truth"; (c) because the configuration of dissociated self-states is always shifting abruptly, the experience of authenticity is inherently unstable; and (d) each self-state excludes other voices that continue to make their presence felt.

To the degree that these other voices cannot fully participate in life, they remain alive as a private torment, in one way or another compromising the person's credibility in his own eyes regardless of whether or not he may be judged as "honest" by any immediate external criterion. Life is not authentically "lived." The present is at best a waiting period—a "masked" search for self-validation as a temporary escape from internal persecution and the moment when he will be ignored, disbelieved, challenged, criticized, disdained, or denounced by the world. He is waiting, in other words, for the always anticipated eventuality when another person he has been foolish enough to trust forms an alliance with one or another of his dissociated self-states and becomes an embodiment of his internal voices.

When an analyst finds himself swept into this enactment, he is encountering simultaneously the source of the greatest turmoil in therapy and the best single pathway to growth; finding and directly engaging the patient's dissociated voices as discontinuous but *individually authentic* expressions of selfhood. It is in this sense that I share with Bass (1993) his belief that "therapeutic experience is found by the patient—it is not provided. . . . Neither patient nor therapist can alone know what is best or what is needed. This is jointly discovered as the therapeutic process unfolds" (p. 165). The therapist's private experience becomes the channel through which the patient's full range of dissociated self-experiences can first achieve linguistic access, but optimal use of this channel depends on the analyst's ability to allow a transitional reality to be consensually constructed between himself and his patient. If this reality is successfully negotiated, an internal linking process will take place through an intersubjective field in which fantasy, perception, thought, and language all play a part, but the patient is not pressured to choose between which "reality" is more "objective" (Winnicott, 1951, 1971b). Within this area of potential space, the judgment of authenticity as an objective reality is moot because the analyst's own subjective experience is serving in part as a "container" (Bion, 1965) for a dissociated aspect of the patient's experience. It is through an analyst's ability to be aboveboard, and not hide behind "objective" interpretations of reality that mask their subjective origin, that a patient can risk gradually reclaiming what belongs to him and thus increase his range of access to linguistically symbolized self-experience (see Harris, 1992). As this process continues, feelings of personal authenticity inherently increase.

I thus see the patient's use of potential space as a dialectic between his ability to preserve the self as it is, while allowing symbolic communication, a little at a time, to be accommodated relationally into the repatterning of representational mental structure. Because this process *inherently* threatens a patient's ability to feel safe in the use of his dissociated organization of self, any patient will systematically oscillate between "restructuring" activity and restoration of dissociation; but I believe that to see this "resistance" as a defensive withdrawal in order to abort or foreclose the therapeutic process is, most of the time, an error. The patient's paramount need is to preserve the dissociative structure while surrendering it, and he hears many voices that are specifically designed to preserve the sense of safety in the old structure.

Distractive activity, for instance (see Goldberg, 1987), is one way of getting the therapist to "back off" at moments when the therapist's involvement in "change" is greater than his recognition or understanding of the patient's need to cope with a myriad of opposing internal voices, some advocating trust and others shouting "stupidity." The therapist becomes aware of the other "voices" at the point the patient is willing to let him participate in his internal world through enactment, but to the extent the therapist is not sufficiently able to enter into an *authentic* relationship with each voice, the patient's "resistance" is bolstered. If given the opportunity, most patients ordinarily can participate in the ambiguous reality co-created by the processing of enactment, but for the experience to be sustained in a safe way, it requires a relationship with an "other" who can exist there as an equal partner. Through the gradual restoration of hope, the revitalization of "collapsed" potential space can then take place (see Smith, 1989; Reis, 1993; Goldberg, 1995).

Dissociation, Symptoms, and Personality Type

I have speculated in chapter 12 that the concept of personality "disorder" might usefully be defined as the characterological outcome of the inordinate use of dissociation and that independent of type (narcissistic, schizoid, borderline, paranoid, etc.), it constitutes a personality structure organized as a proactive, defensive response to the potential repetition of childhood trauma. If, early in life, the developmentally normal illusion of self-unity cannot safely be maintained when the psyche-soma is flooded by input that the child is unable to process symbolically, a configuration of "on-call" self-states is gradually constructed in which the centrally defining hallmark of dissociation is the presence of a concrete state of mind. By "concrete" I mean to indicate that there is thought without a thinker, or rather, without the thinker being aware of the "other" as a thinker in his or her own right with whom it might be possible to share or reciprocate ideas. Thus, each self-state insofar as it exists in dissociation from other self-states is necessarily an island of concreteness. Concreteness has the great virtue of being simple; the threat that the "other" presents is evaded before it can get started and the road is thus opened for obsessional thinking: What we call compulsivity and obsessional thinking may often serve primarily to bolster the dissociative process by filling in the "spaces" and denying that they even exist. There is then a return to the simplicity of concreteness (see chapter 12). Successful use of the external world is preempted by a drivenness to fill in the spaces of existential deadness with "compulsive regimes" (Goldberg, 1995, p. 499). One form this can take has been described by Guntrip (1969) as a schizoid phenomenon he called "compulsive stop-gap fantasying" (p. 230). Guntrip's formulation is virtually identical with my own; he saw this kind of fantasying as derived from a "state of primary ego-unrelatedness which makes it impossible for people to be alone without panic. Then 'compulsive fantasying and thinking,' whether by day or night, whether bizarre or realistic and rational, is part of the struggle to keep oneself mentally alive" (p. 229).

Davies and Frawley (1994) have asserted that "dissociation exists along a broad continuum with coexistent, alternative ego states moving in ever-shifting patterns of mutual self-recognition and alienation" (p. 68). In dissociative disorders, it is not as much a "pseudointegrated" psyche-soma that is perceived by the mind, as a shifting experience of reality that changes in configuration depending on the needs of discontinuous self-states, each holding its own narrative truth. As an extreme example, paranoid schizophrenia may not be so different from less dramatic forms of psychopathology despite the foreclosure of potential space. That is, it might reasonably be seen as a mental state organized by the same processes as in other personality disorders. In fact, as I have suggested in chapter 12, I would hypothesize that the immovably fixed self-narrative found in paranoia is labeled "delusional" because the extreme dissociative isolation of the self-state that holds paranoid "truth" makes it virtually immune to modification through relational negotiation.

I am suggesting, in other words, that "personality disorder" represents ego-syntonic dissociation no matter what personality style it embodies. Each type of personality disorder is a dynamically "on-alert" configuration of dissociated states of consciousness that regulates psychological survival in terms of its own concretized blend of characteristics. In each type, certain self-states hold the traumatic experiences and the multiplicity of raw affective responses to them, and others hold whichever ego resources (pathological and nonpathological) have proven effective in dealing with the original trauma and making sure the pain would never again be repeated (e.g., vigilance, acquiescence, paranoid suspiciousness, manipulativeness, deceptiveness, seductiveness, psychopathy, intimidation, guilt-induction, self-sufficiency, insularity, withdrawal into fantasy, pseudomaturity, conformity, amnesia, depersonalization, out-of-body experiences, trance states, compulsivity, substance abuse).

Most broadly, each personality configuration is shaped by the degree to which pathology of cognition, impulse control, affectivity, or interpersonal functioning is a central feature, but the specific configuration defining each type of disorder might be said to result from a dissociative solution to trauma that was preserved and perfected because it had achieved a balance between safety and need satisfaction that "worked" for that person. As a proactive way of living, however, the subsequent cost of this solution to each individual is always identical—to one degree or another, an unlived life.

A dissociative disorder proper (Dissociative Identity Disorder, Dissociative Amnesia, Dissociative Fugue, or Depersonalization Disorder) is from this vantage point a touchstone for understanding all other personality disorders even though, paradoxically, it is defined by symptomatology rather than by personality style. A dissociative disorder is clinically recognized by the *direct* manifestation of discontinuity between states of consciousness that other types of personality disorders are designed to mask and to express only indirectly and "characterologically"—as a relationally impaired but relatively "enduring pattern of inner experience and behavior that . . . is inflexible and pervasive across a broad range of social situations" (American Psychiatric Association, 1994, p. 275).

There are different likelihoods that a dissociative personality structure will "fail," and I would say that the likelihood is determined largely by the type of personality style in which it is embedded. Sometimes the failure is seen in the return of symptoms; sometimes in a flooding of affect as in hysteria; sometimes in a loosening of the schizoid's hold on reality. A too "successful" dissociative structure can be observed in what I have described as the schizoid's "psychopathology of stability" (Bromberg, 1979), while its failure within the same structure is found in the schizoid's potential for schizophreniform collapse. Fairbairn's (1944, 1952) concept of schizoid withdrawal and Guntrip's (1969) formulation of the "schizoid compromise" each in its own way addresses this same clinical observation. Guntrip (1969), for example, says that some patients' "external object relations have become so weakened by early schizoid withdrawal inside" (p. 129) that such a person faces "the danger of the depersonalization of his ego-of-everyday-life along with the derealization of his environment, and he faces the appalling risk of the loss of definite selfhood" (p. 56). Here Goldberg's (1995) contention that dissociative processes can take bodily and sensory experiences—and emotionality generally—and render them inauthentic as a kind of protective cocoon is, despite its anchorage in the traditionally safe harbor of libido theory, a valuable addition to our understanding of the phenomenology seen in some patients. It adds a somato-sensory dimension to Guntrip's (1969) metaphors of a "halfway-house" and an "in-and-out policy" to describe how a patient tends to negotiate the twin dangers of depersonalization and of feeling that he is "missing the bus and life is passing him by" (p. 62).

Afterward

I began by invoking the ghost of Pierre Janet, banished from the castle by Sigmund Freud a century ago, returning for an overdue haunting of Freud's current descendants. I hope I have made it clear why I feel it is worth talking to this ghost, and indeed finally embracing the value of his legacy—the concept of dissociation and its clinical implications. But it would be wrong if I left the reader with the impression that I believe we can dispense with the memory of Freud or even with his preferred concept, repression. As Kerr (1993) has pointed out, Freudian theory represented a crucial advance in a certain respect over what Janet had to offer. For in truth, Janet, though he well understood the passions and the exigencies of trauma and dissociation, was at a loss to explain why there should be splits in the personality other than by enlisting the now totally antiquated notions of "hereditary weakness" and "hereditary degeneration." It fell to Freud to indicate that the alternation of states of consciousness could best be understood *dynamically*, that is, as reflecting an interplay of motives and countermotives. But Freud's vision in turn was too simple. Though he lent a new coherence to our understanding of disparate mental states, he did so at the cost of bequeathing us the therapeutic fiction that for practical purposes, or at least where psychic conflict was involved, the structure of the self could be assumed to be unitary. Despite Josef Breuer's contrary position and his comprehension of the role of hypnoid states (Breuer and Freud, 1893–1895), Freud's "one-sided anti-Janet stand" (Berman, 1981, p. 285) carried the day for close to 100 years.

So where does this leave us? An increasing number of clinicians representing most schools of psychoanalytic thinking have been persuaded by several decades of renewed theorizing and fresh clinical investigations that the dynamic conceptions of Freud must be understood to be in an ongoing dialectic with a complex latticework of psychic structure, one central organizing principle of which is dissociation. As we seek to find within the patient a self we can talk with and a self who simultaneously can talk to us about the experience of talking, we find ourselves traversing states kept apart from one another by dissociation. That is, the seemingly "unitary self" we meet in our patients is in important ways incapable of true dialogic engagement, and is incapable in other important ways of the experience of intrapsychic conflict. In this context our understanding of character pathology in particular needs to be revamped to take into account the dissociative structure of the mind, or so I would argue.

In summary, I offer the view that psychoanalysis must continue to study the nature of dissociation by examining it as both a process and a mental organization (see also Kirmayer, 1994). First it must be more fully explored as a normal phenomenon of the human mind that is not inherently tied to trauma. Second and concurrently, we must grapple with its multitude of defensive manifestations: (a) as a here-and-now process of unlinking aspects of the self from the sensory apparatus as a protection against potential or actual trauma; (b) as a psychodynamic organization, a configuration of discontinuous self-states—ever-shifting and always "on-alert"—that attempt to mask the dissociative "gaps," compensate for existential deadness by a compulsive search for self-validation, and preserve readiness for the return of past trauma by maintaining an ongoing reality in which potentially unbearable psychic pain is always around the next corner. Third and finally, we must acknowledge the relevance of dissociation as a challenge to the traditional ways of understanding character structure and character pathology that different schools of thought, each in its own metaphor, have relied upon as cornerstones of their theories.

Translated into the traditional metapsychology of "pathological narcissism (see chapter 7), a patient's investment in protecting the insularity of a so-called "grandiose self" diminishes as the need for dissociation is surrendered and replaced by the increased capacity to tolerate the existence of *conflictual* self-states, vitalizing a broadening experience of "me-ness" as simultaneously adaptational and self-expressive—an outcome that, I believe, most contemporary analysts would accept as the foremost criterion of a successful treatment process.

14

RESISTANCE, OBJECT USAGE, AND HUMAN RELATEDNESS[1] (1995)

"Resistance" is not a word I ordinarily use, either conceptually or clinically, and when I might hear it inadvertently pop out of my mouth it is usually when I am feeling grouchy with a patient and unaware that I wish to conceal it. Notwithstanding its illusory advantage in a countertransferential emergency, it is a term that I feel has become largely incompatible with the natural evolution in postclassical analytic thought. In effect, it traps us into preserving intact Freud's (1925) formulation of the function of negation, in which the negativity of resistance is viewed as a barrier between depth and surface designed to prevent repressed images or ideas from entering consciousness. In this sense, it is a remnant of our past that I think can be usefully reframed as part of an enacted dialectical process of meaning construction, rather than an archeological

1. Portions of this essay in earlier versions were presented in February 1993 as a discussion of Christopher Bollas's paper "Preoccupation Unto Death" at a meeting of the William Alanson White Psychoanalytic Society and as part of a November 1993 panel, "Resistance: Obstacle or Steppingstone?" at the William Alanson White Institute's Fiftieth Anniversary Clinical Conference. The chapter was originally published in its present form in *Contemporary Psychoanalysis*, 1995, 31:163–192.

barrier preventing the surfacing of disavowed reality. Freud (1925) observed that

> the content of a repressed image or idea can make its way into con-sciousness, on condition that it is *negated*. Negation is a way of tak-ing cognizance of what is repressed; indeed it is already a lifting of the repression, though not, of course, an acceptance of what is repressed. . . . With the help of the symbol of negation, thinking frees itself from the restrictions of repression and enriches itself with material that is indispensable for its proper functioning [pp. 235–236].

This, of course, bears centrally on the concept of "resistance," which in my view, as I shall discuss, is anchored more fundamentally to disso-ciation than to repression. My conceptualization of resistance, like that of Schafer (1983, pp. 230–231), addresses the *structure* of resistance as an account of transference itself, but as a dyadic experience rather than an individual one—an account of the transference and countertransference matrix, rather than of transference alone. It also addresses the *motiva-tion* of resistance as not simply an avoidance of insight or a fear of change, but as a dialectic between preservation and change—a basic need to preserve the continuity of self-experience in the process of growth by minimizing the threat of potential traumatization. It is a "marker" that structures the patient's effort to arrive at new meaning without disruption of self-continuity during the transition, and gives voice to opposing realities within the patient's inner world that are being enacted in the intersubjective and interpersonal field between analyst and patient. The negativity of resistance thus represents a dialectic tension between realities that are not yet amenable to a self-reflective experience of intrapsychic conflict and are, at that moment, in a discontinuous, adversarial relationship to each other. Optimally, and most simply, it is a dimension of the ongoing process of negotiation between incompatible domains of self-experience.

Consider the following clinical vignette. It is based on a consulta-tion and a dream—a first dream in analysis—which contained an image that configured both the analytic process and my subsequent ability to comprehend this patient, whom I will call Mr. M.

It was a Friday afternoon. The last of Mr. M's three "preanalytic" consultations with me had just ended with an agreement that we would begin an analysis and start work the following Monday. Alone, I found myself in an odd reverie state, complacently daydreaming: "As consultations go," I thought to myself, "these went pretty well, and I think he felt similarly." But I then heard another voice in me saying: "What do *you* know? You're not even sure what you mean by 'pretty well,' much less what *he* thought!" It was obvious that Mr. M's analysis had already begun. Nevertheless, he arrived promptly at 8:00 A.M. on Monday for what was technically his first session, and began by enthusiastically reporting the "brief" dream he had just two hours earlier. It was brief because the alarm clock that had awakened him marked, as he put it, "the end of my dream and the beginning of my treatment." Even though it wasn't until later that we could start to comprehend together his subtle portrayal of reality implied in this seemingly casual remark, the dream he then presented, like my own "daydream," powerfully foreshadowed what was to come:

> "I was leaning out of a window on the top floor of a tall building that was in flames. A fireman was climbing up a ladder to rescue me, and I was throwing rocks at him. Then my alarm went off."

How to look at Mr. M's dream! There are as many potential ways to explore the issue of resistance, and as many ways to talk about the meaning of the concept in the treatment process, as there are schools of psychoanalytic thought. The subject becomes even more complex when comparisons are made across theories of treatment. Like "resistance," the term "treatment" is commonplace in the contemporary analytic literature, but we rarely find analysts talking about what it is they believe they are treating, and even more rarely what they think they are "curing." In other words, how a given school of thought looks paradigmatically at a dream such as Mr. M's, addresses not only its formulation of resistance but also its implicit theory of cure.

I've thus chosen to begin with the above vignette because it gets to the theme of resistance by its most direct and perhaps most informative route: the unique quality of psychoanalytic cure that distinguishes it from any other form of cure, the fact that it is "resisted" as an intrinsic part of its nature. How this quality is understood by a given body of analytic theory is going to inform not only what an analyst does, but what an analyst hears. Obviously, without associations Mr. M's individuality is hidden. Nevertheless, any analyst, regardless of theoretical persuasion, will inevitably, without associations, hear the dream at a metaphorical level that addresses the issue of resistance in whatever way that particular analyst conceives of resistance, and this will to some degree inform the way the treatment gets shaped. As an interpersonal-relational analyst, I frame the metaphor as if the patient were saying "I'm here because I'm in trouble, but the trouble I'm in is not something I need rescuing from, even though it may look that way.

However, I fully expect you to try to 'cure' me and I'm prepared to defeat you. I don't *have* an illness; I *am* my illness and I won't let you cure me of being who I am."

A person may feel himself so psychologically incapacitated and at risk in the world of people, that it is indeed similar to living alone in a burning building from which he needs to be rescued. But that particular burning building is the only one that exists as a self, and one's individual selfhood, no matter how painful or unadaptive, must be protected at all cost as part of any rescue operation. So I suppose what this essay is really all about is why I believe that any patient, with or without such an opening dream, needs to construct, through enactment with his own analyst, his personal meaning for the metaphor of "throwing rocks at the fireman"; if this can't be mutually constructed, then the treatment will, tragically, be nothing more than a well-meaning attempt to "cure the patient of his dream"—who he is to himself—and it will surely fail.

"Resistance," from this perspective, is an enacted communication that an analyst's effort to interpret meaning is being experienced at that moment as requiring the patient to trade off some domain of his own self-experience for something he is being offered that is "not me," and that the analyst's offering is being opposed, in one way or another, because it is not felt as sufficiently negotiable. "This is *not* who I am!" is part of the dialectic between loyalty to old patterns of self-meaning and the consensual construction of new meaning with increased ability to state "*This* is who I am!"[2]

The reason I dislike the term "resistance" should now be fairly clear. The concept to which it refers is inconsistent with how I think about analytic process, and unless I stretch its original meaning beyond recognition, it doesn't fit what I see as taking place between analyst and patient. The concept rests upon an unquestioned positioning of the analyst as arbiter of reality, so that the analyst determines what constitutes resistance on the basis of whatever meaning he attributes to the patient's behavior or to his experience of the patient's attitude towards him at a given time. Moore and Fine (1990) define "resistance" in its broadest sense as "all of a patient's defensive efforts to avoid self knowledge" (p. 168). I am struck with how much ground

---

2. The issue of the dialectic between "no" and "yes" has been explicated in a dialogue between Enid Balint (1991, p. 426) and me (Bromberg, 1991a, pp. 431–433), in which I argue that the patient's capacity to confront the analyst's perceived inaccuracy ("resistance") and the analyst's attuned responsiveness to this confrontation are a unitary interpersonal configuration that *shapes* the potential value of the content rather than simply "carrying" it.

this statement covers and how much latitude it gives the analyst to arbitrate reality on a completely subjective basis. Though most analysts are too sophisticated simply to apply the concept of resistance in that manner, the term itself positions the analyst with regard to the patient as somebody who is trying to "cure" faulty reality.

I would argue that the human personality, in order to grow, needs to encounter another personality as a separate center of subjective reality, so that its own subjectivity can oppose, be opposed, confirm, and be confirmed in an intersubjective context. "Resistance-as-obstacle" functions inherently as a necessary guardian of self-continuity during this process and, in that sense, an obstacle, as opposition, is an intrinsic aspect of the growth dialectic that makes clinical psychoanalysis possible. I proposed in chapter 12 that the human personality possesses the extraordinary capacity to negotiate stability and change simultaneously, and it will do so under the right relational conditions—conditions that preserve every patient's necessary illusion that he can "stay the same while changing." So the question that to me seems most clinically relevant is what role a patient's opposition is playing in his efforts to accommodate new experience at a given moment, not simply what constitutes the best way to interpret it as a defense against insight.

A perception of oneself through the eyes of an "other"—the heart of the interpretive process of self-exploration—is possible only if the other's subjectivity can be accommodated into one's own self-experience. But this is inseparable from the relative presence or absence of a core experience of one's human relatedness. Certain patients enter analysis with so little sense of their own humanness that they can relate only through dehumanizing the analytic relationship and through objectifying intersubjective space. Since it is not possible to empathize with an object, the analyst is exposed to the continuing experience of being himself transformed into one and doing the same thing to his patient. The impact of this on the analyst is so deadening and frustrating (see also Ogden, 1994) that it typically evokes the analyst's need to escape this necrophilic bondage through a variety of his own defensive strategies, including a determined wish to "cure" the patient of his unrelatedness as quickly as possible.

I see this situation and its variations to be not unusual in clinical work. In real life, the quality of a person's capacity for relatedness can be distinguished, often dramatically, by the broadness or narrowness of his field of consciousness, including perceptual consciousness. In analytic treatment this phenomenon is brought into high relief because transference embodies, if nothing else, a powerful narrowing of one's field of consciousness. Its effect on perception and interpersonal behavior is to render the other person into an object—a fixed, concrete representation of another person linked to an equally concrete representation of oneself. Technically, patients like Mr. M do not transferentially have to reduce the analyst to an object, because people are already perceived *only* as objects. They therefore enter treatment lacking a connection to an "analyst as human being" with whom to explore relationally the workings of their mind and, even more importantly, are foreclosed from the possibility of exploring this nonrelatedness as an intersubjective experience in itself. Such a patient's objectification of self and other, often his most pronounced feature, is not initially discernable to the patient by looking at himself through the analyst's eyes. To the patient, his "intersubjective deadness" is who he is, not a feature of his behavior, and he is no more likely to perceive it than a fish is likely to discover the existence of water (Levenson, 1988, p. 566). For indeterminate periods of time, the patient tends to observe his analyst from a hypnoidal state of consciousness that is the hallmark of dissociation—a narrowed, dreamlike field of dehumanized and concretized objectivity.

Dissociation and Object Usage

During these periods the other person exists to the patient as an "object," as distinguished from a subjective center of his own reality. Often, the patient's field of consciousness is so narrow that, regardless of whether the other person is his therapist, his spouse, his friend, his employer, or his child, he "focuses" on them in a dissociated state, as if he were looking at objects through a window. Mr. M, because he entered treatment without the capacity to exist experientially in an intersubjective context through which personal reality could be consensually reconstructed, had to find his own way to "resist" trading off his dream in return for treatment.

From this vantage point, the task for any analyst is to be able to live with paradox (Ghent, 1992; Pizer, 1992). He must not on his own either reject or accept the status of "object," but must learn from his patient how to be a "usable" object for *that* patient—a complex relational negotiation that depends upon remaining alive and related as a person in his own right. But how? What is the fuel for the psychic machinery? Without the concept of "resistance" as a libidinally derived phenomenon, how are we to comprehend why a person, accepted on his own terms, should ever grow and change in analysis (and in life), rather than use the nurturant environment as a secure nest in which to stay safe and accepted forever, not having to bear the discomfort of the new and unfamiliar? For me, the answer must embrace a source of security that provides both "stillness" (in Winnicott's terminology) and the potential for metamorphosis (growth, movement, and transition), without requiring the notion of a separate source of energy (libido) to account for forward movement. But if stillness and movement are to be interlocked in a single aesthetic, how does this inform what we *do* as analysts? With this in mind, I would like now to look at Winnicott's (1969) concept of "object usage," an idea I find extremely evocative in depicting the interpersonal dialectic between letting oneself be used and using oneself.

Let's start with the idea of "usage." Winnicott's concept is not easy to grasp, and its history of being misunderstood is interestingly polarized; some analysts are overly wary of it and others overly enthusiastic about it. One group tends to condemn it as legitimizing the patient's narcissism and the analyst's passivity, while another group tends to enshrine it in an image of the patient's desperate search for empathic recognition met by the analyst's selfless adaptation and nonintrusiveness. Partly because of sociocultural implications attached to the term "use," both groups fail to grasp sufficiently the distinction between an analyst being used as an object and being exploited as a person, and if a patient is to get what he is there for, this distinction is no small matter.

In Winnicott's terms, an analyst permits himself to be "used" as a subjective object and then to be "destroyed" as a projective object. What does this mean in actuality? First of all, the analyst has to comprehend the essential difference between being used as an object and what Ghent (1992) called "object abuse." Secondly, he has to have the ability to be humanly reliable in surviving the patient's attacks on his identity. I do not see this as literally meaning an absence of any quality of retaliation or the absence of any change in attitude toward the patient. In fact, I think of it as largely the opposite; the analyst has to be able to experience and acknowledge his own limitations. A patient does not need a saint as an analyst; he needs authenticity.

Winnicott (1969, pp. 86–89) emphasized the importance of the analyst interpreting so as to convey the limits of his understanding—to place himself outside of the patient's domain of omnipotent control and thus present himself as an object of perception and potential scrutiny. I see this as an effort to engage the patient's capacity for *perception*—to enable a shift from what is behind the patient's eyes (his internal reality) to what is in front of his eyes (cf. Greenberg, 1991a). If the analyst were actually able to be a perfectly reliable object, the analysis would fall victim to its own artificiality and hypocrisy, and the affective interface between unconscious fantasy and perception (the place of analytic growth) would not be reached. I believe that an analyst's "failure" as a usable object is not so much a matter of unreliability as it is of unwillingness or inability to ultimately listen to or hear the patient's overt or covert descriptions of his blind spots, and to make judicious use of the patient's perceptiveness. In other words, "psychotherapy must remain an obstinate attempt of two people to recover the wholeness of being human through the relationship between them" (Laing, 1967, p. 53).

Gross failure of object usage (in Winnicott's sense) results in or perpetuates the experience of *being* an object (in the sense of a created product), suffering a dehumanized hatred of life while envying those who live it. Reflect upon this shattering, transferential accusation of failed responsibility made by one who was so failed (Shelley, 1818):

> I am malicious because I am miserable. . . . Yet, mine shall not be the submission of abject slavery. I will revenge my injuries; . . . and chiefly towards you . . . do I swear inextinguishable hatred [pp. 130–131]. . . . [W]hen I discovered that he, the author . . . of my existence . . . sought his own enjoyment in feelings and passions from the indulgence of which I was forever barred, then impotent envy and bitter indignation filled me with an insatiable thirst for vengence. . . . I knew that I was preparing for myself a deadly torture, but I was the slave, not the master, of an impulse which I detested yet could not disobey. Evil thenceforth became my good. Urged thus far, *I had no choice but to adapt my nature to an element which I had willingly chosen* [pp. 202–203, italics added].

"What a monster!" you might say. And you would be right, because the accused in this case is Victor Frankenstein, and the accusor is Mary Shelley's modern Prometheus, abandoned by his creator, and in turning away from his own longing for human relatedness, becoming the monstrous incarnation of an obsessive hatred of life itself. Shelley's struggle with this moral issue is not hard to comprehend. She was trying to find a way of dealing with the complicated and qualified responsibility that each person must ultimately take for the hateful and dark side of his own nature. Though not absolving the monster in each of us, Shelley's morality tale suggests (at least in tone) that the greatest moral responsibility lies, as it did with Victor Frankenstein, in the caregiver's success or failure in offering adaptational human involvement (whether the caregiver is parent or society)—that is, in his or her commitment to relationship rather than "creationship."

How do we as analysts know when, like Victor Frankenstein, we have crossed the line into self-deception and have become the feared "shrink," delivering reality as if creating life? The hardest part of my own job as an analyst is to struggle against my natural human tendency to be pulled unreflectively into linear thinking and its reassuring certainty of a past, present, and future linked in causal sequence. I am always aware that if I am not vigilant I will find myself organizing meaning along the lines of "that happened then," which led to "this happening now," and (if all goes well) will lead to "so-and-so happening later." Linear organization of meaning is an inevitable dimension of reality, but if I let this mode dominate for too long, it is also inevitable that the work will begin to drain itself of spontaneity, and will potentially stalemate or even die. In other words, I am suggesting that what we do as analysts is, at its best, an ongoing dialectic between the inherent ambiguity of human experience (its nonlinearity) and the equally human "pull" to give it linear meaning.

Bion's (1970) admonition to enter each session "without memory or desire" and Levenson's (1976b) holographic imagery each give me more of a weapon against runaway linearity than does, for example, Bollas's (1992) more "causal" view of a person motivated to create certain types of objects and to fill an "empty present" with projections from the past. I view an "object" as a component of a dynamic structure rather than as a static structure in itself. From this perspective a patient does not simply become attached to a certain "kind" of object as though the object had certain inherent qualities that the patient was looking for; the process through which the object is in fact created is that of interpersonal engagement. The other person, that is, has as much of a role in the creation of the "object" as does the patient, even though the patient's need to perceive the other in a certain way may be the stronger of the two motivating forces. The focus is not on the filling of an "empty" object with projections, but on what a person does with and to other people, with that which he already has (see also chapter 11), and on what sorts of fixed, concrete patterns of relatedness constitute his world of interpersonal mental representation that result from these types of integrations with other people. It is these fixed patterns of relatedness that lead to the mutual creation, between the patient and other people, of a reality that supports his way of being and his way of perceiving himself and others.

In Mr. M's analysis, for example, those qualities in the analyst that were experientially usable were limited to those over which he could maintain omnipotent control by dissociation held in place by systematic unrelatedness to the analyst's other attributes. But for every patient,

it is in the *act* of dissociation itself, in all of its interpersonal manifestations—what the patient does *with* the analyst to make transferential
experience usable—that the work of "object usage" and its analytic
exploration takes place by the mutual creation of an intersubjective
reality that bridges fantasy and objectivity. R. D. Laing (1967) has the
following to say on this issue:

> *Fantasy is a particular way of relating to the world*. It is part of, some-
> times the essential part of, the meaning or sense implicit in action.
> As relationship we may be dissociated from it . . . [and] we may . . .
> refuse to admit that our behavior implies an experiential relation-
> ship or *a relational experience that gives it a meaning*. Fantasy . . . is
> always experiential and meaningful; and if the person is not disso-
> ciated from it, relational in a valid way [pp. 31–32, italics added].

Dissociation, Trauma, and Resistance

Sometimes self-preservation is accomplished almost or entirely at the
expense of growth, and the individual is removed from full involvement (sometimes from all involvement) in the here-and-now experience of life. For certain people, here-and-now experience—the living
present—cannot, in fact, be mentally represented without the felt danger of traumatization. They, in effect, live in a frozen past, a world in
which they are defined primarily by their attachment to a configuration of discontinuous, concrete states of consciousness, each an
embodiment of a discrete representation of self. To sustain this form of
safety while trying to live a life is no easy matter, and as a solution it
leads to a hatred and fear of the living present. Obsessions and preoc-
cupations are usually unavoidable as "fillers" for what cannot be mentally represented, and these function so as to deny the very existence
of the gaps between dissociated self-states. Bion (1970, pp. 19–20; 1978,
p. 3) called this felt presence of an absence a "no-thing," its existence
obscured by what Guntrip (1969, pp. 62–64, 82–84) depicted as stop-
gap fantasy in the service of a "schizoid compromise," and what
Sullivan (1953, pp. 353–354) described as "part of this vast body of
complex performances which we call substitutive activity." Sullivan
(1953) says something quite interesting in this regard.

> Dissociation can easily be mistaken for a really quite magical busi-
> ness in which you fling something of you into outer darkness,
> where it reposes for years, quite peacefully. This is a fantastic over-
> simplification. Dissociation works very suavely indeed as long as it

works, but it isn't a matter of keeping a sleeping dog under an anaesthetic. It works by a constant alertness or vigilance of awareness, with certain supplementary processes which prevent one's ever discovering the usually quite clear evidences that part of one's living is done without any awareness [p. 318].

Dissociation is a phenomenon connected to interpersonal psychoanalysis in a way that is not only deeply rooted but central to its basic model. In fact, Sullivan's (1953) theory of interpersonal analysis, reduced to its essentials is, in my view, a theory of the dissociative organization of personality in response to trauma.

It is not a new version of Freud's theory of repression in response to conflict, and despite some historical misunderstanding, dissociation is not simply Sullivan's word for repression. In disavowing Freudian conflict theory, Sullivan was not just rejecting a concept; he was saying that what structures the development of human mind is a process empirically different from the one Freud came to believe existed. He was referring to the dissociative process, and it is this phenomenon that I suggest was most unfortunately lost when Freud abandoned his recognition that trauma exists as a reality in shaping personality, perception, and memory, and turned exclusively to the concepts of psychic reality, fantasy, and internal conflict to provide virtually the sole source of data. Consider, in this regard, what Laub and Auerhahn (1993) have to say about trauma, defense, and the capacity to process psychic reality:

> [W]e all hover at different distances between knowing and not knowing about trauma, caught between the compulsion to complete the process of knowing and the inability or fear of doing so. It is the nature of trauma to elude our knowledge *because of both defence and deficit.* . . . trauma overwhelms and defeats our capacity to organize it [p. 288, italics added].

Laub and Auerhahn are suggesting, in other words, that resistance is not simply defensive resistance to knowing (as in repression); it is the more primary nature of trauma to "elude" our knowledge because of what they call a deficit—a gap that has to do with the formation of psychic structure into "me" and "not me"—a dissociative gap, by virtue of which the experience of original trauma is relegated to a part of the self that is unlinked to that part of self preserved as a relatively intact "me." It is not the "contents" of the mind that are primarily at issue; *it is the dissociative structure of the mind itself ("me" and "not-me") that resistance is most fundamentally addressing, at least during much of an ongoing treatment.*

Sullivan went back to the wellspring of personality development—its roots in the observable reality of what people do with each other and to each other. In so doing, he restored to psychoanalytic thinking the centrality of the phenomenon of dissociation as the most basic capacity of the human mind to protect its own stability—the cornerstone upon which all else rests—which Putnam (1992, p. 104) referred to as "the escape when there is no escape." I am not willing, however, to discard the concepts of conflict and repression and simply replace them with trauma and dissociation. I believe that dissociation and repression are each based upon phenomena that have their individual integrity, and that the link between them has particular bearing on how we understand resistance. It is my belief that Sullivan's interpersonal emphasis on the "manifestly observable," when additionally informed by the deep respect for the "experientially observable" inner world held by the Independent School of British object-relational thinking, offers a unique possibility of correcting Freud's mistake without abandoning his wisdom.

From Dissociation to Conflict

One ramification of thinking about patients in terms of dissociation is a fresh understanding of the concept of resistance and the differing ability of patients to work in the transference. But for me, it also raises a further question: whether, in certain phases of *all* treatment, we are in fact dealing not with conflict, but rather with a broad range of dissociated states that we may not be acknowledging as such, and we are actually helping (or sometimes interfering with) a patient's ability to move from a dissociative structure to a more conflicted one. If so, this would make certain periods of seemingly intractable resistance, treatment impasse, or sometimes abrupt termination, more a matter of the analyst's failure to identify and confirm the validity of dissociated parts of self, than a patient's stubborn need to avoid dealing with painful conflict, or as it is sometimes put in termination notes, "the patient's need to flee from intimacy." As I've stated in chapter 13, I believe that to see "resistance" as a defensive withdrawal in order to abort or foreclose the therapeutic process is, most of the time, an error. Because the patient's paramount need is to preserve the dissociative structure while surrendering it, many of his inner voices are specifically designed to preserve the sense of safety in the old structure.

From this vantage point, one aspect of resistance can be considered as a way of noting or marking the existence of a dissociated aspect of self with its own reality that has to be accessed and "consulted," rather than simply a defense against taking responsibility for one's own actions. I think this view is particularly supported when "resistance" comes at or near the end of a session, a point at which the need to mark the existence of a self-state that is not sufficiently participating in the therapy is most important as a link to "next time." In this context, it would be as if the patient were saying "internal negotiation is still in progress, and even though I can't use all of what you said this session, it may not be going to waste." That is, despite an analyst's frequent feeling that his patient is simply trying to "undo" the work of that session, the analyst's interventions, rather than "disappearing into thin air" as sometimes seems the case, are potentially enabled by the patient's "resistant" comments to be held for further negotiation till next time, without abandoning or "selling out" the patient's more dissociated self-experience.

It is only through an analyst's joining the intrapsychic battle in his patient's inner world via the interpersonal and intersubjective battle in the analytic process, that a patient's divisions within himself can come to be known. Having to feel your patient's internal world as an analyst, and being required to use your own shifting self-states while holding on to the dissociated pieces of your patient's reality, is the only way an analyst is going to get to the fact that resistance is, in the main, a statement of work going on. It is through resistance-as-obstacle that the essential tension of the dialectic of growth is maintained and that questions are formulated that shape the analyst's experiential understanding of his patient as an ongoing process. Questions such as "Is my patient feeling my presence and involvement, and if so, what is his reaction to the experience? It is conflicted? Is it still dissociated? Or is it perhaps an as yet unintegrated mixture of both-what Winnicott (1971b) designated as the use of 'potential space'?" That is, are patient and analyst at a transitional point, where the patient is beginning to surrender his dissociative structure and is shifting to a more conflicted one? The intersubjective context is particularly significant here, because with such patients the therapist is almost invariably attuned, at least preconsciously, to the relatively greater room for relatedness at these change points than earlier in the work, when his more typical feeling was likely to have been frustration or deadness. It is this "room for relatedness" that turns static, frozen space into "potential space," and allows the creative encounter between a patient's multiple realities and those of his analyst to form something new—a negotiated enhancement of the patient's perceptual capacity and an increased surrender of the dissociative structure of his personality organization.

Dreaming: A "Path of Least Resistance?"

Often emblematic of a transition from dissociation to conflict, are a patient's dreams at this juncture. Schwartz (1994, p. 218) has commented that "the therapist's search for the patient's self is anticipated as the destruction of self by the other, ultimately bringing the therapist into the transferentially dual role of seeker-destroyer." I have observed, for instance, that dreams about one's car or one's apartment being broken into, or dreams about driving a car with defective brakes, or some other metaphor for loss of control, frequently occur at a point when an intrapsychic "war" is heating up between opposing self-states in the patient's inner world—a point when the patient's hope of self-growth is gaining momentum and threatening the control held by the dissociative voices that speak for "safety and stability as a matter of survival." The dreams often suggest that the locus of the action has shifted from the transference-countertransference enactment to a struggle within the patient's internal object world, representing the dread of being robbed of life—a dread that, paradoxically, increases as a response to increased hope that pleasurable growth can really happen. "Life," in this sense, is a metaphor for the wish to continue existing as the same "self," and frequently the fear of "robbery of life" occurs at a point when a patient's own perception of growth potential may be drowning out the voice of self-preservation, and not only at a point when the analyst is being "overzealously therapeutic" in his search. For a patient, the excitement that accompanies genuine hope of being fully "alive" is a complex experience that represents a stress-point in the dialectic between self-continuity and self-growth.

In other words, these kinds of dreams tend to surface or resurface when the hope of inner stability and satisfying human relatedness is greatest, and therefore when the fear of not being able to return to "the old selves" is strongest. At such times they signal the growing ability to experience conflict between states of mind that formerly were incompatible within the same "apartment" or the same "car," and a fear that if these self-states are allowed in the same mental space, the self that now occupies the apartment will "lose control," be ransacked, and "robbed of life." The threat to the patient's dissociative structure is as real as the excitement in growth, and the wish to restore the reliability of past solutions invariably finds its voice—a voice yearning to be able once again to relinquish personal agency and not feel, to find escape from the potential of traumatic loss of self by becoming an object and following rules. To feel, this voice cries, is to die—death being the plunge into the dread of eternal aloneness.

At this point in treatment, the patient is starting to organize a capacity to deal with complex feelings in the here-and-now and is becoming genuinely fearful and angry at the threat to his stability, as if it were an invasion from within that was out of his control. I would like to underline this kind of moment as one in which the analyst must be particularly responsive to the simultaneous existence in his patient of opposing self-states that formerly could not be contained in a single relational context, but are now achieving that potential. Opposing parts of self, individually enlivened through interchange with the analyst, begin to bridge the dissociative gap between them. A first step towards self-cohesiveness starts to take shape, and the analyst's sense of the patient shifts to that of a shadowy whole person emerging, and away from his earlier experience of his patient and himself as "objects" that have no authentic human contact. But this can only happen at the point when the patient has developed some ability to experience the mutual impact of the analytic relationship. He can feel the analyst's new capacity to recognize and care about who he (the patient) *is*, not just about who he wants the patient to *be*—that is, someone more "alive." The patient can feel the analyst's new capacity to care about him but to still be himself, and as I've said in chapter 10, he can respect the analyst's ability to be both "empathic and emphatic." In other words, he perceives that the analyst, too, has changed through the relationship and is a "usable" object.[3]

The analytic relationship, if effective, facilitates a patient's ability to gradually replace the protection of her hard-won dissociative sanctuary from pain with a capacity for self-reflectiveness and a life that includes past, present, and future. Nevertheless, no matter how often I have seen this negotiation take place, I'm still amazed when it happens the next time—that someone is truly willing to dismantle her self-stability for the sake of a dangerous image of hope that is held in the mind of the therapist. The following clinical vignette, I think, captures particularly vividly the resiliency of the human spirit, both in its determination to grow and in its determination to protect itself from betrayal by its own capacity for hope of a trustworthy relationship.

"Well, It's More Fun than a Nightmare"

My patient, whom I will call Clarissa, was a young woman in her early twenties, unmarried, and living alone in a marginal section of lower

---

3. See Slochower (1994) for a compelling depiction of "object usage" that synthesizes this concept with Winnicott's portrayal of the "holding environment."

Manhattan—marginally run-down, marginally unsafe, marginally inconvenient, and marginally unsuited to someone of her background. It is this last point that is the most complex, because although she was raised as a child of affluent parents and smothered in the best that money could buy, she grew up in emotional poverty, her inner life disconfirmed as a matter to be taken seriously. She existed in the eyes of her narcissistic parents as a living cartoon—a prepubescent sexual toy to her father and a source of disdainful amusement, as well as a scatter-brained nuisance, to her preoccupied and competitive mother.

Clarissa at this time had been in treatment about two years; she was at a point where her dissociative mental organization was beginning to shift and she was starting to experience conflict around issues that had been simply enacted through separate and discontinuous states of consciousness. The paramount theme that was starting to surface, in a more fully conscious and self-reflective form, was that of emotional neglect and her feelings about adults who wish to see her only in their own terms. The vignette is organized around a dream and the work following its appearance:

> She dreamt that she was flying through the sky on the back of a white horse with chartreuse and pink polka-dots. She was wearing no underwear and her dress was blowing in the wind, showing all, when she and her horse landed on the terrace of her parents' penthouse, where they were having cocktails with friends. Her mother and father nodded at her, perfunctorily acknowledging her arrival, but did not interrupt their conversation. She just sat there on the back of the horse, waiting for them to finish. That was the dream.

When I asked her what came to mind about it, her first response was a rather contemptuous, *"Well, it's more fun than a nightmare."* She would not elaborate on that or allow the images to touch personal thoughts or feelings, beyond what information she had already told me about her parents' social life-style and her own love of riding as a young girl. The harder I tried to probe for associations the more she treated the subject as something she found humorous. She was not overtly dismissive of me, but rather behaved as though I lacked a sense of humor and she was trying to help me "loosen-up" and appreciate that the dream was only an illustration of her capacity to deal with life in a light-hearted manner. In fact, I *was* starting to feel more and more like an "old fogey," and had just begun (defensively) to get into the "spirit of fun" with her, when I could feel her self-state switch dramatically. Suddenly I was the one making light of her inner life, and she was sitting there looking hurt and pathetic. It was then I had the thought that I may not have been protecting myself from feeling like an *old* fogey, but a *young* fogey—I as the young Clarissa, wanting my feelings to be taken seriously and having them disconfirmed by "Clarissa as father," who was defining reality as my failure to realize that I take things *too* seriously. So *I* switched defensively, and it was only then I could feel my effort at humor as a hollow cartoon, masking the neglected person I did not wish to feel myself being—a person who was now sitting opposite me in her own form.

Slowly, I told her some of what was taking place for me subjectively, and a process began that was initially defined by her switches between self-states, in which she oscillated from being remarkably responsive and forthcoming to being distrustful and frightened. The difference for me was that although I had seen these states many times before, there were now periods in which *both* states of mind had access to her consciousness simultaneously though they were not yet felt as a unitary self-experience. She could now begin to feel the presence of multiple realities as internal voices that were still at war but were now talking to each other. She told me that one reason she had been angry at me—just before she had the dream—was that I was not aware of how frightened she was to take things seriously, and in the previous session, when she was telling me about her current life, I wasn't "getting" how bad it was because she told it as though she was "above it all." She was furious that I was being just like her parents and didn't really want to know about the "marginal" world she really lives in, both inner and outer. This led to a stream of associations beginning with "It's more fun than a nightmare"; nightmare had reference to the horse, the "mare" she rode as a child, on the back of which she could live in her dissociated world, flying magically "above it all"—above the *real* nightmare she feared would flood her if she achieved fuller access to consciousness, and memory of the exploitation, disregard, and neglect that constituted her "objective" reality of relationships with adults. Thus, "don't trust adults" became her secret motif for survival through turning everything, including herself, into a cartoon. But now, one part of herself had enough insight into this process to respond to my parental failure with a dream that, by my entering through enactment, took her to a next step in her growth.

New self-experiential capacity becomes possible when dissociated aspects of self are activated vividly with the analyst, but for the patient these are always moments of "good news and bad news." The "bad news," in one form or another, will be experienced and communicated as such by parts of self that do not feel gratitude for having been relationally "enlivened" but feel threatened at having been "invaded and betrayed." Those parts of self would like to be able to comfortably and routinely return to the familiar dissociated structure—that is, to the ability to see life as a disaster waiting to happen—and to mechanically deal with the potential failure of the environment to protect the patient from trauma. In other words, even during periods of movement from dissociation to conflict, one can feel the dialectic between opposing parts of self; what is good news received with thanks by one part is bad news received, rocks in hand, by another. If an analyst does not listen to the fear and anger in the parts dedicated to preservation of safety and continuity, while he is "celebrating" with the part dedicated to change, the former will "throw rocks at him" and the analyst will call it "resistance." The voice of dissociation will always be heard in one form or another, often in dreams, and the message (which we frequently hear *directly* from certain patients) is "don't celebrate; just listen." Mr. M found his own metaphor in the image of "throwing rocks at the fireman" and found his own way to enact with me his fear that the beginning of his treatment was an "alarm" clock signalling the end of his "dream." Clarissa found hers in the image of riding her nightmare "above it all," while enacting her need for her analyst/parent to engage what she was doing.

Talking about internal object relations and object usage is one way of looking at the dilemma created by the fact that the security of the self is never fully stable, because the natural configuration of the human personality is that of being both fully in, and at the same time separate from, the "world out there." Dehumanization of the self and other is a result of overbalancing in favor of living in one's inner world, but successful object usage doesn't move a person from "inside" to "outside." Creativity and self-expression are not simply a matter of a capacity for "ruthless" object usage, in Winnicott's sense, or of being able to break out of one's inner prison and "do your own thing." They result from being able to find one's own balance between being fully in, and at the same time separate from, the world, and allowing this balance to shift as age and circumstances change. Furthermore, I believe that what constitutes an optimal balance between self-expression and adaptation is always shifting and always tied to the context in which life exists, particularly one's stage of life. After a certain point in one's life, the "need to be oneself" and continue to make one's own statement can be driven by a narcissistic quest for self-validation (a need to confirm a sense of self that doesn't feel sufficiently nourished simply in the act of living), just as surrender to external "rules" at an earlier phase of life can derive from fear and hatred of the living present.

15

HYSTERIA, DISSOCIATION, AND CURE

Emmy von N Revisited [1] *(1996)*

"An hysteric," it has been said, "is someone who goes through life pretending to be who he really is."[2] I've never heard a diagnostic description of hysteria I liked better, except perhaps, "an hysteric is like a glass of water without the glass." Each of these aphorisms, in its own imagery, points a finger directly at the hysteric's most pronounced interpersonal handicaps: his readiness to dramatize his feelings lest they not be taken as "real" by others and his burden of chronic anxiety engendered by the mistrust that is indeed felt by others as to where they stand with him at any given moment. Whether male or female, the hysteric, in other words, suffers not only from reminiscences (Breuer and Freud, 1893–1895, p. 7), but from a

---

1. An earlier draft of this essay, titled "On Treating Patients with Symptoms, and Symptoms with Patience," was presented in May 1995 at "The Psychoanalytic Century: An International Interdisciplinary Conference Celebrating the Centennial of Breuer and Freud's *Studies on Hysteria*," sponsored by the New York University Postdoctoral Program in Psychotherapy and Psychoanalysis.

2. A slightly different version (possibly the original) can be found in R. D. Laing (1962b, p. 34).

tragic inability to convince others of the authenticity of his or her own subjective experience. Comparing this to what Sullivan (1953) labeled "security operations," Laing (1962b) suggested that "the hysteric is engaged in sincerity operations." He noted, however, that

> it is usually others who complain of the hysteric's lack of genuineness or sincerity. In fact, it is regarded as pathognomonic of the hysteric that his or her actions should be false, that they should be histrionic, dramatized, etc. The hysteric, on the other hand, often insists that his feelings are real and genuine. It is we who feel that they are unreal [p. 36].

This issue of the collision between the subjective reality of the patient and the subjective reality of the therapist is, of course, at the heart of every clinical psychoanalysis, and has probably never been portrayed as openly or in as pure a form as it was described in *Studies on Hysteria* (Breuer and Freud, 1893–1895) in Freud's struggle with the use of hypnosis as a technique while attempting to treat Frau Emmy von N, first in 1889 for about seven weeks and then about one year later for an approximately equal length of time.

Friedman (1994) discussed the impact on the history of psychoanalysis of Emmy von N, who, under her actual name, Fanny Moser, was the widow of an affluent Swiss businessman (see Ellenberger, 1977). She was a woman locked in by time, place, and social role to an identity defined by the power of men—in real life an identity defined by widowhood and by what her husband's family said about her[3]; and under her pseudonym, an identity defined by "patienthood" and by what Freud said about her. Friedman (1994) writes that the great lesson of psychotherapy discovered by Freud was that "you cannot fail if you invite the patient to do what she wants to do," and Freud was thus "prepared to obey his patient, Emmy von N, when, in effect, she told him to stop pestering her about the cause of her symptoms and let her talk about whatever she pleased. Freud instantly made her rule his own—in fact, his Fundamental Rule" (pp. 8–9). He took the rule as a key to the storehouse of mental contents—the needed raw data—the ingredients to be placed into the crucible of psychoanalysis, which the analyst would then link together and transform into the substance of

---

3. According to Appignanesi and Forrester (1992), "Fanny's husband died of a heart attack a few days after the birth of her second daughter. Fanny was then twenty-six. Following his death, the children of the first marriage accused Fanny of having poisoned him. An exhumation found no evidence of murder, but his relatives kept up their campaign against her and the rumors persisted" (p. 92).

cure—objective truth. As Friedman put it, Freud "saw that if he could himself make all the necessary connections among the data, then all he would need from the patient is what she was anyway inclined to give him," but he then encountered a new problem with patients—"Freud no longer had to solicit cooperation; but he now had to solicit belief . . . since they could refuse to believe in Freud's inferences" (p. 9). This, as Friedman notes, led Freud to the concept of resistance (see also chapter 14) and led the psychoanalytic situation to be framed for close to 100 years as a struggle between ignorance and objective truth. The problem that psychoanalysis has faced since that time is that although Emmy was correct, and Freud's genius allowed him to recognize this, the human mind was not sufficiently understood to comprehend *why* the Fundamental Rule was useful and that *Emmy's lesson was really a statement about the analytic relationship, not a lesson in analytic technique.* I would argue that this, more than any other single misunderstanding, has slowed the subsequent evolution of psychoanalysis, clinically and conceptually.

Freud (Breuer and Freud, 1893–1895) used the term "waking-state" to distinguish it from Emmy's state of consciousness when she was in a hypnotically induced trance. For example, he says that "in her waking-state she seemed, so far as possible, to, ignore the fact that she was undergoing hypnotic treatment" (p. 51) and that "during this hypnosis I convinced myself that she knew everything that happened in the last hypnosis, whereas in waking-life she knows nothing of it" (p. 55). Similar to the distinction that classical theory has made between dream-life versus waking-life as reflecting the difference between unconscious and conscious, the parallel division between consciousness as "healthy" versus unconsciousness as regressive (in the sense of involving—as in dreams—more "primitive" modes of functioning) has never been seriously questioned. Because of the increased attention now being paid to the normal multiplicity of states of consciousness, an important shift is taking place that is leading away from the unconscious-preconscious-conscious continuum per se, toward a view of the mind as a configuration of discontinuous, shifting states of consciousness with varying degrees of access to perception and cognition. Some of these self-states are hypnoidally unlinked from perception at any given moment of normal mental functioning—lending support to some of Freud's ideas in his *Project* (Freud, 1895) and *The Interpretation of Dreams* (Freud, 1900)—while other self-states are virtually foreclosed from such access because of their original lack of linguistic symbolization.

The major difference between Freud's early view and more recent findings about the nature of the mind is that what Freud called the "perceptual system" is now seen as circumvented or compromised not only during sleep and dreaming, but as a normal developmental response to trauma and as a person's most basic defense against its anticipated recurrence. From this frame of reference, dreaming may be simply the most familiar special case of the more general phenomenon of dissociation—the normal self-hypnotic capacity of the human mind, the voice of other "selves." It might, thereby, be fair to conclude that Freud's willingness to see hypnosis as a phenomenon worthy of his serious attention was startlingly ahead of its time in his treatment of Emmy, but that, in utilizing it, he went about things the wrong way. That is, the key he was looking for is not in hypnosis as a technique (something to be "applied" from outside), but in the fact that autohypnosis is an intrinsic aspect of mental functioning that shapes every human relationship, to one degree or another, without having to be induced.

There are always domains of dissociated self-experience that have weak or nonexistent links to the experience of "I" as a communicable entity, and this is particularly so with patients such as Emmy. Before these hypnoidally inaccessible self-states can be taken as objects of cognitive reflection leading to resolvable intrapsychic conflict, they require that the necessary conditions for cognitive resolution be available. That is, they must first become "thinkable" by becoming linguistically communicable through enactment in the therapeutic relationship. Until this happens, neither genuine repression nor the experience of intrapsychic conflict can take place because each state of consciousness holds its own experientially encapsulated "truth," which is enacted over and over again (see also chapters 12 and 16). The difficulty for psychoanalysts is that they have not had a strong theoretical model to deal with the implications of this, because Freud, in abandoning trauma theory, also dismissed the phenomenon of dissociation and formulated a conceptual system that led to the belief that, except for the most seriously disturbed patients, interpretation of "unconscious conflict" should be sufficient. This belief, as we know, began with his break with Josef Breuer over the issue of how to conceptualize the etiology of hysteria, and it is to one aspect of this controversy—the issue of hypnoid states and splitting of consciousness—that I would like to turn first.

Hysteria and Dissociation

Breuer, essentially agreeing with Charcot and Janet, stated in his theoretical chapter in *Studies on Hysteria* (pp. 185–251), that "what lies at the centre of hysteria is a splitting off of a portion of psychical activity"

(p. 227), but he went even further, in writing that this deserves "to be described as a splitting not merely of psychical activity but of consciousness" (p. 229).[4] In brief, Breuer was advancing the opinion that traumatic hysteria is mediated by a process that can "be classed with autohypnosis" and that "it seems desirable to adopt the expression 'hypnoid,' which lays stress on this internal similarity" (p. 220). The importance of autohypnosis in the genesis of hysterical phenomena, Breuer writes, "rests on the fact that it makes conversion easier and protects (by amnesia) the converted ideas from wearing-away—a protection which leads, ultimately, to an increase in psychical splitting" (p. 220). Almost parenthetically, Breuer adds an observation that in postclassical analytic thinking embodies the heart of our contemporary understanding of normal personality development, its pathology, and its treatment; he writes that, in response to trauma, "*perception too—the psychical interpretation of sense impressions—is impaired*" (p. 201, italics added).

But, while Breuer asserted that the basis of hysteria was the existence of hypnoid states that had the power to create an amnesia, Freud rejected Breuer's concept of self-hypnosis and later contended that he had never encountered a self-hypnotic hysteria, only defense neuroses (Bliss, 1988, p. 36).[5] After *Studies on Hysteria*, Freud was, for the most part, openly contemptuous about the possible usefulness of theorizing about dissociation, hypnoid states, or alterations in consciousness (Loewenstein and Ross, 1992, pp. 31–32). Berman (1981) characterized this as a "one-sided anti-Janet stand" (p. 285) that led psychoanalysis, for the next century, toward an "emphasis on repression at the expense of dissociation" (p. 297).

---

4. Baars (1992), among others, presents research data supporting the conclusion that there is so much evidence for the internal consistency of momentary conscious experience that we are now obliged to go beyond even the idea of divided or dissociated consciousness and must now accept the concept of dissociated aspects of *self*.

5. Eventually, Breuer halfheartedly supported Freud's concept of defense hysteria, "although not without adding that in his opinion defence alone would be hardly sufficient to produce a genuine splitting of the psyche" (Hirschmuller, 1978, p. 167). "Auto-hypnosis," Breuer writes, "has, so to speak, created the space or region of unconscious psychical activity into which the ideas which are fended off are driven" (Breuer and Freud, 1893–1895, p. 236). Thus, while Breuer seemed later to modify his earlier position by including defense as an additional factor in hysteria, he also, "on the other hand, insisted openly that the greater importance should be attached to hypnoid states" (Hirschmuller, 1978, p. 167).

228 • CHAPTER 15

Freud (Breuer and Freud, 1893–1895), who liked to use the term "delirium" to represent the switches from Emmy's "normal" state of consciousness, writes, in a brilliant piece of clinical observation, that

> the transition from a normal state to a delirium often occurred quite imperceptibly. She would be talking quite rationally at one moment about matters of small emotional importance, and as her conversation passed on to ideas of a distressing kind I would notice, from her exaggerated gestures or the appearance of her regular formulas of speech, etc., that she was in a state of delirium. . . . It was often only possible after the event to distinguish between what had happened in her normal state. For the two states were separated in her memory, and she would sometimes be highly astonished to hear of the things which the delirium had introduced piecemeal into her normal conversation [pp. 96–97].

This anecdotal observation is, in fact, empirically supported by current research on dissociative disorders, which confirms that switches between self-states occur quite imperceptibly to the patient, who essentially has amnesia for the switching process itself. Putnam (1988) writes that "it is as if the 'self' that observes and remembers is state-dependent and is suspended during the moment of transition between states of consciousness" (p. 27). It is often also very difficult for the therapist to observe the transitions unless he knows what to look for.

Freud's observation is also, of course, right at the heart of the contemporary controversy about memory, and he is here taking an interesting stand about the reality of subjective experience and the issue of "lying." People with dissociative disorders frequently present with a lifelong history of having been accused of lying, not keeping their promises or, at best, unreliability—very much like Laing's observation about hysterics. Freud said that "in her ordinary life, Frau von N scrupulously avoided any untruthfulness, nor did she ever lie to me under hypnosis. Occasionally, however, she would give me incomplete answers and keep back part of her story until I insisted a second time on her completing it" (p. 98).

Freud's point of view implied a conscious control by his patient over the incompleteness of her answers and that the characterological issue of veracity was somehow independent of the condition itself. From a contemporary vantage point, however, the "incompleteness" of Emmy's answers is consistent with the limited access she had to self-states that possessed additional memories that would have changed not only the content but the meaning of her narrative. Freud's "insisting" may have indeed enabled her sometimes to shift to another self-state, but what was missed in the "successful" result was quite important to the future of psychoanalysis. Freud discovered at this early point in his research that if he pushed hard enough he could get his patient to provide previously undisclosed data that he believed then created a more "complete" story. But, as Lionells (1986) has commented, "the mind of the hysteric shows a particular propensity for dissociation" (p. 587) and what Freud did not recognize was that his patient was already telling the "whole" truth as structured by the dissociated view of reality held by a particular domain of self. In other words, a hysteric's dramatization of feelings is, most of the time, not a performance or an act, and, I might add, this includes many occasions in treatment when the patient herself may be insisting that it *is* an act. Emmy was always reporting not just the *information* held by a particular self-state, but a view of reality defined by the limited part of the self to which Freud was relating at that moment—a hypnoidally discontinuous domain of self with its own dominant affect, its own selectively structured perceptual field, its own range of memories, and its own mode of interpersonal relatedness, including relatedness to Freud.

If an analyst can access and personally engage the particular self-state that is there at a particular moment—what its individual "story" is and how his own here-and-now feelings about his patient are part of that story—he will get not only information (that is, "data"), but, as Rivera (1989) has eloquently put it, he will also facilitate "the erosion of dissociative barriers to a central consciousness that can handle the contradictions of the different voices—not the silencing of different voices with different points of view, but the growing ability to call those voices 'I,' to disidentify with any one of them as the whole story" (p. 28). In other words, it might be said that patients such as Emmy suffer mainly from an "I condition" and that the dissociative symptom Freud referred to as "reminiscences" is just one of the more dramatic consequences of what Rivera called the contradictions between voices.

Trauma, Enactment, and the "Talking Cure"

This brings us to the subject of trauma. Freud (1910) described hysteria as the result of having "been subjected to violent emotional shocks" (p. 10), and in this context, it is not difficult to see how the ordinary experience of surprise becomes phobically associated with traumatic "shock" (see also Reik, 1936). In Emmy's case, it led to what Freud called her "constant fear of surprises" (Breuer and Freud, 1893–1895, p. 59), and Freud in fact proposed that the root of her repetitive "Keep still! Don't say anything! Don't touch me!" was a "protective formula . . . designed to safeguard her against a recurrence of such experiences" (p. 57). I would put it that this type of "safeguard" takes the form of maintaining perpetual readiness for harm by foreclosing any sustained experience of safety. By repeating her formula, she reminds herself that danger is always present and that she must stay on guard; by staying on guard, she is prepared for the ambush she "knows" will come as soon as she feels safe. It is the preparedness (which the formula reinforces) that is the safeguard, so that, if an unanticipated experience happens, it is less likely to be traumatic because her mind is ready to process potential harm. Thus, the continual readiness of the dissociative vigilance is what serves as the protection. It doesn't prevent a harmful event from occurring and, in fact, may often increase its likelihood. It prevents it from occurring *unexpectedly* (see chapter 13).

Freud's technique in treating Emmy was an effort to wipe out the memories of the various events that occurred by surprise—to wipe out the memories of events that caused the shock to the psyche and thus wipe out the negative affect associated with these events. It was not the content of the events that was crucial, but rather their form or structure as something that took place unexpectedly, as with the friend who liked slipping into her room "very softly," or the strange man who opened the door of her compartment "suddenly" (Breuer and Freud, 1893–1895, p. 59). Freud was trying to erase the negative affect being expressed through Emmy's symptoms, and he believed at the time that, if the memories could be rooted out hypnotically, there would be no need for the negative affect. Why did it not work?

Freud wrote: "my therapy consists in wiping away these *pictures*, so that she is no longer able to see them before her. To give support to my suggestion, I stroked her several times over the eyes" (p. 53). He was saying that he was trying to influence the relationship between perception and cognition, but, because he was also attempting to discover empirically what would "work," he could not realize how close he had come to the genuine key (perception), and was inconsistent in his effort. Thus, at other times he tried to influence not perception, but thoughts, in the hope of changing their meaning directly, as for example, when he wrote, "I tried to reduce the importance of this memory, by pointing out that after all nothing had happened to her daughter, and so on" (p. 54).

In what was probably the first instance of Freud's referring to the phenomenon that in later work would be described as "transference," he stated that Emmy "declared that she was afraid she had offended me by something she had said during the massage yesterday which seemed to her to have been impolite" (p. 59). It was here, in the midst of his first preanalytic experiment, that Freud began to think about treating patients with symptoms while treating symptoms with patience. Emmy complained "in a definitely grumbling tone that I was not to keep on asking her where this and that came from, but to let her tell me what she had to say" (p. 63). "I saw," Freud stated, "that my general prohibition had been ineffective, and that I should have to take her frightening impressions away from her one by one. I saw now that the cause of her ill-humour was that she had been suffering from the residues of this story which had been kept back" (pp. 62–63). Acting on this insight, Freud then responded to Emmy's description of her fear of worms by crediting its significance and asking her to tell him some more animal stories, here displaying his emerging recognition that it might be more therapeutic to attend to Emmy's perception of what was meaningful than to continue trying to "figure her out" on his own. Freud, as we know, was accurate, but the shift in his approach was more important than simply being a key to the store-house of hidden memories. It was a relational act that allowed Emmy to experience her own impact in shaping the process that Anna O (Bertha Pappenheim) had called "chimney sweeping" (Breuer and Freud, 1893–1895, p. 30). It might even be said that at this moment in Freud's treatment of Emmy von N, psychoanalysis was presented with its first piece of data that the "talking cure" is therapeutically effective only in a relational context, and is not in fact a catharsis but a negoti-ated "act of meaning" (Bruner, 1990).

What Freud was unable to see at that time was that his failure was not a lack of patience with Emmy's symptoms as symptoms, but a lack of patience with her symptoms as representing her perceptual reality, and in this sense were more than "pieces of pathology" that should or could be "taken away," whether one by one or all at once. Freud writes that through hypnosis he "made it impossible for her to see any of these melancholy things again, not only by wiping out her memories of them . . . but by removing her whole recollection of them, as though they had never been present in her mind. I promised her that this would lead to her being freed from the expectation of misfortune which perpetually tormented her" (p. 61). Ironically, it is this very promise, in its various forms, that I feel most accounts for Emmy's having reacted to Freud over and over in a way that I've referred to in chapter 14 as "throwing rocks at the fireman." Because the anticipation of misfortune is the principal way a traumatized person protects himself from future trauma, the promise of "cure" (which is always implied by a therapist even if not explicitly stated) makes the process of attempting to "free" a traumatized patient from the expectation of misfortune probably the most complex treatment issue a psychoanalyst faces.

Freud (Breuer and Freud, 1893–1895) states that, contrary to his expectations following this intervention, Emmy "slept badly and only for a short time" (p. 62). He expected her to be much better. She was not, of course, better, because his hypnotic suggestion simply addressed one self-state and left the others untouched and, more to the point, unheard. It is the unheard voices of these other dissociated states that in her relationship with Freud were having negative responses to his helpful "technique" and were not only upset but also angry.

Nevertheless, Emmy's angry complaint that she felt "unheard" had a powerful impact in making Freud sit up and take notice, and he subsequently realized he could not just attack symptoms as if hypnosis were an experiential eraser and expect it to have any positive effect. In talking about the origin of symptoms, Freud thus writes that, while pains can be determined organically, pains can also be *memories* of pains—"mnemic symbols," as he puts it (p. 90). He was here foreshadowing the issue of the dissociative split between the mind and what Winnicott (1949) called psyche-soma, preventing the linguistic symbolization of immediate experience by the use of perceptual/conceptual perspective (see chapter 13; also Goldberg, 1995), thus forcing the body to store sensory experience physically, through symptoms.

The essence of dissociation is that the mind is disconnected from the psyche-soma to protect one's illusion of unitary selfhood from the potential threat of traumatically impinging experience it cannot process cognitively. This can frequently lead to symptoms such as, in Emmy's case, agoraphobia, and what Freud interpreted as her inhibition of will (abulia). On the basis of my own clinical observation, I would offer the view that a so-called loss of will can be most usefully understood as an intrinsic outcome of dissociation. Because self-agency is limited to whatever function is performed by the dissociated self-state which at that time has access to the mind, what is most frequently seen by a therapist treating a patient such as Emmy, represents a specific mode of the patient's self-experience that has limited or no access to other aspects of reality, self-expression, or modes of relatedness. In this regard, the ability to act purposefully—what we call willpower—is not inhibited in the sense of a global suppression of will, but is "repackaged" in unlinked states of mind, leading to a personality dynamic whereby certain self-states are dramatically willful while others appear inhibited but are simultaneously "on-alert" (see chapter 13). From this perspective, inhibition of action and hysterical outbursts of action are opposite sides of the same coin, and, as Emmy demonstrated when she was in her unruly state, action not only was possible but was relentless in its power (e.g., her determination to act on her belief that eating and drinking water were harmful to her despite Freud's effort to make her more "reasonable" (Breuer and Freud, 1893–1895, pp. 81–83).

Using Emmy's anorexia as an example of an abulia, Freud concluded that "abulias are nothing other than a highly specialized . . . kind of psychical paralysis" (p. 90), which, in Emmy's history, represented an escape from the fact that "it is impossible to eat with disgust and pleasure at the same time" (p. 89). This formulation speaks directly to the basic adaptational function of dissociation when one's overarching sense of self cannot hold two incompatible modes of relating to the same object at the same time. In its most general form, it protects the person from the felt impossibility of responding self-reflectively with feelings of fear and security toward the same object at the same moment. There is thus, inevitably, a "psychical paralysis" in anorexia simply because the psyche-soma is always disconnected from the mind with regard to the process of eating.

A "True Lady" or a "Woman of Parts?"

Freud concludes the case history of Emmy with an extraordinary addendum that followed his final contact with Emmy in May, 1890. He had received, three years later,

> a short note from her asking my permission for her to be hypnotized by another doctor, since she was ill again and could not come to Vienna. At first I did not understand why my permission was necessary, till I remembered that in 1890 I had, at her own request, protected her against being hypnotized by anyone else, so that there should be no danger of her being distressed by coming under the control of a doctor who was antipathetic to her. . . . I accordingly renounced my exclusive prerogative in writing [p. 85].

Here one can feel the powerful effects of the hypnosis in having subdued Emmy's capacity for self-authorized assertiveness in a relational context. Claiming that to have a relationship with another doctor she first needed to be released from Freud, Emmy felt that she needed to have her paralysis undone by Freud in order to restore self-hood. Whether this was literally true is a matter for speculation, but I think a plausible case can be made for the possibility that this communication was her final effort to bring Freud's attention to bear (as it indeed did) on the fact that his technique of hypnotic suggestion itself evoked an iatrogenic "abulia"—a paralysis of Emmy's experience of herself as a human being entitled to make her own choices. All in all, I agree with the observation made by Appignanesi and Forrester (1992), that "if we draw up the inventory of this early analytic episode, we are struck by Freud's attentiveness to the doctor-patient relationship, even when he is abusing it with tricks and his pride in the shaman-like power granted him over his patients" (p. 102).

Freud had recognized that there was a part of Emmy that was angry (the part he called "her unruly nature") at not being allowed to tell her version of what had happened to her in the past; but he was, of course, not aware of the importance of her immediate reality as material in itself—what she felt was happening to her right then in her relationship with Freud. It was not simply that Emmy needed more time to narrate her history, as Freud believed. She needed a cohesive temporal context that addressed both the past and the present—a context within which Freud would listen to and engage not only her multiple historical narratives as "told," but, equally importantly, would respond to, and engage, her *enacted* self-narrative as responses to his behavior with her in the here-and-now: that is, *her dissociated responses to both his messages and his massages.* From a contemporary perspective, he might have thus comprehended that her formulaic "Keep still! Don't say anything! Don't touch me!" was not simply an echo from the past, but a warning to remain vigilant with regard to Freud himself.

An illustrative case in point can be drawn from my own work with a patient psychologically traumatized in childhood, who described herself as having "a talking vagina." She experienced vaginal pain in situations with older men whom she "trusted" but who made her feel anxious in their efforts to help her. The pain, which sometimes occurred during analytic hours, was eventually connected to her father's overdetermined, overzealous, and frequently inappropriate efforts to teach her how to cope with life. Because she had no one but her father to rely on, she could not process the fact that his compulsive determination to teach her "the facts of life" was, simultaneously, an assault on her mind, and she thereby processed the pain of his disregard for her feelings as though it were an assault on her body. As she grew up, she was always ready to discover this kind of "father" in a man she relied on and was always prepared to deal with his dark side through pain in her "talking vagina." She was thus typically able to forestall potential trauma while keeping the relationship intact by not making the "father" aware of anything about himself that seemed outside of his consciousness. Her vaginal pains were eventually eliminated by our processing this enactment as it played out between us over time. When the pains came during or after a session, our ability to address the phenomenon together was contingent on our being able to confront the dissociative process that prevented her, while she was with me, from recognizing that my efforts to explore her early memories (particularly sexual ones) during a session were felt as potentially traumatic to her. That is, what I was looking at as an "exploration" of the past, was for her an event that pulled her into a reliving of the original feelings in the here-and-now. She was thus always feeling at the edge of traumatic hyperarousal but could not hold that experience in awareness. Because I was needed as someone on whom her security depended and who she felt was genuinely acting in good faith on her behalf, she could not simultaneously hold that aspect of my behavior that was painful and frightening. She thereby dissociated this domain of reality, including the reality that I sometimes did indeed become impatient with her "distractions," leaving only her physical pain to testify to the experience. We arrived, little by little, at the understanding that her "talking vagina" was talking simultaneously about me and to me, and was not simply a symbol of a memory of the past (a "mnemic symbol") but was a representation of her present experience that could not be processed as such. In other words, the connection to her past could not be made real to her without authentic negotiation of the here-and-now intersubjective context being enacted with me that paralleled its initial source in the relationship that caused the original pain—the fact that "physical sexual symptoms mask a more broadly based and significant need for 'personal relationship' in its basic security-giving value" (Guntrip, 1971, p. 168).

Freud wrote about Emmy: "She was afraid that I would lose patience with her on account of her recent relapse" (p. 75). I would say that she was *always* afraid that Freud would lose patience with her, because she felt, accurately, that Freud wished to silence her "unacceptable" voices. Even though she welcomed his trying to "cure" her, she didn't want him to "cure" her of being herself. She was "unruly" because she needed to get all of her selves into a human relationship and was afraid Freud was going to lose patience because she was insisting, through her symptoms, on her right to have him accept that her "crazy" (unruly) reactions to his therapeutic efforts had to do with him as well as with her. I think it is particularly interesting that

Freud's own description of Emmy supports this idea quite dramatically. Apart from the "unruliness" of her symptoms, Freud held her to be totally restrained in her life and in the choices she made living it.[6]

She was, in fact, virtually eulogized by Freud as a model of virtuous self-denial, the perfect Victorian widow, commended for "the moral seriousness with which she viewed her duties, her intelligence and energy, which were no less than a man's, and her high degree of education and love of truth" (p. 103). But most telling is his praise of her as the woman who, after her husband's death, refused to remarry, sacrificing her personal needs (sexual and otherwise) for the protection of her children, bearing forever the scars of unjust victimization by her husband's family. "[H]er benevolent care for the welfare of all her dependents," Freud states, "revealed her qualities as a true lady as well" (pp. 103–104). Small wonder that Emmy's most dramatic vehicle of self-expression with Freud was her "pathology." A case can in fact be reasonably argued that Freud's problem was compounded by his powerful idealization of Emmy—an idealization that contributed to a dissociative process in his own thinking whereby he considered her symptoms as pathology but the woman herself as morally irreproachable. Freud's most imperative reason for the idealization, I would conjecture, was to preclude any possible Janet-like view of her as "degenerate," but in addition, one might also speculate as to whether some part of Freud's need to place her on a pedestal was an unconscious effort to insulate himself from the kind of problem that Breuer had with Anna O.

Freud listened to Emmy, but for the most part he was listening, as he put it, so as to be able to "deliver maxims," and that, in my view, was the heart of the problem. Emmy, limited by her dissociative mental structure in her capacity for relatedness, could only indirectly or symptomatically protest being treated simply as an object to be "cured" (see chapter 14) and was continually enacting, dramatically, her dissociated self-states. All through the treatment there was an underlying, unacknowledged, and unverbalized relationship between Freud and those parts of Emmy's self for whom her illness was an interpersonal reality to be taken seriously. I offer the view that, all told, her "relapses" represented dissociated enactments of self-states that were not authorized to express their existence in a *true lady*—a sane Victorian woman whose character, as depicted by Freud, was defined by "her humility of mind and the refinement of her manners" (p. 103),

---

6. That there was indeed another, more "alive" and (sexually) unrestrained side to Emmy in her life is documented by Appignanesi and Forrester (1992, pp. 97–99).

someone who could not possibly be furious that, in her relationship with Freud, including her relationship to his therapeutic massages, she was allowed to exist only as either a highly moral person who had renounced her sexuality in the interest of motherhood or as a patient possessed by craziness that made her "unruly" or "delirious."

In his evaluation of Emmy's treatment in terms of its outcome, Freud said, very honestly, that "the therapeutic success on the whole was considerable; but it was not a lasting one" and that "the patient's tendency to fall ill in a similar way under the impact of fresh traumas was not got rid of" (pp. 101–102). From my own perspective, the reason Emmy was still susceptible to falling ill was that her need to maintain the dissociative structure of her mind remained her way of protecting herself against trauma that had already occurred—a protection against the future by plundering her life as if it were nothing but a replica of the past. In this context, her "illness" was a foreclosure of the "here-and-now" on behalf of the "there-and-then," effectively preventing her from living life with spontaneity, pleasure, or immediacy. To understand why Emmy's cure was not a lasting one is also to understand that we do not treat patients such as Emmy to cure them of something that was done to them in the past; rather, we are trying to cure them of what they still do to themselves and to others in order to *cope* with what was done to them in the past. As both Breuer and Freud[7] discovered, each in his own way, this is at times a "messy" undertaking, and were Freud alive today it would probably not be difficult for him to appreciate the wry humor in the contemporary quip that "psychoanalysis is a good profession for someone who wants to do something dangerous without leaving the office."

---

7. Hirschmuller (1978) comments that "if Breuer did not in fact treat any more patients by means of the cathartic method, one factor instrumental in bringing this about was probably the fact that he did not wish to become involved in any more doctor-patient relationships with such deep emotional content" (p. 202). (See chapter 10 for a more thorough discussion of the paradoxical relationship between the inevitable "messiness" of some aspects of the analytic situation and Freud's reminder that "between urine and faeces are we born.")

PART IV

STANDING IN THE SPACES

16

"SPEAK!
THAT I MAY SEE YOU"

*Some Reflections on Dissociation, Reality,
and Psychoanalytic Listening[1] (1994)*

To Thine Own Selves Be True

The following clinical vignette was not written by a therapist but by a physicist. It is from a book entitled *Einstein's Dreams* (Lightman, 1993), which has to do with the many possible natures of time and the many possible natures of reality that depend on how we experience past, present, and future:

> Every Tuesday, a middle-aged man brings stones from the quarry east of Berne to the masonry on Hodlerstrasse. . . . He wears a gray wool coat in all seasons, works in the quarry until after dark, has

1. An earlier draft of this essay was presented in February 1994 as "The Second Annual Bernard Kalinkowitz Memorial Lecture," sponsored jointly by Section V of Division 39 (Psychoanalysis) of the American Psychological Association, and the New York University Postdoctoral Program in Psychotherapy and Psychoanalysis. This chapter in its present version was published originally in *Psychoanalytic Dialogues*, 1994, 4:517–547.

dinner with his wife and goes to bed, tends his garden on Sundays. And on Tuesday mornings, he loads his truck with stones and comes to town. . . . And as he passes people on the street, his eyes are on the ground. Some people know him, try to catch his eye or say hello. He mumbles and walks on. Even when he delivers his stones to Hodlerstrasse, he cannot look the mason in the eye. Instead, he looks aside, he talks to the wall in answer to the mason's friendly chatter, he stands in a corner while his stones are weighed.

Forty years ago in school, one afternoon in March, he urinated in class. He could not hold it in. Afterwards, he tried to stay in his chair, but the other boys saw the puddle and made him walk around the room, round and round. They pointed at the wet spot on his pants and howled. . . . A clock with big red hands read 2:15. And the boys hooted at him, hooted at him as they chased him around the room, with the wet spot on his pants. . . .

That memory has become his life. When he wakes up in the morning, he is the boy who urinated in his pants. When he passes people on the street, he knows they see the wet spot on his pants. He glances at his pants and looks away. When his children visit, he stays in his room and talks to them through the door. He is the boy who could not hold it in [pp. 167–170].

What if this man were in analysis! How would we see the nature of his problem? What happened to him that day in school? Is he psychotic? After all, he does hide from his children. Is he "borderline?" Is the therapeutic issue one of shame and pathological narcissism? If so, what is the process through which we might hope to comprehend what he feels as an adult, much less know what he felt as a child? What kind of transference can we expect? I am starting here, because I want gradually to approach the topic of what we imagine we are doing when we do psychoanalysis; what our image is of the human being we are listening to; and what our conception is of the mental apparatus and the personality structure that we are applying our technical skills to engage. In what way was this man's emotional response adaptive to the event, how did it become pathological, and how does one listen to such a man so as to determine why his emotions overwhelmed him and to find a way to help him? Consider what Nesse (1991) has to say about emotions:

[E]motions are set to maximize Darwinian fitness, not happiness, and . . . natural selection has molded each kind of bad feeling to help protect against a specific threat. . . . Emotions adjust a person's response to the task at hand. In that sense they are similar to computer programs, which adjust the setup of the computer to carry out a certain kind of task. . . . The behavioral, physiological and cognitive responses that help a person elude a tiger are different from those that help woo a lover or attack a competitor. Thus, fear, love and anger are highly distinct psychological subroutines gradually shaped by natural selection to improve the person's ability to cope with each challenge. . . . When a tiger bounds towards you, what should your response be? Should you file your toenails? Do a cartwheel? Sing a song? Is this the moment to run an uncountable number of randomly generated response possibilities through the decision rule?. . . . How could you compute which possibility would result in more grandchildren? The alternative: Darwinian algorithms specialized for predator avoidance . . . and upon detecting a potential predator, constrain your responses to flight, fight, or hiding [p. 33].

But human relationships, especially for the young, are sometimes not that simple. What of situations where there are competing algorithms at the same moment? What of a moment when your mother bounds toward you with fangs bared? Or a moment when your father approaches you with penis bared? Or, as in this man's case, where your peer group suddenly becomes a pack of hyenas, stripping *you* bare while you are still alive? The algorithm of flight, fight, or hiding pertains only to escape from predators. What does someone (particularly a child) do when there is another strong algorithm already operating, such as "obedience to a parent or an adult," or "love of one's caretaker," or "being accepted by one's peers"? This is the situation, I suggest, that, at least from an evolutionary standpoint, defines the meaning of trauma, and may explain why natural selection seems to have endowed the human mind with a Darwinian algorithm that helps us cope with trauma by providing what Putnam (1992) has called "the escape when there is no escape" (p. 104)—the mechanism of dissociation. Where drastically incompatible emotions or perceptions are required to be cognitively processed within the same relationship and such processing is adaptationally beyond the capacity of the individual to contain this disjunction within a unitary self-experience, one of the competing algorithms is hypnoidally denied access to consciousness to preserve sanity and survival. When ordinary adaptational adjustment to the task at hand is not possible, dissociation comes into play. The experience that is causing the incompatible perception and emotion is "unhooked" from the cognitive processing system and remains raw data that is cognitively unsymbolized within that particular self-other representation, except as a survival reaction.

Thus, the person retains the capacity to survive by preserving the dissociated "predator" experience in its pure form of deadly assault (or in contemporary terms, "abuse") and also retains the original self-other representations organized by obedience, love, and friendship, but without the capacity to modify them by appropriate courses of action that take self-interest into account.

Dissociation is not inherently pathological, but it can become so. The process of dissociation is basic to human mental functioning and is central to the stability and growth of personality. It is intrinsically an adaptational talent that represents the very nature of what we call "consciousness." Dissociation is not fragmentation. In fact, it may be reasonably seen as a defense against fragmentation, and in this regard, Ferenczi's (1930a, p. 230) struggle with whether fragmentation is merely a mechanical consequence of trauma or may actually be a form of adaptation to it was brilliantly ahead of its time. The answer to his question, however, took 60 years to appear. As I've stated in chapter 12, there is now abundant evidence that the psyche does not start as an integrated whole, but is nonunitary in origin—a mental structure that begins and continues as a multiplicity of self-states that maturationally attain a feeling of coherence which overrides the awareness of discontinuity. This leads to the experience of a cohesive sense of personal identity and the necessary illusion of being "one self." One of the major reasons that this understanding of the normal mind has taken so long to reach full scientific consciousness is that changes of state are, for the most part, difficult to perceive in normal adults. The developmental process that eases the transitions across states of consciousness typically results in a healthy person being able to smooth out awareness of the changes, an achievement that is greatly facilitated by caretakers who, through a process of mutual regulation, help the child attain nontraumatic state transitions by appropriate interactive responsiveness to the child's subjectivity.

For psychoanalysts, this view of the mind has been supported by psychoanalytically oriented infant studies such as those by Emde, Gaensbaure, and Harmon (1976), Sander (1977), D. N. Stern (1985), Wolff (1987), and Beebe and Lachmann (1992), but the most direct support has come from nonanalytic empirical research into normal and pathological adult mental functioning—research representing a wide range of disciplines and research centers. The director of the Dissociative Disorders Research Unit of the NIMH, in a seminal paper discussing nonlinear state changes as a developmental paradigm (Putnam, 1988), speaks to the fact that the most central property of states is that they are discrete and discontinuous. Asserting that "states appear to be the fundamental unit of organization of consciousness and are detectable from the first moments following birth," he describes them as

> self-organizing and self-stabilizing structures of behavior. When a transition (switch) from one state of consciousness to another state of consciousness occurs, *the new state acts to impose a quantitatively and qualitatively different structure on the variables that define the state of consciousness.* The new structure acts to reorganize behavior and resist changes to other states. . . . [S]witches between states are manifest by non-linear changes in a number of variables (Wolff, 1987). These variables include: 1) affect; 2) access to memory, i.e., state-dependent memory; 3) attention and cognition; 4) regulatory physiology; and 5) sense of self. . . . *changes in affect and mood are, however, probably the single best marker of state switches in normal adults* [p. 25, italics added].

Nonlinear switches in discontinuous states of consciousness! The implications are profound. A case could be made, for example, that the reason a state such as depression is difficult to alleviate even with medication is that it is not simply an "affective disorder" but an internally coherent aspect of the self. For many people, it is a self-state with its own narrative, its own memory configuration, its own perceptual reality, and its own style of relatedness to others. It is not simply something one feels—it is who one *is*, at least at certain times. There is, therefore, as much of a need to preserve self-meaning in this state of being as in any other, despite its painful, guilt-ridden, and often suicidal nature—to not allow any domain of one's personal reality to be destroyed as though it were meaningless simply because it is painful. The resistance to losing one's depressive reality is greatest where personality is organized more by a dissociative mental structure than by conflict, because the importance of the feeling of selfhood attached to a given state of mind is greatest when there is least simultaneous access to alternative self-states with other potential perceptual realities and internal self-narratives. So the "curing" of depression must be a process that does not become an effort to cure the patient of "who he is." Thus, the analytic exploration of the suffering in depression, before it can become accessible to a mutual cognitive perspective in the analytic relationship, must be in a dialectic with a multiplicity of different self-narratives, perceptual realities, and adaptational meanings to the patient, each of which speaks with its own voice. To put it a bit more poetically, an analyst must be constantly negotiating with a range of self-states with different voices, even when the voice of pain is louder than the others.

"Speak! That I May See You"

"Speak, in order that I may see you," Socrates is alleged to have said (Reik, 1936, p. 21). Speak, that I may see the speaker hidden in his words. Freud (1913b) implied almost the same thing in formulating his basic rule of the free association method. Speak everything that comes to mind, and I will discover the person you wish to hide. But the process of being seen "into," no matter how benign or well-meaning the motive, evokes what analysts' traditionally have called "resis tance." Socrates, in fact, was invited by the Athenians to retire permanently, and though the descendents of Freud haven't yet been offered the hemlock, most psychoanalysts are wearily familiar with the image of the "headshrinker"—the dangerous "truthsayer" holding a special power to discern hidden secrets inadvertently revealed by the other's unguarded speech.

Here I present an argument that both supports and challenges this image. I hold that when psychoanalysis is successful as a method of psychotherapy, the reason is indeed to be found in Socrates's words, but that in any successful analysis the process is a dialectic between *seeing and being seen*, rather than simply being seen "into." That is, when optimally effective, analysis simultaneously frees our patients to do unto us, with equivalent perceptiveness, what we are doing unto them, to see us as part of the act of listening to us.

Words begin as carriers. In early childhood they are vocal carriers of personal feeling—an articulated form of a cry (Sullivan, 1953, p. 185). With the onset of communicative speech they are more than carriers; they are also building blocks in the relational construction of personal meaning. They shift from a sophisticated vehicle for relatively autistic expression of what one feels and what one needs, to the primary modality for the interpersonal creation of who one *is*. Relationally, words in themselves do not exist in time or space. Only the speaker's meaning exists in time and space; and the speaker's meaning is constructed from a perception of his words framed by the immediacy of the context in which they are spoken. Speaking is an action in an interpersonal context (real or implied). Schafer's (1976) concept of "action language" partly addresses this fact, but words—even "action words"—simply point in the direction of the speaker. Ultimately, the speaker must be seen if the words are to achieve meaning.

"Speaking," in psychoanalysis, is thus not simply a process of delivering content. It is also a relational act that shapes the content of what is spoken about. For patients dealing in a primary way with dissociative experience, this point comes into particularly high relief because words themselves feel more or less meaningless. The person carries a sense of internal isolation as his natural state, and trying to convey this in words is experienced as an exercise in futility. But, in analysis, because he is expected to speak, a communicative route can potentially be constructed, sometimes painfully, through the relationship. In the interplay of silence and words, a patient can, at least potentially, force the analyst to give up his attempts to "understand" his patient and allow himself to "know" his patient—to know him in the only way possible—through the ongoing intersubjective field they are sharing at that moment. It is through this medium that an act of recognition can take place in which words and concepts can symbolize instead of substitute for experience. The analyst has an opportunity to recognize (personally know) the thing that cannot be said in words— the quality of subjective experience that makes verbal communication feel artificial and meaningless. But this can take place only if the analyst does not too quickly attempt to translate recognition into understanding, that is, if he does not substitute interpreted meaning for experientially symbolized meaning.

I recently listened to a case being presented to me in ongoing consultation. It may illustrate what I mean. The patient was a woman who had been in treatment for quite a few years and who had made major changes in her life and her self-experience, except with regard to the thing that had brought her into treatment in the first place, her obesity. She felt her weight as a burden that she would carry unto death, with no hope of relief. At the point I entered the case it was her analyst who was feeling no hope of relief, and that was a major reason for the consultation. The situation was quite an extraordinary one and impressed me once again with the fact that when it comes to certain kinds of enactments, it's really a lot more pleasurable to be the consultant than the analyst. As a consultant I'm spared the experience of being personally dismantled by the patient, a fact I feel is critical to comprehend in working as a therapist from this frame of reference. The analyst's willingness to participate in an enactment does not begin as "willingness" in the usual meaning of the term. It is not something the analyst does voluntarily, nor is it something over which he even has much control. It is, in fact, the opposite of what is usually meant by "technique" (something that one "applies" and has command over). The analyst's initial experience of his participation is much closer to the consternation that accompanies projective identification, and the two at times may actually be the same phenomenon with different names. The person "who you are" is perceived as seriously lacking in some way, with regard to the patient, and the more you try to incorporate what your patient is saying about you and use it within your current stance, the more evidence you seem to be supplying of your deficiencies. What the patient is saying in words does not carry the message; the message is carried by the relationship between the words and the experiential context in which they are heard—the way an analyst begins to feel about himself and about his patient as his position feels more and more uncontainable within his natural stance and sometimes within his self-definition as an analyst.

This phase is not (and should not be) a pleasant experience for the analyst. If it is—if the analyst is feeling satisfaction from his willingness to be "used as an object" (Winnicott, 1969)—he is not really being used at all, at least not yet. The patient's need is to perceive and confront the analyst with what is experienced that has been known but unthought. This process involves a dismantling of aspects of the relationship that patient and analyst have used to define who they are to each other. In effect, it means that the patient is "destroying" aspects of the analyst's identity, who he is to himself, as defined through that relationship. Loewald (1979) calls it "emancipatory murder" (p. 758).

In the case of the patient I mentioned, whose treatment I had been following, the dismantling took place around the analyst's "failure" to mention the patient's weight when she herself wasn't mentioning it. "*You* ought to know," the patient insisted, "that when I'm talking about anything else as long as I'm still fat, it's only my good self that's talking and that I'm doing something self-destructive that you're not even caring about." In fact, the analyst cared a great deal about it, as you might well imagine. It was the one painfully overt sign that something still needed to be "cured" and that talking hadn't helped. So the analyst had decided (on his own) to stop addressing it because he was tired of getting nowhere (kind of "fed up," you might say) and hoped that the patient would then bring it up herself. He allowed long silences to develop in which he hoped that she might ultimately put what she was feeling into words. Well, she did, but not in the way that he had hoped. As he was finding the silences increasingly hard to tolerate, she, without the least regard for logic, told him he had no right to stop trying to find out what she was feeling, and "what did he think he was doing?" This is not a situation in which a therapist can just sit back and comfortably do his work (at least, he *shouldn't* be able to). It was in the course of their dealing with the apparent "no-win" quality of his "failure" that he was able to begin to find a small island of shared experience on which he could plant at least one of his feet. It was at this point that the patient began to be able to "back off" from her concrete state of consciousness and to develop a cognitive perspective through which the "unthought known" (Bollas, 1987) became the thought known and through which the analyst could authentically experience himself as a willing participant.

"Only in my silence," the patient declared, "do I feel real. The only way I can get out of here is to be silent for a year." What she meant consciously by "here" was "here" meaning her inner world, and, unconsciously, meaning the analysis. But let's stay with what, at that moment, she was able to render conscious. How could it make any sense that the only way she recognized that she could release herself from the trap of her dissociated mental structure was without words, by remaining silent for a year? The point she was making was not that silence itself mattered, but silence in the presence of her analyst. Why? Because her silence in his presence could have a communicative impact—*as long as he hadn't given up trying*. This is the essence, I think, of the "projective identification" phase of enactment. The analyst has to get fed up; it is important that he get fed up; he should get fed up. But he shouldn't get so detached from his own "fed-upness" that he cannot perceive the retaliatory component of his behavior. If he is open to that, he will feel the communication from the patient as it is pressed into his soul through her silence as well as into his brain through her words. The patient was ultimately able to put into words this remarkable insight:

> When I'm not talking to you and you don't realize that my silence is talking, I feel like I'm hurting myself and you don't care. I hurt myself by being fat in order to call attention to the inside "me." And if you don't notice or seem not to, it's like you're mad that I'm still fat and will let me hurt myself because I'm fat instead of putting why I'm fat into words. But if I do talk, it's not my fat self that's talking. So you have to find her by noticing the fat and not pretending you don't. If I get thin, no one will ever look for her because if I stop calling attention to her existence you will settle for my good self which looks healthy because it is thin, and you will never know it isn't real to me. I'm like Dr. Jekyll and Mr. Hyde. [Shortly, the HYDE/H-I-D-E pun became clear.] Or, like with Clark Kent and Superman, the two parts never get into the same room at the same time because they're the same person.

In other words, by "noticing," through the impact of forced involvement with what the patient needs to call attention to without communicative speech, the dissociated self can start to exist, and a transition begins to take place to what this patient so evocatively described as a growing awareness of "Mr. Hyde." But the success of the transition depends on the ability of the patient to destroy successfully the analyst's conception of "what this is really all about" and thus destroy the analyst's image of the patient in which Mr. "Hide" is imprisoned. The analyst's own self-image, which is a part of all this, is also destroyed, and it is this destruction he must "survive" in Winnicott's (1969) conceptualization of object usage.

In this context, analytic listening might be compared to approaching a patient's words in the same manner that Henry Adams (1904) advocated in appreciating medieval architecture—as if one were approaching medieval poetry in the troublesome "roughness" of the original language in which it was written. Adams wrote, in his delightful book *Mont Saint-Michel and Chartres*:

> Translation is an evil chiefly because anyone who cares for mediaeval architecture . . . ought to care still more for mediaeval English. . . . Anyone who attacks them boldly will find that the [verses] run along like a ballad, *singing their own meaning*, and troubling themselves very little whether the meaning is exact or not. One's translation is sure to be full of gross blunders, but the *supreme blunder is that of translating at all when one is trying to catch not a fact but a feeling*. If translate one must, we had best begin by trying to be literal, under protest that it matters not a straw whether we succeed [pp. 18–19, italics added].

An interpretation is a translation, and what is reflected in an interpretation is the analyst's personal view of the patient, which is one of many possible realities. At the moment the patient is looking at himself through the analyst's eyes, he's also looking at the analyst in a very personal way. The ability of the patient to accept the image of himself that the analyst is offering is directly influenced by his ability to trust his perception of the person presenting it. So his rejection of the interpretation is not only a rejection of a view of himself but also a rejection of an unpalatable view of the analyst—a view in which he experiences the analyst as asking him to substitute, without sufficient negotiation, the analyst's subjectivity for his own. Within normal limits, this is simply part of the natural process of "trying to stay the same while changing" (see chapter 10), but if the analyst's interpretive posture attempts to conceal his own subjectivity while simultaneously attempting to deny that there is anything there to see, a collusive masquerade takes place. The patient seemingly accepts or resists as "objective reality" the language into which the analyst has chosen to translate the patient's original "verses" (the analyst's personal view of the patient), under the guise of its being a reflection of what is "really there" that the patient does or does not want to see.

Dissociation, Enactment, and Reality

I have essentially been arguing for an interpersonal and intersubjective listening stance, a viewpoint that many analytic writers, myself included, have passionately advanced for some time. In the remainder of this essay I would like to try to develop that position along somewhat different lines and present a few ideas that may help its progress toward what I feel is its most likely next step. To do that I want to return in greater detail to the phenomenon of the human mind as a complex system of discontinuous and shifting states of consciousness and examine the impact of this nonlinear model of the mind on the way we think about psychoanalysis as a theory, and the way we think about psychoanalysis in "how we listen and what we do" while with our patients. As will be clear from the following anecdote, I personally find the normal nonlinearity of the human mind a mystery that continues to amaze me.

I recently took a cab ride that, among other things, cured me forever of complaining about taxi drivers who can't speak English. The driver, who was listening to a radio station broadcasting a soap opera in Spanish, would at each red light pick up a newspaper from the seat next to him and start to read, while at the same time clearly following what was happening in the soap opera. I had just begun to feel irritated that he wasn't even pretending to concentrate on what I was paying him for, his driving, when I looked at the newspaper and saw that it was written in French. My irritation was replaced by a combination of envy and disbelief. "Is the human mind really capable of simultaneously processing different content, through different perceptual channels, in different languages? And even if it were, wouldn't it be more natural (not to mention easier on the brain) to choose one or the other?" So I asked him about it, in English. He replied—in English easily as fluent as mine—that he never thought about it before. He's lived in different places and speaks different languages; that's all. He definitely didn't want to get into a discussion about what language he thinks in, what language he dreams in, and whether he could do the same thing if the radio program or the newspaper were in English. He didn't really want to "speak so that I might see him." I think he had too many other things to do, but also he was afraid I was going to try to nail him for reading while he was driving. So I lost a potentially valuable informant, but I continue to wonder about it.

A recent article in the *American Psychologist* (Barton, 1994) starts with the statement that "a new paradigm for understanding systems has been gaining the attention of psychologists from a wide variety of specialty areas" (p. 5). The paradigm, which describes the behavior of complex systems, is known as nonlinear dynamics, or Chaos Theory. It is a science without an implication of "prescribed" sequences, but rather with *a set of necessary and sufficient conditions to allow the construction of something different from the past pattern, but unpredictable as a future event*. It postulates that complex systems (like the human mind) have an underlying order, but that simple systems (like a human interaction) can produce complex behavior. In theory, you could predict the course of an interaction far into the future, but in fact you can't, because almost immediately very small effects start to make a difference and will eventually lead to unpredictable behavior. Gleick (1987) described the heart of the discovery as revealing that "chaos and instability . . . were not the same at all. A chaotic system could be stable if its particular brand of irregularity persisted in the face of small disturbances" (p. 48). He went on: "[C]haos brought an astonishing message: simple deterministic models could produce what looked like random behavior. The behavior actually had an exquisite fine structure, yet any piece of it seemed indistinguishable from noise" (p. 79).

The new emphasis on nonlinear dynamics in psychoanalytic thinking is particularly well captured by a changing view of mental structure, both normal and pathological. The conceptualization of personality growth as therapeutically mediated by the lifting of repression and the uncovering of unconscious conflict is being reexamined in terms of new types of questions—questions that have to do with such concepts as "self-organization," states of consciousness, dissociation, and the readiness of the human personality to exhibit in Barton's (1994) words, "multiple self states that can change suddenly from one to another when a parameter value crosses a critical threshold" (p. 8).

Even in the most resilient personality, psychic structure is organized by trauma as well as by repression, and an analyst will always encounter domains of dissociated experience that have weak or nonexistent links to the experience of "me" as a communicable entity. Before these "not-me" states of mind can be taken as objects of self-reflection, they must first become "thinkable" while becoming linguistically communicable through enactment in the analytic relationship. Until this happens, neither genuine repression nor the experience of intrapsychic conflict can take place, because each state of consciousness holds its own experientially encapsulated "truth" that is enacted over and over again without the availability of the necessary conditions for cognitive resolution. Chu (1991) has described the issue vividly and succinctly. He states that trauma that has been dissociated is repeated with a compulsive quality that takes on an almost biological urgency, and that patients are thrust back into the traumatic events both in their dreams and while awake. . . . The reliving of the trauma is experienced as a real and contemporary event. That is, the patient does not talk about feeling as if he or she remembers the experience; rather, he or she feels the experience in the present. . . . *Therapists are all too familiar with the difficult task of attempting to help patients keep one foot in current reality at the same time as they experience the past* [p. 328, italics added].

In analytic listening, regardless of whether we use the term "reliving" or "enactment," each state of consciousness is signified by its own relational context. While one narrative is being "told," another is being played out between patient and analyst while the telling goes on. Levenson (1982) has gone as far as to state that "analyzing the relationship between what is talked about and the behavior that goes along with what's talked about *constitutes* the psychoanalytic process . . . and is what *distinguishes* it, essentially, from all other forms of psychotherapy" (p. 11, italics added). This, to me, is also what Winnicott's (1967) concept of "potential space" is all about—the interpersonal construction of reality in which playing with meaning (deconcretizing it) becomes possible. It is why parapraxes are so wonderful! Not because they provide a window into what a patient "really" believes, but because they allow opposing realities held by different self-states to coexist and thereby increase simultaneous access to a fuller range of self through the analytic relationship.

For example: A 40-year-old male patient, a widower early in life, was furious and self-righteous because his current girlfriend had refused to accept his claim that he could not marry again because of his religious conviction that his original marriage was a holy covenant. "She won't believe," he shouted, "that I really care about preserving the '*sanctimony*' [*sic*] of marriage." Did this delightful slip lead him to replace his religious conviction with a new image of it being nothing but self-serving and hypocritical? No! But it was funny enough to each of us that we could work with both words in a way that produced another "slip," which led to the emergence of a dissociated self-state that held the memory of why the religious conviction was so important. The second parapraxis was: "When I think of forgetting my wife, I feel so selfish that I'm afraid God is going to punish me. The world feels like it will come to an end, so I can't cut the '*un-biblical cord*'" [*sic*]. As we "played" with this one together, he became in my presence the traumatized five-year-old boy whose world had felt as if it were ending when he was sadistically punished by his mother for wishing to leave her in order to live with his beloved aunt. To "teach him to be good," he had been placed in a children's home overnight, having been told he would have to stay there "for as long as it took to learn his lesson." He relived, in interaction with me, the terror of this dissociated experience and the pact he had made with God never to be bad again if God would only let him come home. For the first time in his treatment, this 40-year-old man was able to meet the frightened five-year-old who accompanied him to every session and for whom the therapy itself was nothing more than a different version of the children's asylum from which he was waiting to be released.

If an analyst thinks of a person as speaking from different self-states rather than from a single center of self, then the analyst will inevitably listen that way. It demands an overarching attunement to the speaker, an attunement that addresses the same issue described by Schafer's (1983) mode of listening and interpreting in which "the analyst focuses on the action of telling itself . . . [and] telling is treated as an object of description rather than . . . an indifferent or transparent medium for imparting information or thematic content" (p. 228). From a nonlinear perspective, however, this means a special attunement to both the impact the speaker is having on you at any given moment and the *shifts* in that impact as close to the time they occur as possible. Obviously, I am looking at these shifts as representing shifts in states of self that are to be held by the analyst as an *ongoing* focus of attention.

It is a way of listening different from that of hearing the person feel differently at different moments. The latter takes the switches in states of consciousness as more or less normal background music, unless they are particularly dramatic. The former takes them as the primary data that organize everything else you are hearing and doing, including how you approach the issue of unconscious fantasy and the reconstruction of personal narrative. We speak of a person as being in different "moods," or as being emotionally "labile," or as not being "himself." These metaphors are useful, particularly with certain patients at specific moments. But because they are based on a conception of affective shifts as emanating from a unitary, centered self that is temporarily decentered, an analyst's traditional posture and listening stance has tended to focus on the *content* of mental states without particular regard for the basic discontinuity in structural *context*—the states themselves. What an analyst hears has thus tended to be organized by a search for continuity between conscious and unconscious meaning rather than by a dialogue between discontinuous domains of self-meaning held by a multiplicity of states of consciousness, some of which can be told and some only enacted. I am offering the view that for any human being, feeling differently at different moments about the same thing, or "getting into a mood," represents a shift to a state of consciousness with its own internal integrity, its own reality, and sometimes its own "truth."

The challenge for an analyst is in being aware that with every patient some state shifts have a minimal link or no link to other states of consciousness, even to those that may have just preceded the change. The change points are moments that sometimes may indeed signify the presence of an interpretable state of conflict and at other times may herald the emergence of a dissociated domain of experience. In a personality that is significantly organized by dissociative protection against trauma, there is, of course, a greater likelihood that an affective shift signals the presence of a self-state that not only is disjunctive with the one preceding it, but also is relatively inaccessible to it. But even in a patient without a diagnosed dissociative disorder, a shift in self-state may signify the absence rather than the presence of a state of conflict even though the patient may appear conflicted because the *content* has remained the same. In such instances, what the analyst may be conceptualizing as "externalization of conflict" is often precisely the opposite—the presence of a dissociated self-state that cannot yet *experience* intrapsychic conflict, much less externalize it. From a nonlinear listening stance, shifts in states of consciousness are firstly viewed by the analyst as moments of recognition, exploration, and potential negotiation within the transference-countertransference field and only through this process as genuine windows for conflict interpretation and resolution.

Perception, Language, and Change

Once again, language does not merely carry meaning, but constructs it as a relational process. The analyst's goal is not to bring the patient to a point where he can eventually accept a "delivered" interpretation, but rather to assume that if such a point is in fact reached, it means that the interpretation had already been made. It was "made," in the sense that it was "constructed" in interactive exploration of the multiple realities of opposing self-states held by patient and analyst, rather than "made" (as in "delivered") by the analyst. The result is not literally a "new" reality, and most definitely not the correction of a faulty or distorted "old" reality. It represents a linking of opposing subnarratives held by different states of consciousness that have been dissociatively inaccessible to an experience of internal conflict. Psychological "integration," as I have suggested in chapter 12, does not lead to a single "real you" or "true self." Rather, it is the ability to stand in the spaces between realities without losing any of them, the capacity to feel like one self while being many.

The patient's ability to move from dissociation to conflict depends on the analyst's ability to relate to several selves simultaneously while maintaining an authentic dialogue with each. It is through this process that relational bridges are built between self-experiences that could not formerly be contained in a relationship with the same object. An analyst, to utilize the frame of reference discussed here, does not have to abandon his or her own school of thought and work in a new way that is incompatible with his present clinical posture. Historically, the stance of any given analyst has tended to slant toward one of three postures partly organized by individual differences in metapsychology: interpretation of conflict, detailed inquiry, or empathic attunement. It is striking to observe, however, that built into each posture, regardless of differences in metatheory, is an acceptance, based on its own clinical logic, of the fact that the transference-countertransference field is where the action takes place. In other words, any analysis from any theoretical context that has as its goal enduring characterological growth is grounded in this understanding. Why?

Clinically, the transference-countertransference field is characterized by its vividness and its immediacy. But why is this fact so important that it is able to transcend conceptual differences among analysts as to how to best utilize this field? My own answer is that, regardless of a given analyst's metapsychology of therapeutic action, we are all either explicitly or implicitly attempting to clinically facilitate a patient's access to the broadest possible range of consciousness *through enhancing perception*. I am arguing, in other words, that in *every* technical approach, the utilization of transference creates its analytic impact to the extent the patient is freed to see the analyst while the analyst is seeing him. Dissociated domains of self achieve symbolization primarily through enactment in a transference/countertransference context because *experience becomes symbolized not by words themselves but by the new perceptual context that the words come to represent.* "Speak!, that your patient might see you," in order that his dissociated states of mind may find access to the here-and-now of the analytic relationship and be lived within it. Judith Peterson (1993) has addressed this in her cogent observation that

> many steps are necessary in order to move someone from a dissociative state to an integrated one. . . . However, the therapy [does] not consist of Freud and Breuer's definition of abreaction, nor of discharging emotional energy to release repressed ideas. . . . The

focus is not on abreaction but on the change points or moments in therapy where cognitive insights, reconstruction or blending and integration occur [pp. 74–75].

Particularly illustrative of this focus in my own work (see chapters 8 and 10) has been the direct appearance in sessions of the Isakower phenomenon (Isakower, 1938), a dissociated autosymbolic hallucination that typically occurs in the twilight state of falling asleep. When it appears, it is most often reported as a soft, white, amorphous bubble descending slowly upon the person's face and threatening to engulf him. My first experience with it (chapter 8) was in treating a man whose schizoid personality encompassed all the elements of an extreme dissociative disorder. Other patients, like this man, have also had in sessions with me dissociated experiences similar to that of the Isakower phenomenon itself.

I believe that all these perceptual events, including the Isakower phenomenon, may represent an effort to restore a developmentally normal process that was traumatically impaired early in life—the process of perceptual transition to linguistic symbolization of experience. The hallucinatory experience, when it has appeared in my own patients, was at times "blank," at other times "gridlike," and at still other times, imagistic. It is my hypothesis that in the process of moving from dissociation to conflict, the use of language in the act of constructing cognitive meaning from experience is first represented schematically through perception, and this is sometimes manifested by the type of articulation that occurs in transitional perceptual experience when the individual is neither fully awake nor fully asleep. It is a state of consciousness that bridges both and is notably similar to the trance and fuguelike states preceding major dissociative episodes.

The early literature on the Isakower phenomenon is suggestive in this regard. Depending on an author's perspective as to whether the person was believed to be more asleep or more awake when the phenomenon occurred, the event is written about as either a form of dream or as an autosymbolic hallucination. Thus, it has been interpreted by Lewin (1946, 1948, 1953) as what he calls "the dream screen" and by M. M. Stern (1961) as what he has labeled "blank hallucinations." I think it is not unreasonable to suggest that the hallucinations may be a kind of "way station" on the road to the use of language, the individual's attempt actively to restore the linkage of his creative and his adaptational capacities. One of my patients (see chapter 10) actually reported that his earliest childhood memory of the Isakower phenomenon was of trying to cope with it by attempting to write into it, but the bubble was so soft and mushy that his hand went into it and left no impression—a description remarkably similar to that of his early experience with his mother. In treating this kind of patient, one can often see a structural resonance between the autosymbolic visual imagery and the simultaneously occurring enactment in the transference-countertransference field, particularly during phases when dissociative structures are being surrendered.

Trauma and Technique

What about the issue of "technique?" It is in my view too linear a concept; if you do "this" correctly now, then "that" will follow later. It feels too overly based on an "If this, then that" model that looks for linear causes for events, with individuality seen as random "noise" in the system. From the vantage point of nonlinear dynamics, it is the unpredictability that is the very nature of the event, and *proper analytic technique lies in the analyst's ability to beware of its presence*, to be as attuned as possible to those moments when application of "technique" has replaced a stance organized by ongoing involvement with the patient's experience. A pattern of pointless retraumatization in analysis can take as many forms as there are analytic techniques, and any systematized analytic posture holds the potential for repeating the trauma of nonrecognition, no matter how useful the theory from which the posture is derived. Nonrecognition is equivalent to relational abandonment, and it is that which evokes the familiar and often bewildering accusation, "you don't want to know me." In other words, it is in the process of "knowing" one's patient through direct relatedness, as distinguished from frustrating, gratifying, containing, empathizing with, or even understanding him, that those aspects of self which cannot "speak" will ever find a voice and exist as a felt presence owned by the patient rather than as a "not-me" state that possesses him.

Areas of personality that are organized by conflict are always interwoven with areas organized by trauma. Trauma produces dissociation, and dissociation creates retrospective falsification of the past and retrospective falsification of one's ability to predict the future. The linear sequence of time experience is altered as a protective device. Amnesia is produced, at least for the perceptual memory of the events, but experiential memory remains relatively intact. It is as if the person "feels" something happened to him because "he just feels it," but he can't remember it as a perceptual event—an image that can be processed cognitively and thus, temporally, as a piece of the past.

What takes the place of the memory is a "time condensation," a reliving of the past as a frozen replica that structures the person's image of the future and of the present. Instead of being able to deal with "what happened to me," the person enters therapy in order to deal with "what he is sure *will* happen to him and what is happening to him now. Terr (1984) has discussed this issue in the context of her research into the aftermath of various traumatic events, including the kidnapping and burying alive of a busload of schoolchildren in Chowchilla, California:

> Following psychic trauma, disorders of time sequencing may assume various guises: (1) condensations of contiguous events into simultaneity; (2) time-skew; (3) retrospective significances (including omens); and (4) the sense of prediction. These post-traumatic distortions of ordering require sizeable suspensions of reality sense, and they may lead the psychiatrist or psychoanalyst erroneously to conclude that the psychically traumatized patient suffers from a "borderline" or worse condition [p. 644].

The difficulty for psychoanalysts is that they do not have a sufficiently robust theoretical model to deal with the implications of this phenomenon because Freud, abandoning trauma theory, replaced it with a conceptual system leading to the belief that, except for the most seriously disturbed patients, interpretation of intrapsychic conflict (with or without "parameters") should be sufficient. In fact, trauma and dissociation breed in *every* human being discontinuous realities that are not amenable to interpretation. Even though a patient's bleak view of the future is a psychodynamic issue based largely on something that really happened in the past, because of the nature of dissociation, he often has minimal perspective on his pain or his dread. It is an experiential truth that he lives with. Thus, the more an analyst pursues his interpretations, the more a patient frequently feels that the analyst really doesn't want to know him. The "him" that he feels the analyst doesn't want to know is the dissociated self-state holding the experience of trauma that can't be processed as a memory. So the analyst is right but wrong, and in being wrong he is presented with a context to discover the speaker hidden in the words. It is an opportunity for an analyst to live with his patient through an inevitable enactment of the original trauma, thus providing the best chance to have the unprocessed experience become a real memory. How does this occur? There is no answer to that because it takes place differently for every unique patient-analyst dyad. But the approach and the principle can at least be stated.

The essential nature of trauma is that because the person is not prepared to cope with it, the integrity of the ego is passively overwhelmed, and the experience of "being oneself" begins to fragment and depersonalize. It is in this sense that dissociation protects against self-fragmentation and restores personhood and sanity by hypnoidally unlinking the incompatible states of consciousness and allowing access to them only as discontinuous and cognitively unrelated mental experiences. It works, but *the basic problem for the traumatized individual then becomes his own self-cure.* The living present and the image of the future serve largely as warnings designed to protect the person against trauma that has already occurred. The capacity for imagination is perverted into a way of making sure that the unanticipated quality of the unremembered original event cannot be repeated. By consistently mobilizing for disaster, the person is unwittingly contributing to its likelihood, and no matter how bad it turns out to be, the person is already prepared for it and his ego is set to master it. To deal with the original trauma, a dissociated state of consciousness is created that holds the experience as a terrifying, but retrospectively falsified temporal event. The nature of the fear is real enough, but the mind retains it as a dread of what can happen or is happening rather than as a memory of what has happened. The result is that the person, through continual enactment of the experiential memory, creates a world of miniature versions of the original situation and lives in that world as a reality that continues to be substantiated through his ongoing relationships. It is as though he is not to be allowed any peace. Around each corner is potential trauma; peace is simply the calm before the storm, and if he goes too long without verification of the reality of his dread, he needs to find some event that provides evidence that justifies his felt need for vigilance in a world of traumatic reality.

The "truth" that is held by a dissociated state exists as an experiential memory without an accurate perceptual memory of its traumatic origin. It will remain untouched unless a new perceptual reality is created between patient and analyst that has some impact on altering the narrative structure that maintains dissociation as though the past were still a present danger. The quality of the relationship between patient and analyst at any given moment will thus determine the degree to which the content of an interpretation will be heard *as* an interpretation rather than as a verbal disguise for what is experienced as the analyst's repetition of the original abuse or neglect. In other words, for traumatic experience to be cognitively symbolized it has to be reenacted in a relationship that replays the interpersonal context without blindly reproducing the original outcome. If the analyst includes this fact in his working stance, then he is more likely to be attuned to the shifts in states of consciousness—*his own as well as his patient's*—that signal when an enactment is taking place and that a modification in approach is required which may or may not include verbally addressing the enactment at that moment.

All in all, I think the patient's dilemma has been particularly well described in a four-line poem by Emerson (1851) that is in its own way a kind of tribute to the patient. Unfortunately, you can't read it to your patient because he will not only deny its validity but will take it as further evidence that you don't want to know his pain. The poem, called "Borrowing," reads

> Some of the hurts you have cured,
> And the sharpest you still have survived,
> But what torments of grief you endured
> From evils which never arrived!

The Uses and Abuses of Self-Disclosure

With regard to how one approaches analytic intervention with this frame of reference in mind, probably the prime clinical issue that addresses the difference between linear and nonlinear thinking in technique is that of self-disclosure by the analyst. Like any other choice an analyst makes with a given patient, self-disclosure derives its meaning from the ongoing context of the relationship in which it takes place, not from its utility as a "technique." It's usefulness to the analytic process is organized by the quality of its genuineness as a human act, particularly the degree to which the analyst is free of internal pressure (conscious or unconscious) to prove his honesty or trustworthiness as a technical maneuver designed to counter the patient's mistrust. The analyst's self-disclosure must be what Symington (1983) calls an "act of freedom" in which the analyst comfortably retains his right to not disclose or, if he does choose to disclose, to claim his own privacy and set his own boundaries. If it is not an "act of freedom" then it also loses its potential as an "act of meaning" in Bruner's (1990) terms, a relational act through which personal narrative is reconstructed as a perceptual event in a context of interpersonal authenticity.

The subjective experience of freedom to say "no," or the absence of such freedom, inevitably informs the way in which the patient's self-disclosure is shaped, and this is equally true for the analyst. His motivation and affective state become as much a part of what is disclosed as the intended content. In other words, if the analyst's choice is motivated by his need to be seen in a certain way by his patient (such as honest, accommodating, unsadistic, or innovatively "free" as an analyst) then self-disclosure becomes a technique and as a technique is as instrumentally linear as any other intervention based on an "if I do this, then the patient will do that" model. Like any human quality that is "packaged," self-disclosure too can lose its primary relational ingredient (mutuality) and become what Greenberg (1981) has called "prescriptive." When it fails in its purpose, it is usually for that reason. It lacks the authenticity, spontaneity, and unpredictable impact on the future, that make analytic growth possible.

A colleague of mine (Therese Ragen, personal communication) has commented that my viewpoint implies a distinction between genuineness and honesty, and I agree. Genuineness is a human attribute only in a relational context. If you try to turn it into a technique, it loses mutuality and becomes a personal instrumentality called "honesty." Any attempt to turn a therapeutic discovery that emerges from a relational context into a technique that can be "applied" to other patients is an illustration of what I believe to be the single most ubiquitous failing in all analytic schools of thought as methods of therapy, and the shared blind-spot in each of their creators (including Freud, Ferenczi, Sullivan, and Kohut).

For example, Ferenczi's failure with "mutual analysis" as a technique (Dupont, 1988) occurred not because what he did was wrong, but because it failed to be right. What I mean by this is that an analyst who systematically attempts to gratify needs fails the patient, not because gratification is "wrong" or intrinsically harmful, but because it is a form of nonrecognition and for that reason fails, just as does systematic *frustration* of needs. Both are evidence to the patient that the analyst is unable or unwilling to authentically "live with" the patient's state of mind in whatever form it presents itself and attempt to know it without surrendering his right to "be himself" as part of the process. I believe this to be a more accurate assessment than Ferenczi's own statement of his disillusionment, in which he concludes (Dupont, 1988) that "mutual analysis is merely a 'last resort' made necessary by insufficiently deep analysis of the analysts themselves [and] 'proper analysis by a stranger, without any obligation, would be better'" (p. xxii). Ferenczi's concept of "mutual analysis" was based on something he originally perceived as demanded of him by certain patients, particularly by his famous patient Elizabeth Severn, known as RN. At that point, his approach to his patient was genuinely mutual—it was not Ferenczi's technical creation but a co-creation of that particular patient and analyst dyad. Following that, Ferenczi turned it into a technique he called "mutual analysis," at which point, like any other technique, it was no longer a co-creation and, I submit, was in fact no longer mutual. It was something, for better or for worse, applied prescriptively, and it failed because of that.

In fact, the way Ferenczi discovered this "technique" reminds me a bit of the old joke based on Charles Lamb's (1822) essay about the farmer in ancient China whose house burned down with his pig in it. While removing the dead animal, the farmer scorched himself, and when he put his finger into his mouth to cool it, he became so thrilled with the exciting new taste that he called all his neighbors to try it. And so, the joke goes, roast pork was discovered, and on the same day each year until the farmer's death he would gather his neighbors together for a feast and burn down his new house with a pig in it. My own addendum would be that perhaps that joke isn't really about the discovery of roast pork but the discovery of "technique."

I am suggesting, in other words, that the reason Ferenczi was successful with Elizabeth Severn (and perhaps a few other patients later on) when he attempted "mutual analysis" was not because patients in general need soul-searching emotional openness from their analysts, but because that patient at that moment in Ferenczi's work was able to confront his inauthenticity with regard to her. She settled for "mutual analysis" because she could not hope to change his personality. In an ironic way, she asked for what she knew he might be able to give, not for what she really needed. She asked for a demonstration of honesty rather than an effort at mutuality because there was no way to get the real thing. In his own way, of course, Ferenczi did ultimately respond with genuine mutuality even though, ironically, he missed her real message—"I need you to be yourself while recognizing what I am feeling, but since you haven't yet been able to do both, let's see what you can do if I push you to the edge." His courage to try self-disclosure at that point came mostly from his need to control what was going on between himself and his patient, and because it "worked" it prevented him from potentially experiencing and recognizing the complex interplay between what his patient was saying to him and what she was doing with him while saying it. Ferenczi could not register, as part of a single relational configuration, the controlling and intrusive way she was behaving toward him while she was talking about "mutual" analysis as the only way she could "protect herself" *from* him. But he could experience in himself at that immediate moment the presence of the very kinds of feelings toward her that she was accusing him of har-boring. He could feel what she was saying about him as accurate—his reaction to what he called in his clinical diary her "terrorism of suffer-ing" (Dupont, 1988, p. 211)—and he turned toward what she insisted was the only possible path that could validate her feelings and enable her to trust him: that of self-disclosure equivalent to hers. It "worked." And *because* it "worked," he came to believe it was the technique that accounted for the improvement in the treatment relationship. In my terms, he confused authenticity with self-disclosure and kept burning down the house to get the roast pork. But unlike the farmer in the joke, he didn't even end up getting the pork again. His subsequent patients, for the most part, kept reacting as though he were doing something bad to them, and I would have to agree; he was inadvertently retrau-matizing them to no immediate therapeutic purpose. All this could have turned out much better if he had adhered to what he had already written about the importance of trauma in personality development. Don't just attend to the words; try to see the dissociated speaker who is relating to you at that moment, the part of the self that "lives on, hidden, ceaselessly endeavoring to make itself felt" (Ferenczi, 1930b, p. 122).

All this having been said, I must admit that Dupont's (1993) state-ment that "gratifications should only be granted to demands aiming at recognition" (p. 154) doesn't provide much of a place to anchor oneself when a patient is rocking the couch and insisting with absolute con-viction that you are depriving him of the one thing he needs in order to get better. At such a moment an analyst is often floundering and not at all sure of what he thinks. There are very few external guidelines, and it's very lonely with only your doubts to keep you company. All I can say is that, while I do believe that gratification is most often expe-rienced by patients as an empathic abandonment because it is typically a substitute for the more painful effort at recognition, there are in my experience certain patients for whom some directly gratifying response by the analyst is the only way they can trust the analyst's concern for them, at least for a period of time.

With such an individual at such a moment, I sometimes find myself making some compromise that is invariably not satisfying to either of us but almost always seems to move the work ahead. Over the years I've come to believe that it may be the *limitation* in my flexi-bility—the fact that I do implicitly draw a line in the sand—that has the most impact because it emanates from relational authenticity. If I do ultimately move the line, *the process through which that happens is at least as important as the accommodation itself*. It carries the fact that what

I'm doing is not a technique but a personal effort I am willing to make as long as it does not exceed the limits of what I establish as my personal boundaries and is thus part of a genuine relational negotiation. So, all in all, I could probably say that my position on technique feels compatible with Kaiser's (1965) observation that "whenever you feel the need to do something, or to refrain from doing something for the purpose of showing [a patient] your concern, you can be certain that your concern is lacking" (p. 170).

Many different analytic concepts have, each in its own metaphor, addressed the fact that the aesthetics of analytic communication is an ineffable coming together of two minds in an unpredictable way, from which something "new but not new" is constructed. Michael Balint's (1968) "new beginning," Winnicott's (1967) "potential space," and Sullivan's (1953) "parataxic mode of experience" are just a few of the more influential examples. I believe that the logic of conceptualizing the intersubjective field in these ways is strongest in the context of a nonlinear view of mental structure and the discontinuity of self-states. The ability of a patient to take in and seriously consider the analyst's perception of him is possible only if another reality (or truth) being held in a dissociated state is not being invalidated as a tradeoff. The patient doesn't need to be "agreed with" or need a heroic attempt at self-disclosure by the analyst. What is required is that the multiple realities being held by different self-states find opportunity for linkage. The most powerful medium through which this takes place is the analyst's ability to recognize that his feelings about his patient are not his personal property, and that his own feelings and his patient's are part of a unitary configuration that must be linked in the immediacy of the analytic relationship in order for the multiple realities within the patient to become linked through cognitive symbolization by language.

Peterson (1993), whom I quoted earlier, referred to the "change points" or moments in therapy where cognitive insights occur. My view is that these change points occur when an enactment is serving its proper function and the patient's dissociated experience that the analyst has been holding as part of himself is sufficiently processed between them for the patient to begin to take it back into his own self-experience little by little. It is a change point because the patient's processing of the experience continues internally as a state of conflict rather than intersubjectively. In other words, the use of language, instead of being a substitute for experience, allows a new self-narrative to be created. It moves a new experience of reality that begins as perceptual and interpersonal to its most mature level of mental processing by the use of thought and intrapsychic conflict resolution. Put most simply, *"unfreezing" the concrete, literal quality of a patient's states of consciousness allows him to embrace the full range of his self-narratives by first embracing the full range of his perceptual apparatus within a single relational field.* All in all, perhaps Socrates would not mind if the title of this chapter were changed to "Speak! That I may see both of us."

17

STANDING IN THE SPACES

The Multiplicity of Self and the Psychoanalytic Relationship[1] (1996)

Perhaps in some measure due to Freud's fascination with archeology, clinical psychoanalysis has tended to embrace an image of two people on a "quest"—a journey to reach an unknown destination to recover a buried past. Despite the fact that I rather like the image, in my day-to-day work as a practicing therapist, I seem to find my reality shaped more by Gertrude Stein than by Indiana Jones. Stein (1937, p. 298) commented about the nature of life and the pursuit of goals, that when you finally get there, "there is no there there." My patients frequently make the same comment. The direct experience of "self change" seems to be gobbled up by the reality of "who you are" at a given moment, and evades the linear experience of beginning, middle, and end. But linear time does indeed have a presence of its

---

1. Earlier drafts of this essay were presented in October 1995 at the "Fifth Annual Symposium" of the Massachusetts Institute of Psychoanalysis, Cambridge, MA; in March 1996 [with discussant Dr. Edward Corrigan] at the "Twenty-Fifth Anniversary Gala" of the Institute for Contemporary Psychotherapy, NYC; and in April 1996 [with discussant Dr. Adrienne Harris] at the William Alanson White Psychoanalytic Institute, NYC. The chapter in its present version was published originally in *Contemporary Psychoanalysis*, 1996, 32:509–535.

own—like the background ticking of a clock that cannot be ignored for too long without great cost—and it is this paradox that seems to make psychoanalysis feel like a relationship between two people each trying to keep one foot in the here-and-now and the other in the linear reality of past, present, and future. Described this way, it sounds like a totally impossible process. If indeed "everyone knows that every day has no future to it" (Stein, 1937, p. 271), then what sustains a person's motivation for analytic treatment? How do we account for the fact that a patient remains in a relationship with another person for the express purpose of dismantling his own self-image for a presumedly "better" version that he cannot even imagine until after it has arrived? The answer, as I see it, touches what may be the essence of human nature—the fact that the human personality possesses the extraordinary capacity to negotiate continuity and change *simultaneously*, and will do so under the right relational conditions (see chapters 12 and 16). I believe that this attribute is what we rely on to make clinical psychoanalysis, or any form of psychodynamic psychotherapy, possible. How we understand this remarkable capability of the mind, and what we see as the optimal therapeutic environment for it to flourish, are, as I have suggested in chapter 12, the fundamental questions that shape psychoanalytic theory and practice. What I want to talk about here is an outcome of this way of experiencing and thinking about the human relationship we call "psychoanalysis."

For example: A patient is engaged in a passionate sexual moment that she refers to, in session, as "coming in diamonds." She and her lover are "lost" in each other and she, a woman who had entered analysis with "gender confusion," has a visual experience that her lover's penis moving in and out, might be his or it might be hers. She can't tell "whose penis it is, who is fucking whom," and "it doesn't matter." How does the analyst hear and process this "loss of reality testing" at that moment?

Another patient reports having been reading a book in bed, looking down at the book, and noticing that it was wet. She realized she had been crying. What allows the analyst to comfortably conceptualize the fact that she didn't know she had been crying *when* it was happening? Does he think of such a mundane event as even interesting, analytically?

A patient, a woman with an eating disorder, is asked by her analyst to describe the details of last night's binge. She cannot do it. She insists, in a voice without affect, that she has no memory of the step-by-step experience of what she ate, how she ate it, and what she thought or felt as she was eating it. Resistance?

A new referral, perhaps an unanticipated dissociative identity disorder (formerly known as multiple personality), enters a trance state during an analytic session and, seemingly spontaneously, enacts a vivid portrayal of a child in the midst of a horrifying event and then has no memory of that part of the session. How does the analyst perceive the "trance" phenomenon and his patient's subsequent report of amnesia for the event that had just taken place before the analyst's eyes a few moments before? From what stance shall the analyst attempt to engage the patient about any or all of this?

And now to the analyst himself. It is seven forty-five A.M. Steaming coffee container in hand, standing at my window looking down at the street below, I am waiting for the "buzz" announcing my first patient, the cue that launches me into my chair—my haven, my "nest." But my gaze is pulled as if by a will of its own, and inevitably submits as it does each morning. There he is! Just as he has been every day for months—in the same doorway next to my Greek luncheonette, half sitting, half sprawling, clutching an empty coffee container holding a few coins, some of them mine. Why must we share the same coffee container? I focus on the barely discernable blue and white sketch of the Greek amphora and the "personal" greeting in simulated classic lettering: "It's a Pleasure to Serve You." I think, somewhat irritably, "Get lost! It's bad enough to see you when I'm buying my coffee—Do I have to also see you while I'm drinking it? I need this time to relax! I have to get ready to help people!"

I hear a voice: "Why don't you just stop looking out of the window"?

A second voice replies, petulantly: "But it's my window!"

The first is heard again: "Then why don't you give him something every day instead of just once in a while? Maybe you won't feel so angry at having to see him when you get upstairs."

"But if I do that he'll expect it every day," the second voice argues. "He'll tell his friends, and then everyone will expect it. I'll have to give to all of them."

"So what!" the first voice proclaims.

"But his needs are insatiable," complains the second voice. "There's one of him on every corner."

"Have you ever met someone with insatiable needs?" asks the first voice.

"I don't think so," the second voice mutters defeatedly.

"I don't think so either," says the first. "Do you think your patients have insatiable needs? Are you afraid of releasing a demon that will never go back into the bottle and will enslave you?"

That does it! I "wake up" and see myself standing at the window, staring at the man in the doorway across the street. "Do I feel that way with my patients and deny it?" I wonder. "It's a pleasure to serve you, but stay in your bottle? It's a pleasure to serve you for fifty minutes but not to know you personally? Oh, God, what a way to start the day. Ah, saved by the buzz!"

Psychoanalysis and the Decentered Self

In a book entitled *More Than Human*, written in 1953, Theodore Sturgeon, one of the most creative and visionary science fiction authors of the twentieth century, wrote the following: "Multiplicity is our first characteristic; unity our second. As your parts know they are parts of you, so must you know that we are parts of humanity" (p. 232). I think it might be interesting to allow Sturgeon's words to remain in your mind, but to now let yourself hear them in the context of a not dissimilar viewpoint offered by someone seemingly unlike Sturgeon, at least in any obvious way—a classical psychoanalyst whose sensibility is more pragmatic than visionary, and whose "professional self," at least in most of her writing, has embodied a traditionally positivistic approach to the nature of reality. In a paper in the *Psychoanalytic Quarterly*, Janine Lampl-de Groot (1981) reported being so persuaded by the power of the clinical evidence supporting multiplicity of selfhood, that she advanced the then extraordinary hypothesis that the phenomenon of multiple personality is present in all human beings as a basic phenomenon of mental functioning. Whether or not one agrees with her use of terminology, I think it is fair to say that an increasing number of contemporary analysts now share the clinical observations that led her to this conclusion—that even in the most well-functioning individual, normal personality structure is shaped by dissociation as well as by repression and intrapsychic conflict.

Parallel with this development, a noticeable shift has been taking place with regard to psychoanalytic understanding of the human mind and the nature of unconscious mental processes—away from the idea of a conscious/preconscious/unconscious distinction per se, towards a view of the self as decentered, and the mind as a configuration of shifting, nonlinear, discontinuous states of consciousness in an ongoing dialectic with the healthy illusion of unitary selfhood. Sherry Turkle (1978), for example, sees Lacan's focus on the decenteredness of selfhood as his most seminal contribution, and writes that "for generations, people have argued about what was revolutionary in Freud's theory and the debate has usually centered on Freud's ideas about sexuality. But Lacan's work underscores that part of Freud's work that is revolutionary for our time. The individual is 'decentered.' There is no autonomous self" (p. xxxii).

Over the years, isolated psychoanalytic voices offering different versions of this view have been acknowledged, frequently with interest, but although these voices were often those of figures influential in their individual domains, these analysts were typically clinicans who had chosen to work with patients suffering from severe character pathology and thus were considered to some degree outside of the psychoanalytic "mainstream." It could be said that the first voice was in fact *pre*-analytic—that of Josef Breuer (Breuer and Freud, 1893–1895), who argued that the basis of traumatic hysteria was the existence of hypnoid states of consciousness that had the power to create an amnesia. After the publication of *Studies on Hysteria*, however, Freud was for the most part openly contemptuous about the possible usefulness of theorizing about dissociation, hypnoid phenomena, or states of consciousness (chapter 15; see also Loewenstein and Ross, 1992), leaving the future of its analytic viability mainly in the hands of Ferenczi (1930a, 1931, 1933).

In succeeding generations, the torch was passed to seminal figures such as Sullivan (1940, 1953), Fairbairn (1944, 1952), Winnicott (1945, 1949, 1960a, 1971d), Laing (1960), Balint (1968), and Searles (1977), each of whom in his own metaphor accorded the phenomenon of "multiplicity of self" a central position in his work. Sullivan, in fact, in a not too widely publicized remark once wrote (Sullivan, 1950b, p. 221) that "for all I know every human being has as many personalities as he has interpersonal relations."

Winnicott's contribution to this area is, I feel, particularly far-reaching. He not only conceptualized primary dissociation as a psychoanalytic phenomenon in it own right and wrote about it in a manner that brought it directly into the basic psychoanalytic situation (Winnicott, 1949, 1971d), but I would suggest that what we now formulate as psychological "trauma" that leads to the pathological use of dissociation is the essence of what he labeled "impingement." Although not specifically elaborated by him in terms of dissociated states of consciousness, perhaps most significant of all was his vision of a true and false self (Winnicott, 1960a) which emphasized the *nonlinear* element in psychic growth. It is not unreasonable to suggest that Winnicott's "nonlinear leap" in psychoanalytic theory has been a major factor in encouraging postclassical analytic thinkers to reexamine its model of the unconscious mind in terms of a self that is decentered, and its concept of "growth" as a dialectic rather than a unidirectional process.

In this context, a recent research study by Sorenson (1994) discusses the range of theories in which a formerly axiomatic presumption about the nature of human mental functioning is now being rapidly revised—the presumption of a linear, hierarchical, unidirectional model of growth in which integration is necessarily or continuously superior to disintegration. Using Thomas Ogden's reformulation of Melanie Klein's developmental theory as an example, Sorenson says the following:

> Ogden (1989) has argued that Melanie Klein's theory of psychological development from the paranoid-schizoid position to the depressive position is too linear and sequential. Instead of Klein's phases which were developmentally diachronic, he proposed synchronic dimensions of experience in which all components play enduringly vital roles, at once both negating and safeguarding the contexts for one another. Unchecked integration, containment and resolution from the depressive position, for example, leads to stagnation, frozenness, and deadness; unmitigated splitting and fragmentation of the paranoid-schizoid likewise leads to fundamental discontinuities of self-experience and psychic chaos. The paranoid-schizoid position provides the much needed breaking up of a too-frozen integration. . . . I believe we make an error to valorize integration and villainize disintegration, just as Ogden was reluctant to do the same to the depressive and paranoid-schizoid positions, respectively [p. 342].

Another voice speaking to the significance of nonlinear mental states is that of Betty Joseph. Joseph emphasizes, write Spillius and Feldman (1989), "that if one wishes to foster long-term psychic change, it is important that the analyst eschew value judgements about whether the shifts and changes in a session are positive or negative. . . . Nor should we be concerned with change as an achieved state; it is a process, not a state, *and is a continuation and development from the 'constant minute shifts' in the session*" (p. 5, italics added).

Normal Multiplicity of Self

A human being's ability to live a life with both authenticity and self-awareness depends on the presence of an ongoing dialectic between separateness and unity of one's self-states, allowing each self to function optimally without foreclosing communication and negotiation between them. When all goes well developmentally, a person is only dimly or momentarily aware of the existence of individual self-states and their respective realities because each functions as part of a healthy illusion of cohesive personal identity—an overarching cognitive and experiential state felt as "me." Each self-state is a piece of a functional whole, informed by a process of internal negotiation with the realities, values, affects, and perspectives of the others. Despite collisions and even enmity between aspects of self, it is unusual for any one self-state to function totally outside of the sense of "me-ness"— that is, without the participation of the other parts of self. Dissociation, like repression, is a healthy, adaptive function of the human mind. It is a basic process that allows individual self-states to function optimally (not simply defensively) when full immersion in a single reality, a single strong affect, and a suspension of one's self-reflective capacity is exactly what is called for or wished for.[2] As Walter Young (1988) has succinctly put it: "Under normal conditions, dissociation enhances the integrating functions of the ego by screening out excessive or irrelevant stimuli. . . . Under pathological conditions . . . the normal functions of dissociation become mobilized for defensive use" (pp. 35–36).

In other words, dissociation is primarily a means through which a human being maintains personal continuity, coherence, and integrity of the sense of self. But how can this be? How can the division of self-experience into relatively unlinked parts be in the service of self-integrity? I've suggested in chapter 12 that the most convincing answer is based on the fact that self-experience originates in relatively unlinked self-states, each coherent in its own right, and that the experience of being a unitary self (cf. Hermans, Kempen, and van Loon, 1992, pp. 29–30; Mitchell, 1991, pp. 127–139) is an acquired, developmentally adaptive illusion. It is when this illusion of unity is traumatically threatened with unavoidable, precipitous disruption that it becomes in itself a liability because it is in jeopardy of being overwhelmed by input it cannot process symbolically and deal with as a state of cognitive conflict. When the illusion of unity is too dangerous to be maintained there is then a return to the simplicity of dissociation as a proactive, defensive response to the potential repetition of trauma. As one of my patients put it as she began to "wake up," "All my life I've found money on the street and people would say I was lucky. I've started to realize I wasn't lucky. I just never looked up."

---

2. Some examples would be the patient who reported not knowing whose penis it was and that it "didn't matter"; the woman crying into her book and not noticing it; and my own trance-state at the window while waiting for my first patient to arrive.

Slavin and Kriegman (1992), approaching this issue from the perspective of evolutionary biology and the adaptive design of the human psyche, write the following:

> Multiple versions of the self exist within an overarching, synthetic structure of identity. . . . [which] probably cannot possess the degree of internal cohesion or unity frequently implied by concepts such as the "self" in the self psychological tradition, the "consolidated character" in Blos's ego psychological model, or "identity" in Erikson's framework. . . . [T]he idea of an individual "identity" or a cohesive "self" serves as an extremely valuable metaphor for the vital experience of relative wholeness, continuity, and cohesion in self-experience. Yet, as has often been noted, when we look within the psyche of well-put-together individuals, we actually see a "multiplicity of selves" or versions of the self coexisting within certain contours and patterns that, in sum, produce a sense of individuality, "I-ness" or "me-ness". . . . Although the coexistence of "multiple versions of the self" that we observe introspectively and clinically may thus represent crystallizations of different interactional schemes, this multiplicity may also signal the existence of *an inner, functional limit on the process of self-integration.* . . . The cost of our human strategy for structuring the self in a provisional fashion—around a sometimes precarious confederation of alternate self/other schemas—lies in the ever-present risk of states of relative disintegration, fragmentation, or identity diffusion. The maintenance of self-cohesion . . . should thus be one of the most central ongoing activities of the psyche. . . . [but] . . . the strivings of such an evolved "superordinate self" would emanate . . . *not primarily from a fragmentation induced by trauma or environmental failure to fully provide its mirroring (selfobject) functions.* Rather, its intrinsic strivings would emanate from the very design of the self-system [pp. 204–205, italics added].

The implications of this are profound for the psychoanalytic understanding of "self" and how to facilitate its therapeutic growth. In chapter 12 I remarked that health is the ability to stand in the spaces between realities without losing any of them—the capacity to feel like one self while being many. "Standing in the spaces" is a shorthand way of describing a person's relative capacity to make room at any given moment for subjective reality that is not readily containable by the self he experiences as "me" at that moment. It is what distinguishes creative imagination from both fantasy and concreteness, and distinguishes playfulness from facetiousness. Some people can "stand in the spaces" better than others. Vladimir Nabokov (1920), for example, wrote at age 24: "I had once been splintered into a million beings and objects. Today I am one; tomorrow I shall splinter again. . . . *But I knew that all were notes of one and the same harmony"* (p. 77, italics added).

Some people can't "stand in the spaces" at all, and in these individuals we see the prototype of a psyche organized more centrally by dissociation than by repression. The key quality of a highly dissociated personality organization is its defensive dedication to retaining the protection afforded by the separateness of self-states (their discontinuity), and minimizing their potential for simultaneous accessibility to consciousness, so that each shifting "truth" can continue to play its own role without interference by the others, creating a personality structure that one of my patients described as "having a whim of iron."

Time and Timelessness

When pathological dissociation is operating, whether it is central to the personality or an isolated area of serious trouble in an otherwise well-functioning individual, part of the work in any analysis at given points in treatment is to facilitate a transition from dissociation to conflict, so that genuine repression can indeed become possible and its contents accessible to self-reflective exploration, interpretive restructuring, and the experience of owning an authentic past. The issues of a person's shifting experience of time and how the analyst regards the phenomenon of timelessness are especially important here. Bollas (1989) and Ogden (1989) have in fact each developed the idea of historical consciousness as a mental capacity that must be *achieved*. Ogden writes that "it is by no means to be assumed that the patient has a history (that is, a sense of historicity) at the beginning of analysis. In other words, we cannot take for granted the idea that the patient has achieved a sense of continuity of self over time, such that his past feels as if it is connected to his experience of himself in the present" (p. 191). Until then, what we call "resistance" to interpretation is often simply evidence that some dissociated voice is experiencing the analyst's words as disconfirming its existence.

Let me describe such a clinical moment that may serve to illustrate what I mean. It is drawn from my work with a man for whom the ordinarily routine issue of missed sessions and "makeups" was more complex than I had anticipated, and led to an unexpectedly powerful revelation of his fragile link between selfhood and the continuity of past, present, and future. Because of the profoundly dissociated structure of his personality, he was unable to process the physical absence of an object and retain its mental representation with a sense of continuity. It was as if both the object (whether a person or a place) and the self that had experienced it had "died," and nothing was left but a void. His solution, as with many such individuals, depended upon his being able to concretize the events that comprised each day's activity and hold them in rote memory, hoping that the cognitive linkage would lead to some experience of self-continuity that would "get by" socially. The one exception to his "laissez-faire" attitude towards life was his determination to "make up" missed sessions. Because I required him to pay for sessions he cancelled that were not rescheduled, I believed that his fierce insistance that every session be made up no matter when, had to do with issues of power and money, and I particularly felt this as true because most of our discussions about it felt like thinly veiled power struggles.

I can still recall the moment in which it became clear that something much deeper was at stake. We were in the midst of discussing this issue, once again from our usual adversarial frame of reference, when I noticed that, inexplicably, I was feeling increasingly warm and tender towards him, and even had the fantasy of wanting to put my arm around his shoulder. This peculiar change in my own feeling state then led my attention to something in his tone of voice that I hadn't heard until that moment, and I asked him about it. I said that there was something about how his voice sounded at that moment that made me feel like a part of him was sad or frightened but couldn't say it, and I wondered whether he might be aware of anything like that going on. He then began to talk in a voice I hadn't quite heard before—a voice that conveyed, hesitantly but openly, the sadness, and desperation I had heard only as a shadowy presence. He began to confess, shamefully, what he had never before revealed—that his real need was not for me to reschedule sessions that he cancelled, but for me to reschedule *all* sessions, including sessions that I myself wished to cancel, including legal holidays.

Exploring this with him was no easy matter, because as soon as I became directly engaged with the self-state that held the feeling of desperation and longing he fled from the moment, became dramatically more dissociated, and lost all conscious awareness that his wish had any personal relevance other than revealing his propensity to be "impractical." I then told him what I had been feeling towards him that had led me to hear the part of him that until then I had been ignoring. His eyes opened wider, and little by little he began to speak more freely, but now as a frightened and confused child. "If I miss a session . . . ," he said haltingly, "If I'm not at the session . . . I won't know what happened during it . . . And if you don't make it up . . . I'll never know. I'll never have it again."

Time, as you and I know it did not exist for my patient in this state of consciousness, and had it not been for my awareness that my own state of consciousness had shifted in response to his, this unsymbolized self, lost in time, might or might not have been found. Reis (1995) has even gone as far as to argue that "it is the disruption of the experience of time that goes to the heart of the dissociative disturbances of subjectivity" (p. 219).

Dissociation as an Interpersonal Process

Dissociative processes operate in both patient and analyst as a dynamic element in the therapeutic relationship, an observation that traditionally has been made only with reference to the treatment of extreme psychopathology or severe dissociative disorders. I am suggesting however, that this statement is true as a general phenomenon of human behavior and relevant to any therapist working with any patient within an analytically informed frame of reference, regardless of theoretical persuasion.

In this regard, a series of thoughtful papers has emerged from the Anna Freud Center in London, on the developmental relevance of mental states in determining analytic "technique." Peter Fonagy and his associates (Fonagy, 1991; Fonagy and Moran, 1991; Fonagy and Target, 1995a) have offered a perspective on the relationship between conflict and dissociation that places both phenomena within a clinical model that incorporates developmental and cognitive research, object relational thinking, and a postclassical interpersonal sensibility. "We take the position," Fonagy writes (Fonagy and Moran, 1991, p. 16), "that the greater the unevenness in development, the less effective will be a technique which relies solely upon interpretations of conflict, and the greater will be the need to devise strategies of analytic intervention aimed to support and strengthen the child's capacity to tolerate conflict." Similarly, and even more to the point (Fonagy and Target, 1995a, pp. 498–499, italics added), "Interpretations may remain helpful but their function is certainly no longer limited to the lifting of repression and the addressing of distorted perceptions and beliefs . . . *Their goal is the reactivation of the patient's concern with mental states in himself and in his object.*"

Pathological dissociation is a defensive impairment of reflective capacity brought about by detaching the mind from the self—what

Winnicott (1949) called the "psyche-soma." In the analytic relationship, such patients (individuals dedicated to preserving self-continuity at the expense of self-reflection) are in need of "recognition" rather than understanding (see chapter 10), but if an analyst is to help someone who has minimal capacity for reflection in the here-and-now, it is necessary for him to accept that his "act of recognition," both developmentally and therapeutically, is a dyadic process—a "two-way street" of mutual regulation (Beebe and Lachmann, 1992; Beebe, Jaffe, and Lachmann, 1992). Consider what Fonagy and Target (1995a) have to say about this:

> We believe that the developmental help offered by the active involvement of the analyst in the mental functioning of the patient, and *the reciprocal process of the patient becoming actively involved in the analyst's mental state*, has the potential to establish this reflection and gradually to allow the patient to do this within his own mind. . . . *The critical step may be the establishment of the patient's sense of identity through the clarification of the patient's perception of the analyst's mental state.* . . . It seems that gradually this can offer a third perspective, opening up a space for thinking between and about the patient and the analyst [pp. 498–499, italics added].

A space for thinking *between and about* the patient and the analyst— a space uniquely relational and still uniquely individual; a space belonging to neither person alone, and yet, belonging to both and to each; a twilight space in which "the impossible" becomes possible; a space in which incompatible selves, each awake to its own "truth," can "dream" the reality of the other without risk to its own integrity. It is above all an intersubjective space which, like the "trance" state of consciousness just prior to entering sleep, allows both wakefulness and dreaming to coexist. Here in the interpersonal field constructed by patient and analyst, such a space is opened in the service of therapeutic growth, and the implacable enemies,"hope and dread" (Mitchell, 1993), because they can each find voice, can potentially find dialogue. How is this phenomenon possible? My answer, in its most general and oversimplified form, is that the reciprocal process of active involvement with the states of mind of "the other," allows a patient's here-and-now perception of self to share consciousness with the experiences of incompatible self-narratives that were formerly dissociated.

What is the analyst's role in this asymmetrical dyadic process that permits such a space to open? Because of the way dissociation functions interpersonally, unsymbolized aspects of the patient's self are routinely enacted with the analyst as a separate and powerful channel of communication in the clinical process—a channel that is multifaceted and continually in motion.[3] One dimension of the analyst's listening stance should therefore be dedicated to his ongoing experience of the here-and-now at the same time his focal attention may be elsewhere. That is, no matter how "important" the manifest verbal content appears to be at a given moment, the analyst should try to remain simultaneously attuned to his subjective experience of the relationship and its shifting quality. Optimally, he should try to be experientially accessible to (a) the impact of those moments in which he becomes aware that a shift in self-state (either his own or his patient's) has taken place, and (b) *the details of his own self-reflection* on whether to process this awareness with his patient or to process it alone—and if with his patient, when and how to do it. Is he reluctant to "intrude" upon his patient at that moment? Does he feel protective of the patient's need for safety and vulnerability to traumatization? Does he feel pulled in two directions about whether to speak? Does he feel strangely paralyzed by being unable to move in both directions simultaneously, as if he must somehow choose between his own self-expression and his patient's vulnerability? If so, can he find a way to use this very experience of his felt constriction of freedom? Would the act of sharing this entire sequence of thought, along with the moment that led to it, be a useful choice in this instance? I believe that, at any point in time, the questions themselves are of greater value than the answers as long as the analyst remains open to exploring the impact of his choice rather than seeing his choice as either "correct" or "wrong." In my own work, I find that even when I choose not to openly share my experience with my patient, my conscious *awareness* of the shift in the intersubjective field, because it changes my mode of processing what is being heard, is invariably picked up by my patient and eventually becomes "usable" because I am no longer hearing the patient's words and my own in the context I was hearing them before the shift. I am now experiencing their meaning being shaped by the participation of another aspect of the patient's self that has been engaged with an aspect of my own self in enacting something beyond what the words had earlier appeared to be conveying.

---

3. I refer the reader to an interesting commentary by Peter Kramer (1990) on a discussion that took place between Richard Geist (a self psychologist) and me around a critique of self psychology I had recently published (chapter 11). Kramer, describing my analytic stance as embodying an "immediately available sense of two bodies in motion" (p. 6), writes that "the interpersonal analyst is free-moving—has to be, because he or she constantly questions the validity of any viewpoint" (p. 5).

The analytic situation is an ever shifting context of reality that is constructed by the input of two people. Smith (1995, p. 69) has commented that "as long as there are two people in the room each with multiple points of view, there is likely to be no shortage of surprises," thus echoing the words of Theodor Reik (1936, p. 90) who claimed that the "royal road to the unconscious" is the experience of surprise, in that it allows an analyst "to find something new which will then create its own technique."

Take, for example, such a moment of surprise in my work with Max. Max was a twenty-four-year-old male patient, a first generation American Jew, an only child raised in a close-knit, upwardly mobile family. Because his mother could speak only Yiddish, he spoke Yiddish to her, but *only* to her, an issue that became significant to his personality development. As he reached adolescence and began to search for his place in the world, he gradually disavowed all connection to his "Yiddish self" (cf. Harris, 1992; Foster, 1996) which had been shaped in the context of his mother's illusion that his substantial intellectual gifts included a more sophisticated command of the English language than he actually possessed. His mother, whom he deeply loved, idealized him as her contribution to the American intellectual community, and despite his efforts to live up to her image of him, or perhaps *because* of his efforts, he would frequently embarrass himself in public by stretching his use of language beyond the point of his actual familiarity with the words themselves, and would manage to undermine himself in situations where he most wished to shine. In short, he was given to putting his foot in his mouth. He was seemingly unable to learn from these experiences, and was always shocked when he ended up being flooded with shame. My view of Max had been that he was unable to accommodate his mother's image of him into an acceptance of himself as a human being with limitations as well as assets, and that he continually enacted a dissociated self-representation in which he presented himself as who she said he was, while simultaneously demonstrating to himself in every other possible way, that he was not who she said he was, and that he was simply a "typical American boy doing his own thing." To put it another way, because his "Yiddish self" was felt by him as uncontainable within any relationship other than that with his mother, he couldn't begin to negotiate a cohesive sense of identity that represented the creative participation of all of his selves. He dissociated from the self-reflective involvement in living that enables someone to state, with a feeling of personal agency, "this is who I am." He was stuck with being able to state only "this is who I am not," and having to live with the "not-me" experience of his disavowed "Yiddish self" finding a voice through his so-called blunders.

Max and I had been engaged in a struggle around what he felt, I think accurately, to be my somewhat unsympathetic determination to pry him loose from having to be who his mother said he was. He insisted that he was not under his mother's spell, and that his tendency to use the wrong words when he did not really know their meaning was simply a matter of insufficient familiarity with the dictionary rather than an unconscious loyalty to his bond with his mother. I had been giving him my "favorite" interpretation in different ways for a long time, and he had consistently (but deferentially) rejected this view, politely protesting that he was his own person, that he also loved his mother, and that there was no opposition between the two. I was in the midst of delivering the "truth" once again, when he said to me, in a tone of benevolent exasperation, " Because I respect you I really want to accept what you are saying about me, but I just can't, and I feel caught between . . . between . . . Sylvia and the chiropodist." I exploded with laughter, and when I calmed down and wiped the tears from my eyes, I looked up apprehensively, expecting him to be hurt, shamed, or angry at my response. He was none of these. Max looked genuinely bewildered. So I explained why I was laughing and told him what the actual expression (Scylla and Charybdis) was. He replied, hesitantly, "What's that?" and I then told him the myth. I found myself unable to omit a single detail. I included Jason and the Argonauts, the Straits of Messina, the monsters, the rocks, the whirlpool, the whole thing. When I had finished, he paused, tellingly, and allowed that he was "immensely appreciative" because, as he put it, "you just told me something I needed to know all my life." I was astounded not only that he could let himself use sarcasm with me, but that he could hear it so clearly. I was also shocked (and slightly embarrassed) at having been so unaware of my shift in role. But I was totally unprepared for the moment, as we spoke, when he suddenly recognized that his remark was not only an act of shaming but was simultaneously an authentic expression of appreciation. He could feel that he had indeed learned something new and that he was excited about it. Max and I had each discovered, by sharing the experience, that being "exposed" in the other's eyes was complex but not traumatic. Max got something more than a lesson in Greek mythology; he got the joke. When we began to laugh at it together and talk about it together, different pieces of Max's reality and different pieces of my reality could start to be negotiated. Until then, language had little impact in symbolizing his dissociated self-experience because, as Bruner (1990, p. 70) has put it, "being 'exposed' to a flow of language is not nearly so important as using it in the midst of 'doing.'"

Obviously, there are many different ways to formulate this event. In my own way of thinking about it, to one part of him I was his beloved mother (whose name, disappointingly, was not Sylvia) for whom he had to be bright, deferential, and without flaw, already possessing all that he might be expected to know. To another part of him I was the chiropodist—the doctor trying to separate him from his painful "handicap." But in my determination to cure him of his "corns" (his perception of who he "really" is) he hadn't experienced the hope of a "better" reality coming out of our relationship until he made his slip and I responded with more of my own selves hanging out than I had anticipated. Each of us, in the various self-states that comprised our identities at that moment, unexpectedly made intimate contact and felt acknowledged by the other person; an example, perhaps, of Levenson's (1983, p. 157) reminder that "participant-observation should not be delegated to the therapist: it is a mutual effort. Catching the therapist in a self-serving operation may do more for the patient's sense of competence than a lifetime of benevolent participations."

For Max, it was a transformational experience in that he became increasingly free to experiment with multiple ways of being within a single relationship. He began to feel less convinced that he would have to trade-off his self that was constructed through his relationship with his mother in order to become more fully "his own person"—in this case, a bright guy who didn't have to be ashamed of not knowing everything.

As an interesting note, it was shortly after this session that the oedipal dynamic of his rivalry with his competitive father surfaced because it was now safer to challenge me. This included his more fully questioning whether my decision to "enlighten" him about Greek mythology might have included not only professional interest, but also some personal one-upsmanship. He even seemed to remember some slight perception that my hilarity over his slip lasted just a bit too long and that I may have been just a bit too eager to play the role of the educator. And so it went, with his becoming more and more able to hold in a single state of consciousness without dissociation, complex interpersonal events that contained feelings toward the another person that formerly would have collided traumatically and thus been too incompatible with his ongoing self-definition to allow self-reflectiveness and the potential for resolvable intrapsychic conflict. Max and I were able to go back and take a new look at historical ground we thought we had covered earlier, but what was more significant is that in the process we went back over our own relationship and looked together at events we told ourselves we had addressed, but which rep-

resented a collusion to dismiss or placate a voice that was silently crying for recognition. Most importantly, Max engaged and broke out of
the residue of the dissociative mode of relating that masked a shame-
ridden young man who was foreclosed from fully living his own life
because he was dedicated to disavowing a dissociated aspect of his
own selfhood. His ability to accept this part of himself allowed the
work we had already done (including reconstructive work) to feel
authentic because he could then more comfortably "stand in the
spaces" between realities and between past, present, and future, without having to lose any of them.

Dissociation and the "Observing Ego"

This brings me to the question of the so-called observing ego. The
extent to which one's individual self-states are simultaneously accessible to awareness (what has been called the relative presence of an
"observing ego") is the traditional criterion that analysts have used in
determining whether a patient is "analyzable." From my own perspective (see chapter 12), the difference between patients who have classically been defined as analyzable and those who have been seen as
unsuitable for analysis is a matter of the degree to which self-states are
dissociated from one another. What I call the structural shift from dissociation to conflict is clinically represented by the increasing capacity
of the patient to adopt a self-reflective posture in which one aspect of
the self observes and reflects (often with distaste) upon others that
were formerly dissociated. This differs from what classical conflict theory would call the development of an observing ego in that the goal is
more than the pragmatic treatment outcome of a greater tolerance for
internal conflict. There are always self-states that are enacting their
experience because they are not symbolized cognitively as "me" in the
here-and-now of a given moment. For the most part this creates no
problem within normal, healthy human discourse. It is where these
self-states are experienced as "not-me" and are discontinuous with
other modes of defining self and reality that the trouble occurs. For
most patients, though to different degrees, I see the goal as being able
to first accept, as a valid mental state in itself, the experience of observing and reflecting upon the existence of other selves that it hates,
would like to disown, but can't. In some patients this initial shift in
perception is dramatic, and involves a major personality reorganization. In its most extreme form this transition is paradigmatic in the
successful treatment of severe dissociative disorders, but the basic

transition is one that I have encountered in every analysis during all phases. If the transition is successfully negotiated, an opportunity has been provided for an internal linking process to take place between a patient's dissociated self-states by broadening his perceptual range of reality in the transference/countertransference field. In the linking process, fantasy, perception, thought, and language each play their part, providing the patient is not pressured to choose between which reality is more "objective" (Winnicott, 1951) and which self is more "true" (Winnicott, 1960a, 1971b).

Consider, in this context, a clinical vignette presented in a paper by Searles (1977) that vividly illustrates the creative synthesis of this perspective within routine analytic process. Searles writes:

> It may not be deeply significant if a patient occasionally begins a session with the statement, "I don't know where to begin." It may be simply a realistic attempt to cope with, for example, the fact that much has been happening with him of late. But I began to realize some two years ago that the patient who more often than not begins the session with this statement (or some variation upon it) is unconsciously saying, "It is not clear which of my multiple 'I's will begin reporting its thoughts, its feelings, its free associations, during this session." That is, it is not basically that there are too many competing subjects for this "I" to select among to begin the reporting, but rather that there are too many "I's" which are at the moment, competing among "themselves" as to which one shall begin verbalizing. . . . A woman, who had become able, over the course of her analysis, to integrate into her conscious sense of identity many previously warded-off part identities, began a session by saying, in a manner which I felt expressive of much ego strength, in a kind of confident good humor, "Now let's see; which one of my several identities will materialize today? [pp. 443–444].

I recently thought of this example from Searles after a session with one of my own patients that began with an uncharacteristically lengthy silence, broken by her saying quite matter-of-factly, and without any discernible anxiety or defensiveness, "I'm having three different conversations with you today." I replied, "Different in what way?" My question was followed by another silence, this one more obviously organized by self-reflectiveness. "Good question!" she stated. "First I thought that the *topics* were different. But when you asked that question I started to realize that I didn't want to answer because there are really three different moods all at the same time, and I don't know which one I want to answer you from." There could be no more clear evidence than this moment, to show that dissociation is not principally a mode of self-protection (even though it serves as such in the face of trauma). It can be seen here in its intrinsic form as the basis of creativity, playing, illusion, and the use of potential space to further self-growth. It was shortly after this session that, following a typically unsatisfying phone conversation with her father, she described looking at herself in the mirror, hating her father, and watching her face while she was hating—playing with the facial expressions (cf. Winnicott, 1971c), trying them out, enjoying the hateful feelings, but, as she put it, "still feeling like 'me' all the way through it."

Standing in the Spaces

As an enactment begins, an analyst will inevitably shift his self-state when the patient shifts his, but the phenomenon is always a two-way street. An enactment can just as easily begin with the analyst. Dissociation is a hypnoid process, and inasmuch as analyst and patient are sharing an event that belongs equally to both of them—the interpersonal field that shapes the immediate reality of each and the way each is experiencing himself and the other—any unsignalled withdrawal from that field by *either* person will disrupt the other's state of mind (see chapter 13). Thus, when an enactment begins (no matter by whom it is initiated), no analyst can be immediately attuned to the shift in here-and-now reality, and he inevitably becomes part of the dissociative process, at least for a period of time. He is often in a hypnoid state qualitiatively similar to that which his patient is in and sometimes becomes fixated, concretely, upon the verbal content of the session; the words begin to take on an "unreal" quality, and this is frequently what "wakes the analyst up" to the fact that something is "going on." He has been hypnoidally dissociated from that part of himself that was participating in the enactment, but once he regains access to it he will no longer be "asleep" to the fact that the patient, although using words, is equally "asleep" to the here-and-now experience between them. A dissociated self-state of the patient holding another reality—one that sometimes is fiercely opposing the one being talked "about"—may then start to gain a voice.

The analyst's dissociation is not a "mistake" on his part; it is intrinsic to the normal process of human communication unless it becomes a genuine countertransferential issue that prevents him from "waking up" regardless of how often and in how many different ways the dissociated voice cries for attention. One might even choose to extend Winnicott's concept of "object usage" (Winnicott, 1969), and suggest that the analyst is *always* "deaf" to the patient and "wrong" in his interpretations, at least with regard to certain dissociated aspects of the patient's self, thus allowing the patient to "re-create" the analyst as part of the evolving process of self re-creation that constitutes the core of the patient's growth. In other words, the patient is provided with a chance for unsymbolized aspects of self to protest the analyst's "wrongness" (see chapter 10) and for these other voices to become known relationally by the analyst through the enactment.

Kate, a female patient just back from a vacation, was marvelling at how free she felt to do things that she couldn't do freely here, because in New York she has to tell me about them and she's afraid of what I will feel. She said that she didn't know why this should be so because she knew I liked her, and wondered whether that fact itself could actually be the reason—that she was afraid to let herself fully experience my liking her because then she would want too much of it. She compared this possibility to how her allergy to chocolate seemed also not to be in effect when she was on vacation, and she ate chocolate for every dessert without feeling guilty and without getting pimples. "So," said Kate, "maybe the truth is that you are like chocolate to me. No matter what you say about me I can't take it in without getting pimples, because when I start to realize how attached I am to you, the pimples remind me not to trust you too much—to be careful of how much of me I show you. You could suddenly hurt me if I'm not who you expect me to be."

"And yet," I replied earnestly, "you seem to be trusting me enough right now to at least let me in on the fact that there's more to you than meets the eye."

"I think you're saying that," Kate retorted, "because you are trying to *get* me to trust you more than I do. But I don't know if what I'm feeling right now is trust, or just a new feeling of 'I don't care what you think.' Right now, I really don't trust why you just said what you said. If I trust you instead of trusting me, I get pimples, and *that's zit*."

"Come on now," a reader might well protest, "how can you be so sure that's what she said? After all, 'that's it'! and 'that's zit'! are pretty much in the ear of the beholder. And he or she may well be right, particularly because I love unconscious plays on words. I seem to hear them with what I suspect is unusual frequency, and I think it is entirely plausible that in a marginal case such as this I heard what I wished to hear. The fact is that I don't know for certain. What I do know, is that when I began to laugh, she caught on immediately to what I was laughing at, and even though she clearly had no conscious awareness of an intended pun, she was ready to enter into the spirit of play. I think I would be on more solid ground (an uncustomary location for me) if I settled for the probability that what my ear did indeed pick up was her readiness to enter the area of potential space (Winnicott, 1967, 1971b)—to play with an aspect of our relationship that before had been concretized and held in separate and discontinuous states of consciousness. My wish for her to trust me, which she so accurately perceived as part of my response to her, was then acknowledged by me. I also acknowledged her accuracy in her perception that I liked her, and my concern that in the acknowledgment I might be making it more rather than less difficult for her to feel free to be herself. She then told me that I worry too much (which I do). She said she was glad that I said it, but that at this point she didn't really need the verification because she really did feel free to be herself with me in a way she hadn't before, and that my input didn't make her feel she had to "jump ship" in order to protect herself.

The point of this vignette is that I didn't know what to expect from moment to moment; I was as much in potential space as she was, and I would put it that if I were not, the concept has no meaning. I had to find my own place to stand without wedding myself to my own subjectivity as "truth," while still being able to be myself—a concept I've described metaphorically in chapter 10 as the ability of the analyst to maintain dual citizenship in two domains of reality with passports to the multiple self-states of the patient.

Transference and the "Real" Relationship

From this frame of reference there is no single transference reality that can be spoiled or contaminated by making a "technical" error. The analyst, guided by the patient and by his own experience of personal authenticity, allows himself to form relationships with each of the patient's selves or self-states to the degree the patient allows it, and in each relationship he has an opportunity to creatively utilize a range of his own states of consciousness. Often, a particular self-state of the patient has never before been drawn out in its own terms so that it can, without shame, communicate to another human being its unique sense of self, purpose, personal history, and personal "truth." In my own work, this experience has at times led directly to the source of a symptom or behavior pattern that has been until then "resistant" to change, as for example, in the case of a patient who had suffered many years with an eating disorder, and then revealed one day that she finally discovered why she binged. "I do it," she said, "because I feel my brain trying to switch to another consciousness and I want to stop it— so I eat or drink something cold to stimulate me in the moment. I need to stay awake, to stay grounded, and sometimes, when I'm afraid I'm not going to be able to, I eat something heavy like pasta or bagels."

The interplay between confrontation and empathy is interesting and especially relevant when working from the perspective of *multiple real relationships* rather than "a real relationship and a transferential relationship." Each of the patient's dissociated self-states does what it does because it sees a single "truth" that it tries to act upon, but on the other hand each has its own reason for existing and will not rewrite its reality to suit an analyst's personal belief system of what defines "growth." The analytic relationship is in this light a negotiated dialectic between attunement and confrontation, or (to express it in a slightly different frame of reference) between "empathy and anxiety" (see chapter 4). There is no way that one's personal narrative of "who I am" ever changes directly; it cannot be cognitively edited and replaced by a better, more "adaptive" one. Only a change in *perceptual* reality can alter the cognitive reality that defines the patient's internal object world, and this process requires an enacted collision of realities between patient and therapist. The analyst's struggle with his own confusion—his ability to make creative use of contradictory realities within a single analytic field without unduly inflicting his need for clarity of meaning upon the patient, plays as much of a role in the analytic process as does empathy or interpretation individually. In other words, for a patient to develop confidence in his growing ability to move from dissociation to intrapsychic conflict, he must engage with the analyst in what I have called, in chapters 10 and 15, the "messy" parts of the analytic relationship. As the analyst furthers the capacity of the patient to hear in a single context the voices of other self-states holding alternative realities that have been previously incompatible, the fear of traumatic flooding of affect decreases along with the likelihood that opposing realities will automatically try to obliterate each other. Because there is less opposition between aspects of self, there is less danger that any individual self-state will use the gratification of being empathically supported in its own reality simply to further its individual sense of "entitlement" to priority within the personality. Translated into the traditional metapsychology of "pathological narcissism," a patient's investment in protecting the insularity of a so-called "grandiose self" (see chapter 7) diminishes as the need for dissociation is surrendered and replaced by increased capacity to experience and resolve intrapsychic conflict.

Fonagy (1991) labels the capacity to symbolize conscious and unconscious mental states in oneself and others as the capacity to "mentalize," (p. 641) and writes that

> "wholeness" is given to objects only through an understanding of the mental processes that provide an account of the object's actions in the physical world. Before mental states are conceived of, the mental representation of the object will be, by definition, partial, tied to specific situations . . . since the vital attribution of mental functioning is absent. . . . [Consequently], the distortion of mental representations of objects through projection is unavoidable at this early stage. . . . Until the point is reached when mental states may be confidently attributed to the object there can be no capacity to limit this projection [pp. 641–642].
>
> *In individuals where the capacity to mentalize is severely impaired, dealing with this aspect of the transference may be considered a precondition of analytic treatment.* . . . [F]ailure to achieve this may lead patients to treat interpretations as assaults and analytic ideas as abusive intrusions [p. 652, italics added].

Psychoanalysis is at its core a highly specialized communicative field, and what constitutes a psychoanalytically "meaningful" moment is constantly in motion with regard to one's experience of both reality and temporality. The shifting quality of time and meaning reflects the enactment of self-states in both patient and analyst that define the multiplicity of relationships that go on between the patient's selves and the analyst's selves, only some of which are being focused on at any given moment. As an analyst opposes, is opposed by, affirms, and is affirmed by each dissociated aspect of the patient's self as it oscillates—in its cycle of projection and introjection—between his own inner world and that of his patient, the energy the patient has used in sustaining the dissociative structure of his mind will be enlisted by him in vitalizing a broadening experience of "me-ness." Because this less dissociated configuration of selfhood is *simultaneously* adaptational and self-expressive, certain self-states do not have to continue to remain unable to participate in living except as "on call" watchdogs that suddenly and unexpectedly seem to become possessed by an "irrational" need to make a mess.

One final note. Grotstein (1995) wrote that projective identification "saturates the manifest and latent content of all psychoanalyses in its role as projected 'alter egos,' which are signifiers of the self at one remove" (p. 501). He stated that "the analytic relationship, like any couple relationship, constitutes a group entity in its own right as well as a relationship between two individuals. As a consequence, the couple is subject to the laws of group formation" (pp. 489–490). What Grotstein calls "alter egos" is not very different from what I call multiple self-states or multiple selves.

I find Grotstein's observation both astute and interesting, and from time to time I've even had the thought that by experiencing the analytic process in this way, it begins to overlap in a funny way with certain elements of doing couples therapy—sort of like treating a couple (or sometimes a family) in a single body. For instance, in the early phase of couples therapy it is virtually impossible for the therapist to make statements about the couple as a unit, to which both parties can be responsive. The therapist has to develop a relationship with each member of a couple individually while dealing with their problems that pertain to the couple as a single unit. If this complex task is done with skill it becomes possible to slowly speak to the couple as a unit even though each member sees things differently, because there is a context that has been created (the individual relationships to the therapist) that allows the individual subjectivity of each "self" to be negotiable. Through this, each reality can begin to negotiate with other discrepant realities, to achieve a common goal.

Used judiciously, I have found that an approach which addresses the multiplicity of self is so experience-near to most patients' subjective reality that only rarely does someone even comment on why I am talking about them in "that way." It leads to a greater feeling of wholeness (not *dis*-integration) because each self-state comes to attain a clarity and personal significance that gradually alleviates the patient's previously held sense of confusion about who he "really" is and how he came, historically, to be this person. And for the therapist, it is not necessary to work as hard to "figure out" what is going on, what has gone on in the past, and what things "mean." He engages in a dialogue with that self that is present at the moment, and finds out from that self, in detail, its own story, rather than trying to approximate it. All told, it facilitates an analyst's ability to help his patient develop increased capacity for a life that includes, in Loewald's (1972, p. 409) language, a past, a present, and a future as mutually interacting modes of time.

18

STAYING THE SAME
WHILE CHANGING

Reflections on Clinical Judgment[1] (1998)

With apologies offered variously to Jack Benny and Zero Mostel, I'm going to begin this chapter with a story that might be called "A Funny Thing Happened to My Title on the Way to the Conference"—a story that turned out to be an unanticipated example of how I see the issue of clinical judgment. What constitutes sound "clinical judgment" is of course inevitably arrived at by hindsight: an analyst presents clinical material at a meeting and defines it as what he did, and the discussant (no matter how sophisticated his efforts at tactfulness) defines it as what it might have been better to do. However, when I recently received my copy of a conference program (see n. 1), I discovered that the title of the paper I was scheduled to present as part of a panel on clinical judgment was listed as "Staying *Sane* While Changing," not, in fact, the title I had submitted. Someone had already been exercising clinical judgment! In my fantasy the "someone" was a copyeditor who found paradox difficult

---

1. This chapter revises and expands a paper presented as part of a panel on "Relational Aspects of Clinical Judgment" at the 1996 spring meeting of the Division of Psychoanalysis (Div. 39) of the American Psychological Association. The original version was published in *Psychoanalytic Dialogues*, 1998, 8:225–236.

to appreciate. I could imagine the copyeditor looking at my actual title, "Staying *the Same* While Changing," and saying to himself, "Bromberg couldn't really have meant that. A patient can't both stay the same and change. Ah, I know. I'll bet the title is 'Staying *Sane* While Changing,' and his secretary misheard him."

The most interesting part of the story to me (apart from the displaced surfacing of my yearning for a secretary), is that the change in title actually does capture an important element of my own thinking but it overly narrows the conceptual frame of reference that I use, and loses the broader context. As I will spell out further, "staying the same" is, for many patients, tantamount to staying sane. So, as a unilateral act on this imaginary copyeditor's part, the change he made was "right" as well as "wrong." I ended up admiring his clinical judgment, but like a resistant patient in analysis I also ended up feeling that his interpretation was forced into my head, while my soul ached for dialogue that was not to be.

As I reflected upon the concept of clinical judgment I began to recognize how parallel my thoughts were to a related issue I had engaged 17 years ago in an essay (chapter 6) I wrote on "the use of detachment," where I discussed the distinction between the concepts of *choice* and *decision*. In that paper I described a patient (Miss R) who had entered analysis with serious narcissistic issues and who had recently reached a major crisis point in her life in which she was faced with the irreconcilable alternatives of immediate marriage or a highly desired career appointment which required extended business trips for undetermined lengths of time. She was quite involved with her boyfriend and had grown to care deeply for him, but also saw this career opportunity as a long awaited challenge. It was a poignant moment in her analysis for her to recognize that although she knew she could not have both, unlike similar situations in the past she was able to sustain her attachment and involvement with both during a conflictual process of inner struggle, involving grief, joy, loss, and gain, without throwing away any parts of her self. She ultimately took the job and surrendered the relationship, but for her, an equally powerful issue was that she had made a choice rather than a decision, and could feel sorrow and loss without loss of self-esteem or selfhood. Her characteristic pattern had always been to dissociate some part of herself in any experience that was not felt to be totally under her control. Ending a relationship, for example, had invariably been experienced as her "decision." The term *decision* implies personal mastery; a self-sufficient command of "objective reality" and an equally self-sufficient command over the options that must guarantee selection of the "right" one. The term *choice* conveys a difficult selection process in which something of value is gained only by losing something else of value. It involves a capacity to acknowledge that one's own mastery of situations is imperfect and that conflict is a painful but bearable part of being human. An analytic theoretican might say it involves a capacity to experience and process intrapsychic conflict.

Faced with such a difficult trade-off in the past, Miss R typically would detach from one of the options as "wrong," and "decide" on the other which then became "right," thus preserving, through dissociation, the illusion of perfect mastery. She was fond of quoting a line from one of her favorite popular songs: "Freedom's just another word for nothing left to lose." To have felt the reality of having to make a choice would have formerly produced not grief or mourning but the experienced loss of self that follows severe narcissistic injury.

The relation between this vignette and the topic of clinical judgment hinges in the first instance on the inevitable professional narcissism of the analyst, which results in a predilection for making right decisions and being able thereafter to justify them to himself and to colleagues. After all, isn't clinical judgment the cornerstone of what we do as analysts? What will happen to it if we remove the element of right and wrong, and reduce it to choice, each choice embodying both gain and loss! I will argue, and will present two clinical examples from my more recent work to illustrate my argument, that any analyst working from a postclassical two-person paradigm has already changed the meaning of clinical judgment from decision to choice, and that our remaining job is to make this shift conceptually explicit in our theories of therapeutic action.

As one case in point, consider the issue of a patient's "analyzability." This clinical judgment, traditionally, was a "decision" made by the analyst (or some third party) based on an assessment of whether the patient possessed certain ego assets that were believed to be a necessary prerequisite in order for a patient to have a "genuine" analytic experience. Postclassically, however, the patient's ego assets are viewed not as a prerequisite for analysis, not as a set of qualities located within the patient that will determine suitability for analysis based on a unilateral "decision" by an "objective" other, but as qualities that are given meaning within a relational matrix and are of value in determining analyzability only in the context of what *that particular analyst* brings or fails to bring to the relational field as the work is taking place. Obviously, we have thus redefined not only analyzability, but have taken another step in reconsidering how psychoanalysis itself is to be redefined.

In other words, I am suggesting that clinical judgment, like analyzability, is best seen as a relationally negotiated outcome and, except for rare instances, it is never the job of the analyst to "decide" alone and unilaterally as to its rightness or wrongness. These judgments are arrived at not in the analyst's mind alone but through the interpersonal-intersubjective field that mediates negotiation of the analytic situation. The cues are being constantly provided in an ongoing way by the patient as to whether what is being said by the analyst is being cognitively processed not only usefully, but pleasurably and safely. In this regard, interpretation and transference regression (see chapters 3 and 10) are aspects of a mutually constructed event, and it is only when the analyst forgets this, that he becomes "dangerous" in Winnicott's (1963a, p. 189) terms—knowing too much too soon, he invades the patient's experience rather than recognizing it—and *pathological* regression can occur. By contrast, an analyst's admitting that he "does not know" is not only *accurate*, but by sharing his state of mind he is acknowledging that he is not upset by not knowing, and he is thus allowing the state of not knowing to be a valid mental state of its own, not simply a meaningless waiting period between illness (ignorance) and cure (insight). This, for me, is the essence of what a "bridge" between self-states means. The analyst's act of recognition is embodied in his willingness to make his own state of mind explicit by putting it into words. To the extent he insulates himself from this task, and replaces it with some construction about the *patient* only, he subverts the use of language by turning words into objects that substitute for meaning, rather than create it by symbolizing experience. If an analyst makes his state of mind explicit—what it is that is going on in him while he engages with his patient—then he gives language a chance to create what Bruner (1990) calls "an act of meaning" out of the individual "truths" held as lonely, unbridgeable islands of selfhood. Such moments can otherwise easily be plundered of their potential to become a new, co-created reality that neither patient nor analyst has the power to define alone.

As another case in point, consider the issue of a patient's diagnosis. This clinical judgment, traditionally, was also a "decision" made by the analyst (or some third party). It is, of course, linked in the minds of many clinicians with issues of parameters if not analyzability. And I must confess that early in my career I was myself keenly interested in the diagnosis of "schizoid." Lately, however, I am less intent on differential diagnosis though I still think an appreciation of character structure adds a valuable dimension to analytic work.

Some time ago, an incident occurred on a plane trip that pretty much sums up my perspective. Just as the flight attendants were preparing to serve dinner, the loudspeaker came on and a voice said: "For today's menu you have a choice of chicken or lasagna, but I don't want you to be too upset if you don't get your first choice because I've tasted them both and they taste remarkably similar." In my own work, I see the use of diagnosis like airline food. It is good to have on the trip, but I try to avoid taking the label overly seriously and to ingest only enough to keep from feeling uncomfortably empty on the journey. Most importantly, I am rarely surprised or upset if I find along the way that the chicken tastes remarkably like lasagna.

Trauma, Shame, and Clinical Judgment

In recent years it has been my observation that, independent of diagnosis, the therapeutic action of psychoanalysis in facilitating structural personality growth with any patient requires a continuing attunement to the role of trauma in affecting the patient's capacity to endure intrapsychic conflict.

For any patient to benefit optimally from analytic treatment the therapeutic relationship must support his ability to maintain (or develop) the internal structure to regulate potentially traumatic hyperarousal of affect, either globally or in specific areas, as the work progresses. The continuing analytic focus always in mind is for the patient to safely experience his self-structure as one that is stable and sturdy enough to withstand the input from the other person's subjectivity, without it threatening to overwhelm his immediate experience of selfhood by triggering a flooding of shame and panic associated with unrepairable early trauma.

Though space does not permit adequate discussion here, it is my view that *routine* anxiety, the affect that Sullivan (1953) associates with an impending threat to one's "self-esteem" differs not only quantitatively but qualitatively from what he calls "*severe* anxiety." The latter, I would argue, is better called shame, and differs from routine anxiety both subjectively and in its consequences. Shame signals a traumatic attack upon one's personal identity, and typically calls forth dissociative processes to preserve selfhood. Routine anxiety signals a problem in self-image regulation, and allows learning from experience because dissociation is not needed. Sullivan (1953, p. 152) writes vividly: "[S]evere anxiety probably contributes no information. The effect of severe anxiety reminds one in some ways of a blow on the head, in that it simply wipes out what is immediately proximal to its occurrence.

. . . Less severe anxiety does permit gradual realization of the situation in which it occurs."

But having said even that much, I should hasten to add that for individuals experiencing intense shame, no words can capture the assaultive intensity of the experience. It is only through *reliving* the trauma through enactment with the analyst that its magnitude can be known by an "other," hopefully this time an "other" who will have the courage to participate in the reliving while simultaneously holding the patient's psychological safety as a matter of prime concern.

In the face of potential collapse of selfhood, the mind falls back on its ultimate safety measure, its capacity for the defensive utilization of the otherwise normal process of withdrawing consciousness from certain aspects of immediate experience while enhancing other aspects. I am referring to the process of pathological dissociation—the hypnoidal unlinking of incompatible patterns of self-experience, so that the domains of meaning that have been most adaptive to preserving sanity and survival are rescued in uncompromised purity by guarding the self-other modes of interaction that define them. Each is now rigidly boundaried within its specific pattern of interpersonal engagement that gives it self-meaning. This allows personal identity a subjective sense of consistency and continuity *within* each self-state regardless of which one has access to consciousness and cognition at a given moment. The individual states are thus hypnoidally unlinked from one another but "on call" as needed.

Making matters more complicated, one might say that each self-state is an island of narcissism on its own behalf, possessing and protecting its unique sense of "truth" (see also chapter 13). Where there is extreme disparity between what is valued and what is disowned in the self at any given moment, the potential pull toward regressive disruption in analytic treatment is always in the background. The process of experiencing the interface between overvalued and disavowed domains of self is the source of any patient's greatest anxiety, dread, and shame, but it is also his only hope for authentic analytic growth. We sometimes hear a patient say as he first enters treatment that he wishes he could look only at certain aspects of himself and leave the rest alone. Usually, however, he is unable to say what it is he wishes to leave alone, and is typically quite willing to approach most *content* areas as the work moves along. It is only in the relational matrix of what we call clinical *process* that the unconscious meaning of the wish not to look is played out, and it is only through the essentially unpredictable evolution of this process that the act of looking at any one "part" of oneself becomes increasingly equivalent to looking at the whole person. Only then may we properly speak of structural growth.

The analyst's contribution to this evolution is poorly captured by the term "clinical judgment." Rather, the analyst's contribution lies in his maintaining the ability to be as fully his own person as possible, while allowing himself to become immersed in the here-and-now intersubjective field as it is manifested at that moment. He must form authentic relationships with each of the patient's self-states as it then exists—honoring those voices speaking for safety and for continuity as well as those speaking for change and for risk—and engage with each in its own terms, without surrendering his own vision of the present moment as also a way station linking the patient as he used to be (the past) to what he ultimately might become (the future). In other words, the analyst must relate nonlinearly while retaining the capacity to process his perceptual experience of the relationship linearly (that is, in terms of past, present, and future). This leads the patient to the kind of synthesis described by Lacan's (1966, p. 373n) observation that "the subject begins the analysis by speaking about himself without speaking to you, or by speaking to you without speaking about himself. When he is able to speak to you about himself the analysis will be finished." While I do not share Lacan's view that this accomplishment signifies the end of the analysis, I believe as he did that such a moment marks a point of true structural growth in personality, and that such moments occur as part of a cyclical process throughout the course of analysis, signalling steps in the reorganization of mental structure from dissociation to internal conflict. I see these "change points"— Peterson (1993) has aptly noted that they are multiple—as occurring over and over throughout a successful analysis and not simply as *the* point at which the patient has arrived at his ultmate goal.

Dreams, Dissociation, and Clinical Process

I have found that a perspective which takes dissociative processes into account deepens all aspects of the analytic work with every patient and informs even my routine approach to working with dreams. *I believe, for instance, that the need of an analytic patient is not only to "bring in a dream" but to "bring in the dreamer."*[2] If a dream, as I have suggested in chapter 15, is simply the most familiar special case of the more general phenomenon of dissociation, the normal self-hypnotic capacity of

---

2. I wish to acknowledege with appreciation the significant influence on my thinking of James Grotstein's 1979 paper, "Who Is the Dreamer Who Dreams the Dream and Who Is the Dreamer Who Understands It?"

the human mind, then dreaming can be considered among the most routine day-to-day dissociative activities of the mind—its nocturnal function being an adaptational effort to cope with minimal levels of not-me experience without interfering with the waking illusion of central consciousness. One of its manifestations in psychoanalysis is to contain and hold, as a separate reality, unprocessed experience that is not safely containable at that moment within the "I" that defines the analytic relationship for the patient (see also Caligor, 1996). In other words, the use of a dream in analysis might, at one level, be thought of as a transitional experience that allows the potential linking of self-states that are hypnoidally disconnected, permitting the voices of "not-me" self-states to be heard and to find access to the dynamic structure that the patient defines as "I." The process through which this takes place is one that I feel is not adequately described by the term "dream interpretation," but is shaped by the gradual development of a dialogue between the patient and the dreamer through the creative use of a projective/introjective process within the analytic relationship. A similar sentiment has been expressed by Cecily de Monchaux (1978) in a clinically illuminating paper on the nature of dreams (which she calls "night thinking"). In describing her work with a patient who "began to feel like . . . someone who had swallowed their twin" (p. 449), she writes that "dissociation with no access to consciousness, as in the numbing or freezing stages of the primary stress response, gives way to dissociation with partial access to consciousness *via* night thinking, and this provides a trial ground, a way station on the road to integration" (p. 448).

With this in mind, I'd like now to turn to an example taken from my work with a patient I call Henry, a man who was in most ways a well-functioning individual with no manifestation of a dissociative disorder. Henry was a 25-year-old man whose mother and father, each a highly accomplished professional, had unconsciously communicated to Henry their intense need to see their child "grow up" as quickly as possible so that they could get back to their careers, and simultaneously communicated their dread of becoming aware of that need lest they feel unbearably selfish and guilt-ridden. In any situation where Henry showed that he, like his parents, was competently able to think for himself in the world "out there" he was at once rewarded with praise for his maturity, while being happily expelled from his parents' minds in terms of their thinking about what help Henry still might need, what sorts of things might be bothering him, what ways he might still need to rely on them, and so forth. Henry, as you might expect, became unable to negotiate the transition to full self-agency because independence became equivalent to insecurity and aloneness. Authentic self-expression felt like a leap into a void—a dissociated plunge into the deep end of the pool while shutting his eyes and "holding his breath." To open his eyes and allow himself not just to breathe in life, but to breathe *into* it, meant losing all sense of security.

In analysis, Henry allowed himself to reconnect with the self defined by his early object attachments and became "his parents' child" in a manner he had been denied in real life, presenting himself not as helpless and dependent but as a smart and resourceful young man who was "not quite there" yet, and certainly was not yet ready to terminate treatment (in case such an idea might ever enter my mind). I was still needed, as he frequently reminded me, to "connect the pieces" that he "for some reason" could not yet connect on his own, even though he invariably placed the pieces so close together that it was hard to imagine how he could miss the "picture" they formed. This transferential issue was invariably "well understood" when discussed in sessions but had no apparent impact on Henry's external life. When I offered this observation, Henry was "grateful" for my "patience," which in fact was starting to wear a bit thin, and chagrined that he was not ready enough yet to "do" anything with this insight. Henry seemed genuinely lost, and would lament: "When will I ever be able to grow up?" I experienced his pain as authentic, and felt somewhat guilty about the impatient voice in my mind murmuring "Grow up already!"

Henry was a prolific dreamer, but when I would ask for associations to his dreams, they would be vague and lifeless, and if seemingly related to our "stuckness" together, were only so in *my* mind, not in his. For Henry, his dreams and associations seemed to be a transferential "dead end." They would lead apparently nowhere, and the work in that session seemed to dry up. "Why," I would ask myself, "if the transferential meaning is as obvious as I think it is, does he need to dream it rather than think it? Why is the dream necessary? And why is the meaning so 'obvious' to *me* but not to him?" Sometimes I would ask him just that, but to no avail. He would present a rationale for his "denseness" that left me feeling like a long-suffering parent trying to help his child with a school subject he just doesn't seem to "get" but which he is trying "so hard" to learn. I could feel myself participating in an enactment. But of what?

Henry then presented another dream. It had to do with a story he had read, about twin babies who were separated after birth, one of whom was mistreated and died before the other discovered his existence. The tragedy for the living twin was that of having never united with his brother and having to "grow up" alone, knowing it could have been different (cf. Bion, 1967). Like most of his dreams at this point in treatment, his associations were vague and lifeless and I could feel myself becoming more and more frustrated with him. I decided to let him know about the sudden shift in my state of mind that had just taken place, including my frustration that such an interesting dream was drained of life by his associations. He did not respond, but lay silently on the couch, as though in a state of paralysis. It seemed almost as if *he* had died. I could feel a surge in the level of my guilt, and then it hit me; I was living the dream with him. There was an enactment taking place in which the patient who "dreamed" the dream and the patient who "presented" the dream" were speaking with separate voices. The healthy twin, the "dreamer," was now being contained in my own consciousness as part of *me*. I was at that moment the only part of Henry that was "alive" enough to think for itself. It was Henry's "dead" self who delivered the dream—the twin who had "died" before it could live—and I had been "mis-treating" him by wanting him to "grow up" and not "live" his deadness in my mind. As Ferenczi (1930b) put it , "[I]t is no mere poetic licence to compare the mind of the neurotic to a double malformation, something like the so-called *teratoma* which harbors in a hidden part of its body, fragments of a twin-being which has never developed" (p. 123).

Feeling both my impatience and my guilt allowed me to feel the existence of a dissociated self in Henry. That self could only be known by my experiencing the incongruity between two discontinuous aspects of my own identity—my alive thought processes and the subjective deadness of my inability to experientially "connect the pieces" that seemed so "obviously" shouting their meaning. Only by my feeling my own futility, my own paralyzed sense of self-agency that was being thwarted, and my own frustration at not being able to discover why he doesn't "get it" himself while I'm simultaneously feeling guilty about my impatience with his seeming denseness, could I then *use* this experience to engage with Henry through the most alive meaning of the dream—the dream as it was being enacted between us. To use Aron's (1996) concept, as this "meeting of minds" became more and more alive to both of us, the session became one of those "change-points" that allow analytic work to get unstuck, because it allowed Henry to experience in a single relational context the voices of formerly dissociated self-states holding incompatible views of reality and incompatible experiences of who he "really" is.

Dissociation is an inherent part of the process of human communication, and the session with Henry's dream illustrates its complex role in the treatment relationship. Until that moment in his analysis, my "clinical judgment" was a unilateral event. I had been trying to indoctrinate Henry with delivered truth so as to enable him to see the objective reality of how grown-up he "really" was. As Laub and Auerhahn (1989) so trenchantly put it: "What is ultimately traumatic in dreams, as in life, is the inability to affect the environment so as to mediate needs, usually the inability to evoke the aid of a helping other" (p. 397). Because I had been attempting to enliven Henry as an enactment of a parental wish to free my mind from having to contain his deadened self, my own dissociative processes inevitably became part of the enactment and ultimately made me aware of my unavailability to the "other" twin. I offer this session with Henry's dream as simply one example of how an analyst's willingness to accept the inevitability of his own dissociated self-states allows him to use them in the patient's interest by enabling the patient's other selves that are being expressed in an alternate reality of "a dream" to find access to waking consciousness in the here-and-now of the therapeutic relationship. Analytic work with dreams then moves from being a *story* that is "interpreted," to being a *space* for the co-construction of a transitional reality between patient and analyst—a space in which the the one who dreams and the one who reports the dream are both included (cf. Bosnak, 1996).

Safety and Confrontation Revisited

I've argued in chapter 10 that our capacity to heal depends on our ability to abide with our patients in the experiential mess of the analytic work without escaping prematurely into the language of conflict and defense. But what does the term "abide" really mean in this context? Sullivan (1937, p. 17) stated that "one has information only to the extent that one has tended to communicate one's states of being, one's experience." I would add that the progress of the work is estimated on the basis of a patient's movement toward the point where all of his states of mind are explored in detail, and his deepest levels of experience become the reservoir for self-understanding. The wholehearted recognition by the analyst of his patient's state of mind at any given moment, *is* the full acceptance of the patient's self, and it is helpful for an analyst to appreciate that no one self-state is more important than another. Because each self-state is a self, and, more, a special self, no part of the person can be "cured" away, no matter how much pain accompanies it.[3] A self-state can be *opposed* by other parts and kept silent for indefinite periods of time, but its presence will sooner or later be manifested through enactments or symptoms.

Depression, for example, is not simply something that one feels; it's who one is at certain times, and for some people it's who one is for most of the time. Depression, in other words, for certain people is not just an affective "disorder"; it is who they are. The same thing is true about hopelessness, an inevitable, though frequently hidden self-state of people who have experienced early trauma. To be sure, in certain patients it is definitely *not* hidden. I am thinking of people who have an aspect of self organized centrally around hopelessness and the experience of futility—what Schecter (1978a) called loss of trust in the possibility of a good relationship—and fight ferociously not to have this reality ignored. Even at a moment when some other aspect of self is feeling a certain degree of hope, a voice of futility is enacted by forcing itself into the mind of the "helper," thus insisting that it be "recognized."

These are patients who leave little doubt that the therapeutic action of psychoanalysis goes beyond the resolution of intrapsychic conflict and that it requires continual attention to the impact of trauma on mental structure. For these individuals, what therapy is all about— how they *use* their treatment—has to do with the modulation of what we refer to in contemporary terms as "hyperarousal of affect." What makes this so? Such patients typically make clear the fact that their ability to use analytic treatment at all is contingent on its effectiveness in helping them to develop the internal structure to self-soothe. That is, treatment has gradually to diminish a patient's vulnerability to feeling traumatized by input from any source that signals the potential threat of flooding him with unregulatable hyperarousal. Put another way, the core analytic goal to keep always in mind is to facilitate a safe reorganization of self-structure into one that is stable and sturdy enough to withstand the input from another person's mind without it triggering the shadow of early trauma. As long as he remains unable to deal with the mind of an other without the dread of retraumatization, then he has no choice but to rely upon the dissociative "truths" held by each of his unbridgeable self-states in order to keep the other's

---

3. Mitchell (1997a, p. 34), addressing this issue, makes the point that "with patients who complain of dead and lifeless marriages it is often possible to show them how precious the deadness is to them, how carefully maintained and insisted upon, how the very mechanical, totally predictable quality of love making serves for them as a bulwark against the dread of surprise and unpredictability."

subjectivity from overwhelming his own experience of selfhood. The price he pays for this protection is being unable to process and symbolize complex interpersonal experience. In other words, the treatment has to buttress his ability to take in aspects of the other that he can reflect upon and process symbolically in the here-and-now. Is that all that treatment does? No! But I believe it is a significant factor with *every* patient at different points in their analysis, regardless of how central dissociation is or is not to their overall personality structure.

I would put it that the analytic effort is designed to arrive at a place relationally where a patient is able, without dissociating, to receive and process some of his experience of his analyst's traumatizing potential. What do I mean by that? I am again referring to what I said earlier about hanging-in through the "mess" of analytic treatment. I have typically found that there is much mess to live through before a patient can access and retain previously incompatible selves in the same moment of consciousness, and that these points are almost always preceded by a series of stressful enactments. Most often, these enactments involve the claims of single self-states, each disclaiming the existence of any others, and insisting on the right to exclusive attention. In those enactments, the therapist is unable to be a "good object" because the different aspects of the patient's self have different realities about what being a "good object" means. A therapist can offer to provide for different parts of the patient's self at the same time, but this offer can only be taken up by a patient when those parts are accessible to him at the same moment. To return to the issue of clinical judgment, my point is that the therapist, on his own, can never be sure of which parts are available and which are not.

In my own work, it not infrequently happens that early in the treatment a hopeless and angry part of the patient's self is all that I am allowed to be with. When this state of affairs continues too long, it eventually *gets* to me, and I show it. Frequently, in such a situation my every effort to reach out is met by my patient's almost accusatory celebration of my ineffectiveness in altering the "truth" about his reality. "See," he will exclaim, "this is hopeless," as if to say, "there's no way your effort to be nice can really change anything; it can never make me forget that a disaster is always waiting around the next corner." Granted, this is the voice of only one part of the patient, but it is the part that at certain moments is most directly engaged with me—a self-state that almost any therapist I know eventually encounters in some sort of adversarial enactment.

"Trust" is not a word that is easily applied to the personality structure of such patients. What looks like trust is often the unreflective adaptiveness of a still dissociated part of the patient's self that cannot yet hold self-interest and safety in the same relational context. Frequently, this first reaches the threshold of my consciousness through my becoming aware of my own end of the enactment. For example, I might begin to recognize an aspect of my experience as a vague discomfort in feeling that I am giving too much for what I am getting back. This may then attune me to one or another dissociated states of my own. I might find myself suddenly grouchy, or perhaps sleepy or detached. Perhaps I find myself feeling negative about my ability as a therapist, or maybe feeling futile about whether analysis ever really works. If I play with this latter feeling a little further, I can even begin to visualize a scene in which my patient says that he feels totally hopeless about ever getting out of this mess—and I reply with some version of Ralph Greenson's remark (Greenson, 1974, p. 260), when he replied to a patient in a similar moment: "You ain't just awhistlin' Dixie." I can even imagine a confrontation in which the patient accuses me of giving up on him and I reply by sharing some of my own feeling of hopelessness but also the fact that this feeling has *not* made me give up on him. But whatever the scenario I imagine, in my own work with such patients it usually facilitates a direct relationship between each of my selves and each of the patient's selves if I can attend to these inner scenes long enough to begin to search for the adaptive purpose behind what is usually defined as "resistance," so that it can begin to be voiced and recognized. It is through this that authentic trust begins to become possible—not through a patient's telling me he feels hopeless and my "understanding" it, but because my own state of mind is personally impacted by it, and we can both survive the experience and "live to talk about it."

Coda

This vantage point also shapes my way of looking at the concept of clinical judgment in working with patients for whom, in comparison to Henry, the presence of dissociative mental structure is quite extreme. Sometimes, before one can even begin to think about exercising judgment with such patients, one has to undergo a kind of transformation in which the patient's reality is forced upon oneself at the level of perception. Let me illustrate.

Though it has since been broken accidentally, on a bookcase shelf in my office there long sat a piece of ceramic sculpture—a man lying face up over the top of a barrel, his legs dangling down over the side, a hat covering his eyes. It sat there for years, noticed and commented upon by some patients, seemingly unnoticed by others. I liked it a great deal, and not only for its artistry. I felt a kinship with it, and would sometimes seek visual solace from my "man over a barrel" at moments when I felt stuck in a particularly painful treatment impasse with some patient. Then, one day, totally unexpectedly, I began to see what "being over a barrel" *really* meant, and the man in the sculpture was, ironically, a central figure in my enlightenment. The event took place during a session in which the piece of sculpture was observed, apparently for the first time, by a patient to whom nothing looked quite the same as it did to other people, and after that session the piece never looked quite the same to *me* again. My patient, Adam, was a person who protected the "truth" of his reality as a battle to the death with a world determined to destroy his sanity, and I knew this all too well, even as I heard him say from where he was seated across the room: "Oh! Where did you get that statue of a man without a head?" In response to my bewildered, "A statue of *what*?" he replied with even greater self-assurance, "That man without a head!" "Oh," said I, looking at where his eyes were focussed, "That's not a man without a head. Is that what it looks like from where you are sitting?" "That's what it *is*," said he, and I knew right then I was in trouble.

With a different patient it wouldn't have mattered to me if the sculpture had been described as a goldfish swimming in noodle soup, but with Adam, I was at that moment consumed by an uncomfortable sense that I had to defend "personally" my own reality and that I did not know how to go about it. All I could at first think of saying from my "therapist self" was that "I really didn't recall ever owning a statue of a man without a head, and I didn't see one on the shelf at this moment, blah, blah, blah," but I didn't say it. There were at least two other competing parts of me beginning to emerge, each of which felt that to say this was experientially inauthentic; to one, it was as if I saw Adam as mentally incompetent, and to the other as if I myself didn't have my own reality as to what I believed the sculpture "really" was. What I ended up saying was something like "I've never seen that statue as being a man without a head, and I still don't, but I also feel that my saying this to you may get me into big trouble, and I'm not sure what to do about that." I then added, in the face of his stony silence, that "even though I believe I do know what the sculpture 'is,' I am finding that your conviction about your perception is having an unsettling impact on my ability to hold my own reality with confidence!" This, more than anything else I said, seemed to catch his interest.

The point, of course, was that the thing we were talking about couldn't be consensually defined at that point by the reality of either of us, and for me to have continued basing my clinical judgment solely upon a "decision" as to what was right for me or what was right for Adam, would have kept us each frozen in our own truths and unable to find a point of contact at which our perceptions could be negotiated. However, a reality that did not belong to either of us alone slowly began to take shape as we talked—a reality that allowed intersubjective contact to become possible despite the fact that our subjective experiences were directly unknowable (and thus "unprovable") to one another. I saw "a man over a barrel." He saw "a man without a head." Yes, some part of what was taking place had to do with visual perspective, and we did get to that later. I looked at it from where he was sitting, and he looked at it from my seat. We each could then see what the other saw, but what was more to the point was how we got there. I ended up not only being able to see (perceptually) the "man without a head," but I also ended up unexpectedly knowing how it felt to *be* a man without a head, and I shared this experience with him. I let him know that I was able to feel in a small way what it was like for him to live in a world where other people were always making him feel like a man without a head, and where he was always hearing about himself from others (including me) in a way he could not perceive himself, but was being asked to accept as "reality." In the process, not only did I get fully in touch with my feeling that Adam had me over a barrel but also with his feeling that other people had *him* over a barrel; in other words, by perceiving him as a person without a head. Neither Adam nor I had been able to negotiate our individual realities before this time because I was certain of the "truth" about mine, and Adam could not fully conceive of another person as a subject, as the center of his own thought processes, but only as an object. He could not "cut me enough slack" to think about what might have been going on in my mind in the context of his thinking about his own reality.

An analyst's "technique" encompasses and is encompassed by an interpersonal and intersubjective process. No matter whether an analyst believes, at any given moment with any given patient, that his patient's need for safety is paramount and views interaction (including self-disclosure by the analyst) principally in terms of its threat to impinge upon the patient's internal reality, or he holds to the importance of a primarily interactive use of himself (including the value of self-disclosure by the analyst within the analytic field), either of these postures provides the analyst a potentially valid place to stand during intersubjective negotiation with his patient. It is only when an analyst embraces his preferred stance as more than personal sensibility, (i. e., as objectively correct "technique") that he forecloses his ability to function intersubjectively, and prevents his patient from using him analytically. It is in this sense that I believe clinical judgment is always relational, and in exercising it, an analyst is always wrong when he views the choice as his to make on his own. Because he is always working in a complex field of multiple realities (his own shifting self-states and his patient's), the work, at its best, entails immersion in a relational field where the balance between confrontation and safety (the patient's experience of "staying the same while changing") is constantly shifting, and the analyst's preferred stance is always subject to scrutiny and renegotiation.

In other words, *any* given analytic stance is inherently both "right" and "wrong" and must be so, because the analyst cannot, on his own, simultaneously accept the patient as he is now and relate to him in terms of his growth potential. During much of the work in any analysis, the analyst must accept that his clinical judgment (no matter how "right" he feels it is) will be continually greeted by a response from a different self-state of the patient that "this is not me" and "you are not understanding who I am." Only by recognizing that his patient is not a "unitary" self in need of insight or in need of "the right relationship" will an analyst be able to allow the multiplicity of voices that comprise the patient's "self" to form a relationship with him, each in its own terms. This, to me, is what "clinical judgment" really means therapeutically—the analyst's ability to relate to the patient's discontinuous nonlinear realities without forcing any of them to be renounced or recast as simply a "defense" against another more "real" or more adaptive. The analyst's capacity to keep this goal in mind puts a patient's growth potential back into the patient's own hands through allowing him his fullest ability for cognitive symbolization of his subjective experience. He then regains more and more of his capacity for being a person with a past he can remember as a "past," a present he can live open-endedly and spontaneously, and a future into which he can project himself despite the fact that it will ultimately be "terminated."

19

"HELP! I'M GOING OUT OF YOUR MIND"[1]

E dgar Levenson (1992), summarizing how he sees the pragmatics of psychoanalysis, leads us in one succinct paragraph to what I believe is the core of the postclassical paradigm shift that he (and other interpersonalists following him) have been central in shaping:

> Within the safety and containment of the frame, one tries one's best to be a perfect analyst—fails of course—and uses one's deviations from the ideal as participatory data defining the interpersonal field of the therapist and patient; and not incidentally, throwing light on the patient's life outside of the therapy room, since it is axiomatic in psychoanalysis that there is a recursion, a repeating of pattern in the transference and in the material under discussion. What is talked about in therapy is reenacted (in reality or fantasy, depending on one's theory) in the relationship of the therapist and patient [pp. 560–561].

Within Levenson's postclassical interpersonal perspective I have attempted to bring an object relational sensibility to my own clinical work as an interpersonal/relational analyst. I've proposed (chapters

---

1. An early version of this chapter was presented in June 1997 as part of a panel, "Perspectives on Relational Psychoanalysis" (with Lewis Aron and Adrienne Harris), sponsored by the Institute of Contemporary Psychoanalysis, Los Angeles, CA.

10, 12, 16, 17) that the transference/countertransference field can be viewed as an ever-changing map of the patient's internal object world as it is played out with the analyst, and conversely that the process through which the patient's object representations come to exist transferentially in this complex field of projection and introjection is through interpersonal engagement, a two-way interaction. The focus is on what the person does with and to other people that reflects, albeit in a shifting, unpredictable way, the multiplicity of fixed and concrete relational patterns that constitute his world of interpersonal mental representation. In ordinary life, it is these fixed patterns of relatedness that lead to the mutual creation, between the patient and other people, of selective versions of reality that support his way of being and his way of perceiving himself and others. In a treatment conducted from an interpersonal/relational approach, these concrete patterns will readily become engaged, to be sure, but hopefully something beyond this should happen, allowing the patient's inner object world to emerge. I can only agree with Levenson that the analyst *cannot* get it right, and that not getting it right can, with luck, allow what is *really* wrong to emerge.

Central to my understanding of therapeutic growth is the phenomenon of dissociation in all its forms—healthy and adaptive, pathological and self-protective—and the fact that dissociation, as Donnel Stern (1996, p. 256) reminds us, is an active process. For every patient, it is the act of dissociation itself, in its multitude of interpersonal manifestations—what each of the patient's selves does *with* each of the analyst's selves—that makes transferential experience usable, and through which the work of analytic exploration takes place by the mutual creation of a projective/introjective field that slowly bridges fantasy and perception.

Ordinarily, every analyst, at various points in the clinical process, is containing and living-out with each patient, dissociated enactments of that patient's self-experience. The analyst's awareness of "switches" in his own and/or his patient's self-states during a session, is frequently the most powerful cue that an enactment is taking place. If the analyst is able to recognize and acknowledge in himself that which is dissociated by the patient, the patient can begin to "play" with its existence in a relational context without fear of compromising the self he unreflectively defines as "me" at that moment. As the patient's dissociated self-experience becomes sufficiently processed between them, the patient reclaims it, little by little, increasing not only his tolerance for self-reflection and intrapsychic conflict but also his sense of dynamic unity—what I have called "the capacity to feel like one self while being many." But first, the analyst and patient have to live together through the "mess."

Cannibalism as a Human Condition

A particularly dramatic aspect of this perspective took shape in my mind, unexpectedly, as I was listening to a panel (Anderson, Balamuth, Looker, and Schachtel, 1996) at a psychoanalytic conference. The three panelists each presented case material selected to illustrate the process of transference-countertransference enactment through which patient and analyst become embedded in a shared phenomenon that oscillates between physically embodied and linguistically represented experience.[2] The first analyst (Anderson) described her work with a woman, referred because of intractable back pain, who reported a dream about twin rabbits, one sitting inside the dead carcass of its twin and eating it. The second analyst (Balamuth) then spoke of how his male patient, shortly before his father's death, became caught up in a desperate hunger to "know" this man before it was too late, and how his desperation led to a hopeless effort to "penetrate" his father's opaqueness through the taking of a photographic portrait, during which his father refused, even then, to "give" eye contact. He said to his analyst, "I was poised like a cheetah, ready to leap at him, to tear him open and to get inside of him and find out who he is." The third analyst (Looker) followed this by presenting a female patient who, at a moment of felt impasse, complained: "This treatment won't ever work because you will hide what you feel. I've been taking in the treatment through my head while the rest of me is starving."

As I listened to the cases unfold I was stunned that each of the three patients, despite dramatic differences in personality, history, and the language they used, seemed to be possessed by the powerful presence of the same unconscious fantasy—largely unsymbolized by language—that permeated and organized their use of imagery, and as it emerged subsequently, informed the enactments played out with their respective analysts. In this dissociated fantasy, a central aspect of what each felt to be his or her "true" self was being held captive

---

2. For the full clinical context of these examples, I refer the interested reader to the illuminating chapters by each of the three panelists (Anderson, 1998; Balamuth, 1998; and Looker, 1998) to be found in Aron and Anderson (1998), a volume offering a rich variety of relational psychoanalytic perspectives on the body.

inside of the mind of an other—an other who refuses to respond to it—thus denying the patient his right to self-wholeness, the felt unity of psychic and somatic experience that Winnicott (1949) called psyche-soma.

The patient who is denied access to those aspects of himself that are unacknowledged by the "other's" mind and are thereby disconfirmed, is turned into an "object" belonging to the other, and is, thus, also an object to himself. He is unable to "inhabit" himself as a psychosomatic unity, and he feels as objectified and unreal to himself as he feels in the mind of the "other." He hungers for his "wholeness" to be restored, and desperately tries to find a way to penetrate and devour the contents of the other's mind to find himself within it. To the degree that the "other" (the analyst) refuses to grant access by recognizing and revealing his own dissociated experience, the power of the patient's cannibalistic need is increasingly expressed through transference and countertransference enactment. Bit by bit—sometimes it feels more like "bite by bite"—the analyst's image of the patient is eaten away from inside (as in the dream of the twin rabbits) and the analyst is forced to experience and respond to those aspects of the patient he wishes to disavow. As this enactment is lived and processed between them, the patient begins to inhabit a self that feels whole in the analyst's mind, and thus starts to feel simultaneously whole in his own.

If all this sounds like I'm talking about projective identification or about Winnicott's (1969) concept of "object usage," I am—at least in certain of their aspects. I see them as different vantage points for looking at the same process. Benjamin (1995) has an interesting take, similar to my own, on the relationship between the development of intersubjectivity and the process of object usage. She suggests that

> Winnicott's scheme can be expanded to postulate . . . a basic tension between denial and affirmation of the other . . . [and that in] the breakdown and re-creation of the tension between asserting one's own reality and accepting the other's . . . destruction makes possible the transition from relating (intrapsychic) to using the object, to carrying on a relationship with an other who is objectively perceived as existing outside the self, an entity in her own right [p. 39].

In this sense both Benjamin and I are each extending into our individual perspectives the idea of "sadism as a perversion of object usage," a concept offered by Ghent (1990) as a way of clarifying the origins of a certain kind of global yet largely unconscious sadism found in certain patients. Ghent suggested that a principal cause of failure in transitional experiencing from object relating to object usage is the caretaker's defensiveness, which results in the child or patient being made to feel that it is he or she who is destructive, leading to a fear and hatred of the other, and the development of characterological destructiveness. "In short," Ghent writes, "we have the setting for the development of sadism (in what remains a unit self, a self as isolate), the need to aggressively control the other as a perversion of object usage" (p. 124).

But why cannibalism? Is it really necessary to go that far? I use the word because in my own work I have found that at an experiential level the metaphor of mutual psychic cannibalism addresses an aspect of the process that even Winnicott's concept of "ruthlessness" doesn't quite reach. It speaks to a *reclaiming*—not only of something psychic but also of a *physical vitality* that is experienced as having been taken— an image that I believe places into a broader dyadic context the characterological sadism that Ghent identifies (see also Mitrani, 1994, 1995). Secondly, I feel that this way of looking at it reveals particularly vividly the central role played by dissociation and perhaps more importantly, the normal multiplicity of selfhood.

The roots of this kind of cannibalism can be seen in certain patterns of child-rearing. The main source of power that a parent has over a child does not come from telling the child who he *should* be but from telling him who he *is*. This is most effectively done through the way the parent relates to the child rather than by a direct verbal communication. That is, a parent's primary power to shape a child's sense of self isn't through saying (in words) "you are such and such" (though this certainly does take place), but through relating to the child as though he is already "such and such," and ignoring other aspects of his being as though they don't exist. These "disconfirmed" (Laing, 1962a) domains of self remain cognitively unsymbolized as "me" because they have no relational context of meaning to give them life. A child's sense of self thus becomes bonded to the early object through his identity being shaped by who the object both perceives him to be and denies him to be. *From then on, in both his internal object world and in the world "out there," he must somehow find a way to be recognized as that same "such and such" by the mind of the "other" in order for his feeling of personal continuity to remain intact.*

A "joke" from my childhood comes to mind here, one that probably originated around the time of the financial depression of the 1930s. It's a bittersweet anecdote about a man who was unable to sleep because he was worried about not being able to pay his rent, and for the third night in a row was lying awake. Finally, in desperation he picked up the phone at 2:00 A.M., dialed his landlord and shouted into the phone: "I can't pay my rent this month; now *you* stay awake."

Most of us doing clinical work have had the experience of treating someone who forces us in one way or another to think about them whether we want to or not, and often it's "not." It's as though the patient is saying: "*You* stay awake." In my own experience, as long as I don't for too long "stay asleep" to avoid the wake-up call, I am eventually forced to become aware that my patient is in some sort of acute psychological pain that cannot be put into words because it is not pain in the usual sense of the word. It is closer to the unbearable agony of empty isolation and sometimes the literal fear of disappearing. Why isolation? Why disappearing? And why the desperate press to be known by someone else at such times? I would argue that the general form this type of encounter takes is an isomorph of how one's sense of self is shaped in the first place, through the vicissitudes of early interactions with the mind of an "other."

One could suppose, for instance, that the man in the anecdote had his identity shaped largely through parental responses that recognized him in his ability to do what was expected of him during hard times, but failed to acknowledge the existence of his self-expression when it challenged their definition of social "reality" and the one meaningful personal quality that was linked to it, the strength of character to overcome adversity. So, in the "joke," this man's feeling of "social failure" was embodied in a self-state that, at least to some degree, couldn't be comfortably contained within his experience of being "himself"—that is, "himself" as recognized and known by the objects that defined him. Thus, the "self" that he had as a bed partner for those three nights of tossing and turning left him without an experience of inner peace—the peace that comes simply from experiencing yourself as existing in a world that knows you and in which you therefore, for better or worse, are a part. So he calls his landlord and shouts himself into his landlord's mind, just as certain patients call the therapist and shout themselves into the therapist's mind.

Sometimes a therapist's answering machine will serve even better than the therapist will, as long as the patient knows he or she will eventually listen to the message. What makes the therapist, at those moments, equivalent to the landlord in the anecdote is that (despite the therapist's genuine concern for the patient's welfare), in some real way he too would prefer *not* to know fully the self which is shouting its existence. The dissociated link between this experience and the patient's similar experience with his early objects is enacted through the patient's desperate effort to keep *that* self alive by preventing it from going out of the mind of the other. For an analyst, this can be the first step in contacting a patient's dissociated self-states as long as the patient doesn't give up trying to make these voices heard. And in most cases a patient won't give up if he can see that his analyst is sturdy enough to accept his own limitation in defining what he believes to be "the" truth about who his patient "really" is.

Multiplicity of Self, Language, and "Disclosure"

The vicissitudes of confirmation and disconfirmation lead inevitably though not always pathologically to a multiplicity of self-states. Each self-state, uncompromising in its entitlement to being validated in its own truth, must be recognized individually by its personal reality being experienced through the analyst's own subjectivity. Through this relational process it becomes "found," in Winnicott's (1963a, p. 190) sense, as it is representationally created by the participation of two minds, each allowing the experience of the other to be known and symbolized by language.

From this frame of reference, as Ginot (1997, p. 373) has argued cogently, "self disclosure is not . . . a way to promote a sense of intimacy through seemingly similar shared experiences. Rather, the emphasis here is on revealing emotional data growing from and organically related to the intersubjective matrix." The subjective reality of a patient's unsymbolized states of consciousness, especially with regard to a patient's experience of the analyst, must be felt and, in some useful way, acknowledged by the analyst. If there can be said to be an interpersonal/relational analytic "technique," it is mainly in the ability of the analyst, throughout the course of each analysis, to negotiate and renegotiate the meaning of what constitutes "useful" acknowledgment. It is when he abandons this effort and falls back on interpretation as a technical instrumentality, that his interpretations, no matter how accurate, will most typically increase the patient's feeling of deadness and isolation (see also Aron, 1992; Hoffmann, 1994). A patient's experience at such a moment is that something destructive is being done to him by the analyst and that it is not simply transference. To return to the metaphor of cannibalism, when an analyst in his interpretive stance fails to fully apprehend some aspect of the patient's self, he is, in fact, cannibalizing the patient of his potential to discover his full existence, and the patient feels increasingly driven by the need to repossess the hidden "reality" about himself that is dissociatively held within the analyst's mind, as if the analyst had devoured it. As the analytic space becomes filled with energy generated by this enactment of nonrecognition, the patient more and more *becomes* the self that has been expelled from the analyst's consciousness, gradually forcing his way into the analyst's perceptual field, and finally igniting in him or her a personal response to that part of the patient that has until then been dissociated and functionally expelled from interpersonal recognition. By increasing a patient's capacity for one aspect of his self to experience and hold in a single field of consciousness other aspects of self that have been disowned, dissociation as an *automatic* defensive process is gradually surrendered, thereby increasing the patient's ability for engaging in self-reflection, promoting his tolerance for experiencing conflictual self-states, and ultimately developing his capacity for *resolving* intrapsychic conflict. As a hermeneutic process, psychoanalysis depends upon these conditions being met, and repression cannot always be assumed to exist as a mechanism. Let me illustrate:

The following clinical vignette is drawn not from my own work, but from that of the English analyst Enid Balint. Although her psychoanalytic heritage is exclusively British object relational and mine is largely American interpersonal, the bridge between the two is so well embodied in the clinical sensibility she demonstrates here, the vignette may serve to put into relief some of the key issues that have led to my evolving commitment, not simply to an interactional stance per se (see also Ghent, 1995), but to *working analytically at the developmental interface between fantasy and perception*, the area of intersubjective space that Enid Balint called "imaginative perception." Like Sullivan, but in a different way, she believed that "a sense of being someone" is needed for conscious thought. This is only possible if the someone belongs in an environment into which he can project, and whose projections he can use and later relate to. To be conscious there has to be an 'I' and a 'you' (Balint, 1987, p. 481). The "I" and the "you" in turn are linked through the process of imaginative perception. "The first imaginative perception," Balint writes (1989, p. 102), "can only arise out of a state of eager aliveness in two people; the infant with the potential for life and the mother alive inside herself and tuning in to the emerging infant."

The clinical vignette I would like to discuss is the now famous case study that Balint presented in her 1987 paper, "Memory and Consciousness." This case, as she modestly suggested, lends some support to Freud's (1915) speculation that "there is a possibility of there being an infinite series of states of consciousness" (Balint, 1987, p. 482). Which is to say that Balint was not so impressed by the operation of repression in the case as by the extraordinary discontinuities between her patient's self-states. Equally, and closely connected to the foregoing, she was impressed by the sense of extreme distance between herself and her patient. Despite the fact that her patient, Mr. Smith, was a highly successful businessman, during the first phase of his analysis Balint reports that she simply "could not understand how the man who was in my room could be so successful in the business world. I could not at this stage, imaginatively perceive him" (p. 477). Further, in important ways Mr. Smith seemed unable to imaginatively perceive himself. In this context she introduced a new term, "body memories," to describe aspects of this man of which he seemed to have no conscious knowledge:

> During the first few years of his analysis Mr. Smith had no mental or visual memories. He had body memories in so far as his body both looked and behaved in a baby-like way on the couch. There were no words to describe the baby or his environment. He was a baby who could not think or communicate verbally. . . . His conscious thoughts were derived from other peoples' consciousness and did not link up with his own perceptions [1987, p. 482].

Enid Balint's use of the term "body memories," a concept that we now take pretty much for granted, is a shorthand way of talking about the body as having "a mind of its own"—an image that as far back as 1872 led to the evocative comment by the psychiatrist Henry Maudsley that "the sorrow that has not vent in tears makes other organs weep" (cited in Taylor, 1987, p. 87). But it is Mrs. Balint's actual description of the way she worked with Mr. Smith that I find most interesting and most relevant. Standing solidly within her particular British object relational frame of reference, she allowed her clinical self free range. "After about three years of analysis Mr. Smith *became awake enough to perceive*" (1987, p. 482). Balint describes what happened:

> At the end of the session there were at one time three of us present: a "he" (probably the baby), an "analyst," and someone who spoke about him to the analyst, who for a time was called "the narrator." During the sessions, then, and at the end, he (the baby) and the person who was called the narrator—one who made up sentences, who had a voice and not only a body—met. . . . When the narrator spoke about the grown man, the grown man and the baby came together to some extent, because the words were sometimes relished . . . and at those times the baby's mouth seemed to be tasting words, eating words, and spitting them out of his mouth with pleasure. . . . I used the word "babbling" perhaps as Bion (1963) used

"doodling" at some stage, and Mr. Smith liked this word very much. It was right for the baby on the couch, and for the narrator man (and these two became separate). The grown man could perceive himself as a baby when I used the words. The narrator disappeared soon after this, and there was a grown-up Mr. Smith who worked and read, and a baby who he could perceive if I used the right words [p. 478].

Finding the "right words"[3] can be considered one aspect of interpersonal engagement, and as Sullivan knew all too well, can be very hard to do. But other aspects of interpersonal engagement, including the analyst's abiding respect for the patient's experience of safety, are no less important or ineluctable. The specific conditions for analytic growth always differ for each analytic couple, and each dyad must strike its own balance between safety and risk. For some patients particularly, confrontation with the analyst's subjectivity is felt as safe only within the window of the patient's capacity to process it, but for any patient, the key ingredient is neither safety nor confrontation alone. The analyst can never get it "right," but is almost always on safe ground if he is not trying to get his patient to "own" the analyst's perception as an improvement on the patient's reality. Instead, the analyst should be genuinely attempting to get the patient to know what the analyst is feeling while he is remaining genuinely curious about what the *patient* feels. I think this is why many seemingly "fragile" patients are able to "hang-in" while being faced with an openly confrontational stance, and can stand to look at the picture their analyst has of them. Their own "truth" is not at risk through the act of listening to that of an "other." But with some patients the tumult of confrontation is a prelude to real turmoil, and the work as it evolves is far more strenuous than it seemed to be between Mrs. Balint and Mr. Smith.

Hanging-In

How can I best describe the experience of trying to maintain an analytic treatment frame with a patient who feels he is going out of his *own* mind each time he feels he is going out of *yours*? In working with

---

3. The growing need of psychoanalysts to understand more precisely what is meant by the phrase "the right words," has led to the emergence of a new area of multidisciplinary research bridging psychoanalysis and developmental psycholinguistics, as for example the work of Adrienne Harris (1992, 1994, 1995, 1996).

a patient who has this problem to any significant degree, the use of the term "technique" has as much meaning as thinking about Dorothy's unscheduled flight from Kansas to Oz as a "strategic choice." The analyst, like Dorothy, simply has to accept the experience of living somewhere without being sure of where it is or how he is going to get home. The present is not a safe vantage point for looking into the patient's nature or of comprehending his past. For such a patient, the past *is* the present, and the therapist is in fact pressured to accept this despite its often frustrating unreasonableness, without "analyzing" it, without giving up, and without retaliating for not being given more than that. Making matters more complicated, as soon as the therapist tries to "work with" the patient's complaints or accusations as "material," the patient experiences this as the analyst's withdrawal from "knowing" him through their direct connection to one another.

As the title of this chapter suggests, the first awareness a therapist has of a patient's dissociated experience is often through his own sense that the more he tries to "understand," the more he feels as if he is abandoning his patient in some way that he can't grasp. The message, "Help! I'm going out of your mind," is thus often felt first by the therapist through his own sense of failure or futility. On the other hand, when the message is delivered to the analyst as a *verbal* communication, it will typically take the form of an accusation that the therapist doesn't want to hear about the patient's pain, that he doesn't want to hear about the depths of the patient's desperation, that he doesn't want to hear about the patient's depression and loneliness, or an insistence that the therapist is bored or uninterested. From this vantage point, many instances of what analysts label "psychotic transference" are enactments of dissociated self-states within a dissociative personality that the therapist is not aware is dissociative. The therapist believes he is simply seeing a unitary but "crazy" person with no observing ego. As a patient once said to me when he realized I could finally comprehend what he meant, "If it wasn't for reality I wouldn't have any problems."

In its most extreme form, a patient's experience that he is going out of your mind and that you could care less, is not an experience that is accessible to change by exploring it as a transferential expression of the past. It is in large part an intrinsic expression of the current dissociative structure of the patient's self-experience, part of which is his uncommunicable state of isolation and alienation. It is a state of wordlessness that, because it is dissociated, is not directly accessible to symbolization by the interpersonal exploration of meaning—a process that has been referred to over the years as "interpretation." Such an individual needs first to *feel* real in order for new meaning to have "meaning." He is in desperate need of someone recognizing him, knowing what it is to live in his skin—to *be* him. The words he uses to accomplish this are not the real analytic content. They are the building blocks he uses to construct what is the real content: the felt hopelessness of his effort to free himself from the internal prison in which he is trapped unless his state of mind is fully known to someone else. Anything other than that, no matter how significant it may appear to the therapist, is to the patient just one more story about him. Until the unspoken self is engaged, the patient is being asked to inhabit meaning that isn't his and accept some new words or concepts as a substitute for feeling real.

With some patients in particular, if this shared phenomenon of the patient "going out of your mind" is not addressed by the analyst, the patient will continue to experience, in one form or another, a need for violence toward the self and/or the other. The dissociated, lifeless, physical "shell" that the patient experiences as his body, but which unconsciously contains as well the uncomprehending other, can't of course be literally destroyed and gotten rid of without actual death. And this fact can indeed sometimes lead to a wish for (or even, in certain cases, an actual attempt at) suicide or homicide as a perverse expression of rage at being denied life.

Consider, for example, a dream reported by one of my patients who had been consistently defined by his mother as her "special boy." A voice is heard in the dream, "Kill the special boy!" He associated this to the scene from William Golding's (1955) *Lord of the Flies* in which a pack of boys are hunting the outcast boy, "Piggy," and shouting "kill the special boy." The dreamer in this instance was that part of my patient who was becoming aware of another part of himself who venomously hated the special boy—the boy whose existence was defined by his mother's delusion that he belonged to her. The dissociated wish to kill it, hoping he would then feel more real to himself, had indeed sometimes led to dangerously self-destructive behavior.

My use of the term "shell" (see chapter 10) as the outcome of dissociative unlinking of mind from psyche-soma, is not predicated on whether the shell is "false," as in Winnicott's "false self," but on the fact that because the shell has become rigid in order to maintain the dissociative structure of the mind, it prevents a full range of experiencing, relating, and creative living. The patient's wish to force open the "shell" of the cannibalizing other, claim its contents, and thereby redefine selfhood, may well be an act that is driven by the species-specific right to exist fully as a self. Grotstein (1995), citing a personal communication from John Bowlby, writes that "the infant probably keenly senses an atavistic fear of being the potential prey/victim and is simultaneously aware of the need to be the predator/hunter for survival" (p. 484). This right to exist fully as a self can only be actualized when the "other" is alive to one's own subjective experience, recognizing it and cognitively engaging it, creating as Enid Balint (1989, p. 102) put it "a state of eager aliveness in two people." Thus, a patient's wish to rip apart the shell of the other that is "dead" to the patient's full existence and penetrate it to perceive the feelings that are being held by the analyst but are unrevealed and sometimes unthought even if they may be "known" (to borrow Bollas's [1987] concept).

A Case in Point

Let me describe a bit of my work with a patient for whom these issues had a particularly high priority. Christina, a beautiful and talented poet in her early 50s, was a survivor of brutal childhood trauma. She had survived psychologically by an extraordinary ability to deaden the reality of her own human aliveness and that of others through a rigidly maintained dissociative mental structure. She employed her mind and her perceptual apparatus to master the techniques of human behavior as seamlessly as possible, and lived as if she were a wind-up toy shut out of a human world—repudiating the one quality, spontaneity, without which human existence is no more than a facsimile: "Nothing is happening; nothing is happening to me; I see nothing; I know nothing; I want to know nothing; there is nothing to question; things are no more than they seem; If I do what is expected of me, and do it with grace, I will be taken care of." And so she was. As the "special" child, she was well behaved, seemingly happy, and, most important, "normal." She took pride in the fact that the terror and loneliness that were her constant companions and the strategies she employed to keep her mind from collapsing, were her own secrets, never to be revealed. Her first dream in analysis was of hitting someone on the head and causing brain damage:

> This person's mouth opens wide—her tongue comes out and she starts shaking back and forth and keels over in a seizure. The scene switches to a hospital in which the victim is wheeled out in a display case like a doll. There are lots of other dolls around her, with painted faces and fancy clothes. One of them explains to me that they have to keep her that way because her brain damage makes it the only environment she can survive in.

Developmentally, what she had to do to her mind, dissociatively, in order to survive her childhood, was most devastating in its impairment of her ability to symbolize experience—to represent it mentally. Particularly handicapped was her capacity for what Target and Fonagy (1996, p. 469) call "mentalization"—the ability to think about another person's thinking about her, without it becoming an "objective" reality that defines her. This handicap became clearer and clearer in analysis as she slowly began to part with her secrets and described how psychological reality had always been little more than a replica of physical reality, and how she was totally vulnerable to being taken over by the "world out there." Her inner world, such as it was, appeared impossibly chaotic; and yet, it was vulnerable to sudden violent disruption, to lightning, to trucks backfiring, and the like:

> Sometimes I would have dreams, but they weren't dreams. I would see things if I started to fall asleep . . . like abstract paintings. . . . chaotic geometric forms stuck together; but other things would suddenly appear in the forms—like an eyeball would suddenly shoot out. It was terrifying. I've always been afraid of thunderstorms. They felt so close. Sometimes I thought they were coming from inside my head. I used to try to protect myself by putting my hands over my ears at night so if there was a storm coming up I would be prepared for it. I was also afraid of other loud noises— gunfire, firecrackers, trucks backfiring. I might even run in the opposite direction. I thought they might blow up. Oh, oh, I better not think those things about a truck; it might blow up in retaliation. I have to propitiate it. I used to propitiate God if I thought a storm was coming up so he would make it go away. I would sing "Harbor Lights," and then I would feel safe and I could say "I hope the truck blows up." No! I don't mean that. I'm fooling around a little bit, but if I fool around too much it might really blow up. Kind of like sticking my tongue out to see if I can do it. That's how I began to write poems when I was a kid. It was like sticking my tongue out, but it looks like nonsense, so it's safe. Like, instead of saying "I hope it blows up," I might write, "I hope it turns into a thousand oatmeals."
>
> I grew up with my mind being the only part of me that felt real; my body was a dead weight. It was only the words that mattered . . . I could be safe by using the right words. And when words don't do it—like when I'm not successful on the phone with the operator—I'm helpless. And then, sometimes, I become possessed—taken over by something inside of me that wants to destroy the thing that is not responding to my words. Sometimes even my own words take me over. Like, now, I can't get the word

"propitiate" out of my mind. I know *you* used that word once. I want to tell you to make it stop."

Christina was a patient for whom life was a series of rituals to be performed while she was waiting for death, and therapy was simply one more ritual among many. To say she *felt* hopeless does not do justice to her personality. Her very being *embodied* hopelessness. Nothing she did and nothing she felt about anything had meaning to her beyond the concrete moment it occurred. Ogden (1986) has described "a developmental phase of 'it-ness,' wherein the infant is lived by his experience (p. 42). . . . [E]ach event exists in itself, but not for a self existing over time or in relation to anything but itself" (p. 48). Christina seemed stuck in this phase. In the therapy, any seemingly shared increase in emotional closeness during a given session would be foreclosed before the session ended and was certain to be gone the next. Barbara Pizer (in press) writes that the experience of working with such a patient—a person who has "adapted to untenable neglect with counterphobic independence and the appearance of narcissistic retreat," is analogous to being with a certain kind of burn victim, someone who has suffered the burn of frostbite: "As we weather the interpersonal and intrapsychic storms precipitated by my approach, I might ask the person if he or she has ever experienced frostbite. 'You don't feel it so much when you're out in the cold,' I suggest; 'It's when you come inside and get warm that the pain begins, and it can get excruciating.'"

Christina would end each session by testifying that there was no point in talking about anything because nothing would ever change, and she would then begin the following session in a dissociated self-state that would have little or no link to any more related state of mind that might later emerge during the hour or had existed in previous hours. My fantasy was that I was doomed to spend the rest of my life forced to see her session after session with no feeling of continuity between sessions, no feeling of hope, no leverage for human contact, and no way to humanly end the therapy. *She,* at least, could "get through" each session as a ritual while waiting to die; I was not allowed this escape because she always knew when I was dissociating from being with her in the moment, and would let me know about it. Most of this was familiar to me in my work with other patients, and in fact I typically was enlivened by the challenge. Christina was different. Her concreteness, as she shifted from one state of consciousness to another, was oppressive. It went on too long, I felt. I reached a point that I was desperate for a little feeling of continuity, a little feeling that she remembered who we were together from week to week, a little feeling of progress, and more than anything, a little playfulness. Christina wouldn't play. She gradually began to force me to recognize that the problem wasn't just hers, but was also mine. My wish for her to be able to play wasn't simply a therapeutic goal; it was also a personal need to make human contact—a need for Christina to feel familiarly human because I was hating the experience of feeling increasingly dehumanized and "out in the cold." So I tried to *force* play. To her, my "playfulness" was simply facitiousness—evidence that I was not taking her seriously. She was, as always, very perceptive.

It didn't matter that I *write* about the fact (chapter 16) that when a therapist tries to turn spontaneity into a technique, it invariably fails. *My* knowing it didn't make any difference. Christina knew it better than I did, so my efforts at "playfulness" failed, over and over. But it may have been that very fact that ultimately did make a difference. Eventually I began to feel hopeless, and I stopped "trying." It was then—when I had stopped trying to be playful out of my personal effort to feel alive—that I began to experience her as beginning to help *me* along.

I can still recall the session in which she was able to do the impossible—to play with her experience of hopelessness. She stood up to leave, walked towards the door, and I readied myself for her usual exit ritual. "There's no way out," she moaned, referring to the impossibility of ever finding a solution to her real-life problems. "Sure there is," I replied, "right through the door." Miracle of miracles, she laughed. "Sure," she said, "you want me to leave fast so you can see your next patient." She was, as always, accurate, and I (heart somewhat in mouth) acknowledged it, but until that moment there had been no words to symbolize the experience at the door that had been repeatedly enacted without an intersubjective context to give it shared meaning. Although it was the same scene we had played many times before, it was not the same. Part of me was actually enjoying this moment with her, even though another part did indeed want her to get out so I could see my next patient. This time, my need to get her (and her hopelessness) out of the room as fast as possible was not filling up all of the space. Should one choose to ponder whether this scene can legitimately be called "play," consider Frankel's (1998) well-taken point that play is not always benign:

> When our dissociated states emerge in play, we are playing with our own subjectivity, but social play is also a way of playing with someone else's subjectivity. . . . When we play with another person, we are looking for, and evoking, certain states in that other person,

not only states in ourselves. *We can be fascinated by those states in others and by shifts involving these states, which are problematic and disturbing for us* [pp. 176–177, italics added].

About four years into her analysis Christina's long anaesthetized appetite for life began to find voice, whispering that what life had to offer was perhaps worth a risk. She was willing to allow this into the analysis as long as it didn't displace the anhedonic, vigilant, bitter self that still claimed priority in her configuration of selfhood. It was at this point that Christina reported the following dream: She was walking along the top of a seawall that began to get narrower and narrower until she was at a place she couldn't go forward without falling into an abyss. But she couldn't go back because she couldn't turn around. The scene then shifted to her looking at herself in a mirror and suddenly noticing a second head growing out of the side of her own head. The face wasn't there yet, and she was terrified of it appearing. She didn't want to see it.

Christina's state of mind as she told me this dream is not easy to capture in words. In allowing herself to dream the dream, she was conveying that although she felt her analysis might be leading her toward "the black hole" of madness[4] she was no longer accepting the existential deadness of dissociation as the price for escaping potential retraumatization. Theodore Sturgeon (1953), in his novel *More Than Human*, describes his protagonist at a similar point of no return, as being "aware of the bursting within him of an encysted need. It had been a part of him all his life but there was no hope in him that might express it. And bursting so, it flung a thread across his internal gulf, linking his alive and independent core to the half-dead animal around it" (p. 9).

In the sessions that followed, Christina began to reveal openly the existence of other selves that shared her body, that spoke to her as voices, and had done so since childhood. It was a deeply guarded secret, horrifying and shameful, and even with my support she disclosed the details only with great mistrust and misgiving, becoming furious if I suggested that her willingness to take this risk was a sign of progress or if I seemed hopeful about her prognosis.

It was shortly thereafter that she reported a dream of being in a dark subway tunnel, walking and walking, and suddenly seeing a chink in the roof with a ray of light coming through:

---

4. See Grand (1997) for a penetrating clinical discussion of "the black hole" phenomenon that places it squarely within a relational context.

I knew I would have to climb to get to it. I wanted to get out of the tunnel but I felt there was no point of making that difficult climb because I'd never get out anyway. Then *in* the dream I said to myself "someone's telling me there's light at the end of the tunnel." I started to laugh because it's so corny. I don't remember if I actually heard the voice in the dream, but it was as if I did. I laughed because I had the thought in the dream that *you* were the one saying that, and it was such a corny thing to say. But I *knew* it wasn't your voice; it was someone who was in the tunnel with me. Then I woke up. I didn't want to tell you the dream because I knew you'd immediately think I'm feeling hope, which I'm not. I'm not sure if that voice is a friend or an enemy. I'm too old to put myself out there again. I'm strong enough this way. Why should I take a risk and leave myself open to trusting people? Who is there to take care of me but me? Why should I take a risk?

The surrendering of dissociation as a defense is a *serious* risk for a patient such as Christina and is not easily taken, which makes the period of therapeutic transition from dissociation to the subjective experience of intrapsychic conflict and ambivalence a particularly trying time for both patient and analyst. During this period, some patients block the analyst's words and literally render them meaningless—sometimes even voiceless—and this can often go on for quite a while before this "transference phenomenon" becomes "material" that can be explored. Christina, for example, was starting to risk being directly engaged with other people with an increased degree of perception as to what was going on between them, and had moved beyond the point of needing automatically to create a perceptual gap that made the experience feel like it wasn't happening to her. During this period she would often experience me as "just moving my lips" whenever I would attempt to look at what was going on between us, but this did not prevent her from being able to hold the words cognitively so as to appear to be thinking about them—which in fact she was, but without their having any relevance to her own existence in the moment. My words were drained of personal impact through her "switching" to another self-state in which the aspect of herself that I was responding to and starting to talk about, no longer had access to her conscious sense of selfhood—her experience of "I." So even as she was replying to my words, she did not know what in herself I was responding to at the moment, and had rendered both herself and me into lifeless objects that could be discussed intelligently without the risk of traumatic anxiety and shame. It was as if I were talking to her about someone else. I have observed the most frequent instances of this phenomenon to occur in the treatment of individuals who have been discovering their increased capacity to stay fully conscious in the moment *without* being overwhelmed by annihilation anxiety, but then become terrified that they might lose the one escape from madness upon which they had learned to rely.

Christina had spent her life trying to keep from totally depersonalizing (falling into a "black hole," as she put it). She was unable to "breathe into" her own life—make her own choices in living it—without losing the configuration of selves that were defined by the traumatic ruptures in her early object attachments. As Target and Fonagy (1996, p. 470) remind us, "The young child, who does not yet have the capacity to mentalize, to reflect on thoughts and feelings as it were from outside, is forced to believe that his or her thoughts and beliefs inevitably and correctly mirror the real world, even if this involves a discontinuity in experience of the self." In working with Christina, it was sometimes horrifying to feel the depth of her dread that her sanity depended totally on the preservation of discontinuous self-states that cannot be bridged by human relatedness. And in a way, of course, she was right. Her vigilant mistrustfulness had been indeed able to prevent her mind from being overwhelmed by experiences that could not bridge the normal discontinuities of selfhood, but only by paying the price of an unlived life.

Christina's solution had been to keep all of her options perpetually open, awaiting the "some day" when real life would begin. Transitions were felt as impossible; her dread of the black hole always stood between being and becoming, and led her to turn every attempt to move forward into an exercise in controlling her panic that she would stop existing. So her own awareness of growth made one part of her apprehend the therapy itself as a version of the trucks that might "backfire" at any moment. Her solution, at certain moments with me, could be looked at as a kind of "perceptual eating disorder" whereby, in response to increasing evidence to the contrary, she would even *more* staunchly enact her reality that she could not safely "take in" meaning conveyed by the words of an "other," digest them, and still retain her own thoughts and feelings.

After about six years of analytic work Christina began to experience herself as a human being who had been hurt and could *still* be hurt, but was not necessarily a "damaged" human being. It was at this point she reported the following dream: She was driving through the woods in a four-wheel-drive sport-utility vehicle (to her, the most repulsive symbol of materialistic self-interest), and suddenly drove into a swamp that she didn't see in time to avoid. The car sank completely underwater with her in it. She felt in real danger because, in trying to escape, her head was at immediate risk of being trapped under the car. Nevertheless she didn't feel panic. "My head isn't caught yet," she said to herself, "and maybe it won't be." In fact it didn't get caught, she was able to swim out, and the dream ended.

Her associations led her to say to me both with pleasure and some fear, "I guess not everyone who is scared is scarred. They're not the same." Christina was now able to experience anxiety for the first time and distinguish it from the traumatic dread that had been her constant companion, telling her she was always on the edge of the "black hole." She could now recognize anxiety as something unpleasant but bearable—something she *felt* rather than a way of addressing the world. The dream spoke to the fact she no longer felt herself living "on hold" in a world that required perpetual readiness for trauma, and she allowed herself to be aware that she had begun to surrender the armor of her dissociative defense against the potential return of unexpected trauma the moment she feels she is safe. That is to say, she came to understand that hurt is not equivalent to traumatic destruction of selfhood. She recognized that she was now taking the risk of pursuing a life that included self-interest, and that in choosing to live life rather than wait for it, she had accepted the inevitability of loss, hurt, and ultimately death as part of the deal.

My story of Christina ends here, and so does the book, but Christina's analysis did not. It continued for several more years and, as you might expect, involved intense mourning, not only for the loss of early objects, but also for the self whose life had for too long been unexamined and, in a true sense, unlived. Her dread of "going out of my mind" was replaced by a conviction that she had a secure place *within* it, as I did within hers. As the work evolved she became increasingly stronger, less dissociated, more spontaneous, more playful, and more loving. At the point we ended, as far as I could tell she had most of her selves pretty well in hand and she was using them robustly and creatively in a full life, even, as she put it, "at my age."

REFERENCES

Adams, H. (1904), *Mont Saint-Michel and Chartres*. New York: Penguin Classics, 1986.

American Psychiatric Association (1994), *Diagnostic Criteria from DSM-IV*. Washington, DC: American Psychiatric Press.

Anderson, F. S. (1998), Psychic elaboration of musculoskeletal back pain. In: *Relational Perspectives on the Body: Psychoanalytic Theory and Practice*, eds. L. Aron & F. S. Anderson. Hillsdale, NJ: The Analytic Press, pp. 287–322.

———— Balamuth, R., Looker, T. & Schachtel, Z. (1996), Panel presented at annual spring meeting of the Division of Psychoanalysis (39) of the American Psychological Association, New York City.

Appignanesi, L. & Forrester, J. (1992), *Freud's Women*. New York: Basic Books.

Aron, L. (1991), The patient's experience of the analyst's subjectivity. *Psychoanal. Dial.*, 1:29–51.

———— (1992), Interpretation as expression of the analyst's subjectivity. *Psychoanal. Dial.*, 2:475–507.

———— (1996), *A Meeting of Minds: Mutuality in Psychoanalysis*. Hillsdale, NJ: The Analytic Press.

———— & Anderson, F. S., eds. (1998), *Relational Perspectives on the Body: Psychoanalytic Theory and Practice*. Hillsdale, NJ: The Analytic Press.

Baars, B. J. (1992), Divided consciousness or divided self. *Consciousness and Cognition*, 1:59–60.

Bacal, H. (1987), British object-relations theorists and self psychology: Some critical reflections. *Internat. J. Psycho-Anal.*, 68:81–98.

Bach, S. (1977), On the narcissistic state of consciousness. *Internat. J. Psycho-Anal.*, 58:209–233.

———— (1985), *Narcissistic States and the Therapeutic Process*. New York: Aronson.

Balamuth, R. (1998), Re-membering the body: A psychoanalytic study of presence and absence of the lived body. In: *Relational Perspectives on the*

Body: Psychoanalytic Theory and Practice, ed. L. Aron & F. S. Anderson. Hillsdale, NJ: The Analytic Press, pp. 263–286.

Balint, E. (1968), Remarks on Freud's metaphors about the "mirror" and the "receiver." *Comp. Psychiat.*, 9:344–348.

———— (1987), Memory and consciousness. *Internat. J. Psycho-Anal.*, 68:475–483.

———— (1989), Creative life. In: *Before I Was I*. New York: Guilford, 1993, pp. 100–108.

———— (1991), Commentary on Philip Bromberg's "On knowing one's patient inside out." *Psychoanal. Dial.*, 1:423–430.

———— (1993), Enid Balint interviewed by Juliet Mitchell. In: *Before I Was I*. New York: Guilford, pp. 221–236.

Balint, M. (1935), Critical notes on the theory of the pregenital organizations of the libido. In: *Primary Love and Psychoanalytic Technique*. New York: Liveright, 1965, pp. 37–58.

———— (1937), Early developmental stages of the ego: Primary object love. In: *Primary Love and Psychoanalytic Technique*. New York: Liveright, 1965, pp. 74–90.

———— (1952), New beginning and the paranoid and the depressive syndromes. In: *Primary Love and Psychoanalytic Technique*. New York: Liveright, 1965, pp. 230–249.

———— (1959), *Thrills and Regressions*. New York: International Universities Press.

———— (1965), *Primary Love and Psychoanalytic Technique*. New York: Liveright.

———— (1968), *The Basic Fault*. London: Tavistock.

Barrett-Lennard, G. T. (1981), The empathy cycle: Refinement of a nuclear concept. *J. Counsel. Psychol.*, 28:91–100.

Bartlett, F. C. (1932), *Remembering*. Cambridge, England: Cambridge University Press.

Barton, S. (1994), Chaos, self-organization, and psychology. *Amer. Psychol.*, 49:5–14.

Bass, A. (1992), Review essay: M. Little's *Psychotic Anxieties and Containment*. *Psychoanal. Dial.*, 2:117–131.

———— (1993), Review essay: P. Casement's *Learning from the Patient*. *Psychoanal. Dial.*, 3:151–167.

Becker, E. (1964), *Revolution in Psychiatry*. New York: Free Press.

———— (1973), *The Denial of Death*. New York: Free Press.

Beebe, B. & Lachmann, F. M. (1992), The contribution of mother-infant mutual influence to the origins of self- and object representations. In: *Relational Perspectives in Psychoanalysis*, ed. N. J. Skolnick & S. C. Warshaw. Hillsdale, NJ: The Analytic Press, pp. 83–117.

———— Jaffe, J. & Lachmann, F. M. (1992), A dyadic systems view of communication. In: *Relational Perspectives in Psychoanalysis*, ed. N. J. Skolnick & S. C. Warshaw. Hillsdale, NJ: The Analytic Press, pp. 61–81.

Benjamin, J. (1995), *Like Subjects, Love Objects: Essays on Recognition and Sexual Difference*. New Haven, CT: Yale University Press.

Berman, E. (1981), Multiple personality: Psychoanalytic perspectives. *Internat. J. Psycho-Anal.*, 62:283–300.

Bion, W. R. (1955), Language and the schizophrenic patient. In: *New Directions in Psycho-Analysis*, ed. M. Klein, P. Heimann & E. Money-Kyrle. London: Tavistock, pp. 220–329.

——— (1957), Differentiation of the psychotic from the non-psychotic personalities. In: *Second Thoughts*. London: Maresfield Library, 1967, pp. 43–64.

——— (1963), *Elements of Psychoanalysis*. London: Heinemann.

——— (1965), *Transformations*. London: Heinemann.

——— (1967), The imaginary twin. In: *Second Thoughts*. London: Maresfield Library, pp. 3–22.

——— (1970), *Attention and Interpretation*. London: Tavistock (reprinted, London: Maresfield, 1984).

——— (1978), *Four Discussions with W. R. Bion*. Strathclyde: Clunie.

Bird, B. (1972), Notes on transference: Universal phenomenon and hardest part of analysis. *J. Amer. Psychoanal. Assn.*, 20:267–301.

Blatt, S. J. (1974), Levels of object representation in anaclitic and introjective depression. *The Psychoanalytic Study of the Child*, 29:107–157. New Haven, CT: Yale University Press.

Blaustein, A. B. (1975), A dream resembling the Isakower phenomenon: A brief clinical contribution. *Internat. J. Psycho-Anal.*, 56:207–208.

Bliss, E. L. (1988), A reexamination of Freud's basic concepts from studies of multiple personality disorder. *Dissociation*, 1:36–40.

Bollas, C. (1987), *The Shadow of the Object*. London: Free Association Books.

——— (1989), *Forces of Destiny*. London: Free Association Books.

——— (1992), *Being a Character*. New York: Hill & Wang.

Bonanno, G. A. (1990), Remembering and psychotherapy. *Psychotherapy*, 27:175–186.

Boris, H. N. (1986), Bion re-visited. *Contemp. Psychoanal.*, 22:159–184.

Bosnak, R. (1996), *Tracks in the Wilderness of Dreaming*. New York: Delacorte Press.

Brenner, I. (1994), The dissociative character: A reconsideration of "multiple personality." *J. Amer. Psychoanal. Assn.*, 42:819–846.

——— (1996), On trauma, perversion, and multiple personality. *J. Amer. Psychoanal. Assn.*, 44:785–814.

Breuer, J. & Freud, S. (1893–1895), Studies on hysteria. *Standard Edition*, 2. London: Hogarth Press, 1955.

Bromberg, P. M. (1979), The schizoid personality: The psychopathology of stability. In: *Integrating Ego Psychology and Object Relations Theory*, ed. L. Saretsky, G. D. Goldman & D. S. Milman. Dubuque, IA: Kendall/Hunt, pp. 226–242.

——— (1980), Sullivan's concept of consensual validation and the therapeutic action of psychoanalysis. *Contemp. Psychoanal.*, 16:237–248.

——— (1982), The supervisory process and parallel process in psychoanalysis. *Contemp. Psychoanal.*, 18:92–111.

――― (1983), Discussion of "Refusal to Identify: Developmental Impasse" by A. J. Horner. *Dynam. Psychother.*, 1:122–128.

――― (1984), The third ear. In: *Clinical Perspectives on the Supervision of Psychoanalysis and Psychotherapy*, ed. L. Caligor, P. M. Bromberg & J. D. Meltzer. New York: Plenum Press, pp. 29–44.

――― (1986a), Discussion of "The wishy-washy personality" by A. Goldberg. *Contemp. Psychoanal.*, 22:374–387.

――― (1986b), Discussion of "Dialogue on love and hate in psychoanalysis" by L. Epstein & M. Schwartz. *Contemp. Psychother. Rev.*, 3:54–68.

――― (1989), Discussion of "Keeping the analysis alive and creative over the long haul" by G. Friedman. *Contemp. Psychoanal.*, 25:337–345.

――― (1991a), Reply to discussion by Enid Balint. *Psychoanal. Dial.*, 1:431–437.

――― (1991b), Introduction to "Reality and the Analytic Relationship: A Symposium." *Psychoanal. Dial.*, 1:8–12.

――― (1993), Discussion of "Obsession and/or obsessionality: Perspectives on a psychoanalytic treatment" by W. E. Spear. *Contemp. Psychoanal.*, 29:90–101.

――― (1995), Introduction to "Attachment, detachment, and psychoanalytic therapy" by D. E. Schecter. In: *Pioneers of Interpersonal Psychoanalysis*, ed. D. B. Stern, C. Mann, S. Kantor & G. Schlesinger. Hillsdale, NJ: The Analytic Press, pp. 169–174.

――― (1996), Discussion of "The Psychoanalytic Situation" by Leo Stone. *J. Clin. Psychoanal.*, 5:267–282.

――― (1997), Commentary on L. Friedman's "Ferrum, ignis, and medicina: Return to the crucible." *J. Amer. Psychoanal. Assn.*, 45:36–40.

Broughton, R. J. (1968), Sleep disorders: Disorders of arousal? *Science*, 159:1070–1078.

Brown, R. (1965), The principle of consistency. *Social Psychology*. New York: Free Press, pp. 549–609.

Bruner, J. (1990), *Acts of Meaning*. Cambridge, MA: Harvard University Press.

Buie, D. H., Jr. & Adler, G. (1973), The uses of confrontation in the psychotherapy of borderline cases. In: *Confrontation in Psychotherapy*, ed. G. Adler & P. G. Myerson. New York: Science House.

Caligor, L. (1996), The clinical use of the dream in interpersonal psychoanalysis. *Psychoanal. Dial.*, 6:793–811.

Carroll, L. (1871), Through the looking-glass, and what Alice found there. In: *The Annotated Alice*, ed. M. Gardner. New York: Bramhall House, 1960, pp. 171–345.

Carroll, P. V. (1937), Shadow and substance. In: *Five Great Modern Irish Plays*. New York: Modern Library, 1941, pp. 217–232.

Castaneda, C. (1968), *The Teachings of Don Juan: A Yaqui Way of Knowledge*. New York: Ballantine Books.

――― (1971), *A Separate Reality: Further Conversations with Don Juan*. New York: Simon & Schuster.

――― (1972), *Journey to Ixtlan*. New York: Simon & Schuster.

――― (1974), *Tales of Power*. New York: Pocket Books.

—— (1977), *The Second Ring of Power*. New York: Pocket Books.

—— (1981), *The Eagle's Gift*. New York: Simon & Schuster.

Chrzanowski, G. (1977), *The Interpersonal Approach to Psychoanalysis*. New York: Gardner Press.

—— Schecter, D. E. & Kovar, L. (1978), Sullivan's concept of the malevolent transformation. *Contemp. Psychoanal.*, 14:405–423.

Chu, J. A. (1991), The repetition compulsion revisited: Reliving dissociated trauma. *Psychotherapy*, 28:327–332.

Coates, S. W. & Moore, M. S. (1997), The complexity of early trauma: Representation and transformation. *Psychoanal. Inq.*, 17:286–311.

Crowley, R. M. (1973), Sullivan's concept of unique individuality. *Contemp. Psychoanal.*, 9:130–133.

—— (1975), Bone and Sullivan. *Contemp. Psychoanal.*, 11:66–74.

—— (1978), Are being simply human and uniqueness opposed? *Contemp. Psychoanal.*, 14:135–139.

D'Aulaire, I. & D'Aulaire, E. P. (1962), *D'Aulaire's Book of Greek Myths*. New York: Doubleday.

Davies, J. M. (1992), Dissociation processes and transference-countertransference paradigms in the psychoanalytically oriented treatment of adult survivors of sexual abuse. *Psychoanal. Dial.*, 2:5–36.

—— & Frawley, M. G. (1994), *Treating the Adult Survivor of Childhood Sexual Abuse*. New York: Basic Books.

de Monchaux, C. (1978), Dreaming and the organizing function of the ego. *Internat. J. Psycho-Anal.*, 59:443–453.

Dennett, D. (1991), *Consciousness Explained*. London: Allen Lane.

Dickes, R. (1965), The defensive function of an altered state of consciousness: A hypnoid state. *J. Amer. Psychoanal. Assn.*, 13:356–403.

Duncan, D. (1989), The flow of interpretation. *Internat. J. Psycho-Anal.*, 70:693–700.

Duncker, P. (1996), *Hallucinating Foucault*. Hopewell, NJ: Ecco Press.

Dupont, J., ed. (1988), *The Clinical Diary of Sándor Ferenczi*. Cambridge, MA: Harvard University Press.

—— (1993), Michael Balint: Analysand, pupil, friend, and successor to Sándor Ferenczi. In: *The Legacy of Sándor Ferenczi*, ed. L. Aron & A. Harris. Hillsdale, NJ: The Analytic Press.

Easson, W. M. (1973), The earliest ego development, primitive memory traces, and the Isakower phenomenon. *Psychoanal. Quart.*, 42:60–72.

Edel, L. (1980), *Bloomsbury: A House of Lions*. New York: Avon Books.

Ellenberger, H. F. (1977), L'histoire de 'Emmy von N.' *L'Évolution Psychiatrique*, 42:519–540.

Emde, R. N., Gaensbaure, T. J. & Harmon, R. J. (1976), Emotional expression in infancy: A biobehavioral study. *Psychological Issues, 10*, Monogr. 37. New York: International Universities Press.

Emerson, R. W. (1851), Borrowing. In: *What Cheer*, ed. D. McCord. New York: Coward-McCann, 1945, p. 321.

Epstein, L. & Feiner, A. H. (1979), *Countertransference*. New York: Aronson.

Fairbairn, W. R. D. (1940), Schizoid factors in the personality. In: *Psychoanalytic Studies of the Personality*. London: Routledge & Kegan Paul, 1952, pp. 3–27.

———— (1941), A revised psychopathology of the psychoses and psychoneuroses. In: *Psychoanalytic Studies of the Personality*. London: Routledge & Kegan Paul, 1952, pp. 28–58.

———— (1944), Endopsychic structure considered in terms of object-relationships. In *Psychoanalytic Studies of the Personality*. London: Routledge & Kegan Paul, 1952, pp. 82–132.

———— (1952), *Psychoanalytic Studies of the Personality*. London: Routledge & Kegan Paul.

Feiner, A. H. (1979), Countertransference and the anxiety of influence. In: *Countertransference*, ed. L. Epstein & A. H. Feiner. New York: Aronson, pp. 105–128.

———— (1982), Comments on the difficult patient: Some transference-countertransference issues. *Contemp. Psychoanal.*, 18:397–411.

Fenichel, O. (1945), *The Psychoanalytic Theory of Neurosis*. New York: Norton.

Ferenczi, S. (1909), Introjection and transference. *First Contributions to Psycho-Analysis*, New York: Brunner/Mazel, 1980, pp. 35–93.

———— (1913), Stages in the development of the sense of reality. In: *First Contributions to Psycho-Analysis*. New York: Brunner/Mazel, 1980, pp. 213–239.

———— (1928), The elasticity of psychoanalytic technique. In: *Final Contributions to the Problems and Methods of Psychoanalysis*, ed. M. Balint. New York: Brunner/Mazel, 1980, pp. 87–101.

———— (1930a), Notes and fragments II. In: *Final Contributions to the Problems and Methods of Psycho-Analysis*, ed. M. Balint. New York: Brunner/Mazel, 1980, pp. 219–231.

———— (1930b), The principle of relaxation and neo-catharsis. In: *Final Contributions to the Problems and Methods of Psychoanalysis*, ed. M. Balint. New York: Brunner/Mazel, 1980, pp. 108–125.

———— (1931), Child analysis in the analysis of adults. In: *Final Contributions to the Problems and Methods of Psychoanalysis*, ed. M. Balint. New York: Brunner/Mazel, 1980, pp. 126–142.

———— (1933), Confusion of tongues between adults and the child: The language of tenderness and passion. In: *Final Contributions to the Problems and Methods of Psychoanalysis*, ed. M. Balint. New York: Brunner/Mazel, 1980, pp. 156–167.

Ferguson, M. (1990), Mirroring processes, hypnotic processes, and multiple personality. *Psychoanal. & Contemp. Thought*, 13:417–450.

Festinger, L. (1957), *A Theory of Cognitive Dissonance*. New York: Row, Peterson.

Field, E. (1883), Wynken, Blynken, and Nod. In: *The Oxford Book of Children's Verse in America*, ed. D. Hall. New York: Oxford University Press, 1985, pp. 160–161.

Fink, G. (1967), Analysis of the Isakower phenomenon. *J. Amer. Psychoanal. Assn.*, 15:231–293.

Fisher, C., Byrne, J. V., Edwards, A. & Kahn, E. (1970), A psychophysiological study of nightmares. *J. Amer. Psychoanal. Assn.*, 18:747–782.

Fisher, C., Kahn, E., Edwards, A. & Davis, D. (1974), A psychophysiological study of nightmares and night terrors. In: *Psychoanalysis and Contemporary Science, Vol. 3*, ed. L. Goldberger & V. Rosen. New York: International Universities Press, pp. 317–398.

Fonagy, P. (1991), Thinking about thinking: Some clinical and theoretical considerations in the treatment of a borderline patient. *Internat. J. Psycho-Anal.*, 72:639–656.

————— & Moran, G. S. (1991), Understanding psychic change in child psychoanalysis. *Internat. J. Psycho-Anal.*, 72:15–22.

————— & Target, M. (1995a), Understanding the violent patient: The use of the body and the role of the father. *Internat. J. Psycho-Anal.*, 76:487–501.

————— & ————— (1995b), Dissociation and trauma. *Current Opinion in Psychiat.*, 8:161–166.

————— & ————— (1996), Playing with reality: I. Theory of mind and the normal development of psychic reality. *Internat. J. Psycho-Anal.*, 77:217–233.

Foster, R. P. (1996), The bilingual self: Duet in two voices. *Psychoanal. Dial.*, 6:99–122.

Fraiberg, S. (1969), Libidinal object constancy and mental representation. *The Psychoanalytic Study of the Child*, 24:9–47. New York: International Universities Press.

Frankel, J. B. (1998), The play's the thing: How the essential processes of therapy are seen most clearly in child therapy. *Psychoanal. Dial.*, 8:149–182.

Franklin, G. (1990), The multiple meanings of neutrality. *J. Amer. Psychoanal. Assn.*, 38:195–220.

Freud, A. (1946), *The Ego and the Mechanisms of Defense.* New York: International Universities Press.

————— (1969), Discussion of John Bowlby's work. In: *The Writings of Anna Freud, Vol. 5.* New York: International Universities Press.

Freud, S. (1895), Project for a scientific psychology. *Standard Edition*, 1:295–397. London: Hogarth Press, 1966.

————— (1900), The interpretation of dreams. *Standard Edition*, 4 & 5. London: Hogarth Press, 1953.

————— (1910), Five lectures on psycho-analysis. *Standard Edition*, 11:9–55. London: Hogarth Press, 1957.

————— (1911), Formulations on the two principles of mental functioning. *Standard Edition*, 12:213–226. London: Hogarth Press, 1958.

————— (1912), Recommendations to physicians practicing psychoanalysis. *Standard Edition*, 12:109–120. London: Hogarth Press, 1961.

————— (1913a), Totem and taboo. *Standard Edition*, 13:1–161. London: Hogarth Press, 1955.

————— (1913b), On beginning the treatment (Further recommendations on the technique of psycho-analysis, I). *Standard Edition*, 12:121–144. London: Hogarth Press, 1958.

———— (1914), On narcissism: An introduction. *Standard Edition*, 14:67–102. London: Hogarth Press, 1957.

———— (1915), The unconscious. *Standard Edition*, 14:159–215. London: Hogarth Press, 1957.

———— (1923), The ego and the id. *Standard Edition*, 19:3–66. London: Hogarth Press, 1961.

———— (1925), Negation. *Standard Edition*, 19:235–239. London: Hogarth Press, 1961.

———— (1926), Inhibitions, symptoms and anxiety. *Standard Edition*, 20:87–172. London: Hogarth Press, 1959.

Friedman, L. (1973), How real is the realistic ego in psychotherapy? *Arch. Gen. Psychiat.*, 28:377–383.

———— (1978), Trends in the psychoanalytic theory of treatment. *Psychoanal. Quart.*, 47:524–567.

———— (1983), Discussion: Piaget and psychoanalysis, by A. Tenzer. *Contemp. Psychoanal.*, 19:339–348.

———— (1986), Kohut's testament. *Psychoanal. Inq.*, 6:321–347.

———— (1988), *The Anatomy of Psychotherapy*. Hillsdale, NJ: The Analytic Press.

———— (1994), The objective truth controversy: How does it affect tomorrow's analysts? *Internat. Fed. Psychoanal. Educ. Newsltr.*, 3:7–14.

Friedman, L. J. (1975), Current psychoanalytic object relations theory and its clinical implications. *Internat. J. Psycho-Anal.*, 56:137–146.

Fromm, E. (1941), *Escape from Freedom*. New York: Rinehart.

———— (1947), *Man for Himself*. New York: Rinehart.

———— (1956), *The Sane Society*. London: Routledge & Kegan Paul.

———— (1964), *The Heart of Man: Its Genius for Good and Evil*. New York: Harper & Row.

Gabbard, G. O. (1992), Commentary on "Dissociative processes and transference-countertransference paradigms . . ." by J. Davies & M. G. Frawley. *Psychoanal. Dial.*, 2:37–47.

Garma, A. (1955), Vicissitudes of the dream screen and the Isakower phenomenon. *Psychoanal. Quart.*, 24:369–383.

Gedo, J. (1977), Notes on the psychoanalytic management of archaic transferences. *J. Amer. Psychoanal. Assn.*, 25:787–803.

Ghent, E. (1989), Credo: The dialectics of one-person and two-person psychologies. *Contemp. Psychoanal.*, 25:169–211.

———— (1990), Masochism, submission, surrender. *Contemp. Psychoanal.*, 26:108–136.

———— (1992), Paradox and process. *Psychoanal. Dial.*, 2:135–159.

———— ((1994), Empathy: Whence and whither? *Psychoanal. Dial.*, 4:473–486.

———— (1995), Interaction in the psychoanalytic situation. *Psychoanal. Dial.*, 5:479–491.

Gill, M. M. (1979), The analysis of the transference. *J. Amer. Psychoanal. Assn.*, 27 (supplement):263–288.

———— (1984), Psychoanalysis and psychotherapy: A revision. *Internat. Rev. Psycho-Anal.*, 11:161–179.

Ginot, E. (1997), The analyst's use of self, self-disclosure, and enhanced integration. *Psychoanal. Psychol.*, 14:365–381.
Giovacchini, P. (1985), The unreasonable patient: A borderline character disorder. *Psychoanal. Pract.*, 1:5–24.
Gitelson, M. (1962), On the curative factors in the first phase of analysis. In: *Psychoanalysis: Science and Profession*. New York: International Universities Press, 1973, pp. 311–341.
Glatzer, H. T. & Evans, W. N. (1977), On Guntrip's analysis with Fairbairn and Winnicott. *Internat. J. Psychoanal. Psychother.*, 6:81–98.
Gleick, J. (1987), *Chaos*. New York: Viking.
Goldberg, A. (1986), Reply to P. M. Bromberg's discussion of "The wishy-washy personality" by A. Goldberg. *Contemp. Psychoanal.*, 22:387–388.
Goldberg, P. (1987), The role of distractions in the maintenance of dissociative mental states. *Internat. J. Psycho-Anal.*, 68:511–524.
———— (1995), "Successful" dissociation, pseudovitality, and inauthentic use of the senses. *Psychoanal. Dial.*, 5:493–510.
Golding, W. (1955), *Lord of the Flies*. New York: Coward-McCann.
Goleman, D. (1985), Freud's mind: New details revealed in documents. *The New York Times*, November 12, pp. C1–C3.
Goodman, A. (1992), Empathy and inquiry: Integrating empathic mirroring in an interpersonal framework. *Contemp. Psychoanal.*, 28:631–646.
Gottlieb, R. (1997), Does the mind fall apart in multiple personality disorder? Some proposals based on a psychoanalytic case. *J. Amer. Psychoanal. Assn.*, 45:907–932.
Grand, S. (1997), The paradox of innocence: Dissociative "adhesive" states in perpetrators of incest. *Psychoanal. Dial.*, 7:465–490.
Gray, S. H. (1985), "China" as a symbol for vagina. *Psychoanal. Quart.*, 54:620–623.
Greenberg, J. R. (1981), Prescription or description: The therapeutic action of psychoanalysis. *Contemp. Psychoanal.*, 17:239–257.
———— (1986), Theoretical models and the analyst's neutrality. *Contemp. Psychoanal.*, 22:87–106.
———— (1991a), Countertransference and reality. *Psychoanal. Dial.*, 1:52–73.
———— (1991b), Psychoanalytic interaction. Presented at winter meeting of the American Psychoanalytic Association, New York City.
———— & Mitchell, S. A. (1983), *Object Relations in Psychoanalytic Theory*. Cambridge, MA: Harvard University Press.
Greenson, R. R. (1974), Loving, hating, and indifference toward the patient. *Internat. Rev. Psycho-Anal.*, 1:259–266.
Grotstein, J. S. (1979), Who is the dreamer who dreams the dream, and who is the dreamer who understands it? *Contemp. Psychoanal.*, 15:407–453.
———— (1995), Projective identification reappraised. *Contemp. Psychoanal.*, 31:479–511.
Guntrip, H. J. S. (1961a), *Personality Structure and Human Interaction: The Developing Synthesis of Psycho-dynamic Theory*. New York: International Universities Press.

———— (1961b), The schizoid problem, regression and the struggle to preserve an ego. In: *Schizoid Phenomena, Object Relations and the Self.* New York: International Universities Press, 1969, pp. 49–86.

———— (1969), *Schizoid Phenomena, Object Relations and the Self.* New York: International Universities Press.

———— (1971), *Psychoanalytic Theory, Therapy, and the Self.* New York: Basic Books.

Haley, J. (1969), The art of psychoanalysis. In: *The Power Tactics of Jesus Christ and Other Essays.* New York: Avon Books, pp. 9–26.

Harris, A. (1992), Dialogues as transitional space: A rapprochement of psychoanalysis and developmental psycholinguistics. In: *Relational Perspectives in Psychoanalysis*, ed. N. J. Skolnick & S. C. Warshaw. Hillsdale, NJ: The Analytic Press, pp. 119–145.

———— (1994), Gender practices and speech practices: Towards a model of dialogical and relational selves. Presented at spring meeting of Division of Psychoanalysis, American Psychological Association, Washington, DC.

———— (1995), Symposium on psychoanalysis and linguistics: Introduction. *Psychoanal. Dial.*, 5:615–618.

———— (1996), The conceptual power of multiplicity. *Contemp. Psychoanal.*, 32:537–552.

Havens, L. L. (1973), *Approaches to the Mind.* Boston: Little, Brown and Company.

———— (1976), *Participant Observation.* New York: Aronson.

Heilbrunn, G. (1953), Fusion of the Isakower phenomenon with the dream screen. *Psychoanal. Quart.*, 22:200–204.

Held-Weiss, R. (1984), The interpersonal tradition and its development: Some implications for training. *Contemp. Psychoanal.*, 20:344–362.

Hermans, H. J. M., Kempen, H. J. G. & van Loon, R. J. P. (1992), The dialogical self: Beyond individualism and rationalism. *Amer. Psychol.*, 47:23–33.

Hirschmuller, A. (1978), *The Life and Work of Josef Breuer.* New York: New York University Press.

Hoffmann, I. Z. (1983), The patient as interpreter of the analyst's experience. *Contemp. Psychoanal.*, 19:389–422.

———— (1991), Discussion: Toward a social-constructivist view of the psychoanalytic situation. *Psychoanal. Dial.*, 1:74–105.

———— (1994), Dialectical thinking and therapeutic action in the psychoanalytic process. *Psychoanal. Quart.*, 63:187–218.

Horner, A. (1979), *Object Relations and the Developing Ego in Therapy.* New York: Aronson.

Hughes, L. (1941), Evil. In: *The Collected Poems of Langston Hughes*, ed. A. Rampersad. New York: Knopf, p. 227.

Isakower, O. (1938), A contribution to the patho-psychology of phenomena associated with falling asleep. *Internat. J. Psycho-Anal.*, 19:331–345.

James, H. (1875), *Roderick Hudson.* New York: Penguin Books, 1969.

Johnson, B. (1977), The frame of reference: Poe, Lacan, Derrida. *Yale French Studies*, 55/56:457–505.

Kaiser, H. (1965), The universal symptom of the psychoneuroses: A search for the conditions of effective psychotherapy. In: *Effective Psychotherapy*, ed. L. B. Fierman. New York: Free Press, pp. 14–171.

Kamenetz, R. (1994), *The Jew in the Lotus*. San Francisco: HarperCollins.

Kennedy, R. (1996), Aspects of consciousness: One voice or many? *Psychoanal. Dial.*, 6:73–96.

Kernberg, O. F. (1966), Structural derivatives of object relationships. *Internat. J. Psycho-Anal.*, 47:236–253.

—— (1975), *Borderline Conditions and Pathological Narcissism*. New York: Aronson.

—— (1991), Transference regression and psychoanalytic technique with infantile personalities. *Internat. J. Psycho-Anal.*, 72:189–200.

Kerr, J. (1993), *A Most Dangerous Method*. New York: Knopf.

Khan, M. (1971), "To hear with the eyes": Clinical notes on body as subject and object. In: *The Privacy of the Self*. New York: International Universities Press, 1974, pp. 234–250.

Kirmayer, L. J. (1994), Pacing the void: Social and cultural dimensions of dissociation. In: *Dissociation: Culture, Mind, and Body*, ed. D. Spiegel. Washington, DC: American Psychiatric Press, pp. 91–122.

Kirstein, L. (1969), Afterward. In: *W. Eugene Smith: His Photographs and Notes*. New York: Aperture Press.

Klenbort, I. (1978), Another look at Sullivan's concept of individuality. *Contemp. Psychoanal.*, 14:125–135.

Kohut, H. (1966), Forms and transformations of narcissism. *J. Amer. Psychoanal. Assn.*, 14:243–272.

—— (1971), *The Analysis of the Self*. New York: International Universities Press.

—— (1972), Thoughts on narcissism and narcissistic rage. *The Psychoanalytic Study of the Child*, 27:360–400, New York: Quadrangle.

—— (1977), *The Restoration of the Self*. New York: International Universities Press.

Kramer, P. (1990), Così fan tutti. *The Psychiatric Times*, April, pp. 4–6.

Krystal, J. H., Bennett, A. L., Bremner, J. D., Southwick, S. M. & Charney, D. S. (1995), Toward a cognitive neuroscience of dissociation and altered memory functions in post-traumatic stress disorder. In: *Neurobiological and Clinical Consequences of Stress: From Normal Adaptation to PTSD*, ed. M. J. Friedman, D. S. Charney & A. Y. Deutch. Philadelphia: Lippincott-Raven, pp. 239–269.

Kvarnes, R. G. & Parloff, G. H., eds. (1976), *A Harry Stack Sullivan Case Seminar*. New York: Norton.

Lacan, J. (1966), *Ecrits*. Paris: Seuil.

Laing, R. D. (1960), *The Divided Self*. London: Tavistock.

—— (1962a), Confirmation and disconfirmation. In: *The Self and Others*. Chicago: Quadrangle, pp. 88–97.

———— (1962b), *The Self and Others.* Chicago: Quadrangle.

———— (1967), *The Politics of Experience.* New York: Pantheon.

Lamb, C. (1822), A dissertation upon roast pig. In: *Anthology of Romanticism,* 3rd ed., ed. E. Bernbaum. New York: Ronald Press, 1948, pp. 385–388.

Lampl-de Groot, J. (1981), Notes on "multiple personality." *Psychoanal. Quart.,* 50:614–624.

Langan, R. (1997), On free-floating attention. *Psychoanal. Dial.,* 7:819–839.

Lasch, C. (1979), *The Culture of Narcissism.* New York: Norton.

Laub, D. & Auerhahn, N. C. (1989), Failed empathy—A central theme in the survivor's Holocaust experience. *Psychoanal. Psychol.,* 6:377–400.

———— (1993), Knowing and not knowing massive psychic trauma: Forms of traumatic memory. *Internat. J. Psycho-Anal.,* 74:287–302.

Lerner, M. (1990), *Wrestling with the Angel.* New York: Norton.

Levenson, E. A. (1972), *The Fallacy of Understanding.* New York: Basic Books.

———— (1976a), The aesthetics of termination. *Contemp. Psychoanal.,* 12:338–342.

———— (1976b), A holographic model of psychoanalytic change. *Contemp. Psychoanal.,* 12:1–20.

———— (1978), Two essays in psychoanalytical psychology—I. Psychoanalysis: Cure or persuasion. *Contemp. Psychoanal.,* 14:1–30.

———— (1982), Follow the fox. *Contemp. Psychoanal.,* 18:1–15.

———— (1983), *The Ambiguity of Change.* New York: Basic Books.

———— (1988), Real frogs in imaginary gardens: Fact and fantasy in psychoanalysis. *Psychoanal. Inq.,* 8:552–567.

———— (1992), Mistakes, errors, and oversights. *Contemp. Psychoanal.,* 28:555–571.

Levi, A. (1971), "We." *Contemp. Psychoanal.,* 7:181–188.

Lewin, B. D. (1946), Sleep, the mouth, and the dream screen. *Psychoanal. Quart.,* 15:419–434.

———— (1948), Inferences from the dream screen. *Internat. J. Psycho-Anal.,* 29:224–231.

———— (1950), *The Psychoanalysis of Elation.* New York: Norton.

———— (1952), Phobic symptoms and dream interpretation. *Psychoanal. Quart.,* 21:295–322.

———— (1953), Reconsideration of the dream screen. *Psychoanal. Quart.,* 22:174–199.

Lewis, C. S. (1956), *Till We Have Faces: A Myth Retold.* New York: Harcourt Brace Jovanovich.

Lightman, A. (1993), *Einstein's Dreams.* New York: Pantheon Books.

Lionells, M. (1986), A reevaluation of hysterical relatedness. *Contemp. Psychoanal.,* 22:570–597.

Loevinger, J. (1973), Ego development: Syllabus for a course. In: *Psychoanalysis and Contemporary Science, Vol. II,* ed. B. B. Rubinstein. New York: Macmillan, pp. 77–98.

———— & Wessler, R. (1970), *Measuring Ego Development, Vol. I.* San Francisco: Jossey-Bass.

Loewald, H. (1960), On the therapeutic action of psychoanalysis. *Internat. J. Psycho-Anal.*, 41:16–33.

———— (1972), The experience of time. *The Psychoanalytic Study of the Child*, 27:401–410. New York: Quadrangle.

———— (1979), The waning of the Oedipus complex. *J. Amer. Psychoanal. Assn.*, 27:751–775.

Loewenstein, R. J. & Ross, D. R. (1992), Multiple personality and psychoanalysis: An introduction. *Psychoanal. Inq.*, 12:3–48.

Looker, T. (1998), "Mama, why don't your feet touch the ground?" Staying with the body and the healing moment in psychoanalysis. In: *Relational Perspectives on the Body: Psychoanalytic Theory and Practice*, ed. L. Aron & F. S. Anderson. Hillsdale, NJ: The Analytic Press, pp. 237–262.

Lyon, K. A. (1992), Shattered mirror: A fragment of the treatment of a patient with multiple personality disorder. *Psychoanal. Inq.*, 12:71–94.

Mahler, M. (1968), *On Human Symbiosis and the Vicissitudes of Individuation.* New York: International Universities Press.

———— (1972), On the first three subphases of the separation-individuation process. *Internat. J. Psycho-Anal.*, 53:333–338.

———— Pine, F. & Bergman, A. (1975), *The Psychological Birth of the Human Infant: Symbiosis and Individuation.* New York: Basic Books.

Marcuse, J. J. (submitted), And what does this bring to mind? Reflections on techniques of dream interpretation.

Marin, P. (1975), The new narcissism. *Harper's Magazine*, October, pp. 5–26.

Marmer, S. S. (1980), Psychoanalysis of multiple personality. *Internat. J. Psycho-Anal.*, 61:439–459.

———— (1991), Multiple personality disorder: A psychoanalytic perspective. *Psychiat. Clin. N. Amer.*, 14:677–693.

McDougall, J. M. (1987), Who is saying what to whom? An eclectic perspective. *Psychoanal. Inq.*, 7:223–232.

Mead, G. H. (1934), *Mind, Self and Society.* Chicago: The University of Chicago Press.

Merleau-Ponty, M. (1942), *The Structure of Behavior.* Boston: Beacon Press, 1963.

Mitchell, S. A. (1988), *Relational Concepts in Psychoanalysis: An Integration.* New York: Harvard University Press.

———— (1991), Contemporary perspectives on self: Toward an integration. *Psychoanal. Dial.*, 1:121–147.

———— (1993), *Hope and Dread in Psychoanalysis.* New York: Basic Books.

———— (1997a), Psychoanalysis and the degradation of romance. *Psychoanal. Dial.*, 7:23–41.

———— (1997b), *Influence and Autonomy in Psychoanalysis.* Hillsdale, NJ: The Analytic Press.

Mitrani, J. L. (1994), On adhesive pseudo–object relations, Part I. *Contemp. Psychoanal.*, 30:348–366.

———— (1995), On adhesive pseudo–object relations, Part II. *Contemp. Psychoanal.*, 31:140–165.

Modell, A. (1976), The "holding environment" and the therapeutic action of psychoanalysis. *J. Amer. Psychoanal. Assn.*, 24:285–308.

―――― (1978), The conceptualization of the therapeutic action of psychoanalysis: The action of the holding environment. *Bull. Menn. Clin.*, 42:493–504.

―――― (1986), The missing elements in Kohut's cure. *Psychoanal. Inq.*, 6:367–385.

Moore, B. E. & Fine, B. D., eds. (1968), *A Glossary of Psychoanalytic Terms and Concepts*, 2nd ed., New York: American Psychoanalytic Association.

―――― (1990), *Psychoanalytic Terms and Concepts*, 3rd ed. New Haven, CT: American Psychoanalytic Association & Yale University Press.

Nabokov, V. (1920), Sounds. *The New Yorker*, August 14, 1995.

Nesse, R. M. (1991), What good is feeling bad?: The evolutionary benefits of psychic pain. *The Sciences*, Nov./Dec.:30–37.

Ogden, T. H. (1985), On potential space. *Internat. J. Psycho-Anal.*, 66:129–141.

―――― (1986), *The Matrix of the Mind*. Northvale, NJ: Aronson.

―――― (1989), *The Primitive Edge of Experience*. Northvale, NJ: Aronson.

―――― (1991), An interview with Thomas Ogden. *Psychoanal. Dial.*, 1:361–376.

―――― (1994), The analytic third: Working with intersubjective clinical facts. *Internat. J. Psycho-Anal.*, 75:3–19.

Ornstein, P. H. & Ornstein, A. (1980), Formulating interpretations in clinical psychoanalysis. *Internat. J. Psycho-Anal.*, 61:203–211.

Osborne, J. W. & Baldwin, J. R. (1982), Psychotherapy: From one state of illusion to another. *Psychotherapy*, 19:266–275.

Parker, R. B. (1983), *The Widening Gyre: A Spencer Novel*. New York: Dell.

Peterson, J. (1993), Reply to Van der Hart/Brown article. *Dissociation*, 6:74–75.

Piaget, J. (1932), *The Language and Thought of the Child*. New York: Meridian, 1955.

―――― (1936), *The Origins of Intelligence in Children*, trans. M. Cook. New York: International Universities Press, 1952.

―――― (1969), *The Psychology of the Child*. New York: Basic Books.

Pine, F. (1979), On the expansion of the affect array: A developmental description. *Bull. Menn. Clin.*, 43:79–95.

Pizer, B. (in press), Negotiating analytic holding: Discussion of P. Casement's "Analytic holding under pressure." *Psychoanal. Inq.*, Vol. 20, No. 1.

Pizer, S. A. (1992), The negotiation of paradox in the analytic process. *Psychoanal. Dial.*, 2:215–240.

―――― (1996a), The distributed self: Introduction to symposium on "The multiplicity of self and analytic technique." *Contemp. Psychoanal.*, 32:499–507.

―――― (1996b), Negotiating potential space: Illusion, play, metaphor, and the subjunctive. *Psychoanal. Dial.*, 6:689–712.

Plato (4th cent. B. C.), Apology (tr. B. Jowett). In: *The Dialogues of Plato*. New York: Bantam Books, 1986.

Putnam, F. (1988), The switch process in multiple personality disorder and other state-change disorders. *Dissociation*, 1:24–32.

——— (1992), Discussion: Are alter personalities fragments or figments? *Psychoanal. Inq.*, 12:95–111.

Rangell, L. (1979), Contemporary issues in the theory of therapy. *J. Amer. Psychoanal. Assn.*, 27(supplement):81–112.

Reik, T. (1936), *Surprise and the Psycho-Analyst*. London: Kegan Paul.

Reis, B. E. (1993), Toward a psychoanalytic understanding of multiple personality disorder. *Bull. Menn. Clin.*, 57:309–318.

——— (1995), Time as the missing dimension in traumatic memory and dissociative subjectivity. In: *Sexual Abuse Recalled*, ed. J. L. Alpert. Northvale, NJ: Aronson.

Ricoeur, P. (1986), The self in psychoanalysis and in phenomenological philosophy. *Psychoanal. Inq.*, 6:437–458.

Rivera, M. (1989), Linking the psychological and the social: Feminism, poststructuralism, and multiple personality. *Dissociation*, 2:24–31.

Roth, S. (1992), Discussion: A psychoanalyst's perspective on multiple personality disorder. *Psychoanal. Inq.*, 12:112–123.

Rothstein, A. (1980), *The Narcissistic Pursuit of Perfection*. New York: International Universities Press.

——— (1982), The implications of early psychopathology for the analyzability of narcissistic personality disorders. *Internat. J. Psycho-Anal.*, 63:177–188.

Russell, P. L. (1993), Discussion of Peter Shabad's "Resentment, indignation, entitlement: The transformation of unconscious wish into need." *Psychoanal. Dial.*, 3:515–522.

Rycroft, C. (1951), A contribution to the study of the dream screen. *Internat. J. Psycho-Anal.*, 32:178–184.

——— (1962), Beyond the reality principle. In: *Imagination and Reality*. London: Marcsfield Library, 1968, pp. 102–113.

Sacks, O. (1992), The last hippie. *The New York Review*, March 26, pp. 53–62.

Sander, L. (1977), The regulation of exchange in the infant caretaker system and some aspects of the context-content relationship. In: *Interaction, Conservation, and the Development of Language*, ed. M. Lewis & L. Rosenblum. New York: Wiley, pp. 133–156.

Sandler, A-M. (1975), Comments on the significance of Piaget's work for psychoanalysis. *Internat. Rev. Psycho-Anal.*, 2:365–377.

——— (1977), Beyond eight month anxiety. *Internat. J. Psycho-Anal.*, 58:195–208.

Sandler, J. & Sandler, A-M. (1978), On the development of object relationships and affects. *Internat. J. Psycho-Anal.*, 59:285–296.

Schafer, R. (1968), *Aspects of Internalization*. New York: International Universities Press.

——— (1976), *A New Language for Psychoanalysis*. New Haven, CT: Yale University Press.

——— (1983), *The Analytic Attitude*. New York: Basic Books.

Schecter, D. E. (1978a), Attachment, detachment, and psychoanalytic therapy. In: *Interpersonal Psychoanalysis: New Directions*, ed. E. G. Witenberg. New York: Gardner Press, pp. 81–104.

——— (1978b), Malevolent transformation: Some clinical and developmental notes. *Contemp. Psychoanal.*, 14:414–418.

——— (1980), Early developmental roots of anxiety. *J. Amer. Acad. Psychoanal.*, 8:539–554.

Schwaber, E. (1983), Psychoanalytic listening and psychic reality. *Internat. Rev. Psycho-Anal.*, 10:379–392.

Schwartz, H. L. (1994), From dissociation to negotiation: A relational psychoanalytic perspective on multiple personality disorder. *Psychoanal. Psychol.*, 11:189–231.

Searles, H. F. (1959), The effort to drive the other person crazy: An element in the aetiology and psychotherapy of schizophrenia. In: *Collected Papers on Schizophrenia and Related Subjects*. New York: International Universities Press, 1965, pp. 254–283.

——— (1977), Dual- and multiple-identity processes in borderline ego functioning. In: *Borderline Personality Disorders*, ed. P. Hartocollis. New York: International Universities Press, pp. 441–455.

Settlage, C. F. (1977), The psychoanalytic understanding of narcissistic and borderline personality disorders. *J. Amer. Psychoanal. Assn.*, 25:805–834.

Shakespeare, W. (1599–1601), Hamlet, Prince of Denmark. In: *The Complete Plays and Poems of William Shakespeare*, ed. W. A. Neilson & C. J. Hill. Cambridge, MA: Riverside, 1942, pp. 1043–1092.

Shapiro, D. (1965), *Neurotic Styles*. New York: Basic Books.

Shelley, M. (1818), *Frankenstein*. New York: Bantam, 1991.

Shengold, L. (1989), *Soul Murder*. New Haven, CT: Yale University Press.

——— (1992), Commentary on "Dissociative processes and transference-countertransference paradigms . . ." by J. Davies & M. G. Frawley. *Psychoanal. Dial.*, 2:49–59.

Silberer, H. (1909), A method of producing and observing symbolic hallucinations. In: *Organization and Pathology of Thought*, ed. D. Rapaport. New York: Columbia University Press, 1951, pp. 195–207.

Slavin, M. O. & Kriegman, D. (1992), *The Adaptive Design of the Human Psyche*. New York: Guilford.

Slochower, J. A. (1994), The evolution of object usage and the holding environment. *Contemp. Psychoanal.*, 30:135–151.

Smith, B. L. (1989), Of many minds: A contribution on the dynamics of multiple personality. In: *The Facilitating Environment*, ed. M. G. Fromm & B. L. Smith. Madison, CT: International Universities Press, pp. 424–458.

Smith, H. F. (1995), Analytic listening and the experience of surprise. *Internat. J. Psycho-Anal.*, 76:67–78.

Sorenson, R. L. (1994), Therapists' (and their therapists') God representations in clinical practice. *J. Psychol. & Theol.*, 22:325–344.

Sperling, O. E. (1957), A psychoanalytic study of hypnogogic hallucinations. *J. Amer. Psychoanal. Assn.*, 5:115–123.

——— (1961), Variety and analyzability of hypnogogic hallucinations and dreams. *Internat. J. Psycho-Anal.*, 42:216–223.

Spillius, E. B. & Feldman, M., eds. (1989), *Psychic Equilibrium and Psychic Change: Selected Papers of Betty Joseph*. London: Tavistock/Routledge.
Spruiell, V. (1983), The rules and frames of the psychoanalytic situation. *Psychoanal. Quart.*, 52:1–33.
Stanton, A. H. (1978), The significance of ego interpretive states in insight-directed psychotherapy. *Psychiatry*, 41:129–140.
Stein, G. (1937), *Everybody's Autobiography*. Cambridge, MA: Exact Change, 1993.
Steingart, I. (1969), On self, character, and the development of a psychic apparatus. *The Psychoanalytic Study of the Child*, 24:271–303. New York: International Universities Press.
Stern, D. B. (1983), Unformulated experience. *Contemp. Psychoanal.*, 19:71–99.
———— (1996), Dissociation and constructivism. *Psychoanal. Dial.*, 6:251–266.
———— (1997), *Unformulated Experience: From Dissociation to Imagination in Psychoanalysis*. Hillsdale, NJ: The Analytic Press.
Stern, D. N. (1985), *The Interpersonal World of the Infant: A View from Psychoanalysis and Developmental Psychology*. New York: Basic Books.
Stern, M. M. (1961), Blank hallucinations: Remarks about trauma and perceptual disturbances. *Internat. J. Psycho-Anal.*, 42:205–215.
Stolorow, R. D. (1975), Toward a functional definition of narcissism. *Internat. J. Psycho-Anal.*, 56:179–186.
———— Brandchaft, B. & Atwood, G. E. (1987), *Psychoanalytic Treatment*. Hillsdale, NJ: The Analytic Press.
Stone, L. (1961), *The Psychoanalytic Situation: An Examination of Its Development and Essential Nature*. New York: International Universities Press.
Strachey, J. (1934), The nature of the therapeutic action of psychoanalysis. *Internat. J. Psycho-Anal.*, 15:127–159.
Sturgeon, T. (1953), *More Than Human*. New York: Carroll & Graf.
Sullivan, H. S. (1937), A note on the implications of psychiatry, the study of interpersonal relations, for investigations in the social sciences. In: *The Fusion of Psychiatry and Social Science*. New York: Norton, 1964, pp. 15–29.
———— (1940), *Conceptions of Modern Psychiatry*, New York: Norton.
———— (1942), Leadership, mobilization, and postwar change. In: *The Fusion of Psychiatry and Social Science*. New York: Norton, 1964, pp. 149–176.
———— (1948), The meaning of anxiety in psychiatry and in life. In: *The Fusion of Psychiatry and Social Science*. New York: Norton, 1964, pp. 229–254.
———— (1950a), Tensions interpersonal and international: A psychiatrist's view. In: *The Fusion of Psychiatry and Social Science*. New York: Norton, 1964, pp. 293–331.
———— (1950b), The illusion of personal individuality. In: *The Fusion of Psychiatry and Social Science*. New York: Norton, 1964, pp. 198–226.
———— (1953), *The Interpersonal Theory of Psychiatry*. New York: Norton.
———— (1954), *The Psychiatric Interview*. New York: Norton.
———— (1956), *Clinical Studies in Psychiatry*. New York: Norton.
———— (1972), *Personal Psychopathology*. New York: Norton.

Symington, N. (1983), The analyst's act of freedom as agent of therapeutic change. *Internat. Rev. Psycho-Anal.*, 10:283–291.

Target, M. & Fonagy, P. (1996), Playing with reality: II. The development of psychic reality from a theoretical perspective. *Internat. J. Psycho-Anal.*, 77:459–479.

Tauber, E. S. & Green, M. R. (1959), *Prelogical Experience*. New York: Basic Books.

Taylor, G. J. (1987), *Psychosomatic Medicine and Contemporary Psychoanalysis*. Madison, CT: International Universities Press.

Terr, L. C. (1984), Time and trauma. *The Psychoanalytic Study of the Child*, 39:633–665. New Haven, CT: Yale University Press.

Thompson, C. (1953), Transference and character analysis. In: *Interpersonal Psychoanalysis*, ed. M. Green. New York: Basic Books, 1964, pp. 22–31.

——— (1956), The role of the analyst's personality in therapy. In: *Interpersonal Psychoanalysis*, ed. M. Green. New York: Basic Books, 1964, pp. 168–178.

Tolpin, M. (1971), On the beginnings of a cohesive self: An application of the concept of transmuting internalization to the study of the transitional object and signal anxiety. *The Psychoanalytic Study of the Child*, 26:316–352. New York: Quadrangle.

Turkle, S. (1978), *Psychoanalytic Politics: Jacques Lacan and Freud's French Revolution*, rev. ed. New York: Guilford, 1992.

Weiss, J. & Sampson, H. (1986), *The Psychoanalytic Process: Theory, Clinical Observation, and Empirical Research*. New York: Guilford.

Winnicott, D. W. (1945), Primitive emotional development. In: *Collected Papers*. London: Tavistock, 1958, pp. 145–156.

——— (1949), Mind and its relation to the psyche-soma. In: *Collected Papers*. London: Tavistock, 1958, pp. 243–254.

——— (1950), Aggression in relation to emotional development. In: *Collected Papers*. London: Tavistock, 1958, pp. 204–218.

——— (1951), Transitional objects and transitional phenomena. In: *Collected Papers*. London: Tavistock, 1958, pp. 229–242.

——— (1955–1956), Clinical varieties of transference. In: *Collected Papers*. London: Tavistock, 1958, pp. 295–299.

——— (1960a), Ego distortion in terms of true and false self. In: *The Maturational Processes and the Facilitating Environment*. New York: International Universities Press, 1965, pp. 140–152.

——— (1960b), The theory of the parent–infant relationship. In: *The Maturational Processes and the Facilitating Environment*. New York: International Universities Press, 1965, pp. 37–55.

——— (1962), The aims of psycho-analytical treatment. In: *The Maturational Processes and the Facilitating Environment*. New York: International Universities Press, 1965, pp. 166–170.

——— (1963a), Communicating and not communicating leading to a study of certain opposites. In: *The Maturational Processes and the Facilitating Environment*. New York: International Universities Press, 1965, pp. 179–192.

———— (1963b), The development of the capacity for concern. In: *The Maturational Processes and the Facilitating Environment*. New York: International Universities Press, 1965, pp. 73–82.

———— (1965), *The Maturational Processes and the Facilitating Environment*. New York: International Universities Press.

———— (1967), The location of cultural experience. In: *Playing and Reality*. New York: Basic Books, 1971, pp. 95–103.

———— (1969), The use of an object and relating through identifications. In: *Playing and Reality*. New York: Basic Books, 1971, pp. 86–94.

———— (1971a), *Playing and Reality*. New York: Basic Books.

———— (1971b), The place where we live. In: *Playing and Reality*. New York: Basic Books, 1971, pp. 104–110.

———— (1971c), Playing: Creative activity and the search for the self. In: *Playing and Reality*. New York: Basic Books, 1971, pp. 53–64.

———— (1971d), Dreaming, fantasying, and living: A case-history describing a primary dissociation. In: *Playing and Reality*. New York: Basic Books, 1971, pp. 26–37.

———— (1974), Fear of breakdown. *Internat. Rev. Psycho-Anal.*, 1:103–107.

Witenberg, E. G. (1976), To believe or not to believe. *J. Amer. Acad. Psychoanal.*, 41:433–445.

———— (1987), Clinical innovations and theoretical controversy. *Contemp. Psychoanal.*, 23:183–197.

Wolff, P. H. (1987), *The Development of Behavioral States and the Expression of Emotion in Early Infancy*. Chicago: University of Chicago Press.

Wolstein, B. (1971), Interpersonal relations without individuality. *Contemp. Psychoanal.*, 8:75–80.

Young, W. C. (1988), Psychodynamics and dissociation. *Dissociation*, 1:33–38.

INDEX

self-experience *(continued)*
  need to preserve continuity of, 206
  objects that "disconfirm," 11
  putting into language, 128, 145, 146
    incapacity for, 133
  traumatic aspects of, finding a
    voice for, 135
self-other configurations, 181
self-other differentiation, 10, 44–46,
  87–88
self psychology
  criticism of, 157–159. *See also under*
    empathic failures; Kohut, H.
  empathic/introspective stance
    negative side effects of, 158
    neglect of interpersonal, 157–159
    one dimensionality of, 157–158
  vs. interpersonal psychoanalysis
    therapeutic approach, 155,
    157–158
  therapeutic processes in, 149
  interpretation in, 159
  listening and, 154
  minimized input of analyst, 149–150
  objects in, 149
  neglect of real, 149
self-reflective capacity, 6–7, 12. *See
  also* observing ego
self-representation. *See also* ego
  stability; representation
  change in, 35, 40
self-states. *See also* dissociated
  self-states
  access to sufficient range of, 193
  experienced as "me," 195–196
  hypnoidally inaccessible, 226, 285,
    296
  protection afforded by separate-
    ness of, 194
  shifts between, 326
    listening to, 255, 261, 310
    as sign of enactments, 255, 261,
    310
  simultaneous switching of
    patient's and analyst's, 193
  unity-separateness dialectic of,
    272–273

self-system, 40, 145–146
  structural reorganization during
    development, 35–38, 40, 43
self-validation, quest for, 222
selfhood, need to protect stability of,
  6, 9, 11, 66. *See also* shame
  transcendence of, 6
selfobject, as "strategic object," 149
selfobject transference. *See* analyst, as
  usable object; mirroring
  transference; object usage;
  transference, narcissistic
self(ves), 40, 87. *See also* wholeness
  anxiety and development of, 86–88
  capacity to feel like one while
    being many, 186
  central qualities of, 35–36
  collisions between aspects of, 13,
    288
  decentered, 7, 8n., 270–272
  dread of the "not me," 6
  escaping from, 56
  feeling like one while being many,
    10, 12, 256, 310–311
  getting into vs. out of, 55–58, 61
  multiplicity, 270–275. See also
    dissociated self-states; self,
    decentered; unitary self
  language, "disclosure," and,
    315–318
  need to validate, 76
  portrayals of, 7, 7n.
  security of, is never stable, 222
  sense of, 6–7, 10
    continuity *vs.* discontinuity of, 6,
    181–182, 206. *See also under*
    consciousness
  sense of personal identity, 174–175
  separate, 187n.
  "yet to be," 6
separation anxiety, 46
separation-individuation, 77
separations from analyst, patients
  unable to tolerate, 171–172
Settlage, C. F., 43–44, 47, 89
Severn, E., 262, 263
Shakespeare, 169